MAKING THE "AMERICA OF ART"

MAKING THE "AMERICA OF ART"

Cultural Nationalism and Nineteenth-Century Women Writers

NAOMI Z. SOFER

THE OHIO STATE UNIVERSITY PRESS

Columbus

Library of Congress Cataloging-in-Publication Data

Sofer, Naomi Z.
Making the "America of art" : cultural nationalism and nineteenth-century women writers / Naomi Z. Sofer.—1st ed.
    p. cm.
Includes bibliographical references and index.
ISBN 0–8142–0983–1 (cloth : alk. paper)—ISBN 0–8142–9069–8 (cd) 1. American literature—Women authors—History and criticism. 2. Women and literature—United States—History—19th century. 3. Nationalism and literature—United States—History—19th century. 4. American literature—19th century—History and criticism. I. Title.
PS151.S67 2005
810.9'9287'0934—dc22
                    2004020068

Cover design by Dan O'Dair.
Type set in Palatino.
Printed by Thomson-Shore, Inc.

9 8 7 6 5 4 3 2 1

CONTENTS

ACKNOWLEDGMENTS

ACKNOWLEDGING the numerous intellectual and personal debts I have incurred in the process of writing this book is one of the pleasantest tasks I can imagine. Susan Mizruchi has been everything one could wish for in an academic adviser and mentor. Her support of this project from its earliest incarnation as my dissertation has been unflagging. Her friendship and seemingly endless capacity for encouragement have been a mainstay of my academic life over the past decade. Laura Korobkin has been an exemplary second reader who has stayed involved and supportive long after her official responsibilities were fulfilled.

Many others have read parts or all of the book and offered valuable suggestions and criticism, or posed questions that helped clarify my thinking. The members of my short-lived but wonderfully encouraging writing group, Karen Flood, Laura Johnson, Becky Noel, and Andrea Volpe, offered invaluable comments on a chapter, pushed me to think more like a historian, and, most importantly, helped me get the process of transforming the dissertation into a book under way. Gail K. Smith and Melissa J. Homestead each read a chapter and provided incisive comments. My mother-in-law, Tamara K. Mitchell, read the entire manuscript—twice—and offered ideas and encouragement. Joan Hedrick and the anonymous press reader were the ideal informed readers.

Numerous librarians have provided the institutional support that is the mainstay of any research project. Rhoda Bilansky of the interlibrary loan department at Boston University's Mugar Memorial Library was ever patient and resourceful. The staff of the interlibrary loan department at Harvard University's Widener Library was efficient and courteous. Ellen Garrison, Curator of W. S. Hoole Special Collections at the University of Alabama Libraries, and the staff of the Alabama Department of Archives and History were prompt and helpful in supplying materials relating to Augusta Jane Evans. Catharina Slauterback and Sally Pierce of the Boston Athanaeum's Prints department were helpful and informative. Lisa Hatch of the circulation staff at Brandeis University did me innumerable favors in the way of extra renewals. Finally, the reference staffs of the Boston Public Library, the Goldfarb Library at Brandeis University, the Mugar Memorial Library at Boston University, and the Widener Library at Harvard University were all knowledgeable and efficient.

Thanks are also due to individuals and institutions whose support doesn't fall into any of the familiar categories. Roger B. Stein returned a thoughtful, detailed answer to an email query from a complete stranger. Drew Gilpin Faust graciously took time to search her basement for missing newspaper articles. Those articles were eventually tracked down by Melissa J. Homestead who, in addition to being a tireless researcher, has been a most generous friend and colleague. Andrea Volpe has offered endless support and encouragement. Finally, I wish to acknowledge the importance of the Northeast Nineteenth Century Women Writers Study Group and the Society for the Study of American Women Writers as contexts and communities for this project.

Many people at The Ohio State University Press contributed to the publication of this book. Special thanks are due my editor, Heather Lee Miller, for her unflagging support of this project, and to Maggie Diehl, who oversaw the copyediting process in exemplary fashion and shared gardening tips to boot.

My entire extended family has been interested, encouraging, and most of all, patient. My sister, Tamar Sofer-Geri, has an infinite capacity to serve as a sounding board, for which I am grateful. My husband, Jonathan Rubel, deserves my deepest gratitude for being willing to let "the book" come first so many times, and for doing so much extra—everything. My son, Benjamin Rubel, who has known no other life, takes it for granted that mommy's work comes before play. I dedicate this book to them.

MAKING THE "AMERICA OF ART"

Why, John, are you aware that those articles were written for bread and butter, not fame; and tossed to the printer before the ink was dry, or I had time for a second reading? And yet, perhaps there is more freshness about them than there would have been, had I leisure to have pruned and polished them—who knows?
—Fanny Fern (1855)[1]

I hope I shall yet do my great book, for that seems to be my work, and I am growing up to it. I even think of trying the "Atlantic." There's ambition for you! . . . If Mr. L takes the one Father carried to him, I shall think I can do something.
—Louisa May Alcott (1858)

Hurrah! My story was accepted, and Lowell asked if it was not a translation from the German, it was so unlike most tales. . . . People seem to think it is a great thing to get into the "Atlantic," but I've not been pegging away all these years in vain, and may yet have books and publishers and a fortune of my own.
—Louisa May Alcott (1859)[2]

Other magazines took their turn—the "Atlantic," I remember—in due course; but I shared the general awe of this magazine at that time prevailing in New England, and, having possibly, more than my share of personal pride, did not very early venture to intrude my little risk upon that fearful lottery.
The first story of mine which appeared in the "Atlantic" was a fictitious narrative of certain psychical phenomena occurring in Connecticut, and known to me, at first hand, to be authentic. I have yet to learn that the story attracted any attention from anybody more disinterested than those few friends of the sort who, in such cases, are wont to inquire, in tones more freighted with wonder than admiration: "What! Has she got into the Atlantic?"
—Elizabeth Stuart Phelps (1896)[3]

The nation has found its true grandeur by war, but must retain it in peace.
Peace too has its infinite resources, after a nation has once become conscious of itself. It is impossible that human life should ever be utterly impoverished, and all the currents of American civilization now tend to its enrichment. . . . Everything is here, between these Atlantic and Pacific shores, save only the perfected utterance that comes with years. Between Shakespeare in his cradle and Shakespeare in Hamlet there was needed but an interval of time, and the same sublime condition is all that lies between the America of toil and the America of art.
—Thomas Wentworth Higginson (1867)[4]

INTRODUCTION

T O TALK about art, artists, or genius in the postbellum era was
to talk about defining American identity in the wake of the event
that called into question the nation's very existence. Thomas Wentworth
Higginson's belief that it was only a matter of time before the "America
of art" would emerge from the crucible of the Civil War was widely
shared, even as the shape and meaning of "American" art and the identity of its producers were hotly contested. The *Atlantic Monthly* was only
the most prominent site of this contest, which took place in book
reviews, editorials, and essays published in the pages of the nation's
"quality journals"[5] as well as in the pages of fiction produced by some
of the nation's best known writers: between 1859 and 1889 Louisa May
Alcott, Rebecca Harding Davis, Augusta Jane Evans, Nathaniel
Hawthorne, Henry James, Elizabeth Stuart Phelps, Harriet Beecher
Stowe, and Constance Fenimore Woolson all published novels that thematized art and artists and took up the central aesthetic questions of the
day.[6] At stake for all the participants in this conversation were questions
of identity both personal and national; for the women writers who are
the subjects of this book, participating in the conversation about producing an "America of art" signaled a fundamental shift in self-
conception: from "bread and butter" writer to artist working on a "great
book," unwilling to disclaim either "ambition" or "fame" as a motivating force. But rejecting the persona of the writer driven by financial
necessity or the identity of mere medium for a religious message, which
had been the sole justifications for American women seeking literary
careers during the first half of the nineteenth century, required a different rationale for one's artistic work and new models to emulate. That
process of literary self-definition, and the postbellum project of cultural
nationalism that is its context, are the subjects of this book.

American women writers' changing self-conception in the second half of the nineteenth century is reflected in Louisa May Alcott's and Elizabeth Stuart Phelps's responses to their initial publication in the *Atlantic Monthly*. Despite their obvious pleasure at having their work accepted by the preeminent literary magazine of the day, both express a certain ambivalence toward their achievement. Alcott's observation that "[p]eople seem to think it is a great thing to get into the 'Atlantic'" implies that she does not share this common view, despite her 1858 remark that suggests that she views publication in the *Atlantic* as a precursor to attempting a "great book." Her subsequent remark—"but I've not been pegging away all these years in vain, and may yet have books and publishers and a fortune of my own"—strengthens the sense of Alcott's mixed feelings about her accomplishment. Beginning as it does with the qualifier "but," Alcott's comment suggests that she finds people's excitement at her work's acceptance by the *Atlantic* misplaced, since this event is not a guarantee of literary success but rather an (admittedly high) point in a long literary apprenticeship.

Phelps's account of her reaction to her first publication in the *Atlantic* registers a similar mixture of pride and diffidence. Her decision to delay submitting her work to the *Atlantic* until after she had published elsewhere points to Phelps's sense of herself as a writer undergoing a systematic literary apprenticeship; her claim to be confused by the story's acceptance and her somewhat sarcastic depiction of the kind of backhanded compliments such success elicits reveal her determination to view the event as a part of her artistic development rather than its culmination. Alcott's and Phelps's similar ambivalence about the meaning of their first publication in the *Atlantic* is emblematic of the paradoxical project they and their peers were engaged in: creating new professional identities that would allow them to eschew the persona of "bread and butter" writer and claim for themselves the status of literary Artist, and a place in the realm of high literary production embodied by the *Atlantic Monthly*, even as that realm was increasingly defined in opposition to the figure of the popular (female) writer, whose existence and example had enabled their own careers.

Like the nation, which, according to Higginson, had "become conscious of itself" in the wake of the Civil War and therefore capable of producing not only its own Shakespeare but an "America of art," the members of what I call the transitional generation of American women writers—Rebecca Harding Davis (1830–1910), Louisa May Alcott (1832–88), Constance Fenimore Woolson (1840–96), and Elizabeth Stuart Phelps (1844–1911)—had begun to "assume" themselves publicly in the years surrounding the Civil War.[7] These writers' literary careers began in the late 1850s, after female authorship had become an accepted fact in American cultural life but before women writers had regularly begun to produce work that was considered high literary Art, either by the literary establishment or by themselves. Theirs was a generation that was limited most severely not by the narrowly defined notions of acceptable female public speech, but by the absence of diverse and flexible models for female intellectual and artistic work. These writers shared with their predecessors popularity and professionalism, but they differed from their foremothers in their relationships to the literary establishment and male intellectual authority, and in their self-conception as artists and intellectuals. Whereas their predecessors—writers like Harriet Beecher Stowe, Fanny Fern, Augusta Jane Evans, Susan Warner, Maria Cummins—typically highlighted the ethical concerns and financial pressures that propelled them into the public arena and minimized their artistic ambitions, the writers of the transitional generation inverted that relationship. Members of this group typically saw themselves as artists whose inspiration and motivation could be drawn equally from their native talent and ambition and from their religious or social commitments. This difference meant that the dominant model of authorship available to American women writers, the domestic-tutelary, was only minimally relevant to the writers of the transitional generation; consequently, each devoted considerable intellectual energy to revising old models of artistic production and constructing new ones.[8]

I locate the beginning of the process of American women's literary self-definition in 1859, with the publication of Harriet Beecher Stowe's *The Minister's Wooing* and Augusta Jane Evans's *Beulah,* each of which takes up a series of questions about the gendered nature of aesthetic production, the proper relationship between religious faith and art, and the role of art in producing national and regional identity, questions that would be central to their own work and that of their peers for the coming decades. Although the need for national culture had been a subject of concern for American intellectuals since the early days of the republic, the tenor of the conversation about American cultural production began to change in the 1850s, when a number of factors converged to produce a sea change in the frameworks that defined and shaped American literature and art. The 1850s saw the emergence of a group of cultural institutions such as literary and art periodicals (*Harper's Monthly* [1850], *Putnam's Monthly* [1853], the *Atlantic Monthly* [1857], the *Crayon* [1855]) publishing houses (Ticknor and Fields), and libraries (the Boston Public Library [1852]), committed to supporting American art and literature, demarcating a realm of "high" literary production, and making a specific notion of "culture" widely available. Meanwhile, a growing middle class was traveling in increasing numbers to Europe, with the express purpose of viewing, studying, and acquiring its artistic masterpieces; and although European art continued to be viewed as the standard of excellence, the increasingly well traveled American middle class represented a potentially large market for domestic visual art. The number of American artists studying in French and Italian schools also increased during the 1850s, and a growing number of American women, who were generally barred from studying the (nude) human form in the United States, began studying in French and Italian art schools.[9]

At the same time, American conceptions of art and the artist were being transformed. The publication of John Ruskin's writings on art in the United States beginning in 1847, and the subsequent debate about the proper relationship between religious faith and the visual arts, contributed to the shift in American conceptions of the function of art, from the view, dominant in the early national era and shaped by Scottish Common Sense philosophy, that the only justification for producing art (both visual and literary) in the fledgling nation was moral utility, to the view, shaped by British Romanticism and American Transcendentalism and by the weakening of the strict Calvinist prohibition on religious art, that aesthetic ambition and the resulting art were expressions of divinity and that beauty and aesthetic pleasure were valuable in their own right.[10] Although these institutional and conceptual changes affected both the literary and the visual arts, change in the literary arena was more rapid, chaotic, and contested because a large literary marketplace and a body of American literature had both emerged, virtually simultaneously, during the first half of the nineteenth century. Those concerned with producing American literature as a form of high culture, therefore, had to do so not only in relation to foreign traditions, but also in relation—usually oppositional—to the existing body of popular writings by Americans, many of them women, that had already begun to define what "American Literature" looked like.[11]

The *Atlantic Monthly* was central to the linked processes of defining "American Literature" and demarcating a realm of high literary culture that began during the late 1850s and accelerated in the postbellum years.[12] That aspect of the magazine's mission is made explicit in its very first issue, which featured a poem titled "The Origin of Didactic Poetry," penned by the magazine's first editor, James Russell Lowell. In the poem Lowell tells the story of the goddess Minerva's disastrous foray into poetry writing and her subsequent decision to take up Sunday School teaching. Minerva's artistic and professional choices align her with the popular women writers of the day, putting future contributors to the *Atlantic* on notice about the magazine's literary standards: the poem ends by warning that "The Muse is unforgiving" of didactic poetry and urging readers to "Put all your beauty in your rhymes, / Your morals in your living."[13] By privileging "beauty" over "morals," Lowell announces the beginning of a new era in American literature, one that will exclude work produced under the premise that literary activity is an appropriate extension of women's role as guardians of their families', and the nation's, moral character.

The struggle to transform the United States from a nation of "toil" to a nation of "art" and to redefine the most valuable art as that which produces "beauty" rather than "morals" took place over the next three decades in a conversation that focused on the urgent need to produce American culture. This conversation is characterized by a number of recurring themes, even while its contributors differ about specific details of their programs. For example, writers tend to agree that a uniquely American literature is a prerequisite to achieving cultural equality with England and Europe, but regularly disagree about what, exactly, makes a work or a body of literature "American." Other shared themes are the importance of educating children, immigrants, working-class people, and newly freed slaves into an understanding of and appreciation for art (or "civilization," or "culture," or "taste"; the terms are often used interchangeably); and a belief that it is the patriotic duty of the nation's prominent artists and intellectuals to contribute to the production of American culture, especially in the wake of the Civil War.

These two constellations of events—the newly urgent conversation about cultural nationalism in the wake of the Civil War, and the new willingness of a prominent group of women writers to lay claim to the identity of literary artist and to the task of producing "American" art—not only took place roughly simultaneously but were shaped and influenced by each other. Expressed in, on the one hand, an explosion of fiction, most of it by women writers, that thematizes art and artistic creation and, on the other hand, a large body of nonfiction writing on questions of culture and nation, virtually all of it by male writers, these two bodies of writing can appear unrelated. Only a small fraction of the fiction overtly takes up the topic of cultural nationalism, and an only slightly larger fraction of the nonfiction explicitly takes up the subject of female artists. They are, however, part of a single conversation, and focusing on the intersections of these two bodies of writing complicates our understanding of the cultural terrain in the decades surrounding the Civil War. Putting the producers of two apparently disparate bodies of writing back into dialogue with each other reveals that these narratives—the struggle over the territory of American high culture and the emergence of female literary artists—are mutually constitutive.

Although this conversation takes place along rather starkly split gender and genre lines—virtually all the nonfiction is written by men; most of the fiction is written by women—the participants in this dialogue hailed from the same class backgrounds and most moved in the same fairly small social and literary circles. Indeed, many of the women writers I study belonged to the prominent families that formed the core of the white Protestant cultural elite for most of the nineteenth century: Harriet Beecher Stowe belonged to a family of prominent Calvinist clergymen—she was a daughter of Lyman Beecher, a sister of Henry Ward Beecher, and the wife of Calvin Stowe, well-known clergymen all. During her husband's stint as professor of sacred literature at Andover Theological Seminary (1854–63), Harriet lived next door to the Phelps's, and a young Elizabeth Stuart Phelps, herself a daughter and granddaughter of influential Protestant ministers and professors at Andover Theological Seminary, visited the Stowes often.[14] Despite the difference in their ages, Harriet Beecher Stowe, the antebellum era's most famous American writer, and Elizabeth Stuart Phelps, whose *Gates Ajar* (1868) would make her one of if not the most famous American authors of the early postbellum period, developed a friendship that lasted until Stowe's death in 1896.[15] Louisa May Alcott's neighbors in Concord included Ralph Waldo Emerson, Nathaniel Hawthorne, and Henry David Thoreau. Emerson and Thoreau were pallbearers at the 1858 funeral of Louisa's sister, Elizabeth; the Alcotts lived in Hawthorne's house in 1858 while he was in England and later bought Thoreau's house; and Alcott knew Emerson well, borrowed books from his library regularly, and idolized him as a "god."[16] Alcott's father, Bronson, was a well-known educator and public intellectual who hand-delivered her stories to *Atlantic* editor James Russell Lowell—the "Mr. L" of the epigraph. A grandniece of James Fenimore Cooper, Constance Fenimore Woolson had deep New England roots and family connections to Lincoln biographer John Hay and to Samuel Mather, a descendent of Cotton and Increase Mather.[17] And although she grew up in Cleveland, far from the nation's cultural centers, and spent much of her adult life traveling in the United States and Europe, Woolson published extensively in American periodicals and maintained close connections to the postbellum literary scene through correspondence and friendships with such prominent literary figures as E. C. Stedman and Henry James.[18] Not all the participants in this conversation were from prominent New England families, but all were familiar with and to the Boston and New York literary worlds. Born in West Virginia to a modest family, Rebecca Harding Davis became a protégé of James T. Fields after "Life in the Iron Mills" appeared in the *Atlantic* in 1861; she visited Boston as Fields's guest in 1862 and was introduced to all the prominent New England intellectuals of the day. After her marriage Davis lived in Philadelphia, which, along with Boston and New York, was one of the three centers of the nineteenth-century publishing world. Even Augusta Jane Evans, who was born in Georgia and spent much of her adulthood in Mobile, Alabama, had strong ties to the New York literary scene. She kept up her friendship with William Seaver, an editor at *Harper's Monthly* whom she met in 1859, for decades, frequently expressed her desire to enjoy the "genial literary glow" of New York, which she visited as often as she could, and read the prominent periodicals of the day.[19]

In addition to moving in the same social circles, all but Evans published their work in the same group of "quality journals," and all six read one another's work.[20] Stowe, Davis, Alcott, Phelps, and Woolson each published fiction in the *Atlantic Monthly,* though only Woolson and Phelps remained regular contributors after the mid-1860s, when the *Atlantic* "underwent a palpable stiffening of its selection criteria" and stopped accepting the work of Alcott and Davis, both of whom it had earlier featured.[21] Their work was widely reviewed in the "quality journals," almost always by their male peers, and a number of them published one or more books with Ticknor and Fields, which was instrumental in creating and marketing the category of "high" literary art. Although only Stowe and Phelps knew each other well, these writers' interest in and support for their peers is evident from their diaries, letters, and memoirs.[22]

These writers' professional friendships included prominent literary men as well as women. Stowe, Davis, Alcott, Phelps, and Woolson all knew and worked with James T. Fields, whom Phelps described

glowingly in her autobiography: "He advocated the political advancement of our sex, coeducation, and kindred movements, without any of
that apologetic murmur so common among the half-hearted or the
timid. . . . He was incapable of that literary snobbishness which under-
values a woman's work because it is a woman's."[23] They also shared an
antagonistic relationship with the young Henry James, who, as a
reviewer for the *Nation,* wrote often-savage reviews of his female peers'
fiction. Although the subjects of his reviews did not necessarily know
the identity of the author, they clearly recognized the bias against their
work emanating from the *Nation;* writing Rebecca Harding Davis after
James attacked her *Waiting for the Verdict* (1867), Harriet Beecher Stowe
consoles the younger writer by reminding her the *Nation* is like "'a
sneering respectable middle aged sceptic who says I take my two glass-
es & my cigar daily . . . But dont [sic] mind them & dont [sic] hope for a
sympathetic word from them *ever* in any attempt to help the weak &
sinning & suffering.'"[24]

   Although their work was published alongside that of their male
peers, the women in this group rarely contributed the kind of explicitly
theoretical analyses of the central cultural questions of the day that
dominate the pages of the quality magazines in the decades surrounding the Civil War.[25] Women writers' absence from the theoretical debates
taking place in the "quality journals" during this period has contributed
to the impression that they did not have well-thought-out aesthetic programs and did not care to participate in the collective work of defining
U.S. cultural identity in the postbellum era. But even a cursory exami-
nation of the works published by Stowe, Evans, Davis, Alcott, Phelps,
and Woolson between 1859 and 1889 reveals a deep concern both with
the question of national cultural identity and with their own identity as
American artists. Instead of producing nonfiction treatises and essays
like those produced by Hawthorne, Poe, and Melville in the antebellum
years, and by Lowell, Higginson, Samuel Osgood, F. H. Hedge, and others during the postbellum years, the women in this study took up these
questions in their fiction.[26]

   This gender/genre split can be attributed both to the conventions
that determined the acceptable subjects and genres of literary production by women and to the structures of the institutions in which the cultural nationalism conversation was conducted. Although most of the
women I discuss wrote nonfiction essays for a variety of periodicals,
they tended to confine themselves to domestic and social topics and
rarely offered their opinions on aesthetic or theoretical issues. It is not
until the end of the century that we find women writers producing

memoirs in which they articulate their aesthetic vision.[27] There is evidence, however, that all the women writers discussed here viewed their fiction as a primary vehicle for expressing their opinion and shaping public opinion. Alcott makes this point explicitly in a letter to her family from July 8, 1870, in which she describes Theodore Tilton's attempts to persuade her to write for the *Revolution,* Elizabeth Cady Stanton's feminist newspaper: "I think I'd rather keep to my own work and lecture the public in a story, than hold forth . . . in the papers."[28] Although Alcott's "public" is not gendered, her preference for lecturing "in a story" reflects what Nina Baym has suggested was a central function of fiction in this period: "from 1850 until well after the Civil War (some would say until the 1920s) the novel was chiefly a form of literary communication among women."[29] Indeed, that understanding of the difference between fiction and nonfiction as appropriate forms for women's public expression was something of a double-edged sword for members of the transitional generation: it was one of the founding premises of the antebellum models of artistic production that they sought to revise; it was frequently used to denigrate their work and bar it from the realm of the purely literary; and it was a convention these writers regularly took advantage of as they used their fiction to participate in the ongoing conversation about the nature of American artistic production.

The institutions that shaped that conversation were almost exclusively male owned and run. And while a number of the men who occupied positions of cultural power were quite progressive on matters of gender equality—Thomas Wentworth Higginson and James T. Fields are particularly noteworthy in this respect—the writers, editors, and publishers engaged in demarcating a realm of elite literary culture increasingly sought to distance it from the female-dominated legacy of antebellum cultural production—a subject that will be discussed in detail in the second half of this book. Members of the transitional generation were visible contributors to many of the "quality journals" in which these views were promulgated, but no women edited or published any of these periodicals. There were, of course, female editors and publishers: Sarah Josepha Hale edited *Godey's Ladies Magazine* for decades, Harriet Beecher Stowe was an editor of *Hearth and Home* from 1868 to 1875, and women edited periodicals such as the *Lily, Woman's Journal,* the *Revolution,* and *Forerunner.* Most of these publications, however, catered exclusively to female readers or focused on "women's issues" ranging from domesticity to suffrage. Although women were often consulted about editorial decisions by husbands and fathers, no woman edited or published any of the periodicals that shaped the high literary culture of the postbellum years, making fiction the most readily available forum for American women writers to express their views of aesthetic and cultural questions.[30]

My account of the changes to women's "models" of authorship, or of artistic production more generally, is particularly indebted to and in dialogue with the work of Lawrence Buell and Richard Brodhead. In *New England Literary Culture, From Revolution through Renaissance,* Lawrence Buell traces the evolution of American conceptions of authorship from the late-eighteenth century, when literature was held to a highly utilitarian standard and required to serve a clearly visible moral purpose, through the emergence of American romanticism in the 1830s. American romanticism, which was, in Buell's term, "domesticated" by Emerson and transformed into transcendentalism, did not reject the requirement that art have a moral or ethical component, but it redefined the author's role, transforming him from moral instructor and entertainer to divinely inspired visionary.[31] Although Buell's study is one of the earliest to resist the "separate spheres" model of American literary history, his is primarily a study of male writers and of the models of authorship they constructed, models that were simply unavailable to the American women who began to enter the literary scene in large numbers between 1830 and 1850. Indeed, as I argue here, coming to terms with the romantic conception of the artist as divinely inspired genius is central to the project of creating alternative models of authorship.

Conceptions of authorship available to both men and women started to change around the middle of the century. Richard Brodhead's *The School of Hawthorne* traces the institutionalization of the American Renaissance as a literary tradition around which American authors could construct their identities as writers, and *Cultures of Letters: Scenes of Reading and Writing in Nineteenth-Century America* charts the changing literary field in the postbellum period and the concomitant changes to the idea of authorship. Although as Lawrence Levine has demonstrated, by the 1870s the American cultural world was increasingly differentiated into "high" and "low" artistic forms, Brodhead's reconstruction of the "scenes of writing" in the three decades after the Civil War reveals that early in the postbellum era "low" and "high" had not yet become rigid, mutually exclusive categories.[32] During this period of differentiation numerous models of authorship coexisted, allowing writers to choose from among the available models, and enabling some writers to make use of several different models, either simultaneously or over the course of a career. Central to the transformation of authorship at mid-century and beyond was the shift away from the "domestically inflected" values that had shaped American literature in the first decades of the century.[33] As I demonstrate in the second part of this book, this shift away from the domestic model of authorship meant that women writers in particular had to reconstruct their literary self-conception and reimagine themselves in the terms of the emerging models of authorship.

For the past two decades female authorship in this period has been seen through the lens offered by Nina Baym in *Woman's Fiction* (1978), in which she noted a "decline" in "woman's fiction" in the years immediately after the Civil War, and the emergence of serious female literary Artists at the very end of the century. This trajectory has been repeated by countless critics and literary historians and institutionalized by the growing body of excellent scholarship on the women writers who emerged at the end of the century.[34] *Making the "America of Art"* tells the story of the emergence of the self-consciously literary American woman writer, a story that has been largely assumed rather than explicated. By focusing on the period between the heyday of popular women's authorship and the emergence of such self-consciously artistic writers as Sarah Orne Jewett and Willa Cather I uncover the process whereby American women writers revised existing models of authorship and gradually came to proclaim themselves Artists. In identifying a group of women writers who were in dialogue both with each other and with their male peers I revise Elizabeth Ammons's account of the period, though I agree with her sense that belonging to a group—however informally—was essential to these writers' ability to redefine the models of authorship that had enabled their careers.[35]

The most important precursor to *Making the "America of Art"* is Mary Kelley's influential *Private Woman, Public Stage: Literary Domesticity in Nineteenth-Century America* (1984). I am particularly indebted to Kelley's broad outlines of the ways in which antebellum women writers justified their entry into the literary public sphere as driven by financial necessity and religious motivation. In my view one of the most striking aspects of Kelley's study is the tremendous consistency in the language her twelve subjects use to describe and justify their literary endeavors. Whereas to Kelley this consistency bespeaks a set of shared psychic experiences, to me they suggest a shared strategic approach. So, although I rely heavily on Kelley's description of the economic and religiously based explanations for antebellum women's entry into the literary realm, I understand those explanations as themselves cultural conventions employed by women who understood that these justifications—whether based in their actual lived experiences or not—allowed them to engage in activities that were otherwise inconsistent with their prescribed gender roles. Indeed, my understanding of the identity of the antebellum women writer outlined by Kelley as a cultural construction is at the core of *Making the "America of Art"*: for it is my contention that women writers' critical engagement with, and transformation of, the antebellum model of authorship was crucial to their participation in the production of American high culture in the middle decades of the nineteenth century.

More recently, the study of nineteenth-century women writers has been enriched by scholarship that does much to expand and complicate our understanding of the literary culture of the period. Works such as Monika Elbert's collection *Separate Spheres No More: Gender Convergence in American Literature, 1830–1930*, and Aleta Cane and Susan Alves's edited volume *"The Only Efficient Instrument": American Women Writers and the Periodical, 1837–1916*, both contribute to the ongoing effort to dismantle the "separate spheres" view of literary culture in the period, and both collections are unusual in the breadth of their coverage. But although individual essays within these collections contribute to our understanding of female authorship during the period, these essays are limited, by their nature, serving as case studies rather than offering historical narratives. A number of important recent studies of individual writers such as Karen Kilcup and Thomas Edwards, eds., *Jewett and Her Contemporaries: Reshaping the Canon;* Victoria Brehm, ed., *Constance Fenimore Woolson's Nineteenth Century;* and June Howard, *Publishing the Family* have contributed significantly to our understanding of literary culture at the end of the nineteenth century, but these studies all confirm the received historical trajectory, which emphasizes the emergence of self-consciously literary women artists at the end of the century.

My focus on the thirty-year period during which American writers and intellectuals of both genders actively debated what American high culture should look like, who should produce it, and what the rewards of success would be offers a new understanding of a complex, contested, and mostly overlooked period of American cultural history. That debate has been largely overlooked in part because there are relatively few accounts of the literary history of the second half of the nineteenth century, and even fewer of the relationship between the literary culture of the antebellum era and the literary forms and values that came to dominate the postbellum era. Most accounts of the century use the Civil War as their dividing line, giving the impression that there is little, if any, continuity between the literary productions of the postbellum and antebellum periods. Recent examples of this tendency include a number of otherwise excellent studies such as Richard S. Lowry, *"Litttery Man"*: *Mark Twain and Modern Authorship* (1996); Michael Newbury, *Figuring Authorship in Antebellum America* (1997); and Linda Grasso, *The Artistry of Anger: Black and White Women's Literature in America, 1820–1860* (2002). The literary historical view of the second half of the century is dominated by accounts of the rise of realism and its identification with high literary culture; it is only relatively recently that scholars such as Nancy Glazener (*Reading for Realism: The History of a U.S. Literary Institution, 1850–1910* [1997]) and Barbara Hochman (*Reimagining Books and Reading in the Age of American Realism* [2001]) have begun to focus on the years immediately before and after the Civil War, a period that has long been identified with what George Santayana famously derided as genteel literary culture.

Making the "America of Art" is explicitly concerned with the realm of high culture, and it seeks to illuminate the fault lines within what can appear to be a monolithic category. Cultural historians such as Lawrence Levine, Alan Trachtenberg, Richard Wightman Fox, and T. J. Jackson Lears have demonstrated that the institutionalization of high culture in the postbellum period was a response to the perceived threat to social order posed by the demographic and economic changes of the postbellum era, and a mechanism for consolidating the social authority of the Protestant elite whose standing as the dominant national elite was challenged after the war by the rise of a new business class and by the redistribution of political power to immigrants and working people. But these accounts tend to focus on opposition from without. I identify some of the internal struggles taking place between men and women of the same social class, who shared a similar worldview and, most importantly, shared a belief in the high value attributed to "culture" in general and to the literary in particular.

In the following five chapters I trace the process whereby American women writers negotiated their position within the emerging realm of high literary culture, and, in the process, modified existing models of female authorship and challenged the assumptions about women's literary production that had governed their predecessors' entry into the world of literary work. These chapters also outline a series of overlapping conversations in which both the theoretical and the practical

implications of attempting to produce "American" culture were end-
lessly debated, revised, and contested.

The first chapter, "Harriet Beecher Stowe's 'New School' of Protestant Art," focuses on Stowe's attempts to redefine the religious and aesthetic frameworks for American cultural production. In *The Minister's
Wooing* (1859) and *Agnes of Sorrento* (1862) Stowe speaks to an audience
increasingly confronted with scientific and intellectual challenges to
religious faith, and in both novels Stowe aligns religious faith and aesthetic production, suggesting that the solution to the nation's crisis of
cultural identity lies, at least in part, in its religious roots. In her work
from this period Stowe undertakes two, related projects: she critiques
sentimental religion as the primary framework for women's intellectual
and spiritual expression, and she challenges the utilitarian view of art
produced by yoking Puritan suspicion of aesthetic pleasure with Scottish Common Sense philosophy. As an alternative, for both women and
the nation, Stowe imagines the possibility that America will produce "a
new school of art, based upon Protestant principles."[36] Read together,
these two novels offer a blueprint for creating a body of American
national art that revises existing models of female authorship and
argues for the necessity of linking religious belief with artistic originality and cultural nationalism as a way of both restoring faith in a time of
increasing doubt and hastening the arrival of "our American day of art,
already dawning auspiciously."[37]

Chapter 2, "'I Dedicate Myself . . . Unreservedly to Art': Augusta
Jane Evans and Southern Art," focuses on two of Augusta Jane Evans's
best-selling novels from the 1860s, *Macaria* (1864) and *St. Elmo* (1866), in
which she critiques the antebellum model of female authorship, offers
an alternative religious feminist aesthetic, and imagines American high
culture with Southern artists at its center. Evans's aesthetic is influenced
by her reading of Ruskin, whose work is cited frequently both in her
correspondence and in her published writing. Evans's work, like
Stowe's, revises the basic premises underlying antebellum conceptions
of authorship and offers an alternative that is based on equal parts
artistic talent, ambition, and religious faith. But unlike Stowe's Ruskin-
influenced writing from this period, Evans's work is explicitly concerned with the lives and careers of women artists, who are the protagonists of her fiction. Evans's aesthetic vision is distinctly Southern, and
her work from this period is shaped by the tension between her sectional loyalties and her artistic ambitions. As a Southern woman writer
Evans had to overcome limitations of both gender and geography. On
the one hand, Evans was fiercely loyal to the South, which she viewed

as the repository of national virtue and the antidote against Northern materialism and factionalism; on the other hand, she was painfully aware of the South's cultural limitations, deeply drawn to the cultural riches of the North, and determined to contribute to the nation's emerging high culture.

The next three chapters focus on the work of the members of the transitional generation—Louisa May Alcott, Rebecca Harding Davis, Elizabeth Stuart Phelps, and Constance Fenimore Woolson—who continued the conversation about reshaping the terms of women's artistic production begun by Stowe and Evans and participated in the ongoing conversation about the making of an "America of art." These chapters are structured thematically around the three central areas of concern that shaped much of the postbellum conversation about art, culture, and national identity: the place of the popular in the realm of high art; the role of the genius; and the legacy of the Civil War.

The development of an ideal of high literary Art in the postbellum era is the subject of the third chapter, "Exorcising the Popular Woman Writer from 'the Domain of Pure Literature.'" I argue that the obsession with distinguishing literary Art from that produced for the marketplace is driven by the figure of the scribbling woman, whose popularity in the marketplace at once helped to create a broad audience for fiction and threatened to make it impossible for high literary art to survive. The conception of authorship underlying this ideal, which defined and privileged literary writing as an inherently masculine activity separate from the marketplace, posed special problems for a woman writer who wished to produce writing considered "literary," as all the members of the transitional generation did. Working from within a self-conception shaped by the antebellum model of female authorship, which stressed women's economic motivation for writing and required them to support themselves and their families, these writers were faced with an irreducible tension between the emerging conception of high literary art as incompatible with the marketplace and the practical and psychic pressures exerted by the literary self-conception that had made their careers possible. This tension is central to Rebecca Harding Davis's *Earthen Pitchers* (1874) and "Marcia" (1876), to Elizabeth Stuart Phelps's *The Story of Avis* (1876), and to Louisa May Alcott's *Little Women* (1868), each of which depicts the market-driven assumptions of the antebellum model as at once inescapable and enormously destructive to the careers of promising women artists. These works demonstrate that for a woman writer to claim for herself the status of literary Artist is, in more ways than one, to attempt to occupy a position that is defined in opposition to her very existence.

Chapter 4, "Genius, Gender, and the Problem of Mentorship," focuses on the figure of the artistic genius, which elicited considerable ambivalence from observers of the cultural scene in the middle quarter of the nineteenth century: treated with a mixture of reverence for his unique qualities and anxiety about the undemocratic implications of valuing those same qualities, the genius embodied the tensions inherent in the postbellum struggle to create a uniquely American high culture even as demographic changes and technological innovation ensured the democratization of culture. Steeped in the antebellum obsession with genius, postbellum observers attempted to preserve genius for their cultural project by playing down its antidemocratic implications and redefining it in terms of quintessentially American values such as self-control, discipline, and hard work. At the same time, women writers challenged the gender and class assumptions of genius, even as they, like their male counterparts, attempted to preserve the idea of genius as part of the project of reimagining the models of artistic production available to them and claiming their place in the emerging realm of high literary culture. For Louisa May Alcott, Rebecca Harding Davis, and Constance Fenimore Woolson, the figure of the mentor is central to the discussion of genius. The relationships between the genius and her mentor range from neglect to domination, but in each case they underscore the failure of the mentor figure to transform the Romantic conception of genius in order to make it a viable model for American artists.

In the final chapter, "The Civil War and the Making of the 'America of Art,'" I focus on the cultural nationalism that dominated Northern intellectual circles in the decade following the Civil War and produced a flood of essays on the topics of art, culture, and "Americanism." To these observers, bringing the nation's cultural productions up to the level of its industrial and manufacturing achievements was the most pressing concern of the day, and many viewed the cultural project as an extension of the Civil War's political and moral aims. There was a remarkable degree of consensus among the Northern intellectuals engaged in this conversation, both male and female, about the need to produce a national culture and the methods for doing so; but while the women of the transitional generation generally believed in the importance of the postbellum cultural project and sought to participate in it, their analyses consistently challenge its underlying assumptions. For Elizabeth Stuart Phelps, Louisa May Alcott, and Constance Fenimore Woolson, the cultural nationalism of the 1865–85 period presented both an opportunity and a challenge. As members of the educated cultural elite, Phelps, Alcott, and Woolson were insiders. As women, who had not fought in the Civil War and whose cultural authority was historically limited to "feminine" concerns, they were outsiders. This doubled vision is evident in the ambivalence toward the Civil War as a source of national cultural production in Phelps's *The Story of Avis* (1877); in the portrayal of expatriation as necessary for women artists' success in Alcott's "Diana and Persis" (ca. 1879); and in "The Street of the Hyacinth" (1882), Woolson's analysis of the tension between an ideal of a democratically based American art and the reality of creating it. In each case, the cultural productions of women are both defined as essential to the project of creating the "America of art" and shown to be undermined by the institutions—both actual and rhetorical—designed to produce it.

CHAPTER ONE

Harriet Beecher Stowe's "New School" of Protestant Art

A S A TEENAGER, Harriet Beecher Stowe "dream[ed]" of becoming "a poet."[1] As a young woman, she wrote stories and humorous sketches to be read aloud at meetings of the Semi-Colon literary club, many of which were later published in the *Western Literary Magazine*. In 1834 she won a fifty-dollar prize for one of these sketches, and by the late 1830s she was making enough money from her writing to hire a second servant, thus buying herself a few hours each day to write.[2] In 1842 Stowe spent a few months in Boston attending to the publication of her first book; during her absence Calvin Stowe wrote his wife to declare: "You must be a *literary woman*. It is so written in the book of fate." A few months later Harriet wrote Calvin expressing her concern about the cost to her children of pursuing a writing career, but concluding the letter with the announcement that "[i]f I am to write, I must have a room to myself, which is to be *my* room."[3] As these details suggest, Harriet Beecher Stowe had artistic aspirations and understood herself as a professional writer long before the publication of *Uncle Tom's Cabin*. But when children's author Eliza Cabot Follen wrote Stowe in 1852 to request biographical information about her for a sketch she was writing, Stowe replied with a self-portrait that fulfilled every conventional expectation about women writers: "The nursery & the kitchen were my principal fields of labour" in the fifteen years since her marriage; her writing was sent out for publication by "[s]ome of my friends pitying my toils"; her sole motivation for writing has been economic: after purchasing "a *feather bed!*" with her first earnings she discovered that she could turn to her pen "when a new carpet, or a mattress was going to be needed, or when at the close of the year, it began to be evident that my accounts, like poor Dora's, *'wouldn't add up.'"* Having been dragged into the literary arena by "the friends who had thought it best to put my name to the pieces, by way of getting up a reputation," Stowe assures Follen that she has permitted herself to become a national icon "contrary to my natural modesty" and only "by the imperative solicitations of my dear 5000 friends & the public generally."[4] Stowe never publicly revoked this self-portrait, but the novels she published in the late 1850s and early 1860s suggest that although she maintained the public posture of reluctant author, she was deeply concerned with finding a viable artistic self-conception and with articulating her vision for national cultural development.

In addition to tending to the needs of her large household, which included sending her son Fred off to war, Stowe published three novels between 1859 and 1862: *The Minister's Wooing* (1859); *Agnes of Sorrento* (1862); and *The Pearl of Orr's Island* (1862). None of these novels has a contemporary setting: the first is set in Puritan Rhode Island soon after the Revolutionary War; the second takes place in fifteenth-century Italy around the time of Savonarola's rebellion; and the third is the story of the seagoing community of Orr's island, off the coast of Maine, shortly before the War of 1812. Despite their disparate historical settings, these three novels all explore in some way the intersection of two of the late-antebellum era's central cultural and social concerns: the struggle to define a uniquely American art, and the growing difficulty of preserving Christian faith in light of recent scientific discoveries and the higher criticism.[5] In *The Minister's Wooing* and *Agnes of Sorrento* Stowe speaks to an audience increasingly confronted with scientific and intellectual challenges to religious faith, and in both novels Stowe aligns religious faith and aesthetic production, suggesting that the solution to the nation's crisis of cultural identity lies, at least in part, in its religious roots. In these two novels Stowe undertakes two, related projects: she critiques sentimental religion as the primary framework for women's intellectual and spiritual expression, and she challenges the utilitarian view of art produced by yoking Puritan suspicion of aesthetic pleasure with Scottish Common Sense philosophy. As an alternative, Stowe imagines the possibility that America will produce "a new school of art, based upon Protestant principles."[6] Read together, these two novels offer a blueprint for creating a body of American national art that revises existing models of female authorship and argues for the necessity of linking religious belief with artistic originality and cultural nationalism as a way of both restoring faith in a time of increasing doubt and hastening the arrival of "our American day of art, already dawning auspiciously."[7]

Calvinism is central to Stowe's project. Although she struggled with many of Calvinism's harsher doctrines and joined the Episcopal church in the 1860s, Stowe never rejected Calvinism in its entirety.[8] Rather, she celebrated the "mental discipline" it provided its adherents, viewed Calvinism as essential to American democracy, and deeply admired many of its most famous divines.[9] Growing up in the Beecher family, Stowe was conversant with theological questions of all kinds, and although she never chose to emulate her sister Catharine in writing a theological treatise, much of her fiction is deeply concerned with theological questions. Stowe has frequently been cited, and derided, as the quintessential popularizer of the strand of liberal Protestant theology known as "sentimental" or "heart" religion; but she was deeply suspicious of theological positions that obviated the difficult or unpleasant aspects of Calvinism, even while she was drawn to the "common sense" approach to religion promulgated by her siblings Catharine, Edward, and, most famously, Henry Ward Beecher.[10] That suspicion informs the religious aesthetic program Stowe develops in *The Minister's Wooing* and *Agnes of Sorrento*.

In addition to her reservations about the theological simplicity of sentimental religion, Stowe's representations of artists in *The Pearl of Orr's Island* and *The Minister's Wooing* suggest that she found the conception of aesthetic production that developed simultaneously with sentimental religion extremely limited, even deadly for the female artists whose entry into the literary public sphere it authorized. In embracing Calvinism Stowe sought to put the intellectual rigor and ecstatic tendencies of Puritan divines, whose emotional and intellectual energy she identified as essentially identical to those of the great Renaissance artists, at the service of American artists of both genders. The resulting blueprint freed American artists, and women writers in particular, from the extremely limited conception of artistic production authorized jointly by sentimental religion and Scottish Common Sense philosophy, transforming them from mere mediums into "priests of national development."[11]

Stowe's efforts to revise the model of women's literary production authorized by sentimental religion and Scottish Common Sense philosophy must be read in the context of the demarcation of a realm of "high" literary culture in literary magazines, publishing houses, and

literary salons of Boston and New York at midcentury and beyond, and
the changing definition of authorship that accompanied that process.
The most visible of these institutions was the *Atlantic Monthly*. Established in late 1857, the *Atlantic's* mission was "developing and disseminating an American literary and intellectual culture. . . . [Its founders]
hoped that this culture would have a broad and direct influence on the
conduct of personal, social, and political life. . . . [T]hey saw themselves
as teachers and educators whose mission was to civilize and humanize
the new nation."[12] As Richard Brodhead has shown, the *Atlantic* was
almost immediately recognized as the preeminent repository of elite literary culture and played a central role in shaping the new distinction
between "high" and "low" culture and in demarcating a realm of high
literary production reserved almost exclusively for male writers.[13]

This project is announced in a humorous poem entitled "The Origin
of Didactic Poetry," contributed to the magazine's debut issue by James
Russell Lowell, the *Atlantic's* first editor. The poem tells the story of
Minerva who, in her youth, wrote a didactic poem and insisted on reading it aloud to the gods. They all made their escape as quickly as they
decently could, leaving Minerva to admit that "Against the Muse I've
sinned, oh!" and tear up her poem, flinging it to the ground. She then
turned her energies to opening a Sunday school. The last two stanzas
record that the torn verses made their way down to earth, where they
"Killed every fish that bit to [*sic*] 'em"; the pieces that made their way
onto solid earth and rotted, "Sprang up again in copies, / And gave two
strong narcotics birth,— / Didactic bards and poppies." Minerva,
though, learned her lesson from her youthful foray into didactic poetry:

> Years after, when a poet asked
> The Goddess's opinion,
> As being one whose soul had basked
> In Art's clear-aired dominion,—
> "Discriminate," she said, "betimes;
> The Muse is unforgiving;
> Put all your beauty in your rhymes,
> Your morals in your living."[14]

In this final stanza Lowell offers an unambiguous statement about his
aesthetic program. Clearly aimed at the "mob of scribbling women"
that could be expected to flood the new publication with submissions,
Lowell takes pains to inform both his readers and potential contributors
that this is a different kind of magazine. By privileging "beauty" over

"morals," Lowell announces the beginning of a new era in American literature, one that will apparently exclude the work produced by the most popular and successful writers of the day. This is not to say that a work's moral component ceased to matter to American readers and critics: for decades reviews in the *Atlantic* itself continued to look for and comment on a work's moral position. This poem does, however, serve as a warning to women (and men, presumably, though the poem clearly figures women as the main offenders) who specialize in didactic fiction and poetry that they have no place in America's future cultural elite.[15]

A moving force behind the establishment of the *Atlantic* and a contributor to the magazine since its inception, Stowe nevertheless occupied a tenuous position in relation to the realm of high literary culture that the magazine embodied and defined. Ellery Sedgwick credits Stowe with being instrumental in convincing publisher Moses Phillips to bankroll the *Atlantic*.[16] She was not, however, among the people who attended the first of many dinner parties in which the magazine's editorial policy was shaped, a list that included Ralph Waldo Emerson, Henry Wadsworth Longfellow, Oliver Wendell Holmes, James Russell Lowell, Francis Underwood, J. Elliot Cabot, and John Lothrop Motley. Joan Hedrick notes that these dinners, which took place at the Parker House, were "grafted onto" the "series of overlapping men's clubs" that formed the basis of Boston society, effectively excluding women from participating in an editorial capacity in what would rapidly become the most influential organ of the newly differentiated realm of American high culture.[17] But although she was excluded from running the magazine, "[t]he *Atlantic* needed Harriet Beecher Stowe . . . for she had a genius for falling into trends before they had caught on with the general populace."[18] Ironically, Stowe's status as the nation's most famous woman writer, outspoken abolitionist, and member of a prominent theological family meant that she was both essential to the *Atlantic*'s mission of creating American high culture and the embodiment of the very forces in American culture that it sought to supplant.

This tension informs Stowe's attempts to redefine the religious and aesthetic frameworks for American cultural production in *The Minister's Wooing*, which was serialized in the *Atlantic Monthly* beginning in December 1858. In the chapter titled "Which Treats of Romance" Stowe argues that American materialism is indirectly responsible for the growing skepticism of the age, and offers "Romance" as the antidote.[19] In this aesthetic manifesto Stowe defines "romance" as the literary expression of the soul's divinity, critiques the antebellum suspicion of aesthetic production, shaped by the Scottish Common Sense school, and rejects "Byronic bitterness" in favor of a religious aesthetic informed by Puritanism and embodied by the figure of the "soul artist." In the process, Stowe enters the conversation about the character and purpose of American art that had been taking place in the pages of intellectual publications for over a decade, offering her own vision of a religiously based national aesthetic that will be carried out by "romancers" and "soul-artists," who are primarily women.

This conversation centered on a single question, which was expressed in a variety of ways: What was the role of art, and the artist, in American society? This question encompassed the debate about the place of European tradition in American culture, the debate about the proper relationship between art and religion in a country whose religious founders eschewed aesthetic production, and the struggle to overcome the legacy of the Scottish Common Sense school's insistence on Art's utilitarian function, which had initially provided a way to circumvent the Puritan prohibition on aesthetic production but had, by the 1840s, become an obstacle to the development of an American national art competitive with the European.

These discussions were sparked by the emergence of transcendentalism in the 1830s and 1840s and coalesced around the work of Thomas Cole, whose painting reflected Romantic and Transcendentalist beliefs in the divinity of nature, which replaced eighteenth-century views of the imagination as an agent of the rational mind, sorting and arranging sense data through the lens of traditional taste and prescribed aesthetic standards. Cultural observers worried both about the pantheistic implications of American Romanticism and about the nationalistic zeal of those who adopted a Wordsworthian worship of wild, untamed nature as the foundation of an original American art, rejecting European art and cultural traditions as old, polluted, and inferior to the prelapsarian innocence of American nature. The American publication of Ruskin's *Modern Painters I* in 1847, and the widespread acceptance of Ruskin's view in the 1850s, provided critics on both sides of the debate with a way to bridge the gap between tradition and innovation, Europe and America, pantheism and Christianity.

Ruskin appealed to American antebellum intellectuals who wanted to preserve a religious foundation for art because he combined an intense, Wordsworth-inspired love of nature with a strong resistance to pantheism, and a hatred of all things Catholic. To defend his interest in art, and to bring it into line with his religious faith, Ruskin constructed an elaborate theory of art—creating it, critiquing it, and teaching about it—as an essentially moral endeavor. It was this that made Ruskin's formulations particularly appealing to Americans:

> Ruskin was shifting the criteria of artistic judgment from the sensuous, which was suspect and unfamiliar in America, to the moral; from pictures, which were still relatively difficult to see in America, to nature, which was abundant; from the well-established European aesthetic traditions of "taste" to the imaginative insight of the individual observer, as he perceived the moral order of the universe. In effect the critic could be the embodiment of Emerson's American Scholar, his poet-genius, drained of the dangerous overtones of pantheism. . . .The fundamental importance of Ruskin's writing in America in these years before the Civil War was his identification of the interest in art with morality and religion as well as with the love of nature, his ability to build a loose but convincing system where art, religion, and nature were inextricably intertwined.[20]

Ruskin's ideas about the essentially moral nature of aesthetic endeavor, and the American interpretation of those ideas, which tended to minimize Ruskin's specific claims about painting and architecture and focus more generally on the epistemological frameworks that could be derived from them, were particularly useful to a writer whose career, like those of most of her female peers, had been enabled by the yoking of artistic talent and religious faith.[21] By tapping into the Ruskin-inspired discussion of the visual arts to articulate a literary aesthetic, Stowe circumvents the definition of literary art evident in Lowell's "The Origins of Didactic Poetry" and offers an alternative framework for understanding women's aesthetic production, which was almost exclusively literary and predominantly religious during the 1840s and 1850s. She also lays the groundwork for her own and other women writers' subsequent resistance to the redefinition of literary art as secular and masculine, which was to shape the emergence of the realm of high culture in the postbellum years.[22]

Essential to Stowe's transformation of the terms of women's aesthetic production in *The Minister's Wooing* is her critique of American materialism and the Common Sense view of art's social function that had historically been used by women writers to justify their entry into print. Stowe blames what she calls a "utilitarian" view of art[23] for producing "bitter, disenchanted people," who believe that "'the victory that overcometh the world'" consists of submitting to the "dead grind and the dollars that come through the mill," "learn[ing] to be fat and tranquil, to have warm fires and good dinners," and throwing "all but this" into "one waste 'catch-all' . . . labelled *romance.*"[24] Romance, Stowe argues, is not optional, but essential, because it is not only an expression of one's "better nature" (599), but the expression of the divinity of the soul. Asking, "What is romance? Whence comes it?" Stowe cites Plato's belief that:

> "Man's soul, in a former state, was winged and soared among the gods; and so it comes to pass, that, in this life, when the soul, by the power of music or poetry, or the sight of beauty, hath her remembrance quickened, forthwith there is a struggling and a pricking pain as of wings trying to come forth. . . ." And if an old heathen, two thousand years ago, discoursed thus gravely of the romantic part of our nature, whence comes it that in Christian lands we think in so pagan a way of it, and turn the whole care of it to ballad-makers, romancers, and opera-singers?
>
> Let us look up in fear and reverence and say, "GOD is the great maker of romance. . . . HE, who strung the great harp of Existence with all its wild and wonderful and manifold chords, and attuned them to one another,—HE is the great Poet of life." Every impulse of beauty, of heroism, and every craving for purer love, fairer perfection, nobler type and style of being than that which closes like a prison-house around us, in the dim, daily walk of life, is God's breath, God's impulse, God's reminder to the soul that here is something higher, sweeter, purer, yet to be attained. (600)

Stowe's slightly tongue-in-cheek wonder that Christians turn "the whole care of" the soul over to "romancers" lays the groundwork for her subsequent assertion that romance is an essential tool in the struggle to combat skepticism and materialism. Despite her view of romance as expressing the divinity of the human soul and essentially similar to the divinity of natural beauty, Stowe's is not a Romantic vision. Hers is a distinctly Christian worldview, and her defense of romance is partially aimed at the orthodox component of her audience whose "grave heads" she "foresee[s] . . . beginning to shake" as "doubts ris[e] in reverend and discreet minds whether this history is going to prove anything but a love story" (601). Harking back to the Common Sense school's emphasis on utility, Stowe argues that the disappointments of life, rather than producing a deeper immersion in "the dead grind" and the material comforts it produces, can serve a crucial religious purpose when transformed into art:

Therefore, man or woman, when thy ideal is shattered,—as shattered a
thousand times it must be . . . turn not away in skepticism and bitterness, saying, "There is nothing better for a man than that he should eat
and drink," but rather cherish the revelations of those hours as prophe-
cies and foreshadowings of something real and possible, yet to be
attained in the manhood of immortality. (600)

To transform the crises that threaten faith into opportunities to renew
and strengthen it is the work of romance:

By such experiences we are taught the pathos, the sacredness of life;
and if we use them wisely, our eyes will ever after be anointed to see
what poems, what romances, what sublime tragedies lie around us in
the daily walk of life, "written not with ink, but in fleshy tables of the
heart." The dullest street of the most prosaic town has matter in it for
more smiles, more tears, more intense excitement, than ever were written in story or sung in poem; the reality is there, of which the romancer
is the second-hand recorder. (600–601)

Almost imperceptibly, Stowe shifts her focus in this passage from the
religious to the aesthetic. The experience of overcoming the disappointment of "shattered ideals" produces not just an appreciation of "the
sacredness of life," but the ability to discern the aesthetic—"poems . . .
romances . . . sublime tragedies"—that is thinly veiled beneath the quotidian of "dull" streets and "prosaic" towns; Stowe holds out the promise that romance cannot only combat skepticism but also transform
the sensibility of its consumers such that they, too, can join the ranks of
those "anointed to see" the "intense excitement" of "reality," an ability
otherwise reserved for "the romancer." In her emphasis on the romance
of the quotidian Stowe describes both her own work and that of all
"romancers" who specialize in transforming "reality" into art, the kind
of art she believes has the power to combat skepticism. In this way
Stowe preserves the religious grounds that had historically authorized
her own and other women's artistic endeavors while, at the same time,
shifting the rationale of aesthetic production from the utilitarian goal of
producing moral improvement, Christian conversion, or social change,
to the more generally humanistic purpose of enabling individuals to
achieve the "highest honor of [their] being" through aesthetic appreciation (601).[25]

Although Stowe frames her defense of romance narrowly, directly
addressing the "right reverend Sir" and "most discreet Madam" whose

suspicion of her "love-story" she anticipates, she is also addressing the
other part of her audience—the readers of the *Atlantic Monthly*, in which
The Minister's Wooing was serialized, who would have recognized the
broader cultural and national implications of her argument. These
implications become apparent when *The Minister's Wooing* is read in the
context of the ongoing attempt to articulate the basis for a national culture, liberate American aesthetic production from the limitations of the
Scottish Common Sense school, and define the proper relationship
between religion and art. Although these issues were discussed extensively in the intellectual press of the day, Stowe's ideas have particular
resonance with the writings in *The Crayon*—a magazine devoted to
Ruskin's ideas that was published between 1855 and 1861—and with
James Jackson Jarves's *Art-Hints* (1855), the first work of original art
criticism by an American.

In an 1855 editorial in *The Crayon* the writer, probably the magazine's founder and coeditor William J. Stillman, takes up the Common
Sense view of fine artists as "superfluities" that have no "right to exist"
and argues that art and artists must be supported by society rather than
by patronage, that art has a social function just as other forms of production do, and that Americans ignore and devalue art and artists at
their peril.[26] Writing a few months later, Stillman returns to the question
of art's social function, observing that "men now consider Art as a thing
which has no relation to their every-day existences, but which should be
kept apart and visited rarely, and when the mind is idle and listless. We
have an impression that this is all wrong—that the first use of Art, be it
painting, music, sculpture, or architecture, is to mingle with and mollify
all the harshnesses of the working world."[27] He goes on to say that art,
and artists, is responsible for spiritualizing the material age and under-
mining the utilitarian view:

> We are as well aware as it is possible to be, that this is not an age in
> which the beautiful is much cared for or often seen—that all that we do
> is full of things that jar and produce discord perpetually: but this hard,
> angular and groveling age, if you consider it so, has to be worked into
> something beautiful, and graceful, and harmonious, or else Art has no
> utility, and the bread and butter school of philosophers must rule the
> world of thought and feeling. . . . At any rate, with and for the present,
> [Art] must work, and the sooner it is at it the better, for, day by day, the
> material world grows heavier, and the spiritual lighter and less effec-
> tive, wherever the spiritual qualities of Art are not brought into
> operation. . . .

> If Art have an [*sic*] use, it is, not to furnish us with phantasies, how-
> ever beautiful, but to point out that which is beautiful and lovely in the
> things which are nearest us, teaching us to see for ourselves that Nature
> being always the same, and humanity always the image of God, that in
> our day as well as in any other, and in our native village as well as in
> Sparta or Thebes, are worth and beauty, and the seal of Divinity in His
> works, to be found by those who will use their eyes and open their
> hearts. . . .[28]

Like Stowe, Stillman believes that the materialism of the age makes a
public commitment to art essential, even as the legacy of what he calls
the "bread and butter school of philosophers" preserves the common
attitude of art as superfluous to the business of the age. Although it is
couched in less Ruskinian terms, Stowe's argument about the religious
potential of romance is essentially similar to Stillman's belief in "the
spiritual qualities of art" and its ability to help those who "will use their
eyes and open their hearts" to see the divine, whether in nature, painting, or the streets of "prosaic" American towns. The nationalistic implications of Stowe's reference to the aesthetic potential of even the
"dullest streets of the most prosaic towns" become apparent when it is
juxtaposed with Stillman's call for an "Art of the Present" that will
"teach . . . us to see for ourselves . . . that . . . in our native village as well
as in Sparta or Thebes, are worth and beauty." While Stillman and
Stowe focus on the potential for art to protect against the pull of skepticism and materialism, James Jackson Jarves makes an even more dramatic claim for the importance of art in protecting America's political
stability and religious security in an age of scientific discovery and economic expansion:

> Science alone is not sufficient for a nation's prosperity. Religion,
> dwarfed into a panoply of forms, creeds, and restraints, is equally
> insufficient by itself. The two properly combined and understood form
> a strong phalanx, but to make that phalanx impenetrable to the shafts
> of atheism, bigotry, and revolutionary licensce, the mental trinity
> should be complete. Beauty, the sentiment which God has bestowed
> upon man for his ENJOYMENT, mark, not USE or WORSHIP, must be
> superadded.[29]

Although he later mounts an argument for art's social function, Jarves's
initial assertion that art is God's gift for pleasure only, "not use," highlights the widespread need for writers on aesthetic matters to position

themselves vis-à-vis the Scottish philosophers' utilitarian view of art. While the specifics of Stillman's, Jarves's, and Stowe's arguments differ, the general thrust of all three is similar: native art, and the artists who produce it, are essential to American society.

In embedding these arguments in a "romance," Stowe announces her participation in the nationalistic project of producing a native art that will preserve both Americans' religious faith and their political system. By focusing on "romance" instead of the visual arts, Stowe includes "poets and novelists," many of whom were women, in the ranks of those charged with doing "Art['s] . . . work." Indeed, for Stowe, "romance" is a uniquely American category, associated with Puritanism through the figure of the "soul artist." Stowe develops the idea of the "soul artist" in the second half of the chapter on romance, where the focus shifts from the religious effects of aesthetic production to the aesthetic foundation of religious experience. Stowe's "soul artist" is the protagonist of *The Minister's Wooing*, Mary Scudder, a young woman who has inherited both her religious nature and her aesthetic sensibility from her father, George Scudder, a frustrated poet whom Stowe praises for his specifically American style of handling his artistic disappointment: "He had a healthful, kindly animal nature, and so his inwardness did not ferment and turn to Byronic sourness and bitterness" (530). Further identifying George with the United States is the central moral dilemma of his life: his abhorrence of the slave trade, which dooms him to poverty but marks him as a member of the elect, if not in the Puritan theological world then certainly in Stowe's.

Stowe's description of Mary Scudder emphasizes her paternal legacy and underscores her American identity:

> There was something in Mary . . . which divided her as by an appreciable line from ordinary girls of her age. From her father she had inherited a deep and thoughtful nature, predisposed to moral and religious exaltation. Had she been born in Italy, under the dissolving influences of that sunny dreamy clime, beneath the shadow of cathedrals, and where pictured saints and angels smiled in clouds of painting from every arch and altar, she might, like fair St. Catherine of Siena, have seen beatific visions in the sunset skies, and a silver dove descending upon her as she prayed; but, unfolding in the clear, keen cold New England clime, and nurtured in its abstract and positive theologies, her religious faculties took other forms. Instead of laying entranced in mysterious raptures at the foot of altars, she read and pondered treatises on the Will, and listened in rapt attention, while her spiritual guide, the

venerated Dr. Hopkins, unfolded to her the theories of the great
Edwards on the nature of true virtue. Womanlike, she felt the subtile
poetry of these sublime abstractions which dealt with such infinite and
unknown quantities. . . .

When her mother questioned him, anxiously, of her daughter's
spiritual estate, he answered, that she was a child of a strange gra-
ciousness of nature, and of a singular genius; . . . Mary was . . . a recast
in a feminine form of her father's nature. The elixir of the spirit that
sparkled within her was of that quality of which the souls of poets and
artist are made; but the keen New England air crystallizes emotions
into ideas, and restricts many a poetic soul to the necessity of expressing itself only in practical living. (539–40)[30]

The comparison of the Italian and New England spiritual climates
works simultaneously to confirm Mary Scudder's status as the product
of a uniquely American religious tradition and to link her to the religious art of the Italian Middle Ages, which serves as the model for
Stowe's national aesthetic program. As she would do at length in *Agnes
of Sorrento*, Stowe here attempts to balance her admiration for Italian
religious art with her suspicion of Catholicism.[31] This balancing act is
evident in Stowe's assertion that although Mary's aesthetic tendencies,
like her father's, are limited and restricted by "the keen New England
air"—Stowe's shorthand for Puritan culture—they are essentially the
same as those that flourish under the "dissolving influences of [Italy's]
sunny dreamy clime," with its rich tradition of religious art. And
although she aligns Mary's aesthetic sensibilities with Italian religious
art, Stowe rejects the "beatific visions in the sunset skies" of Catholic
practice and emphasizes the rational habits of Mary's "religious facul-
ties" and her ability to "read and ponder . . . treatises on the Will" under
the tutelage of Dr. Hopkins, a famous Puritan divine.

In the figure of the "soul artist" Stowe grafts the aesthetic sensibility of Italian Catholicism onto the intellectual rigor of the Puritan mind
to produce a religiously based aesthetic that can serve as the framework
for the project of developing a national culture. The "soul artist" is a
religious figure whose methods and sensibilities are aesthetic:

Once in every age, God sends to some of us a friend who loves in us,
not a false imagining, an unreal character, but looking through all the
rubbish of our imperfections, loves in us the divine ideal of our
nature,—loves, not the man that we are, but the angel that we may
be. . . .

But these wonderful soul-friends, to whom God grants such perfection, are the exception in life; yet sometimes are we blessed with one who sees through us, as Michel Angelo saw through a block of marble, when he attacked it in a divine fervor, declaring that an angel was imprisoned within it; and it is often the resolute and delicate hand of such a friend that sets the angel free.

There be soul artists, who go through this world, looking among their fellows with reverence, as one looks amid the dust and rubbish of old shops for hidden works of Titian and Leonardo, and, finding them, however cracked or torn or painted over with tawdry daubs of pretenders, immediately recognize the divine original, and set themselves to cleanse and restore. Such be God's real priests, whose ordination and anointing are from the Holy Spirit; and he who hath not this enthusiasm is not ordained of God, though whole synods of bishops laid hands on him.

Many such priests there be among women; for to this silent ministry their nature calls them, endowed as it is, with fineness of fiber and a subtle keenness of perception outrunning slow-footed reason; and she of whom we write was one of these. (606)

In defining an essentially religious quality—the ability to recognize the divinity of one's fellows and work to expose it— by way of aesthetic sensibilities, Stowe asserts the inherent equality of the two kinds of activities. Aligning "soul artists" with Italian art and its creators implies that American religious energy is similar to that of the Renaissance and lays the groundwork for Stowe's suggestion in *Agnes of Sorrento*, which is set in fifteenth-century Italy, that this energy be harnessed for the creation of a national art.

Although Stowe's "soul artist" produces no actual work of art, the term itself is associated with the contemporary project of American cultural development and with the Ruskinian view of the moral nature of artistic production. This association is evident in Jarves's assertion, early in *Art-Hints*, that

The energies which have raised America to the position of an enigma for all nations must still find employment. License, the fruit of misdirected passion, and effeminacy, the canker of luxury, are equally stumbling-blocks in her progress. . . . The right direction to be given to each is the problem to settle. Art looks to America with open arms. How is it to be carried there? Not by misses who run over Europe and bring back a cabin-load of new bonnets, with dresses and trinkets to

> match; neither by women whose aim is display and ruling principle
> vanity. . . . We need Art-students, men of sincerity and labor, who will
> not hesitate to go on their backs and knees, if need be in the dust, to
> read the soul-language of the mightiest minds in Europe.[32]

And Stillman offers this view of artists' national importance: "it is society that suffers by the neglect of the artist; and it is the interest of society, therefore, to give him the position which his share in the soul-culture justifies. . . ."[33] As these examples demonstrate, Stowe's conception of the "soul artist" not only evokes similar terms—"soul-language" and "soul-culture" are just a few examples of the locutions that were widely used to describe Art and the artist's function—but takes on the gendered assumptions underlying American cultural nationalism. Both Jarves and Stillman clearly view the artist, or art student, as male, whether as a habit of language or, as in Jarves's case, as an explicit gesture of distinction from women, who embody Americans' crass materialism. Jarves's depiction of women who, as consumers of European "trinkets," pose an obstacle to the "men of sincerity" who are willing to bring art to the United States on their hands and knees, taps into a longstanding association of women with the marketplace and enables him to define high art not only as masculine, but as embattled by the very group that was largely responsible for the emergence of a broad audience for culture in America: women writers and their female audience. Stowe's characterization of the "soul artist" as a peculiarly female quality is, thus, a potent challenge to the gendered assumptions underlying the project of American cultural nationalism. By appropriating the terminology of Ruskinian notions of the essentially moral nature of art and melding it with her own critique of sentimental religion, an authorizing force for antebellum women writers, Stowe shifts the terms that had historically been used to define women's artistic production, creating the foundation for a new conception of women's aesthetic work.[34]

Stowe's critique of sentimental religion is embedded in the theological plot of *The Minister's Wooing*, which revolves around the crisis of faith sparked by the presumed death by shipwreck of James Marvyn, who is assumed to have died unregenerate because he left no positive evidence of his conversion. The theological side of Stowe's novel, which has received the bulk of the critical attention devoted to this text, is usually understood in terms of the familiar dichotomy between Calvinism and sentimental or "heart" religion. The novel is typically read as a critique of New England orthodoxy in which the unfeeling logic of doctrine, represented by Dr. Hopkins, is contrasted to the sentimental theology of Candace, a former slave who is the only person capable of comforting the bereaved Mrs. Marvyn, whose grief is compounded by the belief that her son is almost certainly ineligible for spiritual salvation. That is—that he will spend eternity in hell. This reading, which figures Mary Scudder as either Puritan saint or sentimental heroine, or both, reduces the complexity of Stowe's religious vision and posits her enthusiastic participation in what one critic has called "Stowe['s] . . . holy war of the Sentimental Love Religion."[35] In fact, Stowe struggled for years to reconcile her Calvinist faith with the more liberal solutions developed by Catharine Beecher, among others. Deeply aware of the need for a more emotionally satisfying response to the tragedies of people's lives than orthodox Calvinism offered, Stowe nonetheless clung to Calvinism, whose "strong mental discipline" she felt was "needed by a people who were an absolute democracy."[36] Stowe's struggle with Calvinism is inscribed in the character of Mary Scudder, whose crisis of faith in the wake of James Marvyn's death has been overshadowed by the more dramatic though finally less productive one experienced by the character of Mrs. Marvyn.

The impulse to view Candace as the embodiment of the novel's religious vision has a long history. In his 1889 authorized biography of his mother, Charles Edward Stowe explains why he devoted so much space to the story of the death of Catharine Beecher's fiancé, Alexander Metcalf Fisher, in a shipwreck off the coast of Ireland in 1822: "Without this incident [the loss of Fisher] 'The Minister's Wooing' would never have been written, for both Mrs. Marvyn's terrible soul struggles and old Candace's direct and effective solution of all religious difficulties find their origin in this stranded, storm-beaten ship on the coast of Ireland, and the terrible mental conflicts through which her sister afterward passed, for she believed Professor Fisher eternally lost.[37] He concludes the section on Catharine's religious struggles by declaring that

> [Catharine's] solution in brief is nothing more than that view of the divine nature which was for so many years preached by her brother, Henry Ward Beecher, and set forth in the writings of her sister Harriet,—the conception of a being of infinite love, patience, and kindness who suffers with man. The sufferings of Christ on the cross were not the sufferings of his human nature merely, but the sufferings of the

divine nature in Him. In Christ we see the only revelation of God, and
that is the revelation of one that suffers. This is the fundamental idea in
"The Minister's Wooing," and it is the idea of God in which the storm-
tossed soul of the elder sister at last found rest. All this was directly
opposed to that fundamental principle of theologians that God, being
the infinitely perfect Being, cannot suffer, because suffering indicates
imperfection. [That is, the view of orthodox Calvinism.][38]

Charles Stowe here instructs his readers how to read *The Minister's Wooing*, directing us to focus on Candace as the bearer of the "direct and
effective solution of all religious difficulties," a solution that is "directly
opposed" to the Calvinism it replaces. Charles's investment in Can-
dace/Catharine/Henry Ward's sentimental religious solution is not
surprising, given that by 1889 it had become a family industry. But the
reading of *The Minister's Wooing* he offers does much to obscure his
mother's ambivalence about her siblings' "direct and effective solution
of all religious difficulties," an ambivalence he documents at length in
the very same chapter of the biography that contains this statement and
which his mother develops in the novel, in the character of Mary Scudder.[39] Many subsequent readers have followed Charles Stowe's direction. The novel is typically viewed as seeking to replace male ministers
with a domestically based feminine ministry, supplanting the paternal
Edwardsian God with a Bushnellian maternal Christ. Candace's ability
to comfort Mrs. Marvyn is regularly cited as the evidence of that substitution.[40] The novel certainly offers a clear-eyed view of Calvinism's
shortcomings and seeks to ameliorate its harshness, making it a more
nurturing faith, especially for women. But the focus on Candace
bespeaks a distinctly binary understanding of Stowe's project: she is
widely understood to be replacing Calvinism with sentimental love religion. But Stowe's project, and her attitude toward Calvinism, is far
more complex: she is, as Charles Foster has observed, saying "both yes
and no" to Calvinism.[41] While James Marvyn's death is clearly the catalyst for religious crisis in the novel, the heart of the novel's theological
vision lies not with Candace's sentimental formula of a loving maternal
Christ but with Mary Scudder's highly individual form of faith, which
she achieves after a lengthy period of thoughtful introspection and
prayer during which she abandons her uncomplicated youthful conceptions of faith and comes to terms with the doubts raised both by James's
death and by Doctor Hopkins's and Mrs. Marvyn's rational approach to
faith. Candace's solution is an emergency measure, not a lifelong alternative. She comforts Mrs. Marvyn by treating her like a child, explaining

that "in fair weather I ha'n't no 'objection to yer hearn' all about dese yer great an' mighty tings he's [the Doctor] got to say" but that "it won't do for you now" (736). While Stowe clearly endorses the healing, indeed life-saving, quality of Candace's approach, she finds it inadequate as an enduring framework for adult women's faith.

All of Stowe's fiction drew heavily on her own and her family's experiences, but *The Minister's Wooing* is perhaps the most deeply autobiographical of all her work. The plot is drawn directly from the experience of Stowe's sister, Catharine Beecher, and of Stowe herself, whose beloved oldest son, Henry Ellis Stowe, drowned while swimming in the Connecticut river in July 1857. Both young men had died without experiencing conversion—the Calvinist prerequisite to election—and both deaths prompted a crisis of faith in the Beecher women left behind. After struggling with the Calvinist doctrines surrounding eternal damnation and election for a number of years Catharine developed her own religious framework, which drew on the ideas of English evangelical writer John Newton, "who stressed God's compassion and His willingness to save even the most reluctant sinner."[42] Her son's death reignited a religious crisis that Harriet Beecher Stowe had struggled with on and off for her entire life, beginning with her first conversion to Christianity at the age of thirteen.

For the daughter of a renowned Calvinist minister, faith was never something to take lightly. Nor was it something that came easily. Stowe describes her first conversion, which occurred in the summer of 1825, in a letter written to one of her sons in 1886. She records that the event took place on a beautiful summer morning, in her father's church. Having entered the church feeling "quite dissatisfied" with herself because of her inability to "feel [her] sins and count them up," the young Harriet settled down to listen to her father's sermon, which she expected to be like his others—"as unintelligible to me as if he had spoken in Choctaw." To her delight, she was drawn in by her father's "pathetic earnestness" as he preached a

> "frame sermon;" that is, a sermon that sprung out of the deep feeling
> of the occasion, and which consequently could be neither premeditated
> nor repeated. . . . Forgetting all his hair-splitting distinctions and dialec-
> tic subtleties, he spoke in direct, simple, and tender language of the
> great love of Christ and his care for the soul. He pictured Him as
> patient with our errors, compassionate with our weaknesses, and sym-
> pathetic for our sorrows. He went on to say how He was ever near us,
> enlightening our ignorance, guiding our wanderings, comforting our

sorrows with a love unwearied by faults, unchilled by ingratitude, till at last he should present us faultless before the throne of his glory with exceeding joy.[43]

What is interesting in this recollection—written long after the fact—is that Stowe's conversion is produced by an inspired sermon given by her father in which he "forget[s]" his Calvinist training and methods, allowing himself to preach a "sermon that sprung out of the deep feeling of the occasion." In so doing, he gives a sermon that is not only accessible to his daughter, but that produces that most desirable of outcomes: conversion. By giving her father the power to effect her first conversion, Stowe grants Lyman Beecher—and through him, Calvinism—pride of place in her religious identity. In making the vehicle for her conversion an unusually emotional sermon that focuses on Jesus as friend rather than on any of the questions of doctrine that are her father's usual subjects, Stowe highlights the limitations of traditional Calvinist theology. Indeed, the sermon Lyman Beecher preaches, in which he urges his listeners to view Christ as their loving, watchful, patient, caring friend, strongly resembles the kind of Christ-centered love religion that a number of his children would adopt and popularize in the coming decades. But in the years that followed her initial conversion Harriet Beecher struggled mightily to reconcile the tension between her father's mostly harsh, unforgiving God and a Calvinist theology that emphasized self-examination and sin, and the more forgiving Christ-focused theology adopted by her siblings Catharine and Edward.[44] The tension arose from Stowe's unwillingness to give up those aspects of Calvinism that appealed to her: its intellectual rigor and its awesome God, who commands respect precisely because he is not a friend but a superior being.

That tension dominated the years following her first conversion, during which Stowe lived in Hartford, studying and teaching at Catharine Beecher's Female Academy. Her struggle with her adolescent angst and religious doubts are recorded in letters to her brother Edward, then studying at the Andover theological seminary, whose religious views she longed to accept but found lacking in some important ways. Writing to Edward in August 1827, Harriet continues their ongoing conversation about her struggle with faith in general, and with the views her brother has been urging on her in particular:

It appears to me that if I only could adopt the views of God you presented to my mind, they would exert a strong and beneficial influence over my character. But I am afraid to accept them for several reasons. First, it seems to be taking from the majesty and dignity of the divine character to suppose that his happiness can be at all affected by the conduct of his sinful, erring creatures. Secondly, it seems to me that such views of God would have an effect on our own minds in lessening that reverence and fear which is one of the greatest motives for us to action. For, although to a generous mind the thought of the love of God would be a sufficient incentive to action, there are times of coldness when that life is not felt, and then there remains no sort of stimulus. I find that as I adopt these sentiments I feel less fear of God, and, in view of sin, I feel only a sensation of grief which is more easily dispelled and forgotten than that I formerly felt.[45]

There is a great deal more in this vein, as Harriet vacillated between accepting the comforting faith her brother urged upon her and finding fault with it. Six months later, in March 1827, she writes: "I think that those views of God which you have presented to me have had an influence in restoring my mind to its natural tone. But still, after all, God is a being afar off. He is so far above us that anything but the most distant reverential affection seems almost sacrilegious."[46] Comforting as she finds her brother's views, Harriet cannot give up on the awesome, distant God of Calvinism. It is precisely this mixture of desire to adopt a less harsh view and distrust of the relative ease offered by Edward and Catharine that informs *The Minister's Wooing*.

Although Stowe enjoyed a period of relative religious peace of mind during the 1830s, when she moved to Cincinnati with her family, began her literary career, and married Calvin Stowe, the 1840s proved considerably more difficult. The pressures of adapting to marriage, frequent childbirth (she had five children between 1836 and 1843, including one set of twins), the expectation of domestic and religious perfection, political and economic crises, a wave of religious revivals, and finally, the suicide of brother George Beecher in 1843 all posed serious challenges to Stowe's religious identity.[47] While she was in Boston in 1842 Harriet wrote Calvin, expressing her fear that she was not a good enough Christian and vowing to do better: "Now by the grace of God I am resolved to come home & live for God. . . . Will you dear husband join with me in simplicity & earnestness to lead a new life?—to live no more as we have—allowing ourselves in sin here & there. . . . are we ready to take the exceeding and eternal weight of glory—what have we done & suffered for Christ?" She longed for "a second conversion that is to the Christian as real an advance, as his first regeneration."[48] A year later, her struggles with "perfectionist strivings" intensified in the face of George's death, and the birth of her fifth child, Georgianna, a few weeks later, precipitated a crisis that had been brewing for some time.[49] As she grieved for her brother, Stowe struggled to accept the Calvinist teaching that George's death was an expression of divine will. She battled her conviction that she was a failed Christian, "berated herself for her inability to make 'an entire IDENTITY of my will with God's,' . . . and urged herself to submit—to give up her 'seperate [*sic*] will' and unite her soul to Christ's; when time and again she proved incapable of such submission, she lashed herself to greater and greater efforts."[50] During the winter of 1844 Stowe wrote her brother Thomas Beecher that she "'often wondered why God would press my soul longing for reunion with a weight of cares that seemed to hold it prostrate on the earth—I felt alone unsupported—& whom in former times I had found *very* present seemed to leave me entirely.'" At this low point, "'When self-despair was final,'" Stowe wrote Thomas Beecher, she finally found "'the long-expected and wished help. . . . My *all* changed. . . . the will of Christ seems to me the steady pulse of my being & I go because I can not help it. Skeptical doubt can not exist—I seem to see the full blaze of the Shekinah every where. I am calm, but full.'"[51] Although Charles Foster characterizes this as Stowe's "'true' conversion," she would confront "Skeptical doubt" and, above all, the inability to submit to the divine will again and again in the coming years.[52] The death of her treasured eighteen-month-old baby Charley, during the Cholera epidemic that swept through Cincinnati in the summer of 1849, would prove another trial, and the death of her eldest son Henry Ellis in 1857 would revive the old struggles again.

Shortly before Henry's death Catharine Beecher's *Common Sense Applied to Religion* was published, and one of its central arguments was that "God saved those who seemed to want to be saved, not merely those who had passed through a conversion experience."[53] For the next year, during which she began writing *The Minister's Wooing*, Stowe alternated between finding comfort in her sister's view, which would allow her to believe that her son had gone to heaven despite having died unconverted, and her commitment to the "calm settled belief" in Edwardian Calvinism which she had adopted after her "true" conversion of 1845.[54] That belief, which she was able to grasp at in her "better moments," dictated that God might send any unconverted adult to hell "with eminent justice."[55] Foster notes that Stowe's religious belief during the year following her son's death was, in fact, deeply contradictory. In effect, she temporarily bracketed her "settled belief" in order to accept Catharine's views and make an exception for her beloved son.[56] There was no neat solution to Stowe's dilemma: adopting Catharine's view required abandoning a faith she had accepted after great turmoil and that she deeply admired; believing the teachings of that faith, however, caused her immeasurable pain and grief. Writing *The Minister's Wooing* enabled Stowe both to come to terms with her grief and her recent religious crisis and to transform them into the source of her own and the nation's artistic and cultural future.

The Minister's Wooing is strongly autobiographical, but its religious concerns are not strictly personal. Its readers were struggling with what James Turner has called the "intellectual crisis of belief," which was prompted by the development of anthropology and the comparative study of religion, by new scientific discoveries, and by the higher criticism of the Bible, emanating from Germany. Anthropology suggested that Christian truths and values were not of divine origin, handed down from on high to Jesus and from there to all Christians, but were, rather, the result of cultural evolution. The comparative study of world religions suggested that "'Christian truths' were, apparently, not unique to Christianity at all."[57] Both developments were profoundly unsettling to Christians and yet were so compatible with each other and with the nineteenth century's increasing emphasis on historical progress that they could not simply be ignored. What was particularly disturbing about the growth of these two new disciplines and the resulting understanding of religion as something that evolves was not so much that it "negate[d] the truth of religion, for it dovetailed with the prevailing belief that God had implanted religious intuitions in the human mind. But the idea was toxic to the central dogma of historic Christianity: that God had intervened in human history to reveal a unique body of religious truths in the career of Jesus."[58]

In the scientific realm, evidence that linked human nature to animals through evolution and new understanding of the workings of the brain and mind all challenged prior assumptions about what it meant to have a knowledge of God. The discovery that the brain was a physical organ composed of a series of electrical impulses made it hard to view the mind as the seat of the soul. Another major source of the intellectual crisis of belief was Darwinian biology and the implications it had for the relationship between science and faith in God. Whereas before Darwin science was a central bulwark of the belief in God, in the shape of the design argument, Darwinian biology "not only torpedoed the argument from design but made clear that the whole enterprise of natural theology had foundered in very deep waters. The whole idea of a scientific natural theology involved now a contradiction in terms. For science qua science, by definition, could now offer no foundation for belief in God."[59] Theologians shifted from showing how science supported the existence of God to insisting that science did not explicitly disprove his existence, though it certainly made clear that the world could have come into being without him. This posed a particular problem because Protestant clergy had been linking science and God for over a century, buttressing religion against increasing challenges and hoping "to capitalize on the rising stock of science, on the ever-growing confidence in its approach to knowledge. . . . Natural theology had invested huge sums of confidence in scientific knowledge. If it now turned out that science could give no knowledge of God, the question had to be asked whether knowledge of God was possible at all."[60]

Even if they hadn't yet read Darwin's *Origins of the Species*, which was published in the same year as *The Minister's Wooing*, by the late 1850s educated Americans were being buffeted by challenges to faith posed by the higher criticism. Originating in Germany during the late-eighteenth century and brought to the United States by renowned Andover theologian Moses Stuart in the 1820s, the higher criticism "used philological and historical expertise to try to determine the dates, authorship, and, ultimately, meaning of scriptural texts."[61] The first casualty was belief in the factuality of the Old Testament and in the existence of Moses, Isaiah, and others as real, individual, historical beings. But so long as the New Testament revelations were left intact, Christians could maintain their faith. That changed in 1846 with the publication of the first English translation of David Friedrich Strauss's "Das Leben Jesu." Strauss argued that "the Gospels did not intend to relate a factual history; rather, they created a myth of a God-man. . . . This Christ-myth embodied profound religious truth, but it could hardly yield any historical knowledge. Indeed, Jesus and his real teachings remained unknowable—assuming that they had actually existed behind the primitive myth."[62] Taken together with a slowly liberalizing theology, which struggled to reconcile fundamental Christian doctrines like the existence of hell and eternal damnation with a new belief in humanitarianism and in a good, benevolent, loving God, with the challenges posed by premature death of children and young people, scientific discoveries and the higher criticism conspired to make religious belief increasingly difficult for Americans at midcentury.

The intellectual crisis of faith is typically viewed as a distinctly male concern, a conversation between ministers, scientists, and cultural observers. In *The Minister's Wooing* Stowe enters into this conversation, insisting on her right to weigh in not only on "feminine" concerns, such as the challenge to faith engendered by the death of a child, but on the theological and intellectual dilemmas that faced all thinking Americans: the difficulty of reconciling faith in God and a rational understanding of the world as it was coming to be known.[63]

The concept of the "soul artist" attempts to do just that. The "soul artist," embodied by Mary Scudder, taps into the artistic sensibilities that Stowe has defined as equivalent to religious energy in order to bridge the gap between the relentlessly rational models of Calvinism and a faith that depends on one's willingness to suspend logic altogether, embodied by both the youthful Mary and by Candace, the bearer of sentimental heart religion. These two theological positions are described in a chapter titled "Evidences," in which Dr. Hopkins, who boards with Mary's mother, questions the young girl about her faith:

> "Mary . . . Do you ever have any periods in which your evidences seem not altogether clear?" . . . with a deepening flush she answered gently, "No, Sir."
>
> "What! never any doubts?" said the Doctor.
>
> "I am sorry," said Mary, apologetically; "but I do not see how I *can* have; I never could."
>
> "Ah!" Said the Doctor, musingly, "would I could say so!" . . . when she saw the man for whom her reverence was almost like that of her God thus distrustful, thus lowly, she could not but feel that her too calm repose might, after all, be the shallow, treacherous calm of an ignorant, ill-grounded spirit, and therefore, with a deep blush and a faltering voice, she said,—
>
> "Indeed, I am afraid something must be wrong with me. I cannot have any fears,—I never could; I try sometimes, but the thought of God's goodness comes all around me, and I am so happy before I think of it!" (700–701)

The irony of a minister seeking to plant doubt where none exists would not have been lost on Stowe's audience, for whom the need to repress doubt was a matter of increasing concern. Mary's admission that she "tr[ies] sometimes" to have fears, only to have her efforts fail as her faith in "God's goodness" surrounds her, is obviously appealing to the minister, but Stowe soon reveals why he is unable to enjoy the kind of ecstatic faith that Mary possesses painlessly:

The Doctor had practised [*sic*] his subtile mental analysis till his instruments were so fine-pointed and keen edged that he scarce ever allowed a flower of sacred emotion to spring in his soul without picking it to pieces to see if its genera and species were correct. Love, gratitude, reverence, benevolence,—which all moved in mighty tides in his soul,—were all compelled to pause midway while he rubbed up his optical instruments to see whether they were rising in the right order. Mary, on the contrary, had the blessed gift of womanhood,—that vivid life in the soul and sentiment which resists the chills of analysis, as a healthful human heart resists cold; yet still, all humbly, she thought this perhaps was a defect in herself, and therefore . . . confessed in a depreciating tone, her habits of unanalyzed faith and love. . . . (702)

It is tempting to read Dr. Hopkins's failing as his lack of emotion, but Stowe carefully notes that he is afflicted not by the inability to feel—"mighty tides" of emotion regularly "moved" within his soul—but by the habits of "subtile mental analysis" he has developed through years of practice. Dr. Hopkins's problem is not that he is a cold and unfeeling Calvinist minister, but rather that the very habits of reason on which the minister's faith relies lead to doubt. The distinction is important because it suggests that Stowe's project is not simply a critique of Calvinism's failure of feeling, but an exploration of the tension between faith and reason that is inherent in Calvinism. Although the novel is set soon after the Revolutionary War, decades before either biblical criticism or scientific discoveries created insuperable challenges to religious faith, Stowe's allusion to the Doctor's habit of analyzing the "genera and species" of every "flower of emotion" and using his "optical instruments" to ensure that the "mighty tides" of emotion are "rising in the right order" underscores his scientific habits of minds and aligns his doubts with those experienced by Stowe's contemporaries.

In contrast, Mary Scudder's ability to experience "God's goodness" is largely dependent on her willingness to abandon rational thought:

In all the system which had been explained to her, her mind selected points on which it seized with intense sympathy, which it dwelt upon and expanded till all else fell away. The sublimity of disinterested benevolence,—the harmony and order of a system tending in its final results to infinite happiness,—the goodness of God,—the love of a self-sacrificing Redeemer,—were all so many glorious pictures, which she revolved in her mind with small care for their logical relations. (733)

Appealing though Mary's "unanalyzed habits of faith and love" might have been to Stowe's readers, they are not a viable model for emulation for those who doubt and question. Modeled in part on Stowe's mother, Roxanne Foote, who had been sanctified in the Beecher family after her death in 1814, Mary is one of the elect from birth; she is incapable of having fears of her own salvation.[64] She is also so good, so pure, so pious as to seem like a stereotypical sentimental heroine, interested only in effecting others' salvation. Upon reading a letter left in her room by James Marvyn on the eve of his departure, Mary is moved not by the declaration of love it contains but by the consciousness that her beloved is far from God: "It was without one particle of exalted vanity, with even a throb of pain, that she read such exalted praises of herself from one blind to the glories of a far higher loveliness" (571). The narrator's observation that Mary was "unknown to herself, one of the great company scattered through earth who are priests unto God,—ministering between the Divine One, who has unveiled himself unto them, and those who as yet stand in the outer courts of the great sanctuary of truth and holiness" further aligns her with other of Stowe's sentimental heroines such as Eva St. Clare and Mara Lincoln, whose lives, and deaths, are devoted to bringing others closer to Christian faith (571). Part Puritan saint, part sentimental paragon, the youthful Mary has little to offer to those readers who insist on analyzing their "habits of faith."

Although she is painfully aware of the doubts that approaching one's religious beliefs logically can engender, Stowe is fundamentally sympathetic to this dilemma. Indeed, she views Calvinism's intellectual rigor as one of its greatest strengths and the cornerstone of American democracy. In an 1858 *Atlantic* essay titled "New England Ministers" Stowe uses the publication of William B. Sprague's *Annals of the New England Pulpit* as an opportunity to argue for the centrality of New England Calvinism to American national identity. Stowe reserves special praise for the ministers' insistence on logically reconciling all the doctrines in which they believe:

> It is a mark of a shallow mind to scorn these theological wrestlings and surgings; [the famous New England divines] have had in them something even sublime. They were always bounded and steadied by the most profound reverence for God and his world; and they have constituted in New England the strong mental discipline needed by a people who were an absolute democracy.[65]

Mary clearly does not "scorn" the Doctor's "theological wrestlings," and her form of faith is initially characterized as a "gift"; but the crisis of faith engendered by James's presumed death and by his mother's rejection of Calvinism will reveal the limitations of her "habits of unanalyzed faith and love" and transform her into a thinking adult entitled to wear the mantle of the "soul artist."

Stowe's respect for the difficulties produced by logical habits of thought, and her understanding that they are not limited to Puritan divines is underscored in the character of Mrs. Marvyn, whose formidable intellect makes her the minister's equal, both in capacity for reason and in capacity for doubt. Mrs. Marvyn is handsome, an efficient housekeeper, and a highly intelligent woman whose mind is "of a finer and higher stamp" than her husband's (589). Her intellectual energies are divided between voracious reading in all disciplines and a deep concern with the metaphysical:

> No pair of eyes followed the web of [the minister's] reasonings with a keener and more anxious watchfulness than those sad, deep-set hazel ones; and as she was drawn along the train of its inevitable logic, a close observer might have seen the shadow deepened over them. . . .
>
> The consequence of all her listening was a history of deep inward sadness. That exultant joy, or that entire submission with which others seemed to view the scheme of the universe, as thus unfolded, did not visit her mind. Everything to her seemed shrouded in gloom and mystery; and that darkness she received as a token of unregeneracy, as a sign that she was one of those who are destined, by a mysterious decree, never to receive the light of the glorious gospel of Christ. (590)

Like Dr. Hopkins, Mrs. Marvyn struggles to reconcile her desire for unquestioning faith with a rational mind that does not allow her to ignore the implications of the minister's reasoning. As a result, she has access to neither the "exultant joy" nor the "entire submission" of her fellow parishioners and is destined to wait without "hope of remedy" for the expression of the divine will (590). Although this is the long-standing problem facing Calvinists, it is also precisely the problem facing rational believers in the mid-nineteenth-century context in which the novel was published: those who, like the minister and Mrs. Marvyn, bring reason to bear on the evidence before them cannot help but acknowledge the implications of that evidence, leaving the believer with little, if any, source of spiritual solace.

What had been a lifelong metaphysical concern becomes a crisis when the news of her son's death at sea reaches Mrs. Marvyn, whose suffering is worsened by the minister's inability to assure the grieving parents that their son's soul will be saved for lack of "evidence" that he became a Christian before his death (725). Asked to stay with the grief-stricken mother, Mary is shocked when the usually reticent and con-trolled Mrs. Marvyn explodes in a paroxysm of religious anguish, which Stowe attributes to her rational habits of mind:

> Hers was a nature more reasoning than creative and poetic; and what-ever she believed bound her mind in strictest chains to its logical results. She delighted in the regions of mathematical knowledge, and walked in them as a native home, but the commerce with abstract cer-tainties fitted her mind still more to be stiffened and enchained by glacial reasonings, in regions where spiritual intuitions are as necessary as wings to birds. (732)

Unlike Mary, whose "creative and poetic" mind protects her from the chill of "glacial reasonings," Mrs. Marvyn appears doomed to die of the cold. Listening to Mrs. Marvyn's analysis of the implications of the doc-trine of election, Mary is suddenly assailed by the doubts she had earli-er assured the minister she didn't know how to have:

> Pale, aghast, horror-stricken, Mary stood dumb, as one who in the dark and storm sees by the sudden glare of lighting a chasm yawning under foot. It was amazement and dimness of anguish;—the dreadful words struck on the very centre where her soul rested. She felt as if the point of a wedge were being driven between her life and her life's life,— between her and her God. She clasped her hands instinctively on her bosom, as if to hold there some cherished image, and said, in a piercing voice of supplication, "*My* God! *my* God! Oh, where art thou?" (734)

Mary's cry, with its emphasis on the first-person possessive, and her subsequent crisis of faith, reveal that the Doctor's incredulity was not misplaced. Mary's tendency to "select . . . points on which [she] seized with intense sympathy, which [she] dwelt upon and expanded till all else fell away" (733) is a pleasant and comforting approach for a child, but it is inadequate for an adult faced with the nineteenth century's most common challenge to religious faith—premature death and the withheld promise of salvation.

Having demonstrated the insufficiency of both Mrs. Marvyn's intensely logical orthodox belief and Mary's selective Calvinism, Stowe devotes the remainder of the novel to exploring the possibility of creating an alternative to both. As a first step, Mary witnesses Mrs. Marvyn's choice of Candace's sentimental faith, which offers comfort in exchange for agreeing "not to stretch our mind with reasonings" (741) over the Doctor's "system" (742). Having come perilously close to losing her faith altogether, Mrs. Marvyn explains to Mary why she chose the sentimental over the rational:

> "There is but just one thing remaining, and that is, as Candace said, the cross of Christ. If God so loved us,—if He died for us,—greater love hath no man than this. . . . Mary, I feel that I must love more, to give up one of my children to suffer, than to consent to suffer myself. There is a world of comfort to me in the words, 'He that spared not his own Son, but delivered him up for us all, how shall he not with him also freely give us all things?' These words speak to my heart. I can interpret them by my own nature, and I rest on them. If there is a fathomless mystery of sin and sorrow, there is a deeper mystery of God's love. So, Mary, I try Candace's way,—I look at Christ,—I pray to Him. If he that hath seen Him hath seen the Father, it is enough. I rest there,—I wait. What I know not now I shall know hereafter." (742)

Although Mrs. Marvyn has apparently achieved "that entire submission" that had eluded her earlier, the sacrifice she must make to reach some degree of "comfort" and "rest" is considerable: she has lost both her child and an essential part of her identity. Mrs. Marvyn is forced to sacrifice her commitment to "logical results" in order to preserve her sanity, and to accept instead the vague promise of knowledge to be gained in the "hereafter." Although embracing Candace's sentimental faith comforts Mrs. Marvyn and prevents her from losing her faith altogether, Stowe does not, finally, endorse sentimental religion as the solution to the problem posed by rational challenges to faith.

Indeed, Stowe privileges the ability to struggle with one's religious beliefs. Although she is acutely aware of the emotional destructiveness of strict Calvinism, she seeks to ameliorate its harshest tenets rather than replace it with a system that obviates the need for intellectual and spiritual struggle. Candace's response to Mrs. Marvyn's crisis of faith demonstrates that simplicity and accessibility are both the strengths and weaknesses of sentimental religion. Candace's theology operates by analogy and can be expressed quite clearly in the down-to-earth language of maternal love. Gathering the grieving Mrs. Marvyn in her arms "as if she had been a babe" Candace explains:

"Why, de Lord a'n't like what ye tink,—He loves ye, honey! Why, jes'
feel how I loves, ye,—poor ole black Candace,—an' I a'n't better 'n Him
as made me! Who was it sweat great drops o' blood?—who was it sid,
'Father, forgive dem'? Say, honey! Wasn't it de Lord dat made ye?—
Dar, dar, now ye'r' cryin'!—cry away, and ease yer poor little heart! He
died for Mass'r Jim,—loved him and died for him,—jes' give up his
sweet precious body and soul for him on de cross! Laws, jes' leave him
in Jesus's hands! Why, honey, dar's de very print o' de nails in his
hands now!" (736)

Articulated by a black former slave, whose "abundant outwardness and
demonstrativeness" (594) Stowe elsewhere associates with childishness,
Candace's theology is powerful but uncomplicated, based largely on
the catechism and a simple faith in God's love coupled with an imaginative streak that allows her to visualize the marks of the nails of the
cross in Christ's hands as "evidence" of James's salvation. Candace's
version of "evidence" points to the weakness of sentimental religion: it
requires that Mrs. Marvyn stop using her powers of reason and find
comfort by making a logical leap between Candace's love and God's.

In making Candace, a black woman, the vehicle of sentimental religion, Stowe simultaneously grants her the important role of "high priest
of suffering" and signals the insufficiency of sentimental religion (282).
For blacks, Stowe had declared in *Uncle Tom's Cabin*, have an innate ability to accept religious teachings without questioning. Describing Tom's
spiritual victory over Simon Legree, Stowe cites "missionaries" who
have observed that "of all the races of the earth, none have received the
Gospel with such eager docility as the African. The principle of reliance
and unquestioning faith, which is its foundation, is more a native element in this race than any other. . . ."[66] This is, of course, meant as praise.
But Stowe's racialist condescension is evident in this description of
Africans' "docility," and the celebration of "unquestioning faith" has a
double-edged quality, coming as it does from someone who had herself
spent years questioning faith and was surrounded by people she
respected and admired (including her husband) who did the same.[67]
Unlike Mary, whose rigorous theological training by one of the most
prominent Puritan divines marks her as a member of America's elite,
Candace is an uneducated former slave who accepts the Doctor's religious teachings for all the wrong reasons. As the narrator explains,
there had been some difficulty in getting Candace to adopt "received
[religious] opinion," and certain parts of the catechism in particular.
When asked to declare that she

had sinned in Adam and fell with him, Candace made a dead halt:—

"'I didn't do dat ar', for one, I knows. I's got good mem'ry,—allers know what I does,—nebber did dat that ar' apple,—nebber eat a bit ob him. Don't tell me!"

It was of no use, of course, to tell Candace of all the explanations of this redoubtable passage,—of potential presence and representative presence, and representative identity, and federal headship. She met all with the dogged,—

"Nebber did it, I knows; should 'ave 'membered, if I had. Don't tell me!" (611)

Underlying the humor of this description is Stowe's conviction that "it was no use, of course" to expect literal-minded Candace to understand and accept the complex, abstract theological reasoning underlying the catechism. Candace finally accepts the Doctor's belief system not because she has come to believe in it, but because she discovers that he has been instrumental in freeing a distant cousin of hers, who was harshly treated by his master. When she hears the news Candace declares "Den I'm gwine to b'liebe ebery word he does." She is as good as her word:

At the next catechizing, the Doctor's astonishment was great when Candace pressed up to him, exclaiming—

"de Lord bress you, Doctor, for opening de prison for dem dat is bound! I b'liebes in you now, Doctor. I's gwine to b'liebe every word you say. I'll say de Catechize now,—fix it any way you like. I did eat dat ar' apple,—I eat de whole tree, an' swallowed ebery bit ob it, if you say so." (612)

The grounds for Candace's conversion, if it may be called that, are unorthodox to say the least. And although Stowe praises the Doctor's antislavery activities as consistent with the teachings of Christianity, good deeds, however noble and praiseworthy, are not adequate grounds for religious faith. Indeed, Candace has clearly not undergone a conversion—she simply makes up her mind to accept the Doctor's teachings because she admires and respects him. In this she resembles Mrs. Scudder, Mary's mother, whose faith is based on "this stable corner-stone,—'Mr. Scudder used to believe it,—I will'" (534). The narrator does not reject this mode of choosing a belief system, addressing the reader to ask: "after all that is said about independent thought, isn't the fact, that a just and good soul has thus or thus believed, a more respectable argument than many that often are adduced?" But her subsequent observation that "two thirds of the faith of in the world is built on no better foundation" suggests that the one-third minority who can find a "better foundation" for faith are to be admired (534).

Mary Scudder is a member of that minority. Although Candace urges her comforting theology on Mary, she chooses to struggle with her doubts. Immediately after the scene in which Candace comforts Mrs. Marvyn she draws Mary aside, saying:

> "Honey . . . don't ye go for to troublin' yer mind wid dis yer. I'm clar Mass'r James is one o' de 'lect; and I'm clar dar's consid'able more 'o 'de 'lect dan people tink. Why, Jesus didn't die for nothin',—all dat love a'n't gwine to be wasted. De 'lect is more'n you or I knows, honey! Dar's de Spirit,—He'll give it to 'em; and ef Mass'r James is called an' took, depend upon it de Lord has got him ready,—course He has,—so don't ye go to layin' on your poor heart what no mortal creetur can live under. . . ." (737)

Candace's effort to preempt the kind of suffering that Mrs. Marvyn has undergone is tacitly rejected. Mary's reply to Candace is not recorded in the novel, and the following chapter, entitled "Mysteries," is devoted to the young woman's months-long struggle to abandon the "habits of unanalyzed faith and love" and confront the contradictory beliefs that she had previously held "with small care for their logical relations." Stowe glosses over what exactly goes through Mary's mind, suggesting that the content of Mary's thoughts is less important, finally, than the process of thinking: "Through that one gap of sorrow flowed in the whole awful mystery of existence, and silently, as she spun and sewed, she thought over and over again all that she had ever been taught, and compared and revolved it by the light of a dawning inward revelation" (743). When Mary finally shares her "revelation" with the women's prayer circle, it becomes evident that her theology is not all that distant from Candace's. Hers, too, is a vision of divine love expressed through Jesus. But whereas Candace had sought to replace the Doctor's "great and mighty things," with Jesus' love, Mary finds unity: she "call[ed] God her Father, and spok[e] of an ineffable union in Christ, binding all things together in one, and making all complete in Him" (747). While Candace views the Doctor's "great an' mighty tings" as useful only in "fair weather," Mary must struggle to make Calvinism a suitable theology for everyday life. In rejecting Candace's proffered solution and requiring that Mary come to her faith in Christ's love through her own intellectual efforts, Stowe registers her conviction that the process of finding religious peace cannot be circumvented. Moreover, the lengthy process of introspection and contemplation that Mary undergoes obviates the suspicion that she is one of those whose "shallow mind . . . scorn[s] the . . . theological wrestlings and surgings" of the great Puritan divines.

Stowe's critique of sentimental love religion highlights her understanding that it is a system that infantilizes its (mostly female) adherents and strips them of an important intellectual experience: the process of struggling with one's faith. Whereas the comfort Candace offers Mrs. Marvyn reduces her to a childlike state, the process of struggling with her faith enables Mary to leave childhood behind. When the "floods" of sorrow washing over Mary finally "grew still," the young woman is transformed, and matured:

> Something wise and strong and sacred gave an involuntary impression of awe in her looks and words;—it was not the childlike loveliness of early days, looking with dovelike, ignorant eyes on sin and sorrow; but the victorious sweetness of that great multitude who have come out of great tribulation, having washed their robes and made them white in the blood of the Lamb. (746)

Stowe here insists that her heroine must give up the "childlike" faith that is predicated on ignorance. The allusion to "early days" confirms the reader's suspicions that although Mary's response to the minister's questions about her faith had a "loveliness" that Stowe and the minister found appealing, it is founded on a "dovelike ignorance" that is incompatible with adulthood. In an age in which relatively few women got more than a rudimentary education, struggling with the logic of theology was an important intellectual exercise, one that, Stowe argues, American women should not abandon. By privileging Mary's paternal heritage, rigorous theological education, and willingness to confront the contradictory nature of her belief, Stowe claims for women the ability to participate in the ongoing conversation about the central intellectual questions of the day. In articulating her theory of the "soul artist" Stowe asserts both her concern with aesthetic matters and her conviction that the nation's Puritan roots are crucial to its cultural future. And by refusing to let Mary die, Stowe revises the sentimental model of authorship that she invoked in her letter to Eliza Follen.

The expectation that Mary will die is expressed by Miss Prissy, the voluble seamstress who is also an authorial surrogate. After Mary speaks at the women's prayer circle, giving the long awaited "utterance" (747) in which she attests to her newfound faith, Miss Prissy rushes to the Scudder home to share the news with Mrs. Scudder and Dr. Hopkins: "'Oh, Miss Scudder,'" Miss Prissy exclaims, "'her afflictions have been sanctified to her!— and really, when I see her going on so, I feel she can't be long for us. They say, dying grace is for dying hours, and I'm sure this seems more like dying grace than anything that I ever yet saw'" (748). Miss Prissy here articulates the Christian logic that associates spiritual transcendence with the ultimate sacrifice—death—voicing the reader's expectation that the only fate available to Mary is a sentimental, beatific death. This scene echoes the one in *Uncle Tom's Cabin* in which Uncle Tom correctly identifies Eva's impending death by virtue of the fact that "she told me, this morning, she was coming nearer,—thar's them that tells it to the child, Miss Feely, It's the angels,—'it's the trumpet sound afore the break o'day.'"[68]

But Stowe undermines her readers' expectations. Mary does not die. Nor is she consigned to a loveless marriage to Dr. Hopkins, which would be virtually the same thing. After Mary accepts both James Marvyn's death and the Doctor's proposal of marriage, the narrator intervenes to explain the import of this decision:

> Then she kneeled by her bedside, and offered her whole life a sacrifice to the loving God who had offered his life a sacrifice for her. She prayed for grace to be true to her promise,—to be faithful to the new relation she had accepted. She prayed that all vain regrets for the past might be taken away, and that her soul might vibrate without discord in unison with the will of Eternal Love. So praying, she rose calm, and with that clearness of spirit which follows an act of uttermost self-sacrifice; and so calmly she laid down and slept, with her two hands crossed upon her breast, her head slightly turned on the pillow, her cheek pale as marble, and her long dark lashes lying drooping, with a sweet expression, as if under that mystic veil of sleep the soul were seeing things forbidden to the waking eye. Only the gentlest heaving of the quiet breast told that the heavenly spirit within had not gone whither it was hourly aspiring to go. (775)

Mary's proposed sacrifice turns her into a kind of walking dead woman. The posture of her sleeping body—complete with peacefully crossed hands and marblelike cheek—is virtually indistinguishable from that of a dead person, and her sacrifice, which Stowe mentions three times in one paragraph, aligns her explicitly with Christ and marks her as the quintessential sentimental heroine. The sacrificial nature of the marriage is intensified when James Marvyn miraculously returns, having survived the shipwreck and achieved conversion. But Mary steadfastly refuses to break her promise, believing that her obligation to the minister must take precedence over her love for James.

The process of intervening in the sentimental plot is accompanied by a series of comments on authority and authorship that suggest Stowe's self-consciousness about her project of revising existing models of female artistic production.[69] Temporarily abdicating authorial control to a surrogate, Stowe teams Miss Prissy, the loquacious seamstress, with Candace, the embodiment of sentimental religion, in order to rewrite the sentimental plot. Discussing the injustice of allowing Mary Scudder to marry Dr. Hopkins after James Marvyn's miraculous return, Candace urges Miss Prissy to speak to the minister, eliciting this rumination on the seamstress's suitability to take on the authorial role:

> "To be sure . . . I have talked to people about a good many things that it's rather strange I should; 'cause I a'n't one, somehow, that can let things go that seem to want doing. I always told folks that I should spoil a novel before it got half-way through the first volume, by blurting out some of those things that they let go trailing on so, till everybody gets so mixed up they don't know what they're doing." (856)

In giving Miss Prissy the belief that she lacks an author's patience to let a plot "go trailing on" and allow characters to "get . . . mixed up" Stowe distinguishes fiction writing from stereotypically female activities: Miss Prissy's love of gossip and inclination to meddle do not an author make, Stowe implies. Those same qualities that disqualify Miss Prissy from professional authorship, however, make her an excellent deus ex machina; in highlighting the fact that Miss Prissy's intervention is a literary device, Stowe both calls attention to her own authorial status and distances herself from the sentimental model of authorship that required women writers to deny aesthetic interest and motivation.[70]

At the same time, Stowe's revision of the sentimental in the novel's resolution is less a wholesale rejection than a subtle rewriting, one that requires the presence of the sentimental for its effect. Candace's support for Miss Prissy's scheme underscores Stowe's commitment to creating art that is a form of religious work: "'Well, now, honey,' said Candace authoritatively, 'ef you's got any notions o' dat kind, I tink it mus' come from de good Lord, an' I 'dvise you to be 'tendin' to't, right away. You jes' go 'long an 'tell de Doctor yourself all you know, an' den le's see what'll come on't. I tell you, I b'liebe it'll be one o' de bes' day's work you eber did in your life!'" (856–67). Although the little seamstress has none of Mary Scudder's spiritual power, Candace's "authoritative" assurance that Miss Prissy's desire to rewrite the sentimental logic of sacrifice "'mus come from de good Lord'" neatly posits the integration of God's work and the artist's work. Candace's role is crucial here: She represents the novel's vision of a sentimental, maternal, Christ-centered religious faith of the kind that authorizes the most conventional plot devices of sentimental fiction, and at the same time, her authority is aligned with that of the surrogate author intent on rewriting those plots.

The significance of Stowe's refusal to let Mary Scudder die is underlined by *The Pearl of Orr's Island*, in which Stowe demonstrates that "true" artists and conventional sentimental plots cannot coexist. The novel, which is, Joan Hedrick argues, "as close as Stowe ever came to writing a fictionalized autobiography," took Stowe ten years to complete.[71] She began the novel in 1852, immediately after the book publication of *Uncle Tom's Cabin*; put it aside to write *The Key to Uncle Tom's Cabin* and help with the compilation of Lyman Beecher's *Autobiography*; then returned to it in 1857 and worked on it for some months before and after the death of her son. She put it aside again in 1858, to write *The Minister's Wooing*. The first seventeen chapters of *Pearl* were serialized in the *Independent* newspaper in 1861, and the second half appeared in 1862, at the same time as *Agnes of Sorrento* was being serialized in the *Atlantic*.[72] The concerns of the first half of the novel, which has been widely praised as containing some of Stowe's best writing, seem to be consistent with those of the other two novels she wrote alongside *Pearl*.[73] In particular, the youthful Mara Lincoln seems to possess both the spiritual qualities of the "soul artist" and the talent of an actual artist:

> Hour after hour the child works, so still, so fervent, so earnest,—going over and over, time after time, her simple ignorant methods to make it "look like," and stopping, at times, to give the true artist's sigh, as the little green and scarlet fragment lies there hopelessly, unapproachably perfect. Ignorantly to herself, the hands of the little pilgrim are knocking at the very door where Giotto and Cimabue knocked in the innocent child-life of Italian art.[74]

Consistent with Stowe's belief in the religious foundation of "true" artists, Mara is one of those unique few "in whom from childhood the spiritual and the reflective predominate over the physical. . . . They are the artists, the poets, the unconscious seers, to whom the purer truths of spiritual instruction are open."[75] It comes as something of a surprise, then, to discover that in the second half of the novel—in which Stowe picks up the story rather abruptly ten years after the first part closes— Mara become not an artist but a consumptive heroine whose sentimental death before her twenty-first birthday echoes that of Little Eva. Mara's life work is not to create the kind of national art Stowe imagines in *The Minister's Wooing* and *Agnes of Sorrento,* but to effect the Christian salvation of her childhood sweetheart, Moses Pennel, through her untimely death.

It is impossible to know why Stowe shifted gears so abruptly, although Joan Hedrick speculates that Stowe had neither the time nor the emotional resources to work through the implications of the "radical portrait of a woman's life" she had begun.[76] What is clear, however, is that *The Pearl of Orr's Island* is a cautionary tale: the *küntslerroman* and the sentimental plot cannot coexist. Stowe's revisionary gesture in *The Minister's Wooing* marks her awareness of the necessity of rewriting the sentimental plot and modifying the model of authorship it authorized; but Stowe is unable to move beyond calling our attention to the need for revision, in part because she was herself in the vanguard of those producing alternative models of artistic production for American women writers. Instead, she chose to focus on articulating a religious aesthetic that is both the basis for new models of women's artistic production and the framework for the national cultural project of the postbellum years. The nationalistic implications of Stowe's aesthetic are made explicit in *Agnes of Sorrento.*

In *Agnes of Sorrento,* set in early Renaissance Italy, Stowe uses an artist who is a Catholic monk as a vehicle to articulate a religious national aesthetic and to imagine a society in which the "artist-prophet" occupies a central role. The differences between *Agnes* and *The Pearl of Orr's Island,* parts of which Stowe wrote simultaneously, suggest that despite, or perhaps because of, her status as the most famous American woman writer of the day, Stowe had to mute the gendered critique inherent in her conception of the "soul artist" and adopt a male voice in order to express her deep engagement with contemporary aesthetic debates. As she would do during the Civil War years in the "House and Home Papers" column, authored by "Christopher Crowfield," Stowe ventriloquizes male authority to insert herself into the newly demarcated realm of high culture that was being defined in opposition to the kind of literary production she embodied.[77]

Written exactly ten years after *Uncle Tom's Cabin*, *Agnes of Sorrento* appeared at a crucial point both in Stowe's career and in the nation's history. Serialized during the first year of the Civil War, *Agnes* was completed before the war began, and it reflects both the vigorous aesthetic debates of the late 1850s and the anxieties about national identity and unity that preceded the outbreak of the war.[78] From a professional standpoint, *Agnes*, which was the second serial Stowe published in the *Atlantic*, is a contribution to a new genre—the international novel— which was itself an expression of the growing American interest in all things European and aesthetic. *Agnes* was the ideal vehicle for the articulation of Stowe's religious aesthetic, since its publication in the foremost intellectual magazine of the day and its genre signaled her profound seriousness about aesthetic questions. On a personal level, Stowe clearly felt that *Agnes* was special: writing *Atlantic* editor James T. Fields, Stowe urges him to accept the story for the *Atlantic*, explaining that it is "'as good as anything I ever wrote. . . . Therefore let us cross the Rubicon—The story will not discredit your paper & if not immediately *ad captandum* has in it materials of great power—At any rate it must be written.'"[79] Her partiality for the story is evident in another letter she wrote Fields, this one accompanying the first installment of *Agnes of Sorrento*. Apologizing for the delay in submitting the story, Stowe explains that "she had held up her 'little darling' so that she might read it through again. 'Authors are apt I suppose like parents to have their unreasonable partialities Every body has—& I have a pleasure in writing this that gilds this icy winter weather—I write my Maine story with a shiver & come back to this as to a flowery house where I love to rest.'"[80] Stowe's feeling that in *Agnes* she has "materials of great power" and a story "that must be written" are a little puzzling in light of the novel's structure—it is a rather disjointed travel narrative—and clichéd plot. It is a much less tightly crafted novel than either *Uncle Tom's Cabin* or *The Minister's Wooing*, and its plot—the story of a young Catholic girl's discovery of the corruption of church authorities and the house of Medici, embedded in a fairy tale in which Agnes is transformed from a poor peasant girl to the daughter of a noble family and marries a prince—strikes most contemporary readers as an exotic version of a familiar plot. Stowe's attachment to the story and her conviction that it "must be written" are not merely the idiosyncratic preferences of an author, however, but a reflection of the fact that in *Agnes of Sorrento* Stowe articulates a detailed religious aesthetic based in the nation's Puritan religious roots and explicitly claims for herself, through the character of Father Antonio, a central role in the task of creating a body of art that has the potential to unify a nation on the brink of civil war.

Stowe's aesthetic vision is indebted to the view, which had become widespread by the 1860s, that the art and architecture of the Italian Middle Ages embodied the pinnacle of religious art, a high point followed by the decline into paganism and sensuality instigated by the rise of the Medici family and the emergence of what we now call the Renaissance.[81] This view, which was originated by French Catholic art historians in the late-eighteenth and early-nineteenth centuries, was popularized by a number of English writers in the first half of the nineteenth century. Chief among them was English art critic Augustus Welby Pugin, an architectural draftsman who converted to Catholicism in 1834 and subsequently became a prominent historian of Renaissance architecture, and John Ruskin, whose Protestantism made him more appealing to American readers.[82] Pugin's views, in turn, were influenced by French Catholic art historians such as Alexis Francois Rio, author of *De la Poesie Chretienne* (1836), and Count Montalembert, an architecture critic and social commentator.[83] In this view of history, the Medici are the source of trends that led to the degradation of great medieval art. In *Contrasts*, his architectural history of the Italian Middle Ages, Pugin included a chapter called the "Revived Pagan Principle" in which he linked the "poison, the obscenity, the sensuality, and nudities, the impieties, and the classicizing tendencies of the Italian fifteenth century," under the leadership of the Medici, with "'the grand *renaissance*, or revival of classic art, which moderns so highly extol in preference to the glorious works produced by faith, zeal, and devotion of the middle ages.'"[84] This view of the Italian Middle Ages and the Renaissance became widely accepted among American intellectuals and art critics, who were influenced by its restatement in work by Ruskin, Anna Jameson, and others. Ruskin's views of the Renaissance, most famously articulated in *The Stones of Venice* (1851), shaped his aesthetic philosophy, which privileged art's religious motivation and emphasized the moral framework of all aesthetic endeavor, and were particularly influential among Americans.

Stowe's use of the Ruskinian view of the Renaissance as the framework for *Agnes of Sorrento* and a vehicle for her own religious aesthetic signals her dissent from the standards of the newly demarcated realm of high literary culture. As James Russell Lowell's warning in "The Origins of Didactic Poetry" to "Put all your beauty in your rhymes, / Your morals in your living" reveals, the shapers of America's high literary Art sought to undo the association of art and morality that had characterized American literature since its inception. In the first decade of the *Atlantic's* existence, the magazine sought to carve out what Thomas Wentworth Higginson called a sphere of "pure literature": "The highest aspect of literature assimilates it to painting and music. Beyond and above all the domain of use lies beauty, and to aim at this makes literature an art. A book without art is simply a commodity; it may be exceedingly valuable to the consumer, very profitable to the producer, but it does not come within the domain of pure literature."[85] Higginson's distinction between "the domain of use," which produces "commodit[ies]," and the "domain of pure literature," which is characterized by its privileging of "beauty" and produces great Art, is a gendered distinction between the popular fiction of the antebellum period, produced mainly by women, and evaluated in terms of its social and religious utility, and the kind of writing that was currently being defined as elite Art. Lowell's and Higginson's privileging of beauty as the sole quality that distinguishes "art" from "commodity" was common in discussions of literature from this period, whereas in the realm of the visual arts calls for privileging beauty above all else were suspect because of beauty's association with materialism and pure sensuality. In using a set of terms and values that were widely accepted among critics of the visual arts but increasingly rejected by members of the elite literary establishment, Stowe registers her discomfort with the secular nature of the literary aesthetic being articulated in the pages of the *Atlantic Monthly,* offering an alternative model of artistic production that both preserves the religious values she felt were essential to creating an American national art and defines great art in terms that include her own work and that of her female contemporaries.

Stowe's analysis of the proper relationship between art and religion in *Agnes of Sorrento* begins with a theoretical assessment of the problem. Describing a marble nymph in the garden of the convent in which Agnes spends much of her time, the narrator observes that:

> The figure and face of this nymph, in their classic finish of outline, formed a striking contrast to the drawing of the Byzantine paintings within the cloisters, and their juxtaposition in the same enclosure seemed a presentation of the spirit of a past and present era: the past so

graceful in line, so perfect and airy in conception, so utterly without spiritual aspiration or life; the present limited in artistic power, but so earnest, so intense, seeming to struggle and burn, amid its stiff and restricted boundaries, for the expression of some diviner phase of humanity.[86]

This passage captures the fundamental dilemma about art facing the American cultural establishment at midcentury, and its resolution is the basis of Stowe's program for national cultural development. The beauty of the classical nymph is compelling; its lack of spirituality regrettable. The alternative is equally unsatisfying: the Byzantine paintings possess greater spiritual intensity but are artistically "limited." This is the dichotomy that Stowe struggles to reconcile throughout the novel. The solution Stowe offers her readers is embodied in Father Antonio, Agnes's uncle and the novel's moral and aesthetic center. A Catholic monk and early convert to Savonarola's movement, Father Antonio is, according to Stowe, "enthusiastic not less in religion than in Art" (98).

It is this notion of an "enthusiast"—a word carrying predominantly religious connotations—that captures Stowe's conception of the ideal balance between art and religion. Father Antonio's vocation is support- ed by the convent he belongs to, Savonarola's San Marco, which Stowe tells her readers was "[i]n its best days as near an approach to an ideal community, associated to unite religion, beauty, and utility, as ever existed on earth" (97). Stowe's vision of this ideal community is worth quoting in full:

> It was a retreat from the commonplace prose of life into an atmosphere at once devotional and poetic; and prayers and sacred hymns conse- crated the elegant labors of the chisel and the pencil, no less than the more homely ones of the still and the crucible. San Marco, far from being that kind of sluggish lagoon often imagined in conventual life, was rather a sheltered hotbed of ideas, fervid with intellectual and moral energy, and before the age in every radical movement. At this period, Savonarola, the poet and prophet of the Italian religious world of his day, was superior of this convent, pouring through all the mem- bers of the order the fire of his own impassioned nature, and seeking to lead them back to the fervors of more primitive and evangelical ages, and in the reaction of a worldly and corrupt Church was beginning to feel the power of that current which at last drowned his eloquent voice in the cold waters of martyrdom. Savonarola was an Italian Luther,— differing from the great Northern Reformer as the more ethereally

strung and nervous Italian differs from the bluff and burly German; and like Luther, he became in his time the centre of every living thing in society about him. He inspired the pencils of artists, guided the counsels of statesmen, and, a poet himself, was an inspiration to poets. Everywhere in Italy the monks of his order were traveling, restoring the shrines, preaching against the voluptuous and unworthy pictures with which sensual artists had desecrated the churches, and calling the people back by their exhortations to the purity of primitive Christianity. (97–98)

That this vision of San Marco's perfect melding of devotion and poetics is utopian is evident from the novel's "Introductory Note," where Stowe declares that she has made no effort at historical accuracy. She describes the story as "a mere dreamland" that "reproduces to the reader the visionary region that appeared to the writer" and observes that "whoso wants history will not find it here, except to our making, and as it suits our purpose" (vi). Stowe's disclaimer of any responsibility for historical accuracy is undoubtedly a response to the proliferation of historical and biographical writing about Savonarola and his role in resisting Medici-inspired paganism that began to appear in large numbers in the 1850s.[87] Ironically, Stowe's disclaimer actually makes her work more historically accurate than most other treatments of Savonarola from this period, which were, as Ronald Steinberg has shown, largely invented and mythologized to serve nineteenth-century cultural and religious purposes. Savonarola was a particularly popular figure among nineteenth-century Renaissance historiographers:

> The historical rehabilitation of Savonarola began in the late eighteenth century and was coincidental with a determination that the Renaissance had its origins in a new Christian spirituality which quickly became endangered by a resurgent paganism. Around the same time there arose the belief that the only true art, the only good art, was one that was directly inspired by God. The inspiring deity rather swiftly became specified as not only the Christian God, but the God of the church of Rome. All this inevitably came together in the nineteenth century among the Romantics to be woven into the legend of Savonarola's salubrious influence on Renaissance art.[88]

Steinberg traces the construction of the Savonarola myth to the work of French Catholic art historian Alexis-Francois Rio, who advanced the story, which was to become a "historical *topos* for the next hundred years," that Savonarola "fought bravely to avert th[e] trend toward paganism and to turn art back to its pristine and pious Christian beginnings."[89] For Stowe, Savonarola is not only a champion of religious art resisting the pagan Medici family, but a direct antecedent of Luther and, as such, of American Protestantism.

Stowe's vision of San Marco as a "retreat" from the "commonplace prose of life" is undoubtedly informed by her own frequently expressed desire for freedom from the pressures of the everyday that would allow her time and space to write.[90] Her association of Savonarola with Luther, whom she describes as the father of American Protestantism, and her remarks about the Italian monk's role as "the centre of every living thing in society about him," indicate, however, that this is not merely the fantasy of an overburdened writer. Stowe's San Marco is a prototype of what she imagines might someday be possible in contemporary American society.[91] Her characterization of Savonarola as a "poet and prophet" suggests that neither term is subordinate to the other, though she does put the artistic element first. As though to assure her readers that her vision of "retreat" does not include withdrawal from engagement with the political and moral issues of the day, Stowe describes San Marco as a "sheltered hotbed of ideas . . . before the age in every radical movement." Stowe's unabashed endorsement of "every radical movement" is hardly surprising, coming from the quintessential poet-prophet of the day. What is striking about the association of artistic endeavor and the "fervid . . . intellectual and moral energy" that is at the base of radical social movements is the forthrightness of Stowe's claim for the agency of the poet-prophet. Abandoning the posture of reluctant author writing to help pay household bills or mere medium who "only put down what [she] saw" in a series of visions, Stowe here imagines the possibility of a society led by religious figures who are not only guides to "statesmen" and inspiration to artists, but poets in their own right.[92]

Stowe's emphasis on the balance between the values of the "poet" and those of the "prophet" is also an attempt to envision a way out of the binary oppositions that had required American artists, and especially women writers, to position themselves firmly in one camp or the other. Stowe's program for healing the chasm between art and faith revealed in the earlier discussion of the difference between the classical nymph and the Byzantine artwork revolves around the potential for bliss inherent in producing art that balances deep religious feeling with great artistic talent:

If perfect, unalloyed happiness has ever existed in this weary, work-day world of ours, it has been in the bosom of some of those old religious artists of the Middle Ages, whose thoughts grew and flowered in prayerful shadows, bursting into thousands of quaint and fanciful blossoms on the pages of missal and breviary. In them the fine life of color, form, and symmetry, which is the gift of the Italian, form a rich stock on which to graft the true vine of religious faith, and rare and fervid were the blossoms. (126)

Stowe's metaphor of the grafted tree underscores her belief in the potential for a seamless union of the two traditions represented earlier as hopelessly separate: in a new creation that will be produce "rare and fervid blossoms," the form and symmetry of the classical nymph can be united with, and compensate for, the spiritual power of the artistically "limited" Byzantine art. Stowe's organic metaphor is a response both to the Common Sense tradition, which had long subordinated art to its religious or moral function, and to the contemporary impulse of the literary elite to define art and religion as occupying separate and mutually exclusive spheres.

The implications for American culture of Stowe's meditation on the artistic and religious life of Italian Catholic monks are revealed when, adopting the role of historian she had earlier disclaimed, Stowe's analysis shifts from the individual to the national level: "it must be remarked in justice of the Christian religion, that the Italian people never rose to the honors of originality in the beautiful arts till inspired by Christianity. The Art of ancient Rome was a second-hand copy of the original and airy Greek, —often clever, but never vivid and self originating" (126). She goes on to explain that "[i]t is to the religious Art of the Middle Ages, to the Umbrian and Florentine schools particularly, that we look for the peculiar and characteristic flowering of the Italian mind" (126). Assuming her readers' familiarity with contemporary views of mediaeval and Renaissance art, Stowe concludes her brief history of Italian art with this analysis:

When the old Greek Art revived again in modern Europe, though at first it seemed to add richness and grace to this peculiar development, it smothered and killed it at last, as some brilliant tropical parasite exhausts the life of the tree it seems at first to adorn. Raphael and Michel Angelo mark both the perfect splendor and the commenced decline of original Italian Art; and just in proportion as their ideas grew less Christian and more Greek did the peculiar vividness and intense

flavor of Italian nationality pass away from them. They became again
like the ancient Romans, gigantic imitators and clever copyists, instead
of inspired kings and priests of a national development. (127)

This is the crux of Stowe's program for "national development"
through art. The choices are quite clear and the price of failure is high:
artistic creation, which is synonymous with "national development,"
requires originality, and originality is predicated on religious faith.
Stowe's view of the degrading effects of Greek influence on Italian art,
and her dismissal of Raphael and Michel Angelo as "gigantic imitators
and clever copyists" in the latter parts of their careers, is not original—
such views were widely held among art historians and intellectuals
influenced by Ruskin's and others' anti-Renaissance views; but her
rehearsal of these views here serves a dual purpose: it identifies her as a
participant in an ongoing, male-dominated conversation about the
proper relationship between religious faith and artistic production, and
it allows her to dissent from the emerging model of high literary culture
being articulated in the pages of the *Atlantic Monthly*, a vision in which
religious motivation and aesthetic value were increasingly viewed as
mutually exclusive. Stowe's emphasis on the importance of Christian-
inspired originality to "national development" is underscored by the
parasite metaphor she employs to describe the dangers that the revival
of the Greek tradition posed to Italian art. The beauty of Greek art is
deceptive, and its dangerous power to suck the life out of the tree she
has so exultantly described earlier is concealed until the tree is long
dead. Stowe warns here against allowing the beauty of secular art, of
whose dangers she is acutely aware since she herself is repeatedly
seduced by it, to smother the young tree of American national
development.

Stowe's insistence that the choice facing Italian artists was between
embracing the originality that made them "inspired kings and priests of
national development" and the descent into imitation plays on the
deep-seated concern of American artists with their own belatedness vis-
à-vis English and European art. Since American artists had long been
dismissed by British cultural authorities as "gigantic imitators and
clever copyists," Stowe speaks directly to that concern, offering American artists a way to differentiate themselves from their own equivalent
of the Greek classical heritage and produce "inspired kings and priests
of national development." Reminding her readers that religion is at the
heart of the American national identity, just as it was at the heart of the
"flowering of the Italian mind," Stowe urges her readers, and especially

the artists among them, to look for the source of artistic originality in their religious roots.

Stowe's definition of originality in terms of religious faith is an early contribution to the debate about the sources and characteristics of originality that would dominate the pages of intellectual periodicals during the 1860s.[93] In offering her own definition of originality, along-side the concept of the "soul artist," and her vision of the "poet-priest," Stowe provides a series of terms that, taken together, produce the foundation of a model of aesthetic production that fundamentally differs from that available to Stowe herself and to her contemporaries of both genders, but especially to women writers. Stowe's aesthetic program, with its emphasis on the inextricable link between religious faith, originality, and the power of the romancer, like the "soul artist," to uncover the divine in the quotidian, has the effect of redefining her own artistic production, enabling her to shed the mantle of mere medium she had, like her contemporaries, adopted, and to don the robes of the "priest . . . of national development."

It is striking, then, that nowhere in these works does Stowe depict a female artist, or speculate explicitly about the conditions necessary for the production of one. Indeed, the closest she comes to depicting a female fine artist is in *The Pearl of Orr's Island*, in the character of Mara Lincoln, whose artistic aspirations are channeled into conventional religious sentimentality when she reaches adulthood. Whether or not Stowe was able to imagine a successful woman artist (or truly interested in doing so) matters less, however, than the effect of her sustained engagement with these aesthetic questions and with their gender implications.[94] Her position as a prominent public intellectual and the most famous and popular woman writer of the day ensured that Stowe's views on aesthetic matters, and the aesthetic program she outlines in *The Minister's Wooing* and *Agnes of Sorrento*, would be, at the very least, widely read and available to her female contemporaries and successors, who, as subsequent chapters demonstrate, enthusiastically participated in the project of redefining the conceptual frameworks for American women's artistic production in the postbellum period.

CHAPTER TWO

"I Dedicate Myself . . . Unreservedly to Art"

AUGUSTA JANE EVANS AND SOUTHERN ART

D URING the summer of 1860 Rachel Lyons, a Charleston debutante whom Augusta Jane Evans had met during an 1859 visit to New York City, was bored and depressed. Writing to rouse Lyons from the "despondence" and "inertia," brought on by "the weary round of fashion and gayety," Evans exhorts her friend to "*work*," and the work she recommends is intellectual: "I do not mean to flatter you . . . but I believe you would write successfully—perhaps I am mistaken; yet such is my conviction and at least you might make the attempt."[1] The previous month Evans had written her friend on the same topic: "I have often wondered why you *did not write*—Of course you know you could if you would"; Evans concedes that "literary women have trials that the world knows not of; are called on to make sacrifices whose incense floats not before the public"; but she assures her bored, dissatisfied friend that the rewards of choosing an intellectual vocation are considerable: "Rachel, beloved, though our Sisterhood work in dark lonely corners, we have joys and encouragements peculiar to the vocation. . . . literary women . . . experience a deep peace and satisfaction, and are crowned with a glory such as marriage never gave."[2] Evans wrote to her friend in this vein repeatedly, and her conviction that elite Southern women could and should fill their excess leisure with serious intellectual work was at the heart of the religious aesthetic program for national cultural development that Evans articulated during the 1860s.

Between 1859 and 1866 Evans wrote novels, newspaper articles, and numerous private letters in which she outlined her aesthetic vision for Southern women and the nation. Evans used her pen and her carefully cultivated relationships with powerful men to insert herself into the ongoing conversations about both Southern and American cultural identity, tirelessly promoting her vision of a religiously based high culture that would be at once intellectually challenging and accessible to readers of popular fiction. Like Stowe, Evans based her aesthetic in Ruskinian ideas about the moral value of culture, but unlike her Northern peer, Evans focuses explicitly on women's roles as cultural producers. Indeed, each of the three novels Evans published between 1859 and 1866 features one or more talented female artists who achieve both popular and critical success without being forced to compromise their religious or aesthetic values.[3] These women are all Southerners, and although slavery is virtually never mentioned explicitly in Evans's novels, she was remarkably clear-eyed about the deleterious effects of slavery on the women of the planter class, who were central to Evans's cultural program. Writing to Confederate congressman J. L. M. Curry in 1863, Evans urges him to abandon his proposed speech on the topic "Is the Character of Southern Women Prejudicially Affected by Slavery?" because the answer is clearly yes. "Southern women"—by which she means the women of the planter class—"are enervated, lethargic, incapable of enduring fatigue, and as a class, afflicted with chronic lassitude" because they have too many servants and too much leisure, Evans points out.[4] This physical enervation has a mental equivalent. For although "Southern women have more leisure for the cultivation of their intellects. . . . Thoroughly educated women are deplorably rare among us," Evans laments, as are "intellectual vigor and originality."[5] And slavery is clearly to blame, Evans concludes: "I do not regard this inertia as inseparably bound up with the system, but as far as my observation extends, I find it the practical and melancholy result. Southern women might be exalted by the institution, but such is not the fact."[6] Evans was a loyal Confederate, and her 1864 novel *Macaria* contains numerous defenses of the Confederacy and virulent attacks on the Union; but rather than attempting to defend slavery on its merits, Evans used her published writing to imagine a type of Southern woman whose talent, ambition, and religious faith enabled her to live up to the promise inherent in the institution of slavery and become a source of cultural authority not only for the South, but for the entire nation.

As a Southern woman writer Augusta Evans had to overcome limitations of both gender and geography. On the one hand, Evans was fiercely loyal to the South, which she viewed as the repository of national virtue and the antidote against Northern materialism and factionalism; on the other hand, she was painfully aware of the South's cultural limitations and of the deleterious effects of slavery on the women of the

planter class to which she belonged by birth, if not by fortune.[7] In addition to the sectional and political tensions shaping her artistic choices,
Evans's gender insured that her professional identity was circum-
scribed by the only model of female authorship that was available to a
woman in antebellum America. As a woman writer who came of age in
the 1850s, Evans (1835–1909) had absorbed both the popular novels by
American women that had their heyday in the 1850s, and the model of
authorship that produced them.

Although she is typically viewed as a member of the group of "literary domestics" identified by Mary Kelley, and her plots often resem-
ble theirs, Evans's conception of female artistic production is a notable
departure from the model adopted by the first generation of popular
American women writers.[8] Indeed, Evans's fiction from the 1860s
mounts a critique of the antebellum model of female authorship and
offers an alternative that defines aesthetic labor as a form of religious
work, but rejects the antebellum practice of hiding one behind the other.
Drawing on her reading of Ruskin and her own deeply felt religious
faith, Evans defines artistic production as an inherently moral activity,
and artists as a special group of "hierophants" doing sacred work that is
distinct from other kinds of work available to women.[9] For Evans, producing literature is not interchangeable with sewing, and economic
necessity alone is insufficient grounds for taking up one's pen. Evans's
conception of authorship as a sacred calling distinct from domestic
labor allows her to align her fictional heroines', and her own, work with
the realm of high literary culture that was being defined in the late
1850s and beyond. In addition, Evans sought to claim for Southern writers—herself chief among them—a central place in the creation of "a
national literature."[10]

The notion of Southern literature was, in the eyes of many Northern
intellectuals, a contradiction in terms, even before the Civil War.
Plagued by high rates of illiteracy, no public education system and a
notoriously inadequate private one, relatively few cultural institutions,
and few nationally respected authors, the South suffered from a long-
standing sense of cultural inadequacy coupled with a deep resentment
of the attitude of superiority emanating from many Northern cultural
institutions.[11] There was a widespread belief among Southern intellectuals that the region lacked the conditions—both material and psychic—

to support the kind of cultural activity produced in the North's urban centers, even as the need to produce an independent Southern literature through which to defend and explain the region's culture—and its centerpiece, the "peculiar institution" of slavery—was a subject of increasing concern. Indeed, for some of the leading pro-slavery intellectuals in the antebellum South, the defense of slavery on moral and religious grounds provided a source of legitimacy for their own existence as intellectuals in a region that was otherwise indifferent to the life of the mind.[12] While these men produced nonfiction essays, speeches, and tracts, virtually all of the popular fiction produced by both men and women in the antebellum South was, in some way or another, a defense of Southern institutions and culture.[13] The relative paucity of critically acclaimed work produced in the South or by Southerners, and the close identification of Southern literature with slavery, meant that Northern attitudes toward the concept of "Southern literature" ranged from muted disdain to downright ridicule. A notice of *Southern Literary Messenger* editor John R. Thomson's intention to compile an anthology of Southern literature comments that although Thomson's credentials are impeccable—he is "a fine scholar and has taste"—the editors "suspect that [the proposed work] will fail of the accomplished editor's intent to show a general unfairness toward southern writing by northern critics. We have nothing to offer here as to the causes, but we hold it to be a maintainable fact that the south has not contributed her part to the intellectual riches of the country."[14] Although the reference to the widely shared belief in the South's failure to produce its share of "intellectual riches" is a staple of comments on Southern literature in Northern publications, the tone of this notice is relatively civil. The editors of *Putnam's Monthly* were much less circumspect. In an 1857 essay titled "Southern Literature," *Putnam's* derides the recent convention in Savannah, Georgia, in which the need to develop Southern Literature was the subject of Resolutions and official declarations. Describing the gathering as a "farce" and a "ludicrous" "spectacle," the writer devotes seven double-column pages to an analysis of what one delegate described as the need for the South "to have a literature of her own to defend her principles and her rights."[15] *Putnam's* mocks the resolutions calling for the exclusion of Northern schoolbooks and "school marms" from Southern schools, and ridicules the various explanations for the South's failure to produce a literature of her own as the work of "droll" "wags."[16] But underlying the essay's sarcastic tone and lampooning content is a serious argument; there is no "literature technically southern," the writer argues, because such a literature, which must, by definition, support slavery, is "uninspired by any spirit of liberty" and based on the censorship and silencing of its opponents.[17] And so the stated purpose of Southern literature—to defend and explain Southern institutions, slavery chief among them—is also the central and defining reason that important Northern literary institutions like *Putnam's* or the *Atlantic*, both of which had expressly abolitionist editorial policies, could not find much to recommend either in the project of creating "Southern literature" or in what might be produced in its name.[18]

Somewhat surprisingly, the ambitious young Augusta Evans, who was deeply loyal to the South, shared the disdain with which Northern cultural observers viewed Southerners' attempts to establish a literature of their own. Instead, she argued in a series of articles published anonymously in the *Mobile Daily Advertiser* in October and November 1859, Southerners must overcome their narrowly provincial project and strive to produce literature that is, like the best writing produced by Northerners, not "local in its character, but national. . . ."[19] This distinction between local and national informs Evans's vituperative attack on Northern literature, for the flaws she attributes to Northern literature are strictly regional, in the sense that they are inextricably linked to abolitionism and to the North's market-driven economy. Her opening salvo is the observation that "it is . . . a fact that, as a general rule, the literature, if it may be dignified by that term, which daily float over the country from northern sources, is a disgrace to its authors and insulting to the intelligence of the American people. This fact, doubtless, arises from a false principle, which underlies the efforts of almost every writer of the north of any prominence" (October 10). Compounding their political delusion is Northern writers' willingness to pander to public taste, "plac[ing] before the reader that matter which an uninstructed, uneducated mind and vitiated taste are thought to demand.—The question with our writers is not what is truth, but, *what will people read?*" (October 10). Of course, what is popular in the Northern newspapers and monthlies that are the focus of Evans's wrath is abolitionist rhetoric.

Although Evans has little good to say about most Northern newspapers and periodicals, she does have praise to bestow on a subset of Northern literary productions, and that praise is couched in terms of nation rather than region. At the very end of the second "Northern Literature" article Evans steps back from her relentless attacks to observe that "American writers have contributed some of the most noble monuments to English literature. Many of these writers have been born and bred in the North, but because of this circumstance the South is not less proud of their productions than the North. Such literature is not local in its character; it is national, and should be treated as such" (October 16). Evans's examples of such admirable productions include "Dictionaries" and "Histories," the work of "political essayists" such as Webster, Calhoun, and Clay, and "the collected writings of Washington, Jefferson, and Madison" (October 16).

Having defined what she views as the worst of American literature as purely Northern, and the best as national, Evans turns her attention to the problems facing Southern literature. Beginning with a rehearsal of the perennial problem of Southern cultural inferiority, which is exacerbated both by Northern prejudice against all things Southern and by Southerners' own lack of interest in and support for their literary institutions, Evans observes that "[w]e are not about to deny that these complaints are well founded" but "propose[s] to look now for the cause of the existence of the fact above mentioned" (October 30). And the cause she finds is not primarily Northern prejudice, but Southern failures. First among these is the growing tendency toward Southern cultural boosterism. Observing that "there is a rapidly growing tendency among Southern writers of the present day to extol with indiscriminate praise whatever proceeds from a Southern pen, and to berate, with unbecoming severity, whatever originates on the other side of "Mason and Dixon's Line," Evans warns that "the principle which would lead Southerners to praise and even glorify everything Southern, regardless of quality . . . is calculated to do us an immense deal of injury" (October 30). The reason for the South's long-standing cultural inferiority, Evans asserts, "lies in these two facts: 1. Southern authors frequently aspire no higher than to create a Southern Literature, and 2. This literature, or rather that which is written under the influence of such an aspiration, is pronounced, without hesitation, to be superior in point of excellence, to anything which has before been committed to paper" (October 30).

Addressing the first point she raised, Evans argues that the cherished project of creating a separate Southern literature in fact produces the very inferiority such a literature is supposed to overcome:

> This idea of *creating* a Southern literature is the incentive, it is true, of all our efforts, but it is one which crushes rather than expands our thoughts, and crushes all the more fetally [*sic*] as it carries with it the ordinary allurements of a deceiver. A writer is likely to reach the goal of his ambition just in proportion to his breadth of view. If an author writes for a particular section, if he appeals to the sympathies of that section, if he professes to have special regard for it, in short, if he localizes himself on any ground, ten chances to one he is pronounced a poor

fellow by the very community for which he professes to feel so deeply, and left after a little time without a reader anywhere. On the contrary, let him rise above special pleading and write for the people who speak the English language, and he will have honor even in his own country. . . . Any book, paper, or other representative of literature, in the production of which there is no higher object in view than that of contributing to a literature purely local, deserves the fate which it is almost sure to meet. (October 30)

Evans lays the responsibility for the narrowness and provincialism inherent in the project of producing "Southern literature" at the feet of the numerous literary institutions devoted to the cause, downplaying the familiar charge of Northern prejudice. "We read too much in our papers and reviews about the necessity of creating a Southern literature, a literature of our own," Evans announces. "Occasionally, it is true, we read earnest and merited denunciations of the North for their insane attempts to fix upon as a provincial stigma," she goes on. "But is not the distinction drawn, in endeavoring to create a distinct Southern literature, calculated to occasion the odious allusions of which we justly complain?" The tendency of Southern literary periodicals to identify themselves as such exemplifies this self-perpetuating provincialism, Evans argues, pointing out that "[w]e do not now call to mind a single newspaper or periodical of any kind in the North which designates by its title, its object to be peculiarly Northern. If there is such a paper, then the tendency of it is to make of the North a mere province and its literature provincial" (October 30).

In the second and final installment of "Southern Literature," Evans finally alludes to slavery, the defense of which both requires the production of a uniquely Southern literature and ensures that such a literature will never escape its current provincial status. Urging her fellow Southern writers to "direct . . . all our energies towards the building of a *national* literature. . . ." so that "what proceeds from Southern pens shall be read wherever the English language is spoken and read," Evans confronts, however obliquely, the central obstacle preventing Southerners from producing "national literature":

The South has shown within the past few years that her power[s] of recrimination are equal to any that may be found in the North, and would it not be well to direct her mental energies to something more noble than that of even successfully answering all the inane matter to which the degenerate press of the North gives circulation? So to speak

let us keep up our end of the national literary reputation, and in such
manner that we shall not feel ashamed of the quality of our own claims.
(November 6)

This is by no means a critique of slavery—Evans supports the need to
press "our own claims" and to pass "strictures upon institutions different from our own" (November 6)—but she seeks to liberate Southern
writers from the narrow focus on defending their institutions as a prerequisite to their participation in producing a *"national* literature."

Indeed, Evans's support for slavery is implicit in her call for the
planter class to shoulder the political and literary burdens facing the
nation: "there is no class of people in the United Sates from whom so
much is to be expected as the Southern planter. There is no other class
which at present can command time to attend properly to the interest of
the country, and there is no class from which we have a clearer right to
demand contributions which shall reflect credit upon our literature"
(November 6). Ironically, the planter class is uniquely suited to the task
of "the proper development of our elements of power as a nation" precisely because it has both the leisure and the money to devote to political and literary endeavors, while "all other classes are earnestly
engaged in acquiring the wealth which this already possesses" (November 6). She does not mention women here, but, as I will show below,
Evans clearly felt that the responsibility to produce literature extended
to the women of the planter class, which included herself. By arguing
forcefully against the long-standing effort to produce a "literature purely local" (October 30), Evans both challenges her peers to escape the
self-imposed provincial ghetto of Southern literature and announces
her intention to devote her own energies to "the building of a *national*
literature." Her vehicles are *Macaria* and *St. Elmo,* both of which feature
protagonists whose artistic successes outside the South enable them to
contribute to the nation's high culture, whether it be the victorious Confederacy that Evans prophesied in *Macaria* or the antebellum nation in
which *St. Elmo* is set.

For Evans, taking up one's pen was a religious and national duty. But
unlike her antebellum peers, who regularly excused their careers in
terms of fulfilling a religious or moral duty, Evans does not hesitate to
acknowledge, either in private or in her published work, that women's

artistic work is an intellectually and spiritually satisfying activity undertaken by choice and pursued not only for the greater social good, but for one's personal benefit as well.[20] "Rachel, beloved," Evans writes her friend in July of 1860, "though our Sisterhood work in dark lonely corners, we have joys and encouragements peculiar to the vocation." And although the rewards are different from those provided by marriage, Evans believes that a writing career could be fulfilling in a way that marriage may not:

> I have thought much of all this, and my deliberate conviction is, that while literary women, as a class, are *not as* happy, as women who have Husbands and Children to engage their attention and monopolize their affections; yet in the faithful employment of their talents, they experience a deep peace and satisfaction, and are crowned with a glory such as marriage never gave. I have spoken of the two as antagonistic; I believe them to be so. No loving Wife and Mother can sit down and serve two Masters; fame and Love. It is almost impossible.[21]

Although Evans believed that a woman's primary obligation was to her marriage and family if she had them, she also believed that educated, intelligent single women were required to do some kind of work, both to occupy themselves and to fulfill their religious obligation to do God's work on earth. Writing to rouse Rachel from her "despondence" and "inertia," Evans exhorts her friend to "*work*"; Rachel's wealth means that she isn't required to work for her living, and it is precisely this leisure, Evans believes, that is the source of her friend's problems; "*work*" Evans continues,

> is the only medicine for a nature like yours. Oh Rachel! Rachel! God gave you talents; and will require them again at your hands. Where— where—have you *buried* your "napkin"? Exhume it dear friend; and begin to increase it. Of the circumstances that surround you, of course I can know very little, but I feel assured you *could* accomplish *much* if you only *would*. I do not mean to flatter you . . . but I believe you would write successfully—perhaps I am mistaken; yet such is my conviction and at least you might make the attempt. I do not believe you will be happy until you faithfully begin God's work, in some of its varied departments—Some are called in the very dawn of life; some hear the summons later; all would hear them were not their ears obstinately closed. You admit that you are restless and dissatisfied with the weary round of fashion and gayety. Oh, my friend; no *true* woman ever yet fed

contentedly on those husks. Our hearts are shrines for holier idols than the world can erect; they must have either *Love* or *Duty*. The fortunate and happiest women have both; but the last can give great comfort, pure joy, perfect serenity.[22]

Evans's belief that no "true woman" can be fulfilled by a life of empty leisure is one with which any number of antebellum women writers would have wholeheartedly agreed. But Evans's forthright suggestion that Lyons take up writing, not because she needs to support her family or has a particular religious or social message to convey, but simply because she has God-given talents to develop and will benefit from the intellectual challenge, is remarkable. Evans explicitly urges her friend to produce literature: "Rachel write a Jewish tale; and make it a substratum on which to embroider your views of life, men, women, Art, Literature. You can do this: Give the world another Raphael Aben Ezra!"[23] In suggesting that Lyons, who was Jewish, model herself after a renowned medieval scholar of both secular and religious topics, Evans encourages her friend to aspire to the highest intellectual reaches and suggests that she views a literary career not primarily as a vehicle for social, religious, or economic purposes, although those goals might be accomplished along the way, but as a fulfilling form of intellectual activity that can "give great comfort, pure joy, perfect serenity" to women whose lives are confined to the domestic realm. But it is her conviction that keeping oneself happy is a form of "doing God's work" that forms the most radical departure from antebellum conventions governing women's authorship.

The claim that in picking up her pen a woman writer was "doing God's work" was a staple of antebellum women writers' public and private descriptions of their motivations, a claim that served to disclaim individual ambition and to cast their literary activities as an extension of their conventional role as the keepers of their families', and the nation's, moral well-being. Catharine Maria Sedgwick, author of *A New England Tale* (1822), *Hope Leslie* (1827), and other popular works, described herself as "but an instrument" of God.[24] Susan Warner, whose Christian bildüngsroman *The Wide Wide World* (1850) was one of the best-selling novels of the nineteenth century, told Dorothea Dix that she deserved no praise: "I do not deserve your commendations, not in anywise. You Say 'God bless me' for what I have done,—nay but I say 'Thank him for it,' and I wash my hands of all desert in the matter." Years later, Anna Warner, Susan's sister and biographer, explained that the novel had been "written in closest reliance upon God: for thoughts, for power, and for words."[25] Harriet Beecher Stowe famously declared that "God wrote [*Uncle Tom's Cabin*]."[26] And Maria Cummins, author of *The Lamplighter* (1854), also a Christian bildüngsroman, subordinated her achievement to the workings of the divine, declaring in a letter to Annie Fields that "[i]f I have ever done anything worth doing, it has been through the motives and spirit" of God.[27] But for all these writers, invoking God, whether as the inspiration or as the actual producer of their works, served to deflect any imputation of artistic ambition, which was considered improper for women both because literary creation was understood as an exclusively male preserve and because women were expected to subordinate their own desires and interests, not nurture them. For Evans, doing "God's work" was not a screen behind which to conceal one's ambition, but a justification for pursuing an artistic career with the nominally selfish goal of meeting the writer's own intellectual needs.[28]

Evans's aesthetic is clearly influenced by her reading of Ruskin, whose *Modern Painters* and *Stones of Venice* she recommends to Rachel Lyons early in their friendship, and whom she refers to frequently both in her correspondence and in her published writing.[29] Evans believed strongly that literature should serve an explicitly didactic purpose, but she did not view didacticism and aesthetic values as incompatible or contradictory, nor did she use her heroines' didactic purposes as a kind of "cover story" behind which to conceal their artistic ambitions.[30] Indeed, like Ruskin, Evans's didactic goals were, to a large extent, aesthetic. Each of Evans's novels from the 1859–66 period seeks to educate her readers by exposing them to a wide array of historical and literary knowledge and by defending their "right to erudition"; these novels also argue for the centrality of female artists to the cultural projects of both the South (*Macaria*) and the entire nation (*St. Elmo*); and, in the postbellum period, Evans uses her fiction to attack the increasing stratification of the Northern cultural establishment and the concomitant devaluation of popular literature written by women for women.

In placing Southern women at the center of the project of producing a "national literature" Evans both upholds and modifies the long tradition that viewed women of the planter class, and the domestic values that they embodied as mistresses of their plantations, as conservers and protectors of Southern values.[31] In urging Rachel Lyons to fill her leisure by writing, Evans echoes the view she expressed in "Southern Literature," that members of the planter class are duty bound to use their leisure and income to contribute to the political and cultural advancement of the nation. This line of reasoning was not, of course, original to

Evans. As Drew Gilpin Faust notes, "the planter frequently invoked the 'learned leisure' permitted by slavery as one defense of his way of life." But that same leisure was also viewed, by those Faust characterizes as the "sharper critics," as a source of the region's intellectual weaknesses, because the wealth and leisure it produced combined with the climate to "seduce . . . the Southerner into 'mental indolence,' a far-from-learned leisure that 'deadens his energies and impairs his vigor.'"[32] Evans was one such observer, and by casting her vision of Southern women's roles in explicitly aesthetic rather than domestic or political terms, Evans enacts her belief, articulated in "Southern Literature," that Southern cultural production must move beyond its single-minded focus on defending the "peculiar institution" from Northern attacks.

Although in her letters to Rachel Lyons Evans does not attribute her friend's depression explicitly to her status as a Southerner, she makes precisely this link in an 1863 letter to Confederate congressman J. L. M. Curry, in the context of discussing his proposed speech on the topic "Is the character of Southern women prejudicially affected by Slavery?"[33] Although "Southern women might be exalted by the institution . . . such is not the fact," Evans reminds Curry.[34] By way of explaining why she does not think Curry should give a speech on this topic—she is "afraid a *rigid analysis* might prove unfavorable to us"[35]—Evans offers her own analysis of the question. "Southern women"—by which Evans means the women of the planter class—are

> enervated, lethargic, incapable of enduring fatigue, and as a class, afflicted with chronic lassitude. . . . Why? Simply because they never *systematically exercise.* Why not? From the fact that having a number of servants always at hand, whom she scarcely knows how to employ, the Southern matron accustoms herself to having every office in the household performed by others; while she sits passive and inert, over a basket of stockings, or the last new novel. The less she exercises, the less she feels inclined to do so; gradually her constitution succumbs,— she finds herself listless, querulous, fretful; an incubus to her Husband, and utterly incapable of properly educating and attending to her children.[36]

In the North, Evans reminds Curry, women who rely on *"white labor"* do not have such complete freedom from domestic tasks, and those who do exercise regularly out of doors, a course from which "we are debarred by climate."[37] In the absence of a more temperate climate (and air conditioning), Evans believes that Southern women must regularly perform some of their own household work as a form of exercise. But doing "a certain amount of *physical labor*" with "*brooms, rolling pins, dashers and hoes*" is, in Evans's view, merely in support of the real work to which leisured Southern women should devote themselves: the "cultivation of their intellects." Although she believes that the "evils" she describes are merely a "practical result" of the institution of slavery and could be "counterbalanced by the advantages which are concomitant," Evans is forced to admit that there is little contemporary evidence to support her belief that Southern women could, if they only tried, live up to their full intellectual potential: "Thoroughly educated women are deplorably rare among us," Evans laments, as are "intellectual vigor and originality."[38] Although the South's climate and labor system has produced no prominent female intellectuals, it could, Evans believes, produce a great aesthetic tradition. Expressing the common nineteenth-century belief in a correlation between climate and character, Evans explains to Curry that

> In tropical climes (where slavery flourishes) women are generally more richly endowed than in colder latitudes; their imagination more vivid and glowing, their susceptibility to emotions or impressions of beauty, or sublimity, infinitely keener; and nature seems to stamp them devotees at the shrine of Aesthetics; noble perfect instruments for the advancement of *Art*. But the sacred mission is not fulfilled; they fold their listless fingers, and failing in requisite *energy*, become the victims of chronic *inertia*.[39]

And so the great potential of the slaveholding South, to serve as the repository of feminine intellectual and aesthetic achievements, is not fulfilled.[40] Evans never published an assessment of Southern womanhood as candid or negative as the one she shared privately with Curry; instead, she created fictional Southern women who live up to the promise inherent in the institution of slavery by cultivating their intellects and dedicating themselves to "the advancement of *Art*," achieving both personal satisfaction and national redemption in the process.

Two such fictional women are the protagonists of *Macaria, or Altars of Sacrifice*, Evans's 1864 novel that is, in Drew Gilpin Faust's words, a "war story for Confederate women."[41] *Macaria* is certainly a war story: it includes a political defense of the Confederacy, battle descriptions, including an account of the battle of First Manassas (Bull Run) that Evans based on her correspondence with General Beauregard, and a call for Southern women to make whatever sacrifices the war effort required. It is also a declaration of Southern cultural independence and a public expression of the feminist aesthetic articulated in Evans's private letters. *Macaria*'s heroines, amateur astronomer and heiress Irene Huntingdon and talented artist Electra Grey, both pursue their own paths to intellectual and aesthetic independence, in the process resisting the patriarchal assumptions of the men closest to them, rejecting offers of marriage from men they do not love, and demonstrating the centrality of its women to the independent Confederacy that Evans believed would be produced by the war.

As she had done in her letter to Curry, which is contemporaneous with the writing of *Macaria*, Evans splits the intellectual and the aesthetic strands of her vision of Southern cultural independence in the novel. Irene Huntingdon, whom Evans described as her "ideal of *perfect womanhood*," is not only wealthy and beautiful, but highly intelligent, well educated, and religious.[42] Irene's qualifications as a paragon are evident from childhood: she carries her own books to school, explaining that she doesn't "choose to be petted like baby or made a wax-doll of," goes for daily horseback rides, weather permitting, stands up to her tyrannical father on numerous occasions, and is determined to have a meaningful intellectual and religious life despite her wealth and numerous social obligations, which she fulfills gracefully, if reluctantly (14). And, lest the reader miss the point, her pet dog is named Paragon. Electra Grey lacks Irene's wealth and high birth—she lives in genteel poverty with her sick aunt, and her family history is clouded by scandal—but she too is beautiful, intelligent, extremely talented, and committed to pursuing her artistic ambitions and fulfilling her duty to "form [the] public taste" of the soon-to-be-victorious Confederacy (369). Although her religious faith is less secure than Irene's, Electra's aesthetic is explicitly Ruskinian, and she embodies Evans's view that "*Laborare est orare*" (Labor is prayer) (204). The women, who are childhood friends, live mostly separate lives for much of the novel: Electra, whose aunt dies soon after the novel opens, moves to New York to pursue her art studies as the protégé of an artist she met when his poor health brought him south for the winter, while Irene is groomed for her life of wealth and privilege at an elite Northern boarding school, to which she has been exiled because she defied her father's prohibition on visiting Electra's aunt, Mrs. Aubrey. The parallel plots are brought together only at the end of the novel, when the two women become nurses in a war hospital and later move back to their hometown of W—, to live and work together after most of their male relatives have been killed in battle. The plot is structured around a series of parallel crises in the two young women's lives, crises that often require confrontation with the significant men in their lives and that provide Evans with opportunities to present her views on women's intellectual and aesthetic accomplishment.

The starting point for Evans's aesthetic is the Romantic model of individual genius, which she rejects on religious and social grounds. Evans is clearly drawn to the Romantic conception of the artist as "Genius" (205), despite her awareness that such a conception has the potential to lead to the kind of unbridled "selfishness" she deplores (184). As part of her artistic maturation, Electra must overcome her Romantic tendencies by adopting a Ruskinian aesthetic. Electra's Romantic qualities are highlighted early in the novel: she is "a dreamer, richly gifted," who has a "passionate nature" marked by sharp emotional contrasts: "There was no serene plateau of feeling where she could repose; she enjoyed keenly, rapturously, and suffered acutely, fearfully" (41). From a very young age Electra had known

> wherein she was gifted, she saw whither her narrow pathway led, and panted to set her little feet in the direction of the towering steeps [*sic*] crowned with the temple of art. To be an artist; to put on canvas the grand and imperishable images that crowded her brain, and almost maddened her because she could not give them tangible form, this was the daydream spanning her life like a bow of promise, but fading slowly as years thickened o'er her head, and no helping hand cleared the choked path. (41)

The language of obsession and madness Evans uses to describe the teenage Electra associates her with the Romantic model of inspired genius and paves the way for Evans's subsequent critique of this model as overly "narrow." Evans prevents Electra from succumbing to the madness of Romanticism by arming her with a Ruskinian notion of the social utility of high art, which she marries, at the end of the novel, to national service, through the establishment of an art school in the soon-to-be-victorious Confederacy. In the interim, Electra finds a "helping hand" in the form of Mr. Clifton, a New York artist who comes to W— for his health, discovers Electra, and offers her a home and an education. After her aunt's death, Electra accepts Clifton's invitation and moves to New York to live with the artist and his mother. After years of steady work and considerable success, Electra is on the verge of a long-awaited trip to Europe when her cousin, Russell Aubrey, now a success-ful lawyer, arrives to invite her to rejoin him in W——, where he can now give Electra a home. Russell is the novel's hero—handsome, successful, proud, and a loyal Southerner, who later dies in the battle of Malvern Hill—and long the secret object of Electra's affections, but his view of women's roles is highly patriarchal, and he is unable to understand Electra's ambition in any but the most conventional Victorian terms.

When Russell arrives, Electra is putting the finishing touches on the painting she is to show in the upcoming annual Exhibition, and the nar-rator pointedly reminds the reader that this is the first step in Electra's path toward fulfilling her artistic ambitions: "The tantalizing dreams of childhood, beautiful but evanescent, had gradually embodied them-selves in a palpable, tangible, glorious reality; and the radiant woman exulted in the knowledge that she had but to put forth her hand and grasp it. The patient work of twelve months drew to a close; the study of years bore its first fruit" (204). When Electra explains that she must go to Europe to complete her artistic training, Russell suggests that she continue her studies in W——, living as his dependent. Electra rejects his offer, informing him that she prefers to earn her own living, as he does. The exasperated Russell argues that there is a fundamental difference between their career paths. His work, he explains, is based in "stern necessity," whereas hers "involv[es] no questions of utility—luxuries, not necessities. Yours is a profession of contingencies; not so mine" (209, 210). Electra challenges Russell's distinction, arguing that "[w]hatever tends to exalt, to purify, to ennoble, is surely useful . . . and aesthetics, properly directed, is one of the most powerful engines of civilization" (211). As the discussion progresses, it becomes clear that Russell's dis-tinction between art and the law is not only practical, but ideological. When Electra asks, "[w]hat has come over you, Russell, hardening your nature, and sealing the sources of genial, genuine appreciation?" Rus-sell offers this conventional Victorian view of the proper relationship of "feminine" aesthetics and "masculine" utility:

> "I love beauty, but I subordinate it to the practical utilities of life. I have little time for aesthetic musings; I live among disenchanting common-place realities. It is woman's province and prerogative to gather up the links of beauty, and bind them as a garland round her home; to fill it with the fragrance of dewy flowers, the golden light of western skies, the low soothing strains of music, which can chant all care to rest;

which will drown the clink of dollars and cents, and lead a man's thoughts to purer, loftier themes. Ah! there is no apocalypse of joy and peace like a happy home, where a woman of elegance and refinement goes to and fro." (212)

Russell invokes the most stereotyped tropes of the cult of true womanhood: his woman is the creator and preserver of hearth and home, agent of beauty, associated with flowers and sweet music, distant from the daily life of money and markets, ennobler of male spirits. And his distinction between the "practical utilities of life" and the "luxuries" of aesthetic pleasure reflects the familiar American view of art (which was then being challenged by artists and writers such as James Jackson Jarves, Harriet Beecher Stowe, and James Russell Lowell).[43] Not surprisingly, when Russell repeats his offer to Electra to return to W— with him, its terms have changed. His initial vision was of a partnership: "'You are ambitious, Electra; so am I, let us work together'" (209), but by the time his visit comes to a close Russell has reduced Electra's vocation to something much more conventional: "You shall twine your aesthetic fancies all about it [the house he intends to build], to make it picturesque enough to suit your fastidious artistic taste," he promises (212). Electra's "Genius," her years of study, and her carefully considered aesthetic philosophy have been diluted into "aesthetic fancies" and "fastidious . . . taste." Electra's rejection of Russell's offer returns the debate to the initial terms of the conversation—her status as a serious, professional artist—and she articulates what are perhaps the most unabashed expressions of female ambition in the entire corpus of nineteenth-century fiction by American women:

"I, too, want to earn a noble reputation, which will survive long after I have been gathered to my fathers; I want to accomplish some work, looking upon which, my fellow-creatures will proclaim: 'That woman has not lived in vain; the world is better and happier because she came and labored in it.' I want my name carved, not on monumental marble only, but upon the living, throbbing heart of my age!—stamped indelibly on the generation in which my lot is cast. . . . Upon the threshold of my career, facing the loneliness of coming years, I resign that hope with which, like golden thread, most women embroider their future. I dedicate myself, my life, unreservedly to Art." (213)

Spoken at a time when female ambition was rarely claimed openly as a motivating factor, this proclamation is truly remarkable. It is not, how-

ever, only a celebration of personal ambition. Electra's statement is carefully structured in such a way that her desire for worldly success is bal-
anced by a desire to do good in the world. In the first sentence Electra
expresses pure ambition: she wants a "noble reputation" that will out-
live her; the middle sentence introduces the component of outward-
looking ambition that is essential to Evans's aesthetic model: alongside
her desire for personal immortality Electra hopes that her work will
make the world "a better and happier" place. The final sentence neatly
combines the two forms of ambition: assuming that her name will be
"carved on monumental marble," Electra expresses her desire for an
additional honor—to be memorialized on "the living, throbbing heart of
my age!" The sentence structure subordinates the tangible tribute to the
artist to the intangible, and even seems to minimize the marble monu-
ment ("not only"); in so doing Evans rather slyly suggests that by the
time of Electra's death, female artists will routinely be memorialized in
"monumental marble," making the additional accomplishment of
achieving significant cultural influence a rare distinction.

In proposing a model of female artistic production that balances
personal ambition and social responsibility, Evans is modifying both the
Romantic model of the artistic genius, whose "narrow path" of ambition leads in only one direction, and the antebellum model of female
authorship, which denies artistic ambition altogether. Electra's insistence that her art has an important social function and that she must be
highly trained in order to become "a more perfect instrument for my
noble work" is at the core of Evans's definition of artistic production as
divine labor (213). By expanding the Romantic genius's path to include
a social function, Evans invokes traditional arguments about moral purpose that authorized women's entry into the public sphere early in the
nineteenth century. Where she departs from these earlier arguments is
in her definition of moral purpose: Electra's "noble work" is to create
art and, in time, to teach others to make and appreciate art in her "own
dear native South," to which she plans to return after her European
education is complete (213). That, for Evans, is sufficient moral purpose,
because she believes, with Ruskin, that the work of producing art is a
form of divine worship and that art itself is moral. Evans's feminist aesthetic takes the terms of existing models of women's artistic production
and revises them in such a way that a woman's artistic career can be
seen as satisfying both her personal ambition, which Evans insists is a
legitimate feminine desire as long as it is kept within certain boundaries, and her moral obligation to society. Evans's embrace of Ruskin
was not unique, of course; as I have shown in chapter 1, Ruskin's con-

ception of art as essentially moral was widely adopted by American cultural observers seeking to overcome Puritan suspicion of art and the Common Sense school's emphasis on moral utility. But Augusta Evans and Harriet Beecher Stowe are unique among their female peers in their use of Ruskin's ideas to revise the religious and aesthetic frameworks that authorized their own literary careers.[44]

By the end of the novel Electra's belief that "aesthetics, properly directed, is one of the most powerful engines of civilization" has been transformed into a dedication to the cause of Southern cultural nationalism. When the Civil War breaks out Electra is studying in Italy, but she cuts her trip short and returns to the South on a small boat running the northern blockade, carrying military dispatches concealed in her paintings. During the trip Electra, rather improbably, discusses the place of art in the postbellum South with the boat's captain. Urging the captain to train his two children to "appreciate the beautiful things in this world, which God has given to gild life with," Electra extols the rejuvenating power of beauty: "There is grief and gloom enough at best, and so much innocent exquisite joy may be extracted from a thousand sources, that it seems philosophic, as well as a sacred duty, to reap the great harvest of happiness which calls to us from a proper appreciation of Beauty" (356). Revisiting the terms of her disagreement with Russell Aubrey, Electra expounds her aesthetic philosophy to the captain:

> "The useful, the practical, and the beautiful are not opposed—are even united. . . . I live, sustain myself by my art, as you by your sailor's craft; it feeds and clothes my body as well as my mind. . . . Oh! Aesthetics is a heavenly ladder, where, like Jacob's angels, pure thoughts and holy aspirations come from and go to God. Whatever tends to elevate and ennoble the soul is surely useful; and love of beauty is a mighty educational engine, which all may handle if they will." (357)

Electra's education in New York and Italy has prepared her to fulfill the role that, Evans believes, Southern women were uniquely suited for—as "noble perfect instruments for the advancement of *Art.*"[45] Electra's Ruskinian faith that the artist is in direct contact with the divine both provides an alternative to the overly selfish tendencies of the Romantic genius and locates female artists at the center of the postbellum project of Southern cultural independence. For although Electra returns to help nurse the wounded, the role Irene envisions for her in the postwar South is to nurture a generation of artists that will produce original art and to embody "Southern genius" (409).

The novel's final chapter finds Electra working on her master-piece—a painting titled *Modern Macaria*—in Irene's palatial home, which has lost only its overseer and some of its richer draperies to the war effort. Although the war isn't quite over, Irene and Electra expect the South to emerge victorious in the near future, and the painting is a celebration of that anticipated victory. It features two monumental female figures in the foreground: "Independence, crimson-mantled, grasping the Confederate Banner of the Cross, who[se] victorious folds streamed above a captured battery, where a Federal flag trailed in the dust," and "Peace" (411); behind them is a battlefield upon which women cradle and mourn their dead or dying sons, husbands, and lovers. Electra's female-centered painting is nothing less than "the first offering of Southern Art" which she intends to "lay . . . upon my coun-try's altar, as a nucleus around which nobler and grander pictures, from the hands of my countrymen and women, shall cluster" (409). The vic-torious South will become, in Electra's vision, a center of art equivalent to Renaissance Italy, drawing "Art-students from all ages pressing like pilgrims, to the Perfected School of the Southern States." Southern art will not only glorify its native region, but the entire nation, Electra tells Irene while taking a break from work on *Modern Macaria*:

> "Our resources are inexhaustible, our capabilities as a people unlim-ited, and we require only the fostering influences which Cosmo De Medici and Niccolo Niccoli exerted in Florence, to call into action ener-gies and latent talents of which we are, as yet, scarcely conscious. Such patrons of Art and literature I hope to find in the planters of the Con-federacy. They have wealth, leisure, and every requisite adjunct, and upon them, as a class, must devolve this labor of love—the accom-plishment of an American Renaissance—the development of the slum-bering genius of our land." (409)

Like her Northern peers whose commitment to the project of cultural nationalism would intensify in the postbellum period, Evans here imag-ines the war as a catalyst for the development of the South's "slumber-ing genius," which will, in turn, provide the foundation for a national culture. In imagining Southern culture as producing an "American Renaissance" equivalent to the Italian one, Evans enacts what she had called for in her 1859 "Southern Literature" articles by defining the imagined victorious South *as* the nation. In comparing the coming "American Renaissance" to the Italian one Evans alludes to the long-standing American sense of its cultural belatedness vis-à-vis Europe and grants the South the privilege of producing the long-hoped-for cultural victory on the world stage. By placing a female artist at the center of this project, both as the producer of its founding work of art and as the educator of the new generation of Southern artists and artisans, Evans transforms the production of high culture from the masculine preserve it had historically been and places women's artistic production squarely in the center of her imaginary postbellum cultural project. And although the planter class will play a central leadership role in Evans's plan, the vision at the end of *Macaria* is not of a leisured elite producing culture, but of Southern cultural independence that is produced by and for the thousands of Southern women left destitute by the war, transforming "the masses" into both producers and consumers of art (410).

Yoking together the practical need to find employment for the thousands "beggared" by "our Revolution" with Electra's grand vision of Southern cultural dominance, Irene cites John Stuart Mill's *Political Economy* to argue that the pool of acceptable "industrial pursuits" available to women must be expanded, since traditionally feminine occupations—millinery, dressmaking, and schoolteaching—are oversubscribed and poorly paid (410). To that end, Irene plans to open a "School of Design for women" under Electra's direction, which will educate its students in drawing, wood engraving, and "the various branches of Design" (410). Although Irene observes that "when calmer days dawn upon us, we may be able to secure some very valuable lecturers among our gentlemen-artists," Electra's art will dominate the institution: her murals will adorn the walls, and a copy of her *Modern Macaria* will be prominently displayed in the building in order "that the students may be constantly reminded of the debt of gratitude we owe our armies" (411). Evans carefully locates her vision between two sources of masculine authority—the "planter class" and the work of John Stuart Mill—but at its core, Evans's vision of Southern cultural independence relies on the Confederacy's women.[46] And those women must be single, Evans asserts, in order to concentrate on the task of developing "the slumbering genius of our land," since married women's first responsibility is to their families:

> "Electra, it is very true that single women have trials for which a thoughtless, happy world has little sympathy. But lonely lives are not necessarily joyless; they should be, of all others, most useful. The head of a household, a wife and mother, is occupied with family cares and affections—can find little time for considering the comfort, or contributing to the enjoyment of any beyond the home-circle. Doubtless

she is happier, far happier, than the unmarried woman; but to the last belongs the privilege of carrying light and blessings to many firesides—of being the friend and helper of hundreds; and because she belongs exclusively to no one, her heart expands to all her suffering fellow-creatures. . . . Remember that the woman who dares to live alone, and be sneered at, is braver, and nobler, and better than she who escapes both in a loveless marriage." (412–13)

Irene offers Electra, and all women who are single either by choice or by necessity, the prospect of a fulfilling and productive life outside of marriage, and freedom from the role of dependent spinster aunt to which antebellum single women were limited. Implicit in Irene's observation that the woman who chooses to remain single is "braver and nobler" than she who marries without love is a challenge to nineteenth-century notions of female selfhood, which assume, as the eponymous heroine of Evans's *Beulah* notes, that "a woman's happiness was . . . dependent on marriage."[47]

By insisting that only unmarried women could do the work of producing Southern culture, Evans justifies both her expansion of women's professional opportunities and her embrace of spinsterhood as a tribute to the Confederate soldiers, whose shadows will, quite literally, hover over the school. When Electra bemoans the loss of Russell Aubrey, her cousin and the object of her unrequited love, Irene pointedly reminds the artist that she has her work:

> "It is true that you and I are very lonely, and yet our future holds much that is bright. You have the profession you love so well, and our new School of Design, to engage your thoughts". . . . "Oh, Irene! my friend and comforter! I want to live different in future. Once I was wedded to life and my art—preeminence in my profession, fame, was all that I cared to attain; now I desire to spend my remaining years so that I may meet Russell beyond the grave. His death broke the ties that bound me to this world; I live now in hope of reunion in God's eternal kingdom." (413)

But Irene has no patience for the artist's focus on the next world, reproving Electra for forgetting that she has work to do: "God's great vineyard stretches before us, calling for laborers," she reminds her grieving friend. "You and I have much to do, during these days of gloom and national trial—for upon the purity, the devotion, and the patriotism of the women of our land, not less than upon the heroism of our armies,

depends our national salvation" (413–14). Irene's impassioned description of the "consecrated work to which we are called" has the desired
effect on Electra: "The eyes of the artist went back to the stainless robes
and seraphic face of her pictured Peace in the loved 'Modern Macaria,'
and, as she resumed her work, her brow cleared, her countenance kin-
dled as in days of yore, bitter memories hushed their moans and fell
asleep at the wizard touch of her profession, and the stormy, stricken
soul found balm and rest in Heaven-appointed labor" (414).

Electra's declaration that she has given up all desire for worldly
fame and success and seeks only to be reunited with Russell in the next
life sounds, at first reading, like a critique of female ambition and a
withdrawal from the carefully crafted balance of the aesthetic vision
Electra articulated in her confrontation with Russell Aubrey, years
before. But Irene's response and the closing vision of Electra as a working artist reveal that the novel rejects Electra's offer to renounce all professional ambition. The structure of Electra's assertion that "once I was
wedded to life and to my Art . . . now I desire to spend my remaining
years so that I may meet Russell beyond the grave" suggests that for
Electra, life and art are equivalent; and ceasing to care about attaining
"preeminence in my profession, fame" is essentially a form of suicide.
Although Evans warns repeatedly against allowing ambition to be
one's sole motivation, she suggests here that to renounce ambition altogether is a form of artistic death and an act of disloyalty to the memory
of the Confederate soldiers whose lives Electra's art is to memorialize.
Electra is forced to give up the hope of romantic love, but she is neither
forced to, nor when she tries, permitted to, give up her life's work—"the
accomplishment of an American Renaissance."[48]

Evans's first postbellum novel, *St. Elmo* (1866), was a huge success. It
was also not obviously about sectarian matters. The novel is set in the
late 1850s and its heroine is a Southerner, but her most deeply held
beliefs are aesthetic rather than political. Edna Earl does, however, sym-
bolically win the war the South had just lost: she takes the New York literary scene by storm and becomes both a best-selling writer and a central participant in the city's high culture, all without compromising her
aesthetic and religious beliefs. In *St. Elmo* Evans sends a young Southern writer North to disprove the conventional wisdom of the important
literary figures of the day and to challenge their increasingly stratified

view of culture. Like her creator, Edna Earl writes erudite, socially conservative, intellectually challenging fiction that sells well and, unlike Evans's fiction, garners accolades from the most prestigious literary magazine of the day.[49] Also unlike her creator, Edna Earl becomes the center of a sparkling New York literary salon, and so has access not only to the predominantly female mass audience that reads her fiction, but also to the mostly male cultural authorities who control the high culture world to which Edna craves admission, though not at any price. As Edna proudly notes, she remains true to her religious aesthetic, to her belief that literature should have a didactic function, and to her faith in her readers' intelligence and willingness to exert themselves when confronted with unfamiliar material. *St. Elmo* foregrounds the gender/genre split I described in the introduction, and explicitly takes up questions of taste and cultural hierarchies, in an attempt to produce a model of female authorship that revises some of the fundamental characteristics of the antebellum model of women's authorship even while it refuses to accept many of the assumptions underlying the emerging high-culture conception of authorship and the literary.

Evans's decision to set *St. Elmo* in the antebellum period has been variously explained as a gesture of healing and as evidence of her ability to overcome the strong antagonism of the war years.[50] But her vitriolic statements about the North after the war—albeit in private letters to fellow Confederate sympathizers—suggest that in 1866 Evans's hostility to the North remained strong.[51] Responding to a fan letter thanking her for *Macaria*, Evans writes that "the strongest wish of my heart is, that I may live to witness and *enjoy* the dire retribution,—the awful Nemesis, which if God reigns in heaven, must descend upon that *Synagogue of Satan*—New England."[52] And soon after the publication of *St. Elmo* Evans wrote General Beauregard describing her impressions of the economic and social upheaval in the North and confiding "What will you think of me,—if I tell you candidly that I *exult* at the rapidly increasing demoralization of American society?" She goes on to describe a society that strikes her as degenerate, corrupt, and caught up in a speculative bubble, and expresses her hope that the "buoyant Greenback shams that now flood the country . . . [will] lure the masses to utter ruin" and that "I may live to witness the retributory decrees."[53] It is more likely that Evans's relative impoverishment and her literary ambition dictated that she appeal to as broad an audience as possible. Setting much of the novel's action in the New York literary scene enabled Evans to focus on an aspect of Northern life that she sincerely admired, even at the height of her sectarian antagonism; it also allowed Evans to imagine a different outcome to the recently ended war, albeit in the cultural rather than military arena. Finally, *St. Elmo* is the culmination of Evans's long-standing engagement with the problem of female artistic production, and her most detailed expression of her religious feminist aesthetic.

In an interview she gave to the *New York World* during a visit to the city, probably in 1878, Evans describes her appreciation of New York's cultural resources: "'How I love New York! Here and not in Florida is Ponce de Leon's fountain to be sought! . . . your galleries of art and your libraries! I could spend a lifetime in the Astor Library with all of Argus' eyes and three brains to store all I could gather. And such splendid people as you have here! The friction of intellectual contact with you New Yorkers is so invigorating!'"[54] Evans's love for New York's artistic treasures and her desire to experience the "friction of intellectual contact" with New Yorkers were not new, as is evident from comments sprinkled throughout letters written both before and after the war. In 1859 Evans wrote Orville James Victor, the editor of the *Cosmopolitan Art Journal*, to thank him for a biographical sketch and review of *Beulah* he had just published; apologizing for having failed to produce an article for the *Journal*, Evans expresses her "hope that I shall yet have the gratification of seeing my name in your list of contributors." Assuring Victor of her interest in promoting "the extended circulation of the Journal at [in] the South," Evans closes the letter with a description of the role the *Journal* plays as a surrogate for the city in which it is published: "All that relates to Art has peculiar charm for me, and since I am debarred from the treasures contained in New York Galleries and Studios, I have learned to regard the 'Cosmopolitan Journal' as my sole medium of communication."[55] Evans's assertion that the *Cosmopolitan Art Journal* was her "sole medium of communication" was probably hyperbole—she read *Harper's Monthly* regularly and almost certainly subscribed to other prominent Northern intellectual periodicals—but the feeling of being isolated from the intellectual companionship and artistic riches available in New York is one Evans expressed often. In a letter to *Harper's* editor William A. Seaver Evans confides: "Amid the host of reminiscences connected with my stay in New York, I assure you none give me more pleasure than the memory of our reunions at the St. Nicholas, and the friendly genial gathering at the tea table. Thank you for remembering me at your Delmonico conclaves"—presumably the site of regular all-male dinners attended by prominent New York writers and artists. She goes on to confide that "I do envy you (*not your dinners*, but) your circle of gifted humorous friends where the icy fetters of formal etiquette are severed and congenial spirits meet."[56] After the war, Evans's enthusiasm for

New York initially cooled; writing of a visit to New York to procure medical care for her wounded brother, Evans assures Confederate congressman J. L. M. Curry that "Nothing but a desire to save my brother's life would have induced me to visit a section, which it is probably unnecessary to tell you I cordially detest."[57] But within the year, Evans had renewed her correspondence with Seaver, reminding him of their "intellectual symposiums over the quiet tea table at the St. Nicholas" and asking to be included, in spirit if not in person, in the New York literary scene: "I pray you, let me not be utterly forgotten at your favorite 'tea-fights,' or your brilliant reunions with literary esoterics at Delmonico's."[58] And some years later, Evans expresses her preference for New York over Boston: "Sometime in thinking of the Astor Library, the Galleries, and the Artists' Receptions which I once enjoyed so keenly, I feel disposed to question whether any other spot in America constitutes such an intellectual hot-bed. In Boston a chronic East-wind chilled me perpetually, even in the sunshine of Longfellow's presence, but Gotham—glorious Gotham is the tropic realm of shivering genius, and ambitious authorlings."[59] New York's literary elite had welcomed Evans as an "ambitious authorling" in 1859, and the memory was one Evans held dear, but her sectional loyalty and physical distance from New York combined to forever exclude her from the circle of literary esoterics. Evans reverses that exclusion in her 1866 novel *St. Elmo*, in which Edna Earl—an "ambitious authorling" from the South—not only becomes a central figure in this world, but successfully challenges many of its fundamental assumptions.

Evans's critique of the Northern high-culture establishment is developed through a series of encounters between Edna Earl—a penniless orphan taken in by the wealthy Mrs. Murray after she survived a train wreck at age twelve—and Douglas Manning, editor of an influential literary magazine in New York City. Manning serves as the mouthpiece for the beliefs that Evans is challenging: that women cannot produce great art, that the public won't read literature that is intellectually or morally challenging, and that didacticism and high art are fundamentally incompatible. In their very first encounter, Manning articulates the conventional beliefs about the inferiority of women's artistic abilities and the proper scope for their talents that had become commonplace by 1866. These views are expressed in a letter, in which Manning responds harshly to a sample chapter of a work Edna had been working on for some years, a comparative study of world mythologies and religions. Edna, who had acquired a full classical education after being taken in by Mrs. Murray, researches and writes secretly for months and eventually gathers up the courage to write Manning, whose literary magazine is "renowned for the lofty tone of its articles and the asperity of its carping criticisms," to ask if he would read a chapter of her book.[60] Manning's response is calculated to stifle, or at least redirect, her literary aspirations. Acknowledging that her work shows "irrefragable evidence of extraordinary ability," Manning warns that "[t]he subject you have undertaken is beyond your capacity—no woman could successfully handle it—and the sooner you realize your over estimate of your powers, the sooner your aspirations find their proper level, the sooner you will succeed in your treatment of some theme better suited to your feminine ability" (150). Manning recommends that Edna "burn the enclosed MS., whose erudition and archaisms would fatally nauseate the intellectual dyspeptics who read my 'Maga,' and write sketches of home life—descriptions of places and things that you understand better than recondite analogies of ethical creeds and mythologic systems, or the subtle lore of Coptic priests" (150).[61] To clinch his argument he reminds her that

> women never write histories or epics; never compose oratorios that go sounding down the centuries; never paint "Last Suppers" and "Judgment Days;" though now and then one gives the world a pretty ballad that sounds sweet and soothing when sung over a cradle, or another paints a pleasant little *genre* sketch which will hang appropriately in some quiet corner, and rest and refresh eyes that are weary with gazing at the sublime spiritualism of Fra Bartolomeo, or the gloomy grandeur of Salvator Rosa. (150)[62]

Manning eventually becomes one of Edna's greatest supporters (he even proposes marriage, twice), but his recommendation that the aspiring author stick to the kind of writing best suited to her "feminine abilities" was commonplace in midcentury America, expressed by writers ranging from the anonymous author of an 1851 essay titled "Female Authors" in the *North American Review*, to Harriet Beecher Stowe, giving advice to aspiring writers in 1869. By the time of *St. Elmo*'s publication, the underlying assumption, expressed by the *North American Review* author, that describing the domestic sphere in fiction is not a transgression but an extension of "the influence [woman] is accustomed to exercise in the narrow sphere of the family," had long authorized women writers to enter the public sphere; and the beliefs that women's writing was "more prone to express emotions than ideas" and that "Fame is hardly ever her object in taking up the pen" were both descriptions and prescriptions.[63] Writing almost two decades later, from her authoritative position as the first woman of American letters, Harriet Beecher Stowe echoes this advice: noting that "the best writing is done by men" because they are better educated than most women, Stowe urges aspiring writers to limit their literary aspirations so that their inferior educations are not readily apparent: "There is a great deal of writing, very charming, very acceptable, and much in demand, which consists simply in painting by means of words the simple and homely scenes of everyday life."[64] Stowe's assertion that that "charming" domestic scenes are "much in demand" alludes to the fact that women's domestic writing had, by the late 1860s, become a very successful business. Of course, only a handful of women writers commanded the kinds of fees that Stowe and Evans did, but the financial rewards of writing could be significant, especially in the absence of any comparably well-paid professional opportunities for middle-class women. It is precisely this formula—limited intellectual aspirations coupled with a strong economic incentive—that Evans challenges in her portrait of Edna Earl.

Manning's suggestion that Edna confine herself to the kind of domestic fiction that women had traditionally excelled at, and his assertion that women "never" produce the kind of "sublime" masterpieces that are most highly valued by the cultural establishment, is essentially a declaration of literary separate spheres, a vision of the literary landscape that Evans is intent on challenging. To that end she mounts a two-pronged attack: she redefines female authorship as a vocation rather than a domestic occupation, and she challenges the gendered nature of the growing gap between high and low artistic production that was being enacted in the pages of the real-life counterparts of Manning's "Maga."[65] Understanding that women's successful entry into the literary marketplace through a single genre had effectively excluded them from participation in all others, Evans distances herself from the existing tradition of women's writing by attacking her fellow women writers:

> Literary women, whose advocation [*sic*] is selected simply because they fancy it easier to write than to sew for bread, or because they covet the applause and adulation heaped upon successful genius, or desire mere notoriety, generally barter their birthright of quiet life-long happiness in the peaceful seclusion of home for a nauseous mess of poisoned pottage that will not appease their hunger; and they go down to untimely graves disappointed, embittered, hating the public for whose praises they toiled, cheated out of the price for which they bargained away fireside joys and domestic serenity. (152)

Evans's attack on her female contemporaries is striking not only for its
venom but because it includes women who choose to write for economic reasons, a motivation that had traditionally been used by women to
excuse their entry into the public sphere and to distinguish themselves
from those who wrote for more selfish or worldly reasons. By erasing
the distinction between women who write as an alternative to sewing
and those who seek fame or "mere notoriety," Evans redraws the line
that defines what is acceptable motivation for women's entry into the
literary sphere.[66] By insisting that authorship is not just another way to
support one's family, but a sacred trust, which should be undertaken
only by the elect few, Evans removes writing from the domestic sphere
where it had resided since American women began to write for public
consumption.[67] Her philosophy of authorship rejects the image of the
woman who "writes her book as she writes a letter," producing "playful
little fable[s]" on moral and philosophical questions that replace the
weighty "tome on the origin of evil and its remedy" and "solves the
question quite satisfactorily for all practical purposes in a few pages."[68]
Evans's writers are a breed apart:

> [Edna's] imagination invested authors with peculiar sanctity, as the real
> hierophants anointed with the chrism of truth. . . .There were times
> when the thought of presenting herself as a candidate for admission
> into the band of literary exoterics seemed to Edna unpardonably pre-
> sumptuous, almost sacrilegious . . . ; for writers were teachers, inter-
> preters, expounders, discoverers, or creators—and what could she, just
> stumbling through the alphabet of science and art, hope to donate to
> her race that would ennoble human motives or elevate aspirations?
> Was she, an unknown and inexperienced girl, worthy to be girded with
> the ephod that draped so royally the Levites of literature? Had God's
> own hand set the Urim and Thummim of Genius in her soul? Above all,
> was she mitred with the plate of pure gold—"Holiness unto the lord?"
> (107)[69]

Evans's theory of authors as "hierophants" casts authorship as both a
profession and a vocation. Unlike the women who choose writing over
sewing because the former is easier, and more lucrative, Evans's women
writers are held to a higher standard: authorship is not, according to
Evans, simply one occupation among many, but a specialized sphere of
action open only to those who have the wisdom to interpret sacred mysteries or arcane knowledge and the divinity of a Levite. Evans's model
of authorship overturns all the assumptions about female authorship

expressed in Manning's letter and abandons all pretense that writing is merely an extension of domestic activities. Instead, Evans claims for women the "right to erudition" (151) and the responsibility to share the knowledge they gain with their readers in their roles as "teachers, interpreters, expounders, discoverers, or creators." Evans's theory of authors as experts and scholars effectively excludes most women writing in 1866 from the hallowed halls of authorship. Those who remain, however, are consecrated to their work as literary exoterics of arcane knowledge and therefore free of the taint of writing for "mere notoriety." In defining authorship as a religious act, and equating authors with the priests of the Old Testament, Evans claims for female artists at once a more deeply religious basis and a broader sphere than that provided by the antebellum model of popular female authorship. Her authors are not merely extending their superior feminine morality from the household into the world, preaching the "feminine" values of love, self-sacrifice, and conversion. Instead, draped with the ancient "Ephod" of the all-male priesthood of ancient Israel, Evans's woman writer has a mission as broadly conceived as any "Genius," and her vocabulary is not limited to the language of domesticity, but includes "the alphabet of science and art."[70] Informed by her Ruskinian view of art as a moral endeavor, and motivated by her own Christian faith, Evans here defines female authorship in terms that simultaneously preserve the antebellum rationale for women's entry into the public sphere and vastly extend the range of acceptable intellectual activity authorized by that rationale. For, as long as she is motivated by her religious faith and not by a desire for "mere notoriety" or by financial need alone, a woman is free, indeed obligated, to pursue any intellectual and aesthetic activities that can "ennoble human motives or elevate aspirations"—a fairly broad realm.

Although she clearly privileges intellectual difficulty and subscribes to the literary standards represented by magazines like Manning's "Maga," Evans's model of authorship does not simply seek to ensconce women writers in the realm of high literary culture. Evans views the social function of artistic production as primarily educational; authors are, in this view, popularizers. This conception allows Evans to imagine a model for bridging the growing gap between the realms of high and popular literature that Manning alludes to in his letter and expands on in his first meeting with Edna. During that encounter, which takes place in the New York home where Edna is employed as a governess, Manning discovers that Edna has continued to work on the manuscript he suggested she destroy. He launches into a lecture on her folly, this time focusing on the obstacles posed by popular taste: "Unless I totally misunderstood your views, you indulge in the rather extraordinary belief that all works of fiction should be eminently didactic, and inculcate not only sound morality but scientific theories. Herein, permit me to say, you entirely misapprehend the spirit of the age." That spirit, Manning believes, seeks only entertainment from its fiction:

> "People read novels merely to be amused, not educated; and they will not tolerate technicalities and abstract speculation in lieu of exciting plots and melodramatic *dénouements*. Persons who desire to learn something of astronomy, geology, chemistry, philology, etc., never think of finding what they require in the pages of a novel, but apply at once to the text-books of the respective sciences." (237)

When Edna points out that her goal is to reach those "habitual novel-readers" who would not "educate themselves thoroughly from the text-books to which you refer," Manning asserts that those people are lost to Edna's educational purpose already:

> "those who merely read to be amused will not digest the scientific dishes you set before them. On the contrary, far from appreciating your charitable efforts to elevate and broaden their range of vision, they will either sneer at the author's pedantry, or skip over every passage that necessitates thought to comprehend it, and rush on to the next page to discover whether the heroine, Miss Imogene Arethusa Penelope Brown, wore blue or pink tarlatan to her first ball, or whether on the day of her elopement the indignant papa succeeded in preventing the consummation of her felicity with Mr. Belshazzar Algernon Nebuchadnezar Smith. I neither magnify nor dwarf, I merely state a simple fact." (237)

Manning's mocking description of a novel reader clearly identifies Edna's target audience as middle-class women who, he believes, lack both the ability and the desire to grapple with the kind of complex material she produces. The writer's counterargument that it is precisely that audience's lack of education that militates in favor of using a popular genre as an educational vehicle suggests that Evans's goal is to transform the American novel, from a form that encourages both its readers and its writers to engage only in the kind of stereotypically feminine literary activities that Manning refers to dismissively, into a form that challenges female readers to exercise their "right to erudition." At the same time, Evans's defense of didactic literature as a genre challenges the view, expressed most clearly in *Atlantic* editor James Russell Lowell's humorous poem "The Origins of Didactic Poetry," that didactic literature is fundamentally incompatible with the kind of high art whose province is "beauty."[71]

Appearing in the founding issue of the *Atlantic Monthly*, in November 1857, the poem depicts didactic literature as the exclusive province of women: Minerva starts writing to keep her from "those twin curses" that afflict women—"idleness" and "flirting—" and her chosen genre is "po—, no, verses." Having completed some verses "full . . . of pious plums, / So extra-super-moral," Minerva ties her manuscript with a ribbon and invites her male peers to a reading, which they attend despite their misgivings: "The Gods thought not it would amuse / So much as Homer's Odyssees, / But could not very well refuse / the properest of goddesses." One by one the gods make their excuses; citing a variety of masculine responsibilities ranging from fighting wars (Mars) to dissipation (Bacchus), the Gods escape the poetry reading given by "the queen of prudes," who, recognizing that "Against, the Muse I've sinned, oh!" tears up her verses "And opened with a mind serene / A Sunday School in Athens." Despite its antique setting, the poem's equation of "proper" femininity with mediocre literary production motivated by boredom and characterized by the kind of sugary moral platitudes that belong in Sunday School is a thinly veiled attack on the kind of writing by women that had reached the height of its popularity in 1857, when the *Atlantic Monthly* was established. The gods' preference for "Homer's Odyssees" defines good literature as a strictly masculine province—written by and for men and those few women, like Edna Earl, who are educated enough to prefer ancient Greek and Latin poetry to the "nice" verses filled with "pious plums" that most of their female contemporaries were producing.

Evans's view of the writer as "hierophant," and of writing as a sacred calling rather than a substitute for flirting, sewing, or even teaching Sunday School, implicitly refutes the view that didactic literature produced by women is incompatible with the kind of high literary art that the *Atlantic* sought to promote. When Edna and Manning's conversation turns to genre, the editor of "Maga" suggests that young writer confine herself to magazine essays, "'where an author may concentrate all the erudition he can obtain and ventilate it unchallenged,'" as opposed to "the world of novel-readers" who, like spectators in "'a huge hippodrome . . . expect you to help them kill time not improve it.'" Literary periodicals like his own have a different social function, he concedes:

> "a certain haze of sanctity envelops the precincts of 'Maga,' whence the incognito 'we' thunders with oracular power; for, notwithstanding the rapid annihilation of all classic faith in modern times which permits the conversion of Virgil's Avernus into a model oyster-farm, the credulous public fondly cling to the myth that editorial sanctums alone possess the sacred tripod of Delphi." (238)

The opposing images of the masculine literary periodicals as guardians of the Delphic oracle and feminine novels as entertainment in the Roman coliseum speak to the developing high-low split in American literary culture and to the gender/genre split that shaped the contemporary conversation about culture.[72] It is precisely this split that Evans is crusading against both in theory and in practice: Edna's, and Evans's own, continuing commitment to producing fiction that assumes its readers possess either a classical education or the willingness to use a library and a dictionary reveals that Evans hopes to do nothing less than reshape the American literary scene and close the growing gap between the male-dominated realm of high literary production and the female-dominated realm of popular fiction.[73]

Evans's sense that at stake in Edna's career is not merely one woman's personal success but the right to define a national literary model is evident from the description of the reception her book receives when it is finally published. The initial reaction is harsh: the reviews are bad, most of them focusing on the work's erudition, which is criticized as "incomprehensible," "shallow," and plagiarized, and the novel is "pronounced . . . a failure" (286). The book's brisk sales and the fact that it had not yet been reviewed by Manning enable Edna to keep her composure, and she is handsomely rewarded when the issue of "Maga" containing the review of her work arrives. Despite his private pessimism about her goals and methods, Manning issues "a withering rebuke" to the "howling" horde of critics who had "so flippantly essayed to crush the young writer." Evans takes pains to assure the reader that despite their close personal friendship,

> Mr. Manning handled the book with the stern impartiality which gave such value to this criticism—treating it as if it had been written by an utter stranger.
>
> He analyzed it thoroughly; and while pointing out some serious errors which had escaped all eyes but his, he bestowed upon a few pas-

sages praise which no other American writer had ever received from
him, and predicted that they would live when those who attempted to
ridicule them were utterly forgotten in their graves. (286–87)

This description of Edna's critical success is at once carefully realistic
and extravagant. Although Edna's work is not free of errors, and
"[s]ome faults of style were gravely reprimanded," the fact that it garners praise such as "no other American had ever received from" Manning, the arbiter of literary quality, is a triumph for a writer who sought
to do nothing less than change the standards by which American
women's literary productions are judged (287). That Evans saw fit to
claim for Edna such high praise is a marker of the breadth of her vision:
Edna is not merely one among many other American women "scrib-
blers"; she is a leader of American literature whose work is unique
among native writers. As further confirmation that Edna's project is a
success despite its unconventional approach, Evans notes that "[w]hile
the critics snarled, the mass of readers warmly approved; and many
who did not fully appreciate all her argument and illustrations, were at
least clear-eyed enough to perceive that it was their misfortune, not her
fault" (287). This evidence that Edna's faith in her readers' intelligence
was justified seems to me to be at the heart of Evans's attempt to imagine a model of American authorship that could bridge the growing gap
between high and popular culture. Although this model was not destined to reverse the trend toward an increasingly fragmented literary
scene, the vision Evans articulates in *St. Elmo* attests to the fact that the
hierarchies that came to dominate the American literary scene by the
end of the nineteenth century were neither inevitable nor uncontested.

The final third of *St. Elmo* is devoted to a description of Edna's successful career, during which she produces a second novel that is even
better received than the first, and numerous articles for Manning's
"Maga." She also becomes an important member of the New York literary scene, to which she is introduced by Manning, and even establishes
a salon of her own, which she holds at the home of her employers-
turned-friends, the Andrews family. The amount of space dedicated to
Edna's career suggests that Evans wished to call attention to Edna's status as a working writer, highlighting central aspects of the aesthetic that
was articulated in Edna's encounters with Manning and defining Edna
as the quintessential Southern patriot, whose success in the cultural
realm is a form of retribution for her region's failure in battle. Although
Edna is described as a loyal Southerner on only one or two occasions, the
terms of her success link her to the series of articles Evans published,

"Northern Literature" and "Southern Literature," in the *Mobile Daily Advertiser* in 1859.

Edna's nationwide popularity, and her prominence in New York literary circles, where her "brilliant and delightful" weekly receptions are populated by "eminent men and graceful, refined, cultivated, Christian women" who "assemble to discuss ethical and aesthetic topics, which all educated Americans are deemed capable of comprehending," achieve precisely this goal (359). The last clause of this description both alludes to Evans's belief that her erudition is not incompatible with a popular readership and suggests that Edna has not forgotten her origins as the daughter of a Tennessee carpenter despite her success in the brilliant milieu of intellectual New York. Indeed, it is those very origins, and her loyalty to her native South, which are mentioned on the next page, that combine to suggest the sectional nature of Edna's triumph.[74] Embodying both nationwide popularity and critical acclaim, Edna's fictional career enacts Evans's 1859 vision for "Southern literature." In holding herself and her readers to the highest intellectual standards, Edna lives up to Evans's 1859 call for the South to "direct her mental energies to something more noble than that of even successfully answering all the inane matter to which the degenerate press of the North gives circulation" and has taken a leading role in producing "a *national* literature" (November 6) that allows her to simultaneously vindicate her region's literary aspirations and transcend the provincialism into which, Evans argued in 1859, attempts to do so inevitably deteriorated.

In addition to answering Evans's challenge to Southern writers to "keep up our end of the national literary reputation" (November 6), Edna functions as a cultural critic whose jeremiads are, somewhat improbably, heeded. The role of Jeremiah is one that Evans herself filled, in her *Mobile Daily Advertiser* articles, and one that male Southern intellectuals frequently adopted as they sought to call attention to what they viewed as the inexorable declension in Southern values. Drew Gilpin Faust argues that the role of Jeremiahs, lonely prophets whose voices were not being heard, was particularly appealing to male intellectual writers such as those who composed the "Sacred Circle," because it allowed them to understand their alienation from Southern society as a form of election: "Like his biblical counterpart, the man of mind was selected by God; his vocation was not his own choice, but a divine calling."[75] And like her male counterparts, Edna views herself as one of the chosen few, whose calling requires that she speak truth in the face of corruption, greed, and political declension. Edna's belief that "she held her talent in trust" convinces her that she is obligated to overcome her feminine modesty and participate in the literary life of the city: "Feeling that a recluse life would give her only partial glimpses of that humanity which she now wished to study, she moved in the circles of cultivated friends who now eagerly stretched out their arms to receive her; and 'keeping herself unspotted from the world,' she earnestly scrutinized social leprosy, and calmly watched the tendency of American thought and feeling" (299). And what she sees does not please her: intellectuals are moving away from the "noble principles" of Scottish philosophy and embracing instead the "materialism" of Mill and Buckle or the "gross atheism" of German idealism; the merchant classes and their wives worship at "altars of mammon"; and the political scene is frightening:

> Statesmen were almost extinct in America—a mere corporal guard remained, battled desperately to save the stabbed constitution from the howling demagogues and fanatics, who raved and ranted where Washington, Webster, and Calhoun had once swayed a free and happy people. Republicanism was in its death-throes, and would soon be a dishonoured and insulted ghost, hunted out of the land by the steel bayonets of a centralized despotism. (299–300)

Relations between the sexes are just as bad: new standards of behavior and dress were "rapidly reducing the sexes to an equality, dangerous to morals and subversive of all chivalric respect for woman," while women themselves are either empty-headed slaves to fashion or misguided woman's rights reformers who, in their zeal to distance themselves from the "inanity of the mass of womanhood" mistake the "sources of evil" and demand "*power*, which as a *privilege*, they already posses, but as a *right* could never extort" (300). Although written after the war, this is a description of the social and political situation in the North in the late 1850s and early 1860s, and its language echoes that of Evans's 1859 *Mobile Advertiser* articles, in which she condemned Northern writers for producing literature that "seeks to render all classes of society dissatisfied with their normal condition" (November 6) by agitating for abolition, woman suffrage, and similar social reforms whose "decided tendency toward evil" (October 10) Evans did not doubt. Northern literature, Evans declared in 1859, has unleashed "the demons of pandemonium" which are "actually prowling through the Northern States, making efforts to tear down fabrics which genius, guided by the wisdom and experience of past ages, has erected" (October 16). The only hope, Evans had argued, lay with "the only class which at present can . . . attend properly to the interest of the country" (October 30), the planter class, to whose sons "we must again look for the talents, learning and statesmanship" that contemporary politics lack (November 6). Being neither a man nor a member of the planter class, Edna cannot enter the political fray, but she can use her pen to advocate for the need to restore the order, stability, and properly hierarchical social relations that are the birthright of the South. And her jeremiads are well received precisely because she avoids sectional questions: "Because she was earnest and not bitter, because the white banner of Christian charity floated over the conference ground, because she showed so clearly that she loved the race whose recklessness grieved her, because her rebukes were free from scorn, and written rather in tears than gall, people turned their heads and stopped to listen" (*St. Elmo*, 300). Edna is one of the few voices crying out in a Northern wilderness that Evans had declared in 1859 was characterized by the "total lack of intellectual culture" (November 6). Evans's knowledge that messages like Edna's had not been heeded does not prevent her from attempting to retrospectively rewrite history, giving Edna both her own political and aesthetic ideas and the social influence among Northern intellectuals that Evans herself lacked. Edna's ability to resist corruption is impressive: even after achieving great success "she had never stooped to conciliate popular prejudice, had never written a line which her conscience did not dictate, and her religious convictions sanction," and it is this steadfastness that makes her the standard bearer of Southern literature and values in the North (*St. Elmo*, 284).

In addition to functioning as a Southern victory in the cultural battlefield, Edna's successful career, and in particular her erudition, which she defends repeatedly and continues to display in her writing, vindicate Evans's program for female authorship. Edna is often called upon to defend her belief in women's "right to erudition" in social situations, where educated women are frequently conflated with "those unfortunate, abnormal developments, familiarly known as 'strong-minded women'"—Evans's shorthand for woman suffrage activists (254). "Erudition and effrontery have no inherent connection," Edna explains to dinner party guests at the Andrews home; moreover, "a woman has an unquestionable right to improve her mind, *ad infinitum*, provided she does not barter her womanly delicacy and refinement for mere knowledge; and in her anxiety to parade what she has gleaned, forget the decorum and modesty, without which she is monstrous and repulsive." Expanding on her view that women can acquire erudition without sacrificing their femininity, Edna invokes the same argument antebellum women had used to authorize their entry into the public sphere: "Does it not appear reasonable that a truly refined woman, whose heart is properly governed, should increase her usefulness to her family and her race, by increasing her knowledge?" (256). Although Edna's commitment to women's right to improve their minds is often "sneered at" by critics, she is vindicated by her popularity, which suggests that the reading public at the very least accepts, and perhaps even relishes, the challenge Edna's work presents. The myriad defenses of feminine education scattered throughout *St. Elmo* and Edna's persistence in writing erudite novels for popular consumption are both a vindication of Evans's own work and essential to her aesthetic vision of literature that speaks to multiple reading publics increasingly defined as separate and incompatible. Edna's popularity crosses both gender and genre lines: her fiction is read primarily by the "wives, mothers, and daughters of America" to whom Edna addresses it, while her nonfiction essays in "Maga," which are initially published anonymously, in keeping with Edna's feminine modesty, are, presumably, read by both women and men.

By virtue of her commitment to women's serious artistic endeavors, Evans belongs to the transitional generation that includes Rebecca Harding Davis, Louisa May Alcott, Elizabeth Stuart Phelps, and Constance Fenimore Woolson. Like her Northern peers, Evans was finally unable to resolve many of the contradictions inherent in the ambition to become a serious female artist in mid-nineteenth-century America, but she is in some way more willing to let stand unresolved the contradiction at the heart of her ambitions. Evans's *Macaria* is one of the only published novels from the 1850–90 period in which the protagonist is alive and working as an artist at the end of the novel, a choice that is undoubtedly shaped by the novel's Civil War context.[76] In *Beulah* and *St. Elmo* the artist-protagonists' careers end when the women marry, reflecting Evans's belief, which her peers shared, that marriage and an artistic career could not coexist, because, as Evans wrote to Rachel Lyons in 1860, "No loving Wife and Mother can sit down and serve two Masters; Fame and Love. It is almost impossible."[77] Evans's insistence that writing is not merely another form of domestic work may be part of the reason why she does not allow her heroines from this period to combine marriage and career; her model of authorship requires complete dedication to one's intellectual work, leaving little time for the domestic labor required to run a nineteenth-century household, even one supported by servants. Allowing her women writers to marry and continue their intellectual work would, inevitably, place that work back in the domestic sphere from which Evans is so determined to remove it.

Evans's decisions to marry off her heroines and end their careers has been viewed by twentieth-century critics as reflecting her inability to reconcile the subversive implications of her intellectual, independent, successful heroines with her conservative views about women's proper social roles;[78] but I see these decisions as evidence of the seriousness of Evans's aesthetic aspirations both for herself and for her heroines.[79] For to be a serious artist, as Evans and her peers knew all too well, was incompatible with the demands of marriage and motherhood. Rather than focusing on the struggle to reconcile marriage and career as Davis, Phelps, and Alcott all do, Evans focuses on her heroines' intellectual development and successful artistic careers, signaling her pessimism about the possibility of reconciling marriage and career by requiring her artists either to remain single or to give up their careers for marriage. Twentieth- and twenty-first-century readers find Evans's refusal to even attempt to balance marriage and career troubling, but her peers' portraits of such attempts as universal failures suggest that Evans's fictional choices are, in fact, her solution to the dilemma facing the serious woman artist.

At the core of this solution are, however, irreducible tensions, which take a physical toll on Edna, whose hereditary heart condition worsens as her literary career flourishes. By the end of the novel Edna is on death's doorstep, and is widely expected to die while touring Europe with her young invalid charge, Felix. But it is Felix, not Edna, who dies abroad, and upon her return to the United States Edna confides to Manning her intention to write a children's book. Before she can begin this project, Edna marries the now-reformed St. Elmo Murray, who announces the end of Edna's career immediately after their wedding. While Edna lies fainting on a couch, St. Elmo declares: "To-day I snap the fetters of your literary bondage. There shall be no more books written! No more study, no more toil, no more anxiety, no more heart-aches. . . . You belong solely to me now, and I shall take care of the life you have nearly destroyed in your inordinate ambition" (365). In ending Edna's successful and productive career by fiat Evans confirms her oft-expressed belief that a woman could not combine marriage and career without doing damage to both. Moreover, St. Elmo's directive absolves Edna from the need to produce a children's book. Nina Baym has argued that in the 1870s "woman's fiction" was transformed into "girl's fiction" as it declined in popularity.[80] And as Louisa May Alcott would discover within a few years of the publication of *St. Elmo*, writing successful children's literature and pursuing a career as a serious literary artist were mutually exclusive. Although Evans mounts an argument for the importance of bridging the growing gap between the "masculine" realm of high literary culture and the "feminine" realm of popular domestic fiction, and Edna is able to inhabit both worlds successfully, the split is represented in Edna's own career and exacts a physical toll from the ailing author. Edna cannot write her third book because it would have killed her: not because of the work involved, but because writing a children's book would have upset the delicate balance between literary worlds on which Edna's career was founded, forcing Evans to confront the widening divide that she works so hard to bridge in *St. Elmo*.

Evans's detailed portrayal of Edna's career suggests that how it ends is less important, finally, than the fact that it existed. Here I agree with Susan K. Harris, who argues that the conventional beginnings and endings of popular nineteenth-century novels are part of these novels' "over plots" and that the middles of these novels contain the more substantive, interesting, and potentially transgressive material to which nineteenth-century readers responded.[81] And it is in the middle of *St. Elmo* that Evans depicts a woman writer who is motivated by deep religious faith and rigorous aesthetic standards, who garners both popularity and critical acclaim, who crosses boundaries of gender and genre by writing both fiction and nonfiction, and whose influence reaches both New York intellectuals and the "poor woman of the land" (360). In so doing Evans rewrites the familiar narrative of the popular woman author, revising many of its terms and offering a model of women's artistic production that places women writers firmly at the center of the nation's emerging high culture. In this effort Augusta Evans's vision is strikingly similar to Harriet Beecher Stowe's: both resisted the sacralization of art that was already under way in the late 1850s, insisting that the nation's highest art must be informed by religious faith. Although they disagreed profoundly on most political matters, these two most popular writers of their day each developed a vision of American culture that granted women an equal, if not a leading, role in creating the "America of Art."

CHAPTER THREE

Exorcising the Popular Woman Writer from "The Domain of Pure Literature"

W HEN THE anonymous author of "Woman in the Domain of Letters" declared in 1864 that "in glancing over the recent publications, we confess to having been somewhat surprised by the great numerical superiority of female over male authors," he expressed the common belief that women writers dominated the literary market.[1] The writer goes on to say that "[i]t is certainly not beyond the truth to say that, generally speaking, the best and the most saleable light reading now springs from female brains. That is, the average merit of the sexes as novel-writers is decidedly in favor of woman."[2] The writer's identification of women with novel writing and with popular success are truisms, which he uses merely to set the stage before moving on to defend women's encroachment on "the domain of letters, once sacred to man," and to welcome their increasing visibility in areas of intellectual activity beyond that of "light reading." Although this writer distinguishes between "light reading," produced mostly by women, and "literature" produced mostly by men (his canon includes Shakespeare, Dickens, Scott, and Thackeray), he does not view this distinction either as reflecting women's innate inferiority or as a threat to the development of "literature" in the United States. Many contemporary observers, however, were far less sanguine than the *Knickerbocker* writer, either about women's perceived dominance in the literary marketplace or about the equation of popularity and quality implicit in the writer's observation. Indeed, the belief that popularity and literary quality were in any way correlated was already being challenged by writers and intellectuals, and by the early postbellum period this view, which was quite common in the antebellum period, would be entirely discredited in the elite literary forums concerned with demarcating a realm of high literary culture.

Any discussion of the relationship between literature and the marketplace in the American context is, whether explicitly or implicitly, a discussion of women writers. Although recent research has demonstrated that women did not, in fact, dominate the literary market in purely numerical terms, women were responsible for producing some of the most famous and successful books to appear during the first half of the nineteenth century, and as the *Knickerbocker* author's remarks suggest, in the popular imagination women did dominate the antebellum literary marketplace.[3] As a result, the woman writer was a powerful symbolic figure for observers of the literary scene throughout the nineteenth century. And I would argue that women writers—both actual and imagined—were inseparable from the development of the ideal of American literature in the postbellum era, an ideal that was rhetorically and conceptually framed in opposition to popularity. The development of an ideal of high literary Art in the postbellum era, and especially that ideal's obsession with distinguishing literary Art from that produced for the marketplace, is driven by the figure of the scribbling woman, whose popularity in the marketplace at once helped to create a broad audience for fiction and threatened to make it impossible for high literary art to survive. Thus, for a woman writer to claim for herself the status of literary Artist is, in more ways than one, to attempt to occupy a position that is defined in opposition to her very existence.[4]

One of the defining characteristics of American literature is that it developed simultaneously with a market for it. As historians have long noted, American literature was made possible by the printing press, steam engines, railroads, and the rising rates of literacy. While these changes were crucial to the development of a mass-produced literature in England too, they were more rapid and more decisive in producing a body of literature in the United States, where virtually none had existed before. Whereas England had a famous literary tradition that technology transformed by making it accessible to the masses, the American literary tradition became available to the masses essentially from the moment of its birth. As a result, the market had traditionally been viewed as essential to the development of American literature, rather than antithetical to it.[5] Early American reviewing practices reflect this relationship: unlike their postbellum peers, antebellum reviewers did not automatically view popularity and artistic merit as mutually exclusive. Indeed, they assumed just the opposite—that only a popular novel could be characterized as a great work of art, though, of course, not all successful novels were judged great works of art. Antebellum reviewers did worry about the public's ability to differentiate between good and bad fiction, and many were actively engaged in efforts to elevate the public's taste, but they reconciled the tension between these two beliefs by "suppos[ing] that the people['s] inherent instincts for quality, increasingly called out by opportunity, would make them appreciate better books as these were called to their attention."[6] At the same time, authorship was understood in terms of "genteel amateurism": the ideal author was a leisured, educated man who wrote for his own pleasure and for the edification and entertainment of others, not because he needed to make a living. Popularity, in this model, was desirable because it suggested the quality of the work and gave the author the opportunity to influence more readers.[7] Similarly, publishers conceived of themselves as "Gentlemen publishers": they prided themselves on maintaining friendly, even familial relationships with their writers, both male and female; they embraced an ethos of noncommercialism even though they were engaged in publishing books as a business venture; and they conceived of themselves as guardians of public morals and made editorial choices that conformed to their moral standards.[8] As Susan Coultrap-McQuin has shown, the ideal of "genteel amateurism" that dominated antebellum conceptions of authorship and publishing was, in many ways, compatible with notions of feminine respectability: like publishers and writers, middle-class women were supposed to be motivated by social and moral rather than worldly concerns. Since women, in particular, had been socialized to value familial relationships and moral virtue above all else, antebellum women writers "often affirmed noncommercial values while competing for a good income."[9]

The 1830–60 period was also characterized by emergence of the possibilities of being both a "full-time 'serious' artist and a full-time 'commercial' artist," though these possibilities were not necessarily available to the same people.[10] The tension between these two visions of the artist's function is evident in Emersonian and Transcendentalist conceptions of art, which, as Lawrence Buell has demonstrated, both resist commercialization and are emblematic of it. On the one hand transcendentalists idealized art, resisted its commoditization, disparaged merely popular writing, and described the writer's vocation in terms of prophecy. On the other hand, "the prophetic-didactic view of art was eminently marketable in antebellum America," and large numbers of writers—including Emerson—"found it to their economic advantage to present themselves as harbinger of moral uplift." Buell also points out about Emerson's years on the lecture circuit, "Transcendentalism in his hands became an eminently marketable commodity that (as legions of late-century imitators found) lent itself to mass production. Of course, the commodity was saleable only on condition that it disguise its ultimate design on its audience."[11] In the antebellum era, then, commercial popularity and literature that was generally considered to be of high moral and aesthetic quality coexisted, however uneasily, and by midcentury the popular female-authored novel had become a fixture of the publishing world and a point of reference among observers of American culture.

Beginning in the 1850s, however, a realm of high literary culture began to be demarcated by writers such as Herman Melville, publishers such as James T. Fields, and periodicals such as the *Atlantic Monthly*. And this realm centered on a new definition of the "literary"—one that distinguished between moral purpose, popularity, and aesthetic value and which, more often than not, conceived of the first two terms as incompatible with the third. This conception of the "literary" as a special category of imaginative writing came into being in mid-nineteenth-century in the United States thanks primarily to the efforts of James T. Fields, who used both his publishing house, Ticknor and Fields, and the house magazine, the *Atlantic Monthly*, to "establish 'literature' as a market category. . . . Fields found a way to identify a certain portion of [imaginative writing] as distinguished—as of elevated quality, as of premium cultural value; then to build a market for that writing on the basis of that distinction."[12] The new category of the literary that Fields identified and then institutionalized enabled a new conception of authorship, one that "made it possible to write for, and to find support in, a differentiated realm of literary writing" and, at the same time, "made it possible that such writing could establish, for its creator, a previously unimaginable level of cultural prestige."[13] And that new conception was masculine in its assumptions about the kinds of labor involved in producing "literature" and the relationship of the literary to the popular.

This shift is exemplified in Herman Melville's changing conception of authorship. Although he had begun his career writing for a popular market, with considerable success, by the time *Mardi* was published in 1849, his popularity was declining, just as his literary aspirations were increasing, in part as a result of his somewhat belated reading of some of the central Romantic theorists: Coleridge, Lamb, and Carlyle.[14] Around the time he wrote *Mardi* Melville started to develop an idea of writing as "'a certain something unmanageable in us, that bids us do this or that, and be done it must—hit or miss,'" in other words, as motivated by internal aesthetic or spiritual motivations rather than pecuniary ones.[15] This represents a profound shift from his earlier conception of writing to please his audience: *Typee* (1846) and *Omoo* (1847) were "calculated for popular reading, or for none at all."[16] Although he continued to write for the popular market—both *Redburn* (1849) and *White Jacket* (1849) were written quickly for strictly financial motivations—Melville's views of this kind of writing changed dramatically. Writing to Lemuel Shaw, his father-in-law, after the publication of these two fairly successful books, Melville expresses his disdain for them:

> But no reputation that is gratifying to me, can possibly be achieved by either of these books. They are two jobs, which I have done for money—being forced to it, as other men are to sawing wood. . . . I have felt obliged to refrain from writing the kind of book I would wish to. . . . Being books, then, written in this way, my only desire for their "success" (as it is called) springs from my pocket, & not from my heart. So far as I am individually concerned, & independent of my pocket, it is my earnest desire to write those sort of books which are said to "fail."[17]

By the end of the 1840s, Melville had engendered a high-low split in his mental conception of his audience, marking a distinction between works whose goal is "amusement" and those designed for "achievement," and between the audience that can provide popularity and that which provides "permanent reputation."[18] Alongside this split comes an inversion of the relationship between popularity and literary quality; good books are now, in Melville's view, those that "can be said to 'fail'" in the marketplace. In privileging market failure and aligning it with literary value Melville implicitly distances himself from the "mob of scribbling women" whose books "occupied the public taste" and went into "innumerable editions."[19] Although Hawthorne's statements were made in private letters, Melville expressed his new conception of authorship publicly in "Hawthorne and His Mosses" (1850).

In the essay Melville expresses a profound ambivalence toward popularity. American authors are plagued, in his view, by having both too many readers and too few: on the one hand, there are only a "few men" who "have time, or patience, or palate" to read the great literary geniuses—Shakespeare and Hawthorne—"deeply," and on the other hand he castigates the American reading public for not supporting its native genius, calling on America to "prize and cherish her writers" and to prefer native "mediocrity" to foreign excellence.[20] Hawthorne's popularity itself is, in Melville's view, based on readers' erroneous identification of the author with the feminine: Hawthorne is not, Melville argues, a "flowery" "pleasant writer, with a pleasant style—a sequestered, harmless man. . . ."[21] He is "a man, as yet, almost utterly mistaken among men," whose "blackness" and depth are overlooked by those who mistake for effeminacy his unwillingness to stoop to "all the popularizing noise and show of broad farce and blood-besmeared tragedy" that makes Shakespeare's masculinity unmistakable.[22] And masculinity is a defining feature of originality, which is, in turn, a characteristic of "American genius." Dismissing "that graceful writer . . . that very popular and amiable writer"—Washington Irving—who "perhaps owes his chief reputation to the self-acknowledged imitation of a foreign model, and to the studied avoidance of all topics but smooth ones," Melville reminds his readers that "[i]t is better to fail in originality than to succeed in imitation. . . . Failure is the true test of greatness."[23] The title of original genius is readily available to anyone who is able to "write like a man, for then he will be sure to write like an American."[24] But even the most manly and original writer needs to eat, and to support his family; so Melville temporarily sets aside his belief that "Failure is the true test of greatness" and that genius does not need "patronage in order to expand" because it is the "explosive sort of stuff [that] will expand though screwed up in a vice," and admits that the "American genius" might be driven to "appeal to the people for more recognition." Such an appeal, however, "is not always with selfish motives, but patriotic ones."[25] By defining the literary genius's attempt to seek "more recognition" from the book-buying public as a form of patriotism, Melville distances him from the mob of scribbling women, characterizing their oft-cited motivation for entering the literary marketplace—the need to support their families—as merely "selfish." Because a writer's masculinity is confirmed not by his ability to support his family, but simply by his ability "to write like an American," which is, in turn, to "write like a man," Melville's male genius can both demand popular acclaim as his nationalistic due and remain uncontaminated by the effeminacy of the popular.[26]

Melville's literary manifesto articulates an elite notion of authorship that would become central to the postbellum conception of high literary culture. That conception of authorship, which privileged literary writing as an inherently masculine activity separate from the marketplace, posed special problems for a woman writer who wished to produce writing considered "literary," as all of the members of the transitional generation did. The division of readers in Melville's essay, into a mass and an elite audience, leaves open the possibility of writing for both, and as Richard Brodhead has shown, writing for more than one audience simultaneously was something numerous authors did at mid-century. However, by the early postbellum period the distinctions between the realm of high literary production and the other available literary markets had become much more rigid, and writing for numerous audiences at once while retaining one's credentials as a "literary" author was no longer possible.[27] Working from within a self-conception shaped by the antebellum model of female authorship, which stressed women's economic motivation for writing, and often required to support themselves and their families, these writers were faced with an irreducible tension between the emerging conception of high literary art as incompatible with the marketplace and the practical and psychic pressures exerted by the literary self-conception that had made their careers possible. This tension is central to numerous artist fictions by women from the postbellum period, which depict the market-driven assumptions of the antebellum model as at once inescapable and enormously destructive to the careers of promising women artists.

The specter of the popular woman writer haunts Thomas Wentworth Higginson's essay "Literature as an Art," which is an analysis of what it means to produce literature that will be held to purely aesthetic, rather than moral and economic, standards. In this essay, and numerous others he wrote for the *Atlantic* during the early postbellum years, Higginson articulates the philosophical and theoretical frameworks for the emerging realm of high culture.[28] An ordained Unitarian minister, Higginson was a vocal abolitionist, outspoken reformer and champion of many liberal causes, including women's rights, a lyceum lecturer, and a writer. As a regular contributor to the *Atlantic*, Higginson frequently wrote on the topic of American culture, especially in the postbellum years, when abolition ceased to be the central focus of his public speaking and writing.[29] In "A Plea for Culture" (January 1867), Higginson identified the creation of the "America of Art," as both the challenge and the reward facing the nation emerging from war. In the companion piece, "Literature as an Art," which was the lead essay in the December 1867 issue of the *Atlantic*, Higginson defines the incompatibility of popularity and high art as fundamental to the postbellum project of cultural nationalism.

Higginson's essay begins with an attack on materialism, a call for making the pursuit of art and science the primary activities in American life, and an analysis of the state of the arts in America (bad). Like Stowe, Higginson identifies the utilitarian approach to art that is the legacy of the Scottish Common Sense school as the central stumbling block in the emergence of a new conception of Literature as an Art: "We are now outgrowing this limited view of science, but in regard to literature the delusion still remains; if it is anything more than an amusement, it must afford solid information; it is not yet owned that it has value for itself, as an art."[30] Since presumably many of his readers still held such utilitarian a view of art, Higginson takes pains to explain its limits:

> Of course, all true instruction, however conveyed, is palatable; to a healthy mind the *Mécanique Céleste* is good reading; so is Mill's "Political Economy," or De Morgan's "Formal Logic." But words are available for something which is more than knowledge. Words afford a more delicious music than the chords of any instruments; they are susceptible of richer colors than any painter's palette; and that they should be used merely for the transportation of intelligence as a wheelbarrow carries brick, is not enough. The highest aspect of literature assimilates it to painting and music. Beyond and above all the domain of use lies beauty, and to aim at this makes literature an art.
>
> A book without art is simply a commodity; it may be exceedingly valuable to the consumer, very profitable to the producer, but it does not come within the domain of pure literature.[31]

In the last section of this passage Higginson reveals that the marketplace is the real enemy behind the utilitarian approach to art. In opposing "art" and "commodity" rather than art and craft, Higginson refers both to the history of American literature as it had emerged in the first half of the nineteenth century and to the future he is helping to create. For as Higginson and his contemporaries understood, the utilitarian rationale for art that developed initially as a way to circumvent the Calvinist prohibition on art led directly to the contemporary literary market, in which creative productions were evaluated by market, rather than aesthetic criteria. Although Higginson's formulation leaves open the possibility that a book *with* art might succeed in the marketplace too, by the end of the essay this small window is slammed shut and boarded up, leaving the American literary scene bifurcated in both theory and practice.

Higginson's vision of what it means to be dedicated to literary art emphasizes the disjunction between commercial success and "true" art:

> Indeed, a man may earn twenty thousand dollars a year by writing "sensation stories," and have nothing to do with literature as an art. But to devote one's life to perfecting the manner, as well as the matter, of

one's work; to expatriate one's self long years for it, like Motley; to overcome vast physical obstacles for it, like Prescott or Parkman; to live and die only to transfuse external nature into human words, like Thoreau; to chase dreams for a lifetime, like Hawthorne; to labor tranquilly and see a nation imbued with one's thoughts, like Emerson,— this is to pursue literature as an art.[32]

Not surprisingly, Higginson's canon includes no women, and his definition of art implicitly assumes that the artist has either an independent income or a spouse or children prepared to support him, as the Alcott women did for Bronson Alcott.[33] The quotation marks surrounding the reference to "sensation stories" suggest that the term serves here as a shorthand reference to any fiction that achieves quick and widespread popular success. In addition to aligning great art with financial failure, Higginson valorizes isolation and exile, as if anticipating Henry James's later career. Although he never asserts that a woman cannot be a great artist, Higginson's definition of great art is implicitly gendered male and aligned in opposition to many of the characteristics of female authorship as it had emerged in the antebellum period: rapid production in a domestic environment; a focus on quotidian and conventional subjects; a requirement of financial success; and an understanding of writing as a lucrative profession rather than a spiritual or aesthetic vocation.[34]

As though anticipating readers' objections to this somewhat dreary view of the artist's life, Higginson later returns to the subject of rewards, both financial and otherwise: He assures the reader that "there is no other pursuit so increasingly delightful" as creating art, "[b]ut," he continues,

> the literary man must love his art, as the painter must love painting, out of all proportion to its rewards; or rather, the delight of the work must be its own reward. Any praise or guerdon hurts him, if it brings any other pleasure to eclipse this. The reward of a good sentence is to have written it; if it bring fame or fortune, very well, so long as this recompense does not intoxicate. The peril is, that all temporary applause is vitiated by uncertainty, and may be leading you right or wrong. Goethe wrote to Schiller, "We make money by our poor books."[35]

Although he opens a small crack toward admitting the possibility that good art might bring financial rewards, Higginson is quick to warn against the "intoxicat[ion]" of "fame or fortune."[36] Like a drug, popular success is a kind of addictive substance which, once tasted, may be impossible to give up. Higginson's fear of the marketplace is palpable in this passage—he is no longer occupying the moral high ground of the essay's early pages; here he is desperately trying to convince the reader that while financial success in moderation might be acceptable, it is more likely to signal the advent of a "poor book" and lead to hopeless addiction.

Higginson cements his warnings against the invidiousness of the marketplace by invoking "genius," which he defines as the patience to wait out the market. After a detailed survey of Hawthorne's career, which illustrates the truism that great artists are often overlooked in their own lifetimes, Higginson concludes: "Therefore the writer, when he adopts a high aim, must be a law to himself, bide his time, and take the risk of discovering, at last, that his life has been a failure." He observes that

> since this recognition may not even begin till after his death, we can see what Rivarol meant by his fine saying that "genius is only great patience," and Buffon, by his more guarded definition of genius as the aptitude for patience.
>
> Of all literary qualities, this patience has thus far been rarest in America. Therefore, there has been in our literature scarcely any quiet power; if effects are produced, they must, in literature as in painting, be sensational, and cover acres of canvas. As yet, the mass of our writers seek originality in mere externals; we think, because we live in a new country, we are unworthy of ourselves if we do not Americanize the grammar and spelling-book. In a republic, must the objective case be governed by a verb? We shall yet learn that it is not new literary forms we need, but only fresh inspiration, combined with cultivated taste.[37]

Higginson's program for national cultural development requires patience, a willingness to bypass the market, and a quiet confidence that originality is the natural outgrowth of cultivation. Time is the single most important factor in this plan, but time is, as Higginson undoubtedly knew, a luxury most working artists could ill afford. In his emphatic rejection of the marketplace as a force shaping art and artists, Higginson simply ignores the practical question of physical survival. In articulating this highly idealistic vision of the terms for artistic success Higginson defines a narrow, rarefied zone within which literary art is produced, essentially excluding most of the existing body of American literature. As postbellum writers knew all too well, to embrace financial success was to doom one's artistic ambition, but to embrace artistic production on these terms was to doom oneself to starvation.[38] The resulting dual ambivalence—toward the marketplace and toward the cultural authorities who vilified it—is a hallmark of each of the women writers in this study. Of course, ambivalence toward the marketplace is typical of many nineteenth-century authors. What is unique to my subjects is their complicated relationship to the cultural authorities who were defining artistic quality as antithetical to the marketplace. The gendered terms of this definition, and the legacy of the antebellum model of female authorship, combined to make either complete acceptance or complete rejection of this program difficult, if not impossible, for postbellum women writers.

Revising the domestic model of authorship required confronting the economic expectations it had engendered. The dual justification for women's entry into the public sphere in antebellum America had been moral imperative and financial need. Once the notion that women might resort to their pens to support their families was accepted, and the popularity and financial viability of fiction by women became evident, women writers frequently depicted themselves as producers of a commodity first and artists second, if at all. As long as the popular remained a category that coexisted with literary quality, however uneasily, this formulation provided women writers with a viable identity. But for members of the transitional generation, who were more willing than their antebellum predecessors to claim for themselves the identity of Artist, coming to terms with the legacy of women writers' financial success was central to the development of new models of authorship.

All the women studied here needed to support themselves and their families, and Alcott and Davis in particular spent much of their careers writing stories, articles, and essays that could be produced quickly for a lucrative market, frequently bemoaning their limited opportunities to produce the kind of work that would receive critical acclaim. This sustained frustration at their inability to produce high-quality work is new for women writers, and its public or semipublic expression reflects their determination to construct their public identities as artists first and foremost.[39] Although antebellum writers often remarked on the artistic compromises they made to meet publication deadlines, they did not present themselves as artists whose great work was being delayed or denied while they wrote for the popular market. Fanny Fern's autobiographical character Ruth Hall even suggests that hastily produced work has appeal that more self-consciously literary work lacks. Responding to a fan letter urging her to collect and reprint her columns in a book, Ruth Hall speaks directly to the reader:

> "that's a thought that never entered this busy head of mine, John Stokes. I publish a book? Why, John, are you aware that those articles were written for bread and butter, not fame; and tossed to the printer before the ink was dry, or I had time for a second reading? And yet, perhaps there is more freshness about them than there would have been, had I leisure to have pruned and polished them—who knows?"[40]

Ruth Hall's response to her fan's suggestion simultaneously confirms the woman writer's conventional claim that she is not interested in literary fame and slyly suggests that her own hastily written columns possess a freshness absent from the carefully crafted work produced by those who do seek it. This self-confidence masquerading as humility is entirely absent from the comments of her successors, who clearly believe, with Higginson, that producing good writing takes time, even as they struggle with the financial limitations of producing that kind of writing.

Early in her career Alcott tells herself that her popular writing is a form of literary apprenticeship: "Wrote two tales for L. I enjoy romancing to suit myself; and though my tales are silly, they are not bad; and my sinners always have a good spot somewhere. I hope it is good drill for fancy and language, for I can do it fast."[41] After finishing one of her novels, Alcott registers her perpetual sense of failing to live up to her own standards: "Finished 'Work,'—twenty chapters. Not what it should be,—too many interruptions. Should like to do one book in peace, and see if it wouldn't be good."[42] Another journal entry reveals Alcott's awareness that literary acclaim rarely provides life's necessities: "Wrote a little on poor old 'Success' but being tired of novels I soon dropped it & fell back on rubbishy tales, for they pay best & I can't afford to starve on praise, when sensation stories are written in half the time & keep the family cosy."[43] In the same vein, Sharon Harris writes that Rebecca Harding Davis took up writing for *Peterson's* and later for other popular periodicals purely for economic reasons and that she clearly distinguished between the two venues: "writing for *Peterson's* was to earn money; the *Atlantic* was for artistry."[44] Elizabeth Stuart Phelps, too, alternated "between writing popular literature to produce income that would pay for a new house or new dress, and writing carefully crafted fiction for a serious audience."[45] But the ability to work in both markets was increasingly limited as the postbellum period wore on; the *Atlantic Monthly,* the preeminent literary magazine of the day,

> underwent a palpable stiffening of its selection criteria in the mid-1860s as evidenced by the fact that Rebecca Harding Davis, whose "Life in the Iron Mills" and *Margret Howth* it had featured, was now dropped and left to the drudgery of popular-commercial writing. At the time of this hard-to-document change, the *Atlantic* also began not finding Alcott an author of its sort. Having taken four of her stories between 1859 and 1863, the *Atlantic* ceased accepting Alcott's fiction after 1864.[46]

And Alcott clearly understood that change was in the air; in a journal entry for July 1864 she records: "Went home and wrote a story, 'an Hour,' for the Atlantic, & sent it. As I thought it good was pretty sure they wouldn't take it."[47] She was right. The story never appeared in the *Atlantic.* Alcott's observation that she doesn't expect the *Atlantic* to take her story *because* she "thought it good" both indicates how attuned she was to the changing literary currents and attests to a degree of resignation about those changes. As Alcott's comments in particular reveal, members of the transitional generation enjoyed the financial benefits of the market for women's writing that their antebellum predecessors helped create, but they struggled with the legacy of that generation's self-conception as "bread and butter" writers.

The difficulty of overcoming the financial expectations governing a woman's artistic career is a theme that runs through virtually every artist-fiction by a woman published after 1860. Indeed, the sacrifice of a woman's artistic aspirations to the support her family is an ironic rite of authorship for the writers in this study. While every member of the transitional generation focuses on this problem, Rebecca Harding Davis's portrait of an artist's sacrifice in her 1873 novella *Earthen Pitchers* is a particularly stark analysis of the social assumptions and economic structures governing women's artistic careers. The failure of the protagonist, Audrey Swenson, to achieve her artistic goals can be attributed to numerous sources: the absence of a community of artists (of both genders) to share her artistic interests and provide emotional and artistic support; the power of the antebellum convergence between women's artistic work and the marketplace; and the resistance of other women to the notion that Audrey might invert antebellum models of women's artistic production. The gendered split at the heart of this novella, between Audrey's male mentors, who accept her identity as serious artist, and her female relative and peer, who resist it, reveals that while reversing existing models of artistic production enables women to articulate an artistic self-conception that is familiar to, and supported by, male cultural authorities, it runs the risk of challenging the status quo in ways that women find threatening because it undermines the power and authority they had accumulated since the beginning of the nineteenth century.

Earthen Pitchers is the story of a few days in the lives of four young people: Jane (Jenny) Derby, a struggling journalist in Philadelphia who would rather be "in trade" but has chosen writing because it is one of the only professions open to women;[48] her cousin, Christopher (Kit) Graff, a Delaware farmer who regularly tries to convince Jenny to abandon her career and put herself under his family's protection; Niel Goddard and Audrey Swenson are the other members of the quartet, and the action revolves around two love plots: Christopher's for Audrey (who is a distant cousin) and Jenny's for Niel. The novella is set primarily in the Delaware seacoast farming community that is Audrey's and Christopher's home, where Niel has gone to lay claim to some family property to which Jenny is the true heir. Knowing that Niel (who is also her distant cousin) will not marry until he can afford to support a wife, Jenny conceals her own claim to the property—which would make her independent and liberate her from the work she hates—telling Niel that he is the long-lost heir. Jenny hopes that once he is financially independent Niel will marry her, formalizing the loose understanding that has long existed between them. Jenny's plan is complicated by the fact that Audrey, who is beautiful, reserved, and talented, has become the object of Niel's fickle attention, and much of the plot revolves around her desperate machinations to protect her sacrifice and prevent Niel from marrying Audrey.

Audrey, however, has no intention of marrying either Niel Goddard or Kit, who has always assumed that she will, eventually, move into his home and settle into learning the arts of canning and preserving from his mother, Ann. Instead, Audrey intends to devote her life to composing music, for which she has a great talent. The scene in which Audrey accepts her artistic vocation emphasizes the difference between Audrey's work and that of antebellum women artists. After being drawn outdoors by the "voice" of nature, which is as "real" to her as canned peaches are to her Aunt Ann, Audrey realizes that she is ready to accept the "uncomprehended message" she has often heard (262). Although the precise message she is to deliver remains obscure to

Audrey, she is confident that "[s]ome day she would reach it," and in the meantime, she accepts the burden placed upon her:

> Messages of high meaning were given to a few men to deliver to the world, as of old to the prophets; they wrote or painted, or cut them out of stone. Audrey knew that she had no utterance but in song. . . .
>
> Strains of simple, powerful harmony were heard, unknown before by her; whether she sang them or not she did not know. If she could make audible to the world the meaning of this night to her? How angry storm and prophetic sea, the malignant wind, and the gracious, comforting earth to its smallest green leaf, summoned alike the unwilling soul to the work which God had given it, and forbade it to accept any other. If she could find fit utterance for even so much as this, her life were cheaply given. (263)

Like Harriet Beecher Stowe, who claimed that God wrote *Uncle Tom's Cabin*, Davis depicts Audrey as being "summoned." Unlike Stowe and other antebellum authors who adopted the posture of medium for a religious message and disclaimed artistic ambition, Audrey believes that she has a rare talent and that her artistic ambition is divinely authorized. Davis's characterization of Audrey as one of the "few men" not only literally genders Audrey male, but also bestows upon her the authority associated with biblical prophets and Romantic artists and aligns her with Stowe's "priests of national development" and with Evans's "hierophants."[49] Further distancing Audrey from antebellum formulas is the fact that her "message of high meaning" is strictly aesthetic—the task of expressing the divine in "song" of her own composition—and that her artistic vocation is not interchangeable with "any other" work.

This vocation scene comes shortly after Audrey's encounter with the writer Niel Goddard, in which Audrey is proclaimed a "true artist" in terms that echo Higginson's and confirm her difference from other women (273). In her meeting with Goddard, who is the first person other than her Uncle Tom to take her talent seriously, Audrey asks the writer "'to tell me what my voice, touch, and knowledge of music are worth. These are only my tools, to be sure, but I must know whether they are good tools or not'" (249). Goddard answers, "'It would need five years, at least, of severe study to give you such power of expression as would content you.' She nodded gravely. 'I thought it would be longer. Well, I can give that.'" When Goddard points out that in five years she will be at the stage of life that "most women give to dreams and fancy, and to—love," Audrey explains that she is not like other women: "'I don't believe,' she continued with a grave simplicity, 'that God made me to be a wife or mother'" (249). As though to test her assertion, Goddard proposes marriage the very next day. Audrey refuses, reminding him that she "can never marry" because her life is dedicated to her art, which "'is all there is of me'" (272). Goddard mounts the conventional argument that the central event of a woman's life is a love relationship, arguing that Audrey's art will suffer because she lacks "experience of life" and will be unable to "teach by her art" if she allows "half [her] nature to lie fallow," but he soon changes his mind (272). Having given up his suit, Goddard asks that Audrey "bid me a farewell in your own way"; she sits at the piano, but stops after hitting a single note, explaining that:

> "There is nothing for me to say to you. How can I play?"
> To her amazement, his countenance was at once irradiated. "But this is the feeling of a true artist! On such an idea Mozart, Beethoven, Mendelssohn built their divine work—the necessity of utterance. They wrote no score for a royalty of filthy dollars. You did right to reject me. Let me be sacrificed to art. Better so! better so!" (273)

The scene is quite comic: Goddard, who is ludicrously self-absorbed, proceeds to transform Audrey into a "perfect type of the vestal virgin to dedicate to Art" and a source of inspiration for himself, much to Audrey's surprise (273). Although Davis mocks Goddard, she also uses him, and his authority, as "one of the most promising men of the day" (221), to confirm Audrey's status as a "true artist" and to undermine the arguments he had earlier made about the necessity of love and marriage in women's lives. In comparing Audrey to the great male composers whose music was "divine work" free of the taint of "filthy dollars," Goddard echoes the narrator's earlier assertion that Audrey is one of the "few men" given a prophetic gift and validates Audrey's and her uncle's conviction that the young composer's work must remain outside the realm of the marketplace.

Being anointed a "true artist" and the bearer of a divine gift, however, is not enough to spare Audrey the familiar fate of women artists of this period: Audrey ends up "mak[ing] a market of [her] birthright" after she agrees to marry (284). Audrey's failure reveals the limitations of adopting a self-conception that requires so radical a reversal of existing models of female identity without access to any kind of social support. Although Higginson's portrait of those who "pursue literature as an art" stresses isolation and individualism, his true artists—all men of the same class, from the same part of the country, with similar educational backgrounds—form a community composed of each other. And it is just such a community that Audrey lacks:

> There was a great unknown world of men and women beyond, which she had meant to reach some day. The welcome and the friends waiting for her there had grown real things to her in her lonely fancies. Surely there was there some one for whom fish and tomatoes and household drudgery were not the best of life? She had something to say to such a one—something which ached and pained in her breast now. It would give her a share in their joy or their sorrow. Some day she would be able to utter it clearly.
>
> Until that day nothing should turn her from her work. (279)[50]

Audrey's conviction that she is different from the women around her, whose lives revolve around "fish and tomatoes and household drudgery," inspires the resistance and resentment of those same women. What, exactly, should Audrey's work be is the subject of debate for the two other female characters in the novella, who contest Audrey's conviction that her status as a divinely inspired artist exempts her from the distractions of domesticity and her work from the pressures of the marketplace.

Most critical of Audrey's self-conception is Jane Derby, who supported herself as a journalist before marrying Niel Goddard and becoming a successful businesswoman. Her labor now supports his artistic endeavors, which, after eight years, have yet to produce the long-promised great work. It is from Jane that we learn about the struggle surrounding Audrey's decision to commercialize her talent after her marriage. Jane recalls that

> [Audrey's] old uncle opposed her bitterly, and made a queer speech in Jane's hearing. "Don't make a market of your birthright," he said, "hide it, bury it in a napkin if you will. You sold yourself, but don't sell that for your own selfish ends, or God will punish you." . . .
>
> Jane always thought the old man half crazy before that, and was not particularly grieved to hear, soon afterwards, that he was dead. "People with such odd notions," she said, "were better in some other sphere and society than this. Not take your talent into the market, indeed! What were we commanded to do with them [*sic*], except to trade, and to trade for usury too?" (284–85)

Uncle Tom's description of Audrey's determination to "make a market of [her] birthright" as "selfish" echoes Melville's formulation in "Hawthorne and His Mosses" and underscores the complete reversal of terms that Audrey's ambition represents. As Jane's scorn for Uncle Tom's warning that divine punishment will result from Audrey's commercializing her talent reminds the reader, female artists had long presented themselves as divinely "commanded" to take their talents to the marketplace. At the same time, Audrey's inability to do anything *but* take her talent to the marketplace reveals that such reversals must overcome not only the absence of community but the resistance of those who benefit from the status quo.

Jane's ridicule of the idea that Audrey's talent should be kept out of the marketplace is ironic in light of the fact that she devotes much of her hard-earned income to ensuring that her husband, the once-promising writer Niel Goddard, is spared the necessity of "sell[ing] whatever original power [he] ha[s] for mere food and clothes" (233). Her assessment of Uncle's Tom's dismay at the prospect of Audrey selling her "birthright" as "odd" and out of step with social and economic realities stems not just from her own hypocrisy, however, but from the cultural expectations about the relationship between artistic production and the marketplace, which authorized, however indirectly, Jane's own career as a journalist.[51] Jane's belief that "we"—presumably women—are "commanded"—presumably by God—to trade their talent in the marketplace reflects the history of women's entrance into the American literary marketplace as producers of saleable commodities first and artists second, if at all. Like Audrey's Aunt Ann, who once warned her niece that "'you are a woman. You cannot shirk your real work for any whim'" (278), Jane believes that she knows what Audrey's "real work" is; for these two women, Audrey's and her uncle's conception of her as a serious artist, divinely inspired and, therefore, to be shielded from both domesticity and the marketplace, challenges existing conceptions of the appropriate relationship between female artistic production, religion, and the marketplace, and undermines the social order in ways that both women find threatening. Jane Derby and Aunt Ann resist Audrey's attempt to define her "work" as purely aesthetic because it reverses antebellum formulas, which defined artistic work as an extension of domestic labor and, at least rhetorically, valued them both equally. The characters of Jane and Aunt Ann underscore the complexity of the task facing postbellum women writers: not only did they have to overcome the resistance of male cultural authorities, who could, and did, place institutional barriers in their paths; they had to dismantle a deeply entrenched social and economic system, which had benefited large numbers of American women—including themselves—for decades.

Audrey's decision to marry despite her understanding that marriage and an artistic career are, for a woman, incompatible, is expressed in economic terms that underscore the inescapable power of the market. Arriving at what she thinks is the deathbed of her cousin Kit, who has been injured in a train wreck, Audrey initially resists the "breathless pressure" exerted by Aunt Ann's plea for a deathbed marriage to ease her son's dying hours (281). Audrey is spared by the appearance of her Uncle Tom, who announces that Kit will live and chastises his niece for contemplating a marriage that will "interfere with [her] career as an artist" (282). Just when Audrey seems able once again to withstand the "breathless pressure" exerted by her injured lover and his mother, her uncle expresses the opinion that Kit would be better off dead, since he has just lost the better part of his property in a lawsuit, settled the day before, and has been blinded by the accident. It is this last piece of news that seems to tip the scale for Audrey. "'He has nothing left then? Nothing?'" she asks her uncle. "Her uncle replied, but she did not seem to hear his answer. She was looking at the sea and at the shore, as one who goes from them inland to see them no more." Audrey then goes into Kit's room and offers to marry him if "it [would] make your life worth more" (282).

That her husband is oblivious to her sacrifice is evident in the novella's closing scene, which takes place eight years later. Hearing his wife sing a lullaby to their daughter, Kit remarks

> "Your uncle and that Goddard . . . used to think you had a pretty talent for music, Audrey. You were going to teach the whole world by your songs, I remember. But that little tune is all you ever made, eh?"
>
> "That is all."
>
> "And nobody ever heard it but Baby and me. However, it's very pretty, very pretty. And it was lucky your uncle taught you as thoroughly as he did. Your scales and notes helped us over a rough place. They served their purpose very well, though your voice is quite gone with teaching."
>
> He got up presently, and strolled up the beach. (286)

Kit's careless observation that Audrey's musical training "served [its] purpose very well" crystallizes the critique of the commercialization of women's talents that underlies this novella. What Kit cannot or does not wish to understand is that their marriage is based on an economic transaction in which Audrey exchanged the "worth" (249) of her talent to make his own life "worth more" (282). Kit's belief that the only "purpose" of Audrey's talent was to support their family when he could not underscores the logic, embodied by Niel, that requires that a male "genius" be coddled and supported by his women so that he won't have to "sell whatever original power [he] ha[s] for mere food and clothes," while Audrey, like other talented women, is expected to enter the marketplace and reduce her gift to its monetary "worth," regardless of the loss of "original power" that inevitably accompanies such transactions (233).

Davis's reference to the need to preserve an artist's "original power" by protecting him from the marketplace alludes to the postbellum anxieties about originality and mechanical reproduction that formed separate, though related, strands of the gendered conversation about cultural nationalism. The problem of originality—or lack thereof—had plagued Americans since the early years of the republic. Sydney Smith's rhetorical question from 1820: "In the four quarters of the globe, who reads an American book?" was only the most famous expression of the widely held view that American literature was but a poor imitation of its British forerunners and American visual art was entirely derivative of European masterpieces.[52] By the early postbellum period the long-standing American anxiety about originality had a new focus, as technologies for the mass reproduction of visual arts—photography and lithography—were developed. Questions of originality have special resonance for women writers because the antebellum conception of authorship was predicated on the assumption that women were motivated strictly by the desire to serve as mediums for a divine message, and women writers had long disclaimed any desire to express their own original aesthetic vision because such ambitions were widely considered unfeminine. At the same time, the inextricable link between their artistic endeavors and the marketplace meant that women writers could not afford to keep their "birthright" out of the market even if they wished to do so, as the members of the transitional generation increasingly did. To claim the right to protect one's "original power" from the market then was to distance oneself from the antebellum posture of medium whose vision is, by definition, not original, and for whom popular success is desirable, because it allows the widespread dissemination of the author's religious message. The concern about preserving one's "original power" also aligns the writer with the postbellum cultural project, in which originality was privileged as a central characteristic of an American high art that was conceived as oppositional to the marketplace, either because, as in Melville's and Higginson's views, it is eclipsed in the market by the "sensation stories" that appeal to the lowest common denominator of the mass audience, or because the need to support oneself forces the artist into the marketplace where the sheer labor of teaching music, writing popular fiction, or painting portraits destroys the artist's "original power."

The question of the possibility of producing an original American art had troubled American cultural observers since the early days of the republic. The debate about the proper relationship between American art and its European forerunners was especially heated in the visual arts world in the early-nineteenth century, where views were strongly divided between members of the cultural nationalist camp, who wanted American artists to shun all European influences and focus exclusively on the American landscape for their inspiration and subject matter, and those who feared that American art could not develop without learning from, and being influenced by, the great tradition of European art.[53] By the middle of the century the discussion about originality, imitation, and national identity centered around a number of ideas that had become truisms and were repeated, in various forms, for decades. One of these was the equation of originality—which was rarely defined as anything but the absence of imitation—with national identity.[54] Harriet Beecher Stowe expresses this idea frequently in *Sunny Memories of Foreign Lands,* her account of her grand tour of Europe in the early 1850s. Describing her visit to the graves of Scottish martyrs, Stowe observes that their sacrifices produced the great Scottish literature of Sir Walter Scott; she then states, clearly with her own country's political struggles in mind, that "a vigorous and original literature is impossible except to a strong, free, self-respecting people. The literature of a people must spring from the sense of its nationality; and nationality is impossible without self-respect, and self-respect is impossible without liberty."[55] A second common theme was the belief that influence and imitation were virtually indistinguishable. Commenting on the pervasive influence of the ancient Greeks on European art, Stowe praises the original and damns all subsequent art as mere imitation:

> Nothing could be more glorious and beautiful than the Grecian development; nothing more unlike it than the stale wearisome, repetitious

imitations of it in modern times. The Greek productions themselves
had a living power to this day; but all imitations of them are cold and
tiresome. These old Greeks made such beautiful things, because they
did *not* imitate. That mysterious vitality which still imbues their
remains, and which seems to enchant even the fragments of their mar-
bles, is the mesmeric vitality of fresh, original conception.[56]

As I have discussed in chapter 1, in Stowe's view only religious faith
can protect the artist from the falling prey to "stale" imitation—that
bugbear of American culture. But for other observers, tapping into the
"mesmeric vitality of fresh, original conception" requires a faith not in
the divine, but in America. And as Higginson declared in no uncertain
terms, "When [the artist] loses this faith, [he] takes rank among the
copyists and the secondary, and no accident can raise him to a place
among the benefactors of mankind."[57] In "Originality and Imitation"
(1868), Ralph Waldo Emerson defined originality simply as American-
ness: "And what is Originality? it is being, being one's self, and report-
ing accurately what we see and are."[58] And for Higginson, originality
and cultural nationalism are explicitly linked:

> We need to become national, not by any conscious effort, implying atti-
> tudinizing and constraint, but by simply accepting our own life. It is
> not desirable to go out of one's way to be original, but it is to be hoped
> that it may lie in one's way. Originality is simply a fresh pair of eyes. If
> you want to astonish the whole world, said Rahel, tell the simple truth.
> It is easier to excuse a thousand defects in the literary man who pro-
> ceeds on this faith, than to forgive the one great defect of imitation in
> the purist who seeks only to be English.[59]

As these examples suggest, to invoke originality is to insert oneself into
the ongoing conversation about American cultural nationalism. And
producing the kind of art that will enable the United States to take her
rightful cultural place among nations requires that originality be distinguished not only from imitation, but from popularity. Whereas Melville
demanded that Americans acknowledge Hawthorne's original genius
by making him into a best-selling author, Higginson wishes to make the
distinction between the popular and the original impermeable. Discussing the need for a national culture in his first postbellum essay on
the subject, Higginson explains that "as the value of a nation to the
human race does not depend upon its wealth or numbers, so it does not
depend even upon the distribution of elementary knowledge, but upon

the high-water mark of its highest mind. Before the permanent tribunal, copyists and popularizers count for nothing. . . . So long as the sources of art and science are still Transatlantic, we are still a province, not a nation."[60] And copyists and popularizers are, primarily, women, whose writing had far more appeal to a popular audience than that produced by the "highest mind[s]" of the nation, and whose ability to be original visual artists had long been limited by the prevailing assumption that women were best suited to copying, rather than creating, original paintings.

But even as Higginson and his contemporaries were privileging originality as the defining characteristic of high art, the value of the original was being threatened by technological developments such as photography and lithography, which enabled the mass reproduction and dissemination of art on a previously unknown scale. Writing just two years after Higginson dismissed "popularizers and copyists" as meriting no place in the "permanent tribunal," James Parton—prominent publisher and writer and husband of popular writer Fanny Fern—defended Louis Prang, the "most eminent lithographer of the United States," against charges that widely available, inexpensive lithographs "lessen the demand for excellent original works."[61] On the contrary, Parton argues, the ability to reproduce art fulfills two, related public functions. First,

This art of chromo-lithography harmonizes well with the special work of America at the present moment, which is not to create, but to diffuse; not to produce literature, but to distribute the spelling book; not to add to the world's treasures of art, but to educate the mass of mankind to an intelligent enjoyment of those which we already possess.[62]

The "mass of mankind" Parton has in mind are the European immigrants and

emancipated slaves of the south [whom] it devolves upon us of this generation and the next to convert into thinking, knowing, skilful, tasteful citizens. . . . By [Prang's] assistance we may hope to diffuse among all classes of the people that feeling for art which must precede the production of excellent national works.[63]

In addition to its function as an educational tool, helping to create the kind of citizens that, public intellectuals agreed, were a necessary prerequisite to the development of American culture, lithography would add value to rather than detract from the original works of art that American artists did produce. Parton points out that the market for lithographs, good-quality full-color reproductions that sold for "the price of a pair of slippers," is entirely different from the market for original art, and argues that one does not cannibalize the other: "We may rely upon it, that the persons who now buy expensive works will continue so to do, and that these chromos will enhance, rather than diminish, the value of originals; because the possession of an original will confer more distinction when every one has copies. . . ."[64] Finally, Parton points to the economic benefit that mass reproduction offers the artist: "Nor is it a slight advantage to an artist to have in his works two kinds of property, instead of one; the power to sell them, and the power to sell the privilege of multiplying copies of them."[65] Parton's emphasis on the didactic function of American art, his argument that originality and mass reproduction can coexist productively, and his analysis of the financial constraints facing fine artists capture the kind of balancing act that antebellum women writers regularly practiced. But for postbellum women this balancing act was becoming increasingly untenable, as originality and popularity were being defined as mutually exclusive categories, and the role of copyist or popularizer was deemed socially valuable but essentially inferior to the role of original artist. Whether because a book requires mass reproduction in order to be read at all, or because the ideal of a high literary art was being developed as a market category, anxiety about the devaluation of the original through reproduction was expressed almost exclusively in terms of the visual arts.[66] And it is through the figure of the female visual artist that Nathaniel Hawthorne and Elizabeth Stuart Phelps articulate competing visions of the possibility of feminine originality and of the place of original works by women in the pantheon of American art.

It is unlikely that his female peers were aware of Hawthorne's private diatribe against the "mob of scribbling women" whose work, he knew, would inevitably edge out his own: "I should have no chance of success while the public taste is occupied with their trash" he wrote his publisher William D. Ticknor, "and should be ashamed of myself if I did succeed."[67] It is, however, likely that all the writers discussed in this study would have been aware of Hawthorne's views of American female artists expressed in *The Marble Faun* (1860), which was conceived and written while he was in self-imposed exile in England, waiting for the public taste to change. Although he undoubtedly found the popularity of feminine "trash" distressing, his portrait of Hilda, the artist turned copyist, suggests that it was the possibility that women artists might turn away from the market, to the province of Art, that was ultimately more troubling to Hawthorne.

His portrait of Hilda reveals Hawthorne's awareness of American women's changing understanding of their artistic identities. And although Hilda is a painter, he explicitly equates her artistic ambitions with those of American women writers. Introducing Hilda as an artist who had "early shown what was pronounced by connoisseurs a decided genius for the pictorial art," Hawthorne implies that he is willing to accept the young woman's claim to "genius" on faith, though he finds this characterization questionable.[68] He goes on to cast doubt on Hilda's talent, observing that "[h]ad Hilda remained in her own country, it is not improbable that she might have produced original works, worthy to hang in that gallery of native art, which, we hope, is destined to extend its rich length through many future centuries" (55). The double negative "not improbable" underscores the skepticism suggested by the narrator's insistence that it is not he but "connoisseurs" who have "pronounced" Hilda talented. The narrator goes on to suggest that while European travel is potentially damaging to all artists' self-confidence, it is particularly dangerous for women artists. Since arriving in Rome, Hilda "seemed to have entirely lost the impulse of original design, which brought her thither" (56). This transformation is attributed to "the gift of discerning and worshipping excellence," which Hilda possesses "in a most unusual capacity" (56). Hilda's gift is manifested as a unique ability to understand another's work, a quality that, in Hawthorne's view, is particularly feminine:

> She saw—no, not saw, but felt—through and through a picture; she bestowed upon it all the warmth and richness of a woman's sympathy; not by any intellectual effort, but by this strength of heart, and this guiding light of sympathy, she went straight to the central point, in which the Master had conceived his work. Thus, she viewed it, as it were, with his own eyes, and hence her comprehension of any picture that interested her was perfect. (56–57)

Here Hawthorne applies terms traditionally used to describe women's moral superiority—"the guiding light of sympathy" and "strength of heart"—to suggest that they are incapable of producing original art. Instead, Hilda's feminine ability to feel rather than see or think about a work of art makes her the perfect copyist: she is a vessel or medium through which the male Master can live again. Hawthorne's insistence that Hilda's ability to understand art is a great gift is accompanied by his barely disguised contempt for her original ambitions:

> All the youthful hopes and ambitions, the fanciful ideas which she had
> brought from home, of great pictures to be conceived in her feminine
> mind, were flung aside, and, so far as those most intimate with her
> could discern, relinquished without a sigh. All that she would hence-
> forth attempt—and that, most reverentially, not to say religiously—was
> to catch and reflect some of the glory which had been shed upon can-
> vass from the immortal pencils of old.
>   So Hilda became a copyist. (57)

The narrator's characterization of Hilda's relationship to her work as
"reverential" and "religious" evokes the posture of women writers,
who had historically cast their entry into the male preserve of public
artistic speech as an extension of their socially sanctioned religious
activities. Unlike Stowe and Evans, however, who were transforming
this formula and expanding the definition of acceptable female artistic
activity, Hawthorne uses this formula to limit women artists to the role
they had historically occupied. The terms of Hilda's transformation
suggest that having made their artistic endeavors acceptable by casting
themselves as mediums for a religious message rather than original creators driven by an aesthetic vision, women cannot now change the
terms under which they produce art. That Hilda comes to terms with
the realization that her "feminine mind" is best suited to copying rather
than creating "without a sigh" suggests that her previous ambitions
were a form of false consciousness that can be "relinquished" without
loss—either to Hilda or to the "gallery of native art" from whose walls
Hilda's work will be absent.

At the end of the chapter describing Hilda's transformation from
artist to copyist, Hawthorne editorializes on the subject of feminine
originality: "It strikes us that there is something far higher and nobler in
all this—in her thus sacrificing herself to the devout recognition of the
highest excellence in art—than there would have been in cultivating her
not inconsiderable share of talent for the production of works from her
own ideas" (60). Noting that Hilda's original creations would have
"fall[en] short, if by ever so little, of the best that has ever been done,"
the narrator praises Hilda for choosing "the better, the loftier, and more
unselfish part, laying her individual hopes, her fame, her prospects of
enduring remembrance, at the feet of those great departed ones, whom
she so loved and venerated" (60). Echoing Melville's distinction
between "selfish" and "patriotic" motivations for seeking popular suc-

cess, Hawthorne here rewards Hilda for her "unselfish" decision by giving her a role in the patriotic cultural project of the day—the education and elevation of the American masses who cannot travel to Europe to view for themselves the "best that has ever been done." Praising Hilda for her "generous self-surrender, and her brave, humble magnanimity in choosing to be the handmaid of those old magicians, instead of a minor enchantress within a circle of her own," Hawthorne ends the chapter with this revealing question: "Would it have been worth Hilda's while to relinquish this office, for the sake of giving the world a picture or two which it would call original; pretty fancies of snow and moonlight; the counterpart, in picture, of so many feminine achievements in literature!" (60–61). Hawthorne does not need to answer the question he poses; he has already done so in his portrait of Hilda. His sudden introduction of women writers into a discussion that has, ostensibly, nothing to do with literature reveals just what is at stake in Hilda's character. Acknowledging the existence of women who create "minor" works that the misguided "world . . . would call original," Hawthorne here attempts to contain the emerging specter of female "genius" by insisting that women adhere to the terms that first enabled their entrance into the realm of art. Motivated by their essential sympathy and religious nature, not driven by intellect, women artists must function as mediums for others' messages, not creators with their own unique visions. The dismissive language Hawthorne uses to describe feminine artistic production reveals his belief that the "gallery of native art" that he hopes to see established is destined to remain empty so long as women and "connoisseurs" continue to believe that women's "not inconsiderable share of talent" may be appropriately employed in creating original art.[69]

Hawthorne's praise for Hilda's decision to become a copyist may reflect his belief, shared by countless others during this period, that exposure to great European art was essential to the creation of American culture. For those unable to travel to Europe, viewing reproductions of the paintings of great Masters was the only alternative, and so the work of copyists was essential to the project of "civilizing" the American middle and working classes.[70] And although hand-painted reproductions had been the norm for centuries, the middle of the nineteenth century saw the perfection of lithography techniques, which enabled high-quality, full-color reproduction of paintings, which were produced cheaply and in large quantities.[71] In reducing Hilda to the role of copyist Hawthorne at once grants her a central role in the period's central cultural project and limits her role to producing copies of European art rather than original American art.[72]

Elizabeth Stuart Phelps's *The Story of Avis* (1877) is in many ways a
feminist rewriting of *The Marble Faun*. It is also, however, an analysis
that demonstrates that female artists are particularly vulnerable to the
kinds of economic pressures that devalue originality, both of the art
object itself and of the artist's mind. Phelps's eponymous heroine
appears to be ideally suited to become an important American artist:
she has talent, a rigorous European education, financial security as the
only daughter of a professor at a prestigious New England college, and
a mandate from the well-known French teacher Couture, to "make a
reputation" for herself."[73] She is also determined to produce original art:
when her father dismisses her intention to "paint pictures all my life" as
"womanish apings of a man's affairs" and praises her "pretty little
copies" by way of consolation, Avis fiercely replies "I do not want to
make pretty little copies" (34). And by the time she returns from years
of study abroad Avis, whom Phelps repeatedly identifies as "a Yankee
girl" (36) and a "New England girl" (38), seems poised to achieve artistic "glory" (80), graced as she is with the rare quality of originality that,
her American teacher points out, "we lack in this country" (205).

Like Davis's Audrey Swenson, however, Avis Dobell is forced to
take her talent to the marketplace to help support her family after she
agrees to marry, against her better judgment, a former suitor badly
wounded at the battle of Bull Run.[74] Although her husband, Philip
Ostrander, had promised that Avis would be free to continue her career,
it soon becomes clear to Avis that their limited financial resources pre-
clude hiring sufficient household help, and she is forced to become
what she had sworn she would never be—a housekeeper. Avis finds it
increasingly difficult to carve out time for her painting, and when her
first child is born, her infrequent visits to the studio cease almost completely. From that point on, Avis paints only to meet pressing financial
needs, which become more extreme when Philip loses his professorship
shortly after their second child is born. Philip's already fragile health
worsens under the humiliation of being fired, and he insists that he
must go to Europe to recuperate. Avis dutifully scrapes together the
money to send him, and as soon as he is gone, returns to the studio to
begin her career as sole breadwinner for the family. While she is there
Frederick Maynard, Avis's old teacher, pays her a visit to bring the good
news that her painting of the Sphinx—the only "good picture" (78) she
had produced since returning from Europe—has been sold within
hours of reaching Goupil, a New York art dealer, and that the New York
art critics are praising the painting highly. Almost immediately, Maynard warns Avis against allowing the printer-publisher to reproduce

her work: "Mind you don't let Goupil photograph it. You can't afford to photograph a fledgling. *You* have a future. 'The Easel' says it is a work of pure imagination" (205). Before leaving the studio, where Avis is working on a portrait commission, surrounded by her children, Maynard reminds Avis of her responsibility to the nation: "'You are to make no more portraits, you understand . . . you'll never be a portrait painter. You must create: you cannot copy. That is what we lack in this country. We have no imagination. The sphinx is a creation. I told Goupil so when I took it on [*sic*]. He bowed politely. And now he comes asking for a photograph!'" (205). The suggestion that Avis is destined for "Yankee . . . glory" becomes a reality in this passage, however briefly. Giving Maynard the explicit claim for Avis's importance as an original artist allows Phelps to ventriloquize male authority for her view that female artists are essential to the project of creating an American national art. And Maynard's warning against reproducing the Sphinx allows Phelps to suggest that a female artist's responsibility is primarily to her art, not to her family's financial needs, rejecting the antebellum conception of women as producers of "bread and butter" art, and aligning herself with the view articulated by Higginson, that original Art and commerce simply cannot coexist.

Although she initially heeds Maynard's advice about reproducing the Sphinx, Avis is eventually forced by continuing financial pressures to allow Goupil to photograph the painting. When she tells her husband of her decision he asks, "'Was it best for you, best for the picture, to let the photographs go?' 'Not best for the picture,' said Avis, with her instinctive honesty, 'but best for me, best for us all now. And there is indeed nothing to regret. I shall not paint another picture—at present'" (215). Selling the rights to reproduce the painting marks the end of Avis's career and her forced capitulation to the antebellum model of female artistic production; it also registers Phelps's disagreement with Parton's view that mass reproduction and original art can, indeed must, coexist in order to both protect native art and fulfill its nationalizing function. Phelps's belief that mass reproduction is not in Avis's professional best interests flies in the face of decades of conventional wisdom about the primary function of art produced by women, and underscores the special tension facing American women artists who attempt to define themselves in terms other than those provided by the antebellum model of artistic production.[75]

❖

By outlining the destructive effect of financial pressures on female artists' careers, Phelps and Davis distance themselves from their antebellum predecessors and align themselves with the values of the male-dominated literary elite, which viewed art and the marketplace as fundamentally incompatible. But, as Phelps, Davis, and Louisa May Alcott knew from their own experience, few artists could afford to ignore the marketplace altogether, even if doing so was a prerequisite for acceptance by the high-culture establishment. Of the women writers discussed in this chapter, only Alcott is able to imagine an escape from the haunted house of domestic fiction. Her solution is a vision of widespread private philanthropy, which will provide the financial buffer necessary to help "[a]mbitious girls . . . [who] often have to see youth, health, and precious opportunities go by, just for want of a little help at the right minute."[76] Alcott's model is a rebuke to the high-culture vision of art and artists, which privileges art over the marketplace while blithely ignoring the practical question of how such artistic dedication can be sustained.

Alcott's plan is firmly anchored in social and economic realities: she proposes a kind of mutual aid society through which members of America's growing leisure class can find meaningful ways to spend their extra money, while members of the only slightly smaller class of middle-class women artists can support themselves while developing their talents. An essential component of Alcott's vision is the personal involvement of its sponsoring class: Alcott's patrons come not from the ranks of the newly rich culture seekers who thronged Europe in the postbellum years, but from the ranks of the artistically disappointed: those who have discovered that they lack genius and must reconcile themselves to a life on the sidelines of artistic greatness. Alcott theorizes her vision in *Little Women* (1868), and she provides an example of how such a community might operate in practice in a chapter of *An Old Fashioned Girl* (1870).

The vehicle for Alcott's model of community support is Amy March, an aspiring painter modeled after Louisa's sister May Alcott. In the second volume of *Little Women* Amy is invited to join her aunt for the much-coveted trip to Europe, where she plans to study European art and return to the United States ready to embark on an artistic career. Her encounter with the great masters has a similar effect on Amy as it does on Hawthorne's Hilda: she tells Laurie Laurence, the March family's neighbor and an aspiring composer, who is on his own grand tour, that Rome has taught her that "'talent isn't genius, and no amount of energy can make it so. I want to be great, or nothing. I won't be a common-place dauber, so I don't intend to try any more'" (390). Although she decides to give up painting, Amy does not lose her interest in the arts. Instead, she marries Laurie, who has also come to the realization that he possesses talent but not genius, and the young couple decide to become patrons of the arts, with a special interest in talented but poor "gentlefolks" (442). Laurie wants to help men like the "talented young fellows making all sorts of sacrifices, and enduring real hardships, that they might realize their dreams" whom he encountered in his travels: "'Those are people whom it's a satisfaction to help, for if they've got genius, it's an honor to be allowed to serve them, and not let it be lost or delayed for want of fuel to keep the pot boiling, if they haven't, it's a pleasure to comfort the poor souls, and keep them from despair, when they find it out'" (442); Amy has her own special interest group:

> "Yes indeed; and there's another class who can't ask and who suffer in silence; I know something of it, for I belonged to it, before you made a princess of me. . . . Ambitious girls have a hard time, Laurie, and often have to see youth, health, and precious opportunities go by, just for want of a little help at the right minute. People have been very kind to me, and whenever I see girls struggling along, as we used to do, I want to put out my hand and help them, as I was helped." (443)

The young couple's philanthropic plans allow Alcott to imagine a way to meet the needs of numerous groups at once: those who have "genius" will be nurtured, and their work will fill Hawthorne's "gallery of native art";[77] Amy's focus on "ambitious young women" will relieve some of the economic pressures facing female artists, pressures that drive them to produce "rubbish" because, as Jo March observes, "[f]ame is a very good thing to have in the house, but cash is more convenient'" (260). Finally, Amy's announcement that she wishes to "help as I was helped" and Laurie's careful inclusion of his desire to "comfort the poor souls" who discover that they have talent but not genius point to Alcott's belief in the mutual benefit to be gained from this highly specific kind of philanthropy. Helping others who may have genius but lack the financial wherewithal to find out will allow both Laurie and Amy to feel that their own years of pursuing the dream of artistic success were not wasted. Although they are not destined to be "great," they are uniquely suited to assist that class from which Alcott clearly believes most of America's artists must come—"poor gentlefolk" who "won't ask" for help (442).

Alcott's concern about the dangerously unequal power relations inherent in situations of mentoring and sponsorship (which is discussed in detail in the next chapter) is also addressed in the young couple's plans: Laurie's humble assertion that "it's an honor to be allowed to serve" those who have "genius" suggests that what he has in mind resembles the National Endowment for the Arts more than it does traditional patronage arrangements. To Laurie, aspiring artists are a national resource, and cultivating them is a kind of privileged duty bestowed on a chosen few. Perhaps not accidentally, Alcott's plan for a philanthropic structure that would liberate aspiring artists from financial pressures appears in part 2 of *Little Women*, whose success simultaneously liberated her from genteel poverty and introduced a new kind of financial pressure—a large audience clamoring for more stories. Although the tremendous popularity of *Little Women* coincided with Alcott's exclusion from the high literary culture to which she aspired, it also provided an influential platform from which she could critique the structural forces preventing talented artists from producing original American art. Alcott was fully aware of her power to reach a vast middle- and upper-middle-class audience, and she used that power to suggest a model of artistic patronage that would remove some of the economic barriers preventing artists from developing their talent and help produce a significant body of original American art.[78]

Alcott's interest in alleviating the financial pressures facing aspiring artists did not end with *Little Women*. Her post-1868 work is sprinkled with portraits of artistic communities that are powered by a mixture of philanthropy and self-reliance. One such portrait appears in Alcott's 1870 novel *An Old Fashioned Girl*. The first half of the novel, which is aimed at the *Little Women* audience, outlines the trials and tribulations of Polly, an energetic country girl who comes to spend a winter with her wealthy urban cousins. The novel takes up familiar Alcott themes: Polly's chief trial is her jealousy of her cousins' wealth; she soon overcomes her jealousy when she observes the disparity between her cousins' wealth and their unhappy home life, and she gradually understands that happiness and wealth are not always, or, in Alcott's vision, even usually, directly correlated. In the second half of the novel Polly, a talented singer, returns to the city as a young adult to earn her living teaching music. "The Sunny Side" appears in the second half of the novel and describes a visit Polly and her wealthy cousin Fanny pay to Polly's friends, a small group of women artists. This chapter is rather odd in that the characters introduced in it haven't appeared before and rarely, if ever, appear again. It is also notable because the novel itself is not about artists per se. Polly is a gifted singer, but there is no hint that she aspires to use her musical talents for anything but her family's pleasure and her own support. But Polly's talent is incidental to "The Sunny Side." Indeed, Alcott seems to have inserted this chapter primarily because she needed a forum to articulate her vision of a feminist artists' community.

Part of Alcott's purpose in "The Sunny Side" is to rebuke America's leisured rich for the emptiness of their lives and for their failure to engage in the kind of philanthropy Amy and Laurie chose as their life's work at the end of *Little Women*. The chapter begins with Fanny petulantly complaining to Polly about her boredom and dissatisfaction. Polly replies that she "pit[ies] you rich girls" because "you have so may opportunities and don't seem to know how to use them," pointing to her own landlady as a model of "a rich woman who knew how to get happiness out of her money."[79] Using the same terms Amy and Laurie employed, Polly explains that Miss Mills "was poor till she was nearly fifty, then a comfortable fortune was left her, and she knew just how to use it. That house was given her, but instead of living in it all alone, she filled it with poor gentlefolks who needed neat, respectable homes but couldn't get anything comfortable for their little money" (237). Like the Laurences, Miss Mills uses her wealth to aid impoverished "gentlefolk," and she too gives to those whose fate she once shared. In keeping with Alcott's theory of the importance of the sponsor's involvement, Miss Mills's house is not merely a place to live; it is a community. The house's inhabitants each pays what she can afford on a kind of sliding scale, and as Polly explains, Miss Mills "'does a thousand things that money can't pay for[;] . . . we feel her influence all through the house'" (237).

After showing Fanny the women's cooperative in which she lives, Polly takes her cousin to visit her friends: a group of women artists who have formed an informal community composed of artists and crafters who "help . . . one another" and share everything from artistic advice to one another's good fortune (238). The artistic community includes Rebecca Jaffrey, a sculptor, and Lizzie Small, an engraver, whose relationship is a model of egalitarian friendship: they "work, eat, sleep, and live [in the studio], going halves in everything" (239). Other characters are Anna, an artist who has the good fortune of being selected by a Miss Burton to accompany her to Italy, and Kate King, a successful writer who brings the news of Anna's trip. Kate reminds her friends that Anna "has been longing to go, working and hoping for a chance and never getting it, till all of a sudden Miss Burton is inspired to invite the girl to go with her for several years to Italy" (242). Kate's characterization of

Miss Burton as "inspired" implies that the wealthy single woman has had an epiphany about her power to aid her poorer sisters who "can't ask" for help.[80]

Although philanthropy provides the financial backbone of Alcott's vision, the members of her community practice self-reliance too, working to support themselves and trading goods and services among themselves: Kate, whose successful novel has made her something of a celebrity, distributes complimentary tickets to cultural events she has received from well wishers, and Polly gives free music lessons to a neighbor's child who "has talent, loves music, and needs help" (246). Alcott's vision of an artistic community powered by a mixture of self-reliance and philanthropy stands in stark contrast to the Romanticism-inspired model of artistic production espoused by Higginson. Although Alcott shares the artistic elite's conviction that freedom from market pressures is essential to the production of serious art, her financially based artistic community challenges the prevailing emphasis on individuality, isolation, and the invisible labor of women as the building blocks of successful artistic careers, and provides a prototype of how talented women might escape the seemingly irresistible pull of the antebellum model of women's artistic production.

By relying on private philanthropy Alcott's vision ignores the marketplace in its own way just as willfully as Higginson's. But the portraits of female artists' relationship to the marketplace that fall along the spectrum between these two extremes suggest that for American women in the middle quarter of the nineteenth century, adopting the identity of serious artist required killing not the Angel in the House, but the popular woman writer who had left it for the marketplace. As the portraits of failure discussed here also suggest, however, dismantling a conceptual framework that had become enormously influential in a relatively short period of time required not only overcoming the material conditions that had produced it, but giving up the very real benefits that it had conferred on women.

CHAPTER FOUR

Genius, Gender, and the Problem of Mentorship

O N SEPTEMBER 27, 1855, the New York Association of Book Publishers hosted "The Complimentary Fruit and Flower Festival to Authors" in the Crystal Palace building in New York City. The festival's subtitle, displayed in a huge gaslit banner in the banquet hall, was "HONOR TO GENIUS."[1] The glittering event—a lavish banquet followed by hours of toasts—was attended by many of the nation's authors, editors, and publishers, and coincided with the booksellers' association's first joint sale of books, which was devised in an attempt to bring order to a chaotic book market and improve profitability for both publishers and authors. Although the festival was conceived as an annual event, it was never held again.[2] This singular event occurred at the heyday of what one critic has called the American "cult of genius," decades before the figure of the genius, and the assumptions about artistic production that it embodied, were challenged by the emerging aesthetic of realism in the 1880s.[3] In the intervening years, the figure of the artistic genius elicited considerable ambivalence from observers of the cultural scene: treated with a mixture of reverence for his unique qualities and anxiety about the undemocratic implications of valuing those same qualities, the genius embodied the tensions inherent in the postbellum struggle to create a uniquely American high culture even as demographic changes and technological innovation ensured the democratization of culture.

Efforts to Americanize the figure of the genius were central to the postbellum project of cultural nationalism. And although the realist aesthetic would ultimately define itself in opposition to the concept of genius, the critical engagement with the figure of the genius that pre-

139

ceded the emergence of realism is a crucial, if often overlooked, aspect of the creation of an American high literary culture.[4] The ideal of genius continued to dominate the American literary scene until the 1880s and beyond, but in the years surrounding the Civil War numerous writers challenged some of its underlying assumptions. For some observers the problem was its un-American-ness: genius, in the Romantic conception, is an innate trait and therefore a function of neither merit nor hard work. For these observers, efforts to reclaim genius focused on endowing it with democratic qualities and insisting that genius was merely a starting point to be built upon by hard work, even as they acknowledged and celebrated the uniqueness and superiority of the genius. Another group of writers was troubled by the gender and class assumptions of the Romantic genius figure. Building on long-standing beliefs about women's biological incapacity to create art, "genius" was at once defined as masculine and used as a priori evidence that none but a few "unwomanly" women could possess genius. Not only were women believed to be biologically incapable of the kind of original creativity privileged in the genius, but their social roles were fundamentally incompatible with the egotism that underlay the Romantic vision of genius. And although the Romantic conception understood genius as an inborn trait that could, at least in theory, be manifested by individuals from any social class, it was, in fact, a highly class-bound notion that presupposed the kind of leisure and education typically available only to middle- and upper-class men. The exclusive character of genius was particularly troubling to observers who believed that a truly American art required native artists drawn from all strata of American life, and to those who were themselves neither male nor wealthy and leisured. Grappling with the figure of the genius was thus essential both to the theoretical descriptions of what a uniquely American high culture would look like and to the process of redefining antebellum models of female authorship.

Between 1865 and 1882, Louisa May Alcott, Rebecca Harding Davis, and Constance Fenimore Woolson all produced works in which they explored the possibility of a female artist adopting the identity of "genius." These works assess the gender and class assumptions underlying the concept of genius and conclude that not only is the identity of genius unavailable to female and non-middle-class artists, but that attempts to occupy the role of "genius" are almost always destructive to them. For each of these writers, the figure of the mentor is central to the discussion of genius. The relationships between the genius and his or her mentor range from benign neglect to deadly domination, but in each case they underscore the failure of the mentor figure to transform the Romantic conception of genius in order to make it a viable model for artists who are neither male nor privileged. The prevalence of the mentor figure in fiction that takes up the problem of genius is no coincidence: indeed, the mentor embodies precisely those qualities that make the category of genius both attractive and destructive to women and other cultural outsiders. The mentor is a necessity for adopting the identity of genius, because genius must, by definition, be identified by someone whose status as a cultural authority qualifies him to anoint the "genius"; but the mentors depicted in these works always fail to live up to their roles precisely because their status as cultural authorities, or, in some cases, as a genius, is threatened or challenged in some way by the appearance of the genius who is neither male nor elite. In their depictions of the tragic consequences of women artists' attempts to occupy the identity of genius Alcott, Davis, and Woolson challenge the very project of Americanizing genius by demonstrating that exclusivity and elitism are inherent in the category of genius and dramatizing the futility of outsiders attempting to occupy it. These women writers' analyses of the viability of genius as a useful category in the production of a national culture are starkly different from those of their male counterparts. The male writers, to whom the Romantic category of genius is already available, seek only to transform, or contain, what they perceive as its un-American qualities; the women writers simultaneously suggest that female artists must be able to occupy the category of genius in order to achieve public recognition of the highest order, and, at the same time, demonstrate that the category itself is not a viable one for women and, presumably, non-elite male artists, because it is predicated on a system of class and gender privilege. Although they offer no alternatives—the portraits of female genius from this period are uniformly tragic—analyses by Alcott, Davis, and Woolson suggest that the category of genius and the project of cultural nationalism are fundamentally incompatible.

The term "genius" is etymologically derived from the Latin *genius*, "the male household spirit, inseparable from the land owned by a particular clan" and thus historically associated with both geographical location and masculinity: "Genius is tied not only to a sense of place and ownership of place, but specifically to individual male ownership of place and to a sense of male potency and fertility."[5] The British Romantics added to the historical association of genius with place and with male generativity the belief that the genius was a special kind of person. According to Raymond Williams, during the eighteenth century "*[g]enius,* from meaning 'a characteristic disposition,' came to mean 'exalted ability,' and a distinction was made between it and talent. As *art* had produced *artist* in a new sense, and *aesthetics aesthete,* so this produced *a genius,* to indicate a special kind of person."[6] And this special kind of person, was, by definition, male, not only because of the historical association with male virility, but also because, in the Romantic conception, genius was the exclusive preserve of men. Although the characteristics privileged by the Romantics as evidence of genius—"emotion, sensibility, intuition, and imagination" are stereotypically "feminine"—these qualities were defined as evidence of the male artist's superiority both to women and to other men. "Biological femaleness" the Romantics believed, "mimics the psychological femininity of the true genius," allowing male artists to transcend their biology and leaving women trapped in theirs.[7] The Romantic conception of genius had both psychological and practical implications, since genius was defined in terms that were inherently incompatible with domestic relationships. Marlon Ross points out that Tom Moore's memoir of Lord Byron states unequivocally what is often a submerged premise in the works of the Romantic poets:

> "It is, indeed, in the very nature and essence of genius to be for ever occupied intensely with Self, as the great centre and source of its strength. To this power of self-concentration, by which alone all the other powers of genius are made available, there is, of course, no such disturbing and fatal enemy as those sympathies and affections that draw the mind out actively towards others, and, accordingly, it will be found that, among those who have felt within themselves a call to immortality, the greater number have, by a sort of instinct, kept aloof from such ties, and instead of the softer duties and rewards of being amiable, reserved themselves for the high, hazardous chances of being great."[8]

This kind of self-centeredness was, of course, incompatible with nineteenth-century female gender roles, which emphasized selflessness and the primacy of familial and social relationships. As I have discussed in previous chapters, antebellum conceptions of women's authorship built upon rather than challenged those roles, viewing artistic production as subordinate to women's domestic, social, and religious responsibilities, making the kind of egotism required of the Romantic poet/genius appear deviant if embodied by a woman. George Sand, whose genius was widely granted, was frequently described by American reviewers in the antebellum period as a "biological monstrosity," a shorthand reference to the widespread belief that genius and femininity were, by definition, incompatible.[9]

That incompatibility is dramatized in Louisa May Alcott's vexed relationship to genius. In December 1860 Alcott records in her journal that "Mr. Emerson invited me to his class when they meet to talk on Genius; a great honor, as all the learned ladies go."[10] This image of Alcott and the other "learned ladies" of Concord being lectured on "Genius" by the man who embodied that trait captures Alcott's understanding of the unequal, gendered power relations on which "genius" is based. Elsewhere in her journal Alcott makes explicit that she views herself as the eternal pupil of great men: "Good news of [Theodore] Parker in Florence [who was traveling in hopes of curing his consumption],—my beloved minister and friend. To him and R. W. E. I owe much of my education. May I be a worthy pupil of such men."[11] In these comments, which are typical of ones sprinkled throughout the *Journals,* Alcott depicts genius as a male trait that it is defined by and dependent on an unequal relationship between the genius and his audience, student, or mentee.

Alcott's ambivalence about granting women the identity of genius can be seen in the portrait of Jo March at work in the chapter of *Little Women* titled "Literary Lessons." On the first page of the chapter the reader learns that every few weeks, Jo "'fall[s] into a vortex,'" and "writ[es] away at her novel with all her heart and soul, for till that was finished she could find no peace."[12] During these fits of creativity Jo is left to her own devices by the family, which supplies food and drink and keeps an eye on her from a distance, stopping by her room periodically to ask "'Does genius burn, Jo?'" Alcott insists that Jo

> did not think herself a genius by any means; but when the writing fit came on, she gave herself up to it with entire abandon, and led a blissful life, unconscious of want, care, or bad weather, while she sat safe and happy in an imaginary world. . . . Sleep forsook her eyes, meals stood untasted, day and night were all too short to enjoy the happiness which blessed her only at such times, and made these hours worth living, even if they bore no other fruit. The divine afflatus usually lasted a week or two, and then she emerged from her "vortex" hungry, sleepy, cross, or despondent. (257)

Alcott's assertion that Jo does not "think herself a genius" is necessary both because she had earlier announced that her dearest wish was to have "Genius" (129) and because her creative "attacks" fit the stereotype of "genius." The feeling of compulsion and the pure joy of creation that drive Jo's writing evoke the Romantic model of artistic production, in which the artist/genius is driven to write and cannot rest until the explosion of creativity has run its course. Jo's ability to work without interruption for long stretches and to be "blissful[y] . . . unconscious" of the external world further aligns her with male artists and distances her from stereotypes of antebellum female writers, who famously wrote in spurts, during brief periods of time snatched from their domestic duties.[13]

Alcott returns to the question of Jo's "genius" at the end of this chapter, when her much-revised first novel is published to a mixture of acclaim and censure that confuses and discourages the young writer. Struggling to recover from the emotional turmoil produced by the book's reception, Jo remarks: "'Not being a genius, like Keats, it won't kill me,'" and vows to continue her quest for fame and fortune (262). Alcott's assertion that Jo isn't like Keats is necessary because she has described her literary alter ego in terms that strongly suggest that she *is* like Keats. The two denials of genius that bracket the chapter, and the description of Jo's creative "fits," suggest that Alcott is struggling to find a way to give her character what she wants more than anything— "Genius"—without simply stepping into the preexisting category of "genius" represented here in shorthand by Keats.[14]

In addition to masculinity, another qualifying requirement of Romantic genius was originality. Whereas Classical conception of great art emphasized imitation—of models and of nature—the Romantics demoted imitation to the level of mere mechanical reproduction: "An Original may be said to be of a *vegetable* nature; it rises spontaneously from the vital root of genius; it *grows*, it is not *made*; Imitations are often a sort of *manufacture*, wrought up by those *mechanics*, art and *labour*, out of pre-existent materials not their own."[15] The privileging of originality over "manufacture"—the bedrock of industrialization—was a specific response to the social and economic changes affecting England during the late-eighteenth and early-nineteenth centuries.[16] But a new definition of genius as a special person characterized by originality had particular resonance for American intellectuals in the Antebellum era, perhaps because, as Margaret Ervin suggests, originality, is, in some crucial way, linked to place of origin: "To say that a work or an artist evidenced genius was to say that the writer's country (place of origin) was capable of engendering (originating) people and works, that were wholly original, wholly a product of that nation's genius."[17]

The figure of the genius has had special resonance among American intellectuals since the early days of the republic. Driven by anxiety about the new nation's cultural independence and the conviction that only with the emergence of a native genius would American culture begin to take its place among Western nations, genius was widely invoked, both descriptively and prescriptively, among cultural commentators.[18] Writing early in the nineteenth century, Massachusetts Congressman Fisher Ames observed that "Few speculative subjects have exercised the passions more or the judgment less, than the inquiry, what rank our country is to maintain in the world for genius and literary attainments. Whether in point of intellect we are equal to Europeans . . . whether the muses, like the nightingales, are too delicate to cross the salt water, or sicken and mope without song, if they do."[19] Ames's comments reflect the widespread concern with genius as a hallmark of cultural independence that was to become a mainstay of writings on the subject of American cultural nationalism in the first half of the nineteenth century. By the middle of the century, Emerson and Hawthorne were widely understood as examples of native genius, and the elements of genius—masculinity, originality, and location—had become familiar enough that Melville could invoke them without comment in "Hawthorne and His Mosses" (1850), his paean to Nathaniel Hawthorne's American genius.

Published as a book review in Evert Duycknick's *Literary World*, a periodical dedicated to American literary nationalism, "Hawthorne and his Mosses" serves as a declaration of Melville's own fairly new conception of himself as an aspiring genius writing for an elite audience; it is also a useful snapshot of the conception of literary genius that would soon be called into question by men and women concerned with both their own and the nation's literary identity. For Melville, genius is a universally masculine quality—embodied by "men of genius" and shared by a worldwide "brotherhood" represented in the essay by Shakespeare and Hawthorne.[20] American genius's masculinity and originality are both a function of place: "no American writer should write like an Englishman, or a Frenchman; let him write like a man, for then he will be sure to write like an American. . . . Let us boldly contemn all imitation, though it comes to us graceful and fragrant as the morning; and foster all originality, though, at first, it be crabbed and ugly as our own pine knots."[21] The opposition between "graceful and fragrant" imitation and originality that is "tough and ugly" as a pine knot defines American genius as both strictly native and masculine—a definition that would be repeated, with variations, for the next three decades.[22]

Beginning in the 1880s, genius—both the person and the quality— began to fall from favor among an influential group of literary arbiters—writers, editors, and publishers—that championed realism as the preferred form of American high literary culture.[23] The realist aesthetic was consciously theorized in opposition to the antebellum model of the artist-prophet, which realists viewed as unprofessional and elitist, qualities embodied, for the realist, in the concept of genius. At the heart of the realists' rejection of genius was the Romantic emphasis on writing as a form of inspiration rather than labor, and the understanding of the artist as separate from, and typically above, the economic fray of American middle class life. The realists' rejection of genius was inherent in their self-conception as professionals, which, according to Christopher Wilson, meant not only earning a living from their literary efforts but viewing "their craft predominantly as a product of technical expertise rather than inspiration."[24] Not only did they reject inspiration as the grounds for their own work, but late-nineteenth-century realists viewed "genius" as the root of much that was wrong with American literature:

> Howells labeled [genius] a superstition that had its roots in the aristocratic domination of the literary arts. Antidemocratic to the core, the concept of genius boosted a favored class of writers whose 'innate' abilities allowed them to parade their gifts before an overawed and subservient readership. . . . Norris argued that the frequency with which 'genius' was used to explain the writing process only indicated its uselessness in analysis.[25]

At the heart of the realists' rejection of genius and inspiration was their commitment to writing as a form of market-driven labor that could be regularized and systematized. Although the equation of the writer with the factory laborer was a considerable overstatement, the realists' emphasis on work served the ideological purpose of nationalizing literary authorship and aligning both the writer and his products with the most treasured of American values—the productive worker.[26] In the decades between the midcentury celebration of "GENIUS" and the emphatic rejection of genius by realists at century's end, genius remained central to the postbellum project of cultural nationalism. Anticipating the realists' critique of genius as an antidemocratic holdover of European culture, writers in the years surrounding the Civil War attempted to preserve genius for their cultural project by playing down its antidemocratic implications and redefining it in terms of Victorian American values such as self-control, discipline, and hard work.

Writing on the subject of genius during and immediately after the Civil War was typically characterized by a mix of unalloyed admiration for genius and belief that it was a prerequisite to production of a great national literature familiar from the antebellum era, and a somewhat inchoate anxiety about its incompatibility with American values. Whereas female observers such as sculptor Harriet Hosmer, and writers Louisa May Alcott, Rebecca Harding Davis, and Constance Fenimore Woolson have no illusions about the myriad ways in which Romantic model of genius could be destructive to women artists, male commentators are more uncertain, and their analyses are often contradictory or inconclusive.

Writers on the subject differed about what, exactly, were the dangers that genius posed to American values, but all agreed that these dangers existed. In the lead article in the February 1864 edition of the *Atlantic Monthly* simply entitled "Genius," J. Brownlee Brown worries that the Romantic definition of genius as divine will lead to excessive emphasis on individuals and to pantheism.[27] To forestall that tendency, Brown suggests that genius proves the existence of an organizing intelligence in the universe: "We suspect integrity in Nature. Can this canebrake, in which we are angled with care, fear, and sin, be after all single and sincere, a piece of intelligent kindness? Genius is the opening of this suspicion to certainty."[28] From this observation Brown builds an entire theory of genius as subordinate to divinity, de-emphasizing the artist's original creative impulse and subordinating it to the divine:

> The man must feel to do, and what he does from overmastering feeling will convince and be forever right. The work is organic which grows so above composition or plan. After you are engaged by the symphony, there is no escape, no pause, each note springs out of each as branch from branch of a tree. . . . it cannot be otherwise conceived. Why could not I have found this sequence inevitable, as well as another. Plainly, the symphony was discovered, not made,—was written before man, like astronomy in the sky.[29]

In Brown's view, genius is a medium, a vessel through which the divine operates, with little or no active participation by the chosen human tool. Brown resists the pantheistic tendencies of Romantic genius, using genius to shore up faith in God in an age of increasing uncertainty. He then goes on to redefine genius as a communal rather than individual quality, in an attempt to addresses the dangers that excessive individualism poses to the cohesion and unity required of a nation at war. True genius, according to Brown, is selfless, community minded, and entirely lacking in personal ambition—in short, precisely the opposite of the stereotypical Romantic genius:

> Good should grow with sharing,—more for me when all is given. . . .
>
> Presenting truth, I declare it as freely yours as mine. Every act of genius proclaims that the highest gift is no monopoly of singularity, no privilege of one, but the birthright of the race. . . .
>
> He is supreme poet who can make me a poet, able to reach the same supplies after he is gone. . . .
>
> The poet is one who has detected this latency of power in every breast. His delight is a feeling that all doors are open to all, that he is no favorite, but the rest are late sleepers, and he only earlier awake. Depth of genius is measured by depth of this conviction. Egotism is incurable greenness. An artist is one who has more, not less, respect for the common. The seer points always from his own to a public privilege, says never, "I, Jesus, have so received," but "The Son of Man must so receive."[30]
>
> Genius is an eye single and serene. Good speech carries the sound of no man's, of no angel's voice. Good writing betrays no man's hand, but he is as if traced by the finger of God.
>
> Original will signify, therefore, not peculiar, but universal. The original is one who lives from the Maker, not from man.[31]

Brown struggles to reconcile his deep discomfort with the individualistic implications of the Romantic conception of genius with his equally deep conviction that genius *is* materially different from other qualities and that that difference can be harnessed to promote the development of "the race." The degree of Brown's anxiety about unchecked individualism is somewhat unusual, but the fear that the Romantic conception of genius is incompatible with the contemporary needs of American society is shared by other writers.

In a February 1868 *Atlantic* essay titled "Characteristics of Genius," Frederic Henry Hedge also defines genius as an expression of divinity, and he shares some of Brown's concern with the individualistic tendencies of genius, though he is less resistant to the Romantic project as a whole.[32] Hedge's article is explicitly engaged in reconciling the essentially un-American qualities of the genius with the postbellum project of cultural nationalism. He defines "genius" in the following way:

> It is this involuntary, incalculable force that constitutes what we call *genius*. . . . Genius is the higher self, and common to all then. . . . I only contend that genius is not a special faculty which he who has it employs at will, as the painter his brush or the sculptor his chisel, but the higher nature, the man of the man. . . . So viewed, its great and distinguishing characteristic is originality.[33]

Hedge here vacillates between defining genius as a universal characteristic—simply "the higher nature" that is "common to all" and a unique quality available only to a select few men, those distinguished by "originality." Unlike Brown, however, Hedge soon finds a way to transform genius into a national asset. After a survey of genius in science, Hedge turns to its place in the arts: "In beautiful art, as in mechanical, the mark of genius is still originality," he declares; "And here this trait is most conspicuous in the great transitions by which art passes from its rude and elementary stages to its full development,—transitions which culminate in some marked individual, who bursts the trammels of convention, and leads his age by one decisive step from bondage to freedom."[34] Rather than threatening to undermine America's democratic values, genius has been reimagined as a liberating force, a kind of Moses figure leading his nation from cultural bondage into freedom. The dangerous individual tendencies inherent in genius and originality are here neatly contained and transformed into tools in the service of the project of producing the "full development" of the nation's "art."

Hedge goes on to give a systematic analysis of the characteristics of genius in the arts, and in this section such quintessentially middle-class qualities as self-control, productivity, and rationality come to the forefront.[35] Hedge observes that "[n]ext to originality, the most distinctive characteristic of genius is a right proportion between the productive and regulative forces of the mind,"[36] stressing the importance of achieving this balance through training:

> But though the raw capacity is universal, the trained faculty is peculiar. Out of this unorganized prose imagination the conscious artistic power must develop itself, like the winged bird from the senseless egg. The

artist differs from the common man, not so much in the amount of
mind possessed as in the amount taken up into consciousness. Imagination alone does not constitute genius.[37]

Here Hedge finds a way to bridge his two, mutually contradictory defi-
nitions of genius. By emphasizing the transformation from "raw capacity" to "trained faculty," Hedge engages in the ongoing discussion
about the pressing need for higher education as a prerequisite to cultural development. Even as he insists that the "raw capacity is universal"
and that the artist and the "common man" differ only in degrees of
intellectual development, Hedge undermines his own democratic
impulse and argues for a definition of genius that stresses exceptionality over a vision of genius as something that is "common to all."
Although some of Hedge's contemporaries were imagining a time
when all would have equally well "trained faculty," Hedge clearly
understands that his vision of genius assumes an inevitable split
between a handful of trained artists and the untrained masses.[38]
    As though to soften the elitist implications of asserting the artist's
difference from "the common man," Hedge assures the reader that
genius still requires work, and as such, presumably retains its democratic credentials: "With the grandest themes [masters in art] combine the
most diligent details. For genius is quite as apparent in elaboration as in
conception. It has not only to create the soul of a work, but to mould,
part by part, the body that soul is to inhabit."[39] Further subordinating
genius to American middle-class values, Hedge assures his readers that
"[h]owever imagination may soar, reason must hold it in check. However passion may seethe and foam, a reconciling thought must span the
tumult, as the rainbow spans Niagara."[40] Nervous about the potentially
destabilizing effects of the genius's exceptionality and originality,
Hedge takes steps to rein in these qualities by invoking hard work, reason, and self-control. The specter of the genius running amok in society
seems to haunt this essay, as Hedge continually vacillates between a
Romantic notion of the great artist as accountable to no one and nothing
and a specifically American need to press artists into public service.
    Hedge's insistence that genius cannot prosper without hard work is
explicitly linked to cultural nationalism later in the essay, where he raises the perennial question: "To an American jealous of national fame the
question presents itself, What is our part and lot in this matter [of
genius]?"[41] Hedge answers his own question with the familiar lament
that while there is plenty of evidence of American genius in fields such
as science, the military, and industrial inventions, Americans lag behind

in the area of artistic genius:

> But in literature, it must be confessed that, while we excel in productive
> energy, we are poor in finished products, and can boast of few master-
> pieces in proportion to the whole amount produced. The national mind
> is too diffusive as yet to admit of supreme excellence. . . . Our mental
> energy, like our physical, lacks the restraining power. . . . Flashy, impa-
> tient, unskilled to wait, [the American mind] does not take conditions
> enough with it. It shrinks from careful elaboration; it spends itself with
> a flash. But without careful elaboration, literary eminence was never
> yet attained.[42]

In Hedge's formulation it is not genius per se that American writers
lack, but the discipline and patience to harness their "productive energy" in the interest of the "careful elaboration" that produces "masterpieces." The failure to implement the American work ethic in the literary arena—a failure engendered by the assumptions underlying the
concept of genius itself—is at the heart of Americans' inability to
achieve "literary eminence." But for Hedge and his contemporaries, the
solution lies not in rejecting genius, but in applying the American work
ethic to it.

In deploying work to Americanize genius Hedge taps into a
rhetoric that would have been instantly familiar to his readers.
Although the changes in American work patterns had been under way
since before the Civil War and were significantly accelerated by the
rapid industrialization in the North during the war years, the equation
of work with moral virtue and its identification as a defining national
trait were unchanged. Despite the erosion of the viability of the ideal of
the independent, free worker who owned his own labor and the development of a permanent class of wage laborers, "Mid-nineteenth-
century politicians and poets alike in the North dwelled expansively on
the dignity of labor and the moral worth of those who worked."[43] After
the Civil War, widely viewed as the triumph of Northern "free" labor
ideology over the Southern slave labor system, the rhetoric of "free"
labor, and the belief in work as the cardinal virtue of American life
intensified, even as industrialization irreversibly changed the world
that had produced that ideology. As Eric Foner explains, "the world that
spawned the free labor ideology remained close enough in time, and its
assumptions authentic enough in the experience of men like Lincoln
and the millions of small-town and rural men and women who still
made up the majority of the North's population, for the ideology to

retain a broad plausibility."[44] Hedge's celebration of work, self-discipline, and productivity relies on the cultural resonance of the free labor ideology and the long-standing association between labor and moral (and national) virtue developed by the Puritans and solidified in the eighteenth and nineteenth centuries by intellectuals, politicians, popular fiction, and foreign observers.[45] To assert that no genius can prosper without working, and, at the same time, that national genius exists but must be developed through hard work, is, then, to American-ize genius, transforming it from an elitist, foreign construct developed by intellectuals in nations in which rich national literatures already exist, into the essential value in a democracy urgently in need of a national literature of its own.

Despite his attempts to reconcile the characteristics of genius with such quintessentially American values as work and discipline, Hedge does not hide his distaste for that other mainstay of the American sys-tem—the marketplace. Like Higginson, for whom the market and great literature are fundamentally incompatible, Hedge firmly believes that genius and popularity cannot coexist:

> The bane of American genius is popularity, the pursuit and the tyranny of the popular vote. Without the popular vote no American is great or blest. Our heaven is an elective privilege; to be popular is the American hell. So the custom of the ballot extends its sway over letters and art; no standard of success is acknowledged but a numerical one. So many readers, so many copies sold, so much merit. As if intellectual pre-eminence, like political, could be conferred by the ballot box. The writer will never prosper with the prosperity which the genius artist desires, who has the fear of the majority before his eyes, or thinks more of his readers' judgment than his own. The best works are never popular. . . . Let him who seeks popularity renounce the higher walks of art.[46]

Like many of his contemporaries who hailed from the ranks of the northeastern Protestant elite, Hedge's concern for democracy is limited by his conviction that the "higher walks of art" cannot be pursued through the democracy that is the marketplace. Hedge's attack on pop-ularity, like Higginson's, is elitist in its assumption that the writer who aspires to "intellectual pre-eminence" possesses the independent income required to free him from the constraint of worrying about his readers' opinions. Hedge's rejection of the popular is also a reflection of the widespread belief—at least among members of the literary elite—that the absence of a stable educated elite that would support the works of the genius as Hedge conceives of him here posed a significant barrier to the development of a body of serious American literature.[47] Finally, Hedge's attack on the popular is gendered, insofar as "popularity" and women writers were inextricably linked at midcentury and beyond. For Hedge, as for Melville, genius is "the man of the man."[48] J. Brownlee Brown expresses a similar view of the relationship between masculinity, genius, and popularity:

> Sentimentality is initial genius. Its complaint seems to contradict the cheerfulness of wisdom, yet it enjoys complaining; though life be not worth having on these conditions, it bottles every tear. A weak sadness fills every space in literature, stocks the circulating library, and counts its Werthers by the thousand in every age. Now we expect this malady, as we look for mumps and measles in the growing child. It is feminine—unwilling to be weak, yet not able to stand and go. The strong quickly leave it behind.
>
> In his first novel Goethe burned out for himself this girlish greensickness, and by a more vigorous demand began to take what he wanted from the world.[49]

Brown's "initial genius" resembles a stereotypical middle-class woman: it "enjoys complaining," "bottles every tear," and revels in the "weak sadness" that permeates that most feminine of nineteenth-century literary spaces, the circulating library. His vision of sentimentality as a kind of "girlish" childhood disease to be overcome on the path to adult manhood is a practical formula for the work facing the nation anxious to leave behind its cultural childhood. Popularity, for Brown, is a form of false consciousness from which men must be rescued by genius: "Popular literature is some description of a state which men think they might enjoy: it is no record of joy."[50] In Brown's progressive narrative, sentimentality and popularity, like youthful indiscretions, should be forgiven and put in their proper place—the past—as the mature male genius is free to "vigorous[ly]" assume his rightful place in the world, liberated from the "girlish green-sickness" that threatened to undermine his masculinity and drown the nation's literature in tears.

Hedge's emphasis on hard work is also a way of gendering genius as "masculine." The American work ethic described by Daniel T. Rodgers, which was developed by and for the middle class, was, by definition, masculine, because married middle-class women had not been expected to work outside the home since early in the nineteenth century, and most did not unless driven by financial necessity.[51] Of course, middle-class women continued to perform the bulk of their domestic work themselves, and working-class women worked, as they always had, both for pay and in the home. But the popular image of middle-class women was of idleness and leisure filled with reading popular fiction, gossiping, and shopping, and it is this image that Harriet Beecher Stowe and Catherine Beecher sought to counter in works such as *The American Woman's Home* (1869), in which they bemoaned the decline of a work ethic among women and extolled the earlier era of hardworking, productive women whose "faculty" allowed them to accomplish a prodigious amount of household work without appearing to work at all.[52] Regardless of the large numbers of women in the workforce, at midcentury and beyond, the rhetoric of work figured the worker as male.

The gendered assumptions underlying the rhetoric of work were evident to American sculptor Harriet Hosmer, whose 1864 *Atlantic Monthly* essay titled "The Process of Sculpture" is a defense of herself and of other women sculptors who had been accused of cheating because they employed assistants at various stages in the sculpting process. The widespread public misapprehension that male sculptors create their sculptures entirely with their own two hands had been used by an unidentified "brother sculptor" to support his accusation that Hosmer was an "imposter."[53] Hosmer's essay seeks to dispel the misconceptions that a sculpture is produced entirely by hand by the artist and, more generally, to call attention to the ways in which the American work ethic was used to delegitimize American women who sought to enter such "masculine" artistic arenas as sculpting.

Hosmer begins the essay by announcing her willingness to sacrifice some of the mystique of art in order to clear the record: "I feel disposed to raise the veil upon the mysteries of the studio" in order to enable "those who are interested in the subject to form a just conception of the amount of assistance to which a sculptor is fairly entitled," Hosmer explains (734). She proceeds to provide a detailed description of the stages in the life of a sculpture, from small clay model, molded entirely by hand by the sculptor, to large clay model, supported by an elaborate iron frame, to plaster cast, and finally, to finished product in marble, emphasizing that in each step after the initial creation of the small clay model the artist requires considerable assistance from a variety of skilled workmen who need not possess "imagination or refined taste" in order "to copy the small model before [them]" (735). The accusations against Hosmer and her female peers focus on the process of "preparing the clay" for the creation of the large model, and Hosmer takes pains to explain this process in detail, in order to demonstrate both how labor-intensive this stage of the sculpting process is and how much of it is simply mechanical, involving little, if any, artistic talent. The first step is the production of a "skeleton of iron . . . corresponding to the size of the figure to be modelled" (734). This process requires both "strong hands and arms" and "the blacksmith with his forge" who must hammer, wire, and weld together the iron rods and wires to produce a framework strong enough to support the clay (735). Next the clay must be attached to the iron skeleton, "with strong hands and a wooden mallet, until, from a clumsy and shapeless mass, it acquires some resemblance to the human form" (735). It is only then, "[w]hen the clay is properly prepared, and the work advanced as far as the artist desires, his own work is resumed" (735). Employing skilled helpers during this preparatory process in no way detracts from the originality or integrity of the artist's vision because it is simply the work of skilled craftsmen:

> the work on which [the assistant] is employed, however, obviously requiring not the least exercise of creative power, which is essentially the attribute of the artist. To perform the part assigned to him, it is not necessary that the assistant should be a man of imagination or refined taste,—it is sufficient that he have simply the skill, with the aid of accurate measurements, to construct the framework of iron and to copy the small model before him. But in *originating* that small model, when the artist had nothing to work from but the image existing in his own brain, imagination, refined feeling, and a sense of grace were essential and were called into constant exercise. (735)

As though to confirm Brown's concern that the tendency of genius is to lead to hierarchy, Hosmer describes the relationship between the sculptor and the craftsmen who create the final marble statue in these terms:

> much depends on the workmen to whom this operation [carving the marble] is intrusted [*sic*]. Still, their position in the studio is a subordinate one. They translate the original thought of the sculptor, written in clay, into the language of marble. . . . But whether skilled or not, the relation of these workmen to the artist is precisely the same as that of the mere linguist to the author who, in another tongue, has given the world some striking fancy or original thought. (735–36)[54]

As though in direct rebuttal to Brown, Hosmer gives someone else the task of medium, reserving for the artist the divine role as creator. At the same time, she offers a different definition of "work," comparing the function of the sculptor's assistants to that the printer fulfills for the poet and the stone mason for the architect. Hosmer's emphasis on the physical strength required to produce a sculpture, and her explanation that sculptors of both genders routinely employ such assistance, serves to bracket the question of labor altogether, making it irrelevant to the evaluation of the sculpture's originality and artistic merit. By relegating the person who actually performs the labor to the status of translator or medium, Hosmer offers her own definition of genius, one that has little, if anything, to do with the capacity to perform specific physical labor. In so doing Hosmer attempts to shift the terms of the conversation away from labor per se and toward intellectual abilities, which were increasingly coming to be seen as relatively equally distributed between the sexes.[55]

Hosmer concludes by moving from a general description of the "process of sculpture" to a rebuttal of the specific charges leveled not only against her, but against all "women-artists":

> the question when the clay *is* "properly prepared" forms the debatable ground, and has already furnished a convenient basis for the charge that it is never "properly prepared" for women-artists until is it ready for the caster. I affirm, from personal knowledge, that this charge is utterly without foundation,—and as it would be affectation in me to ignore what has been so freely circulating upon this subject in print, I take this opportunity of stating that I have never yet allowed a statue to leave my studio, upon the clay model of which I had not worked during a period of from four to eight months,—and further, that I should choose to refer all those desirous of ascertaining the truth to Mr. Nucci, who "prepares" my clay for me, rather than to my brother sculptor, in the *Via Margutta,* who originated the report that I was an imposter. (736)

The importance of work in the American imagination is such that the implications of sloth that accompany the charge of failure to do one's own work have the power to seriously damage an artist's public standing. Hosmer's vigorous defense relies on the dual strategy of stressing the essential role of originality and minimizing the importance of physical labor. Labor, even skilled labor, is, according to Hosmer, merely a commodity produced by a series of anonymous workmen. Instead of valorizing the physical work of the common man, Hosmer urges Americans to learn to value intellectual work:

> It is high time that some distinction should be made between the
> labor of the hand and the labor of the brain. It is high time, in short,
> that the public should understand in what the sculptor's work prop-
> erly consists, and thus render less pernicious the representations of
> those who, either from thoughtlessness or malice, dwelling upon the
> fact that assistance has been employed in certain cases, without defin-
> ing the limits of that assistance, imply the guilt of imposture in artists,
> and deprive them and more particularly women-artists, of the credit
> to which, by talent or conscientious labor, they are justly entitled.
> (737)

Hosmer's analysis of the "pernicious" ways in which the American
obsession with work has been used against female sculptors allows us
to recognize the gendered terms of the entire discussion of labor and
genius. Just as Higginson's portrait of the artist as a reclusive individual
with no domestic obligations, possibly living in exile, is incompatible
with contemporary expectations about women's lives and responsibilities, the accusation that women artists don't do their own work invokes
a rhetoric of work that equates virtue with the ideology of free labor—
the quintessential model of doing one's own work—and taps into contemporary stereotypes of women as idle and unproductive.

Hosmer's article is not only a personal defense. By virtue of the
terms it employs and its publication in the preeminent cultural magazine of the day, her argument about the proper relationship between the
"labor of the hand" and the "labor of the brain" is a contribution to the
ongoing conversation about the project of transforming the "America of
toil" into the "America of art."[56] And although Hosmer's contribution of
a nonfiction essay is unusual for a woman artist in this period, the questions she raises are not. In fiction published in the 1860s, 1870s, and
1880s Rebecca Harding Davis, Louisa May Alcott, and Constance Fenimore Woolson foreground the figure of the female genius, focusing
specifically on her relationship to the cultural establishment that simultaneously calls for the emergence of native genius and struggles to contain the threat such genius poses.

In her 1876 short story "Marcia," Rebecca Harding Davis takes up the
question of the proper relationship between genius and work, but in
her view it is the myth that genius does not require work that is most

pernicious to aspiring women artists. In this story Davis goes much further than either Brown or Hedge in her critique of the Romantic concept of genius; whereas they were primarily concerned with the danger that the individualistic nature of genius posed to the social fabric, Davis is concerned with the social, educational, and economic inequalities that such a concept is based upon. Davis shares Hedge's emphasis on the importance of labor in artistic production, but she views work not as a way to anchor genius rhetorically within American democracy but rather as an essential element of making artistic production available to those members of the population whose upbringing does not include the kind of intellectual development that make genius appear to be a "natural" eruption instead of a result of birth, education, and training, however informal.

"Marcia" is the story of a young woman who grew up on an isolated plantation in Mississippi with a father who views women as "mares—only useful to bring forth children" and a mother who has "one of the finest minds in the world" and takes snuff and opium to dull her mental pain.[57] Despite the lack of education, books, or contact with the outside world, Marcia knows that her mind, while "not of as high order as [her mother's] . . . is very different from that of most women" and is determined to "do something for us both" (311). Deciding that she has a vocation as a writer, Marcia leaves the plantation and goes to Philadelphia, expecting to find help and support there. She describes her disappointment to the narrator, a "middle age[d]" (310) woman editor to whom she sent her manuscripts:

> "As soon as I knew that I was a poet I determined to come to Philadelphia and go straight to real publishers and real editors. In my country nobody had ever seen a man who had written a book. Ever since I came here I find how hard it is to find out any thing about the business of authorship. Medicine, or law, or blacksmithing—every body knows the workings of those trades, but people with pens in their hands keep the secret of their craft like Freemasons." (311)

Marcia's comparison of writers and editors to the Freemasons is an indictment of the contemporary American cultural elite and the publishing world it dominates. The absence of any opportunities for training, apprenticeship, or mentoring essentially means that cultural production is limited to those who, by virtue of their class position, education, or family connections, can gain entrance into the secretive "business of authorship." Lacking all three, Marcia is doomed to peddle her manuscripts from one "real" editor to another, amassing a pile of "printed forms of rejection from every magazine and literary newspaper in the country" (311–12). Much to the narrator's surprise, Marcia does not lack talent. Despite her ignorance and the "atrocious" spelling and "errors of grammar in every line," her work suffers from none of the flaws typical to novice women writers:

> But for all her ignorance, mistakes, and weaknesses there was no trace
> of imitation. She plagiarized nobody. There was none of the usual talk
> of countesses, heather, larks, or emotions of which she knew nothing.
> She painted over and over again her home on the Yazoo . . . It was a pic-
> ture which remained in the mind strong and vivid as a desert by
> Gérôme or a moor by Boughton. (312)

Indeed, Marcia has the prerequisites to be an American genius: she possesses that cardinal virtue of originality, and she writes on strictly American subjects, which she describes with great vividness and strength. Her innate artistic talent is further evident when she visits the Academy of Design for the first time and is enthralled by what she sees there. "She had a keen, just eye for form and color; and the feeling of a true artist for both" the narrator observes (313). She is, then, an example of the kind of native genius described by Melville, Higginson, and countless others. All that Marcia lacks is the education to harness her talent and overcome the technical weaknesses of spelling and grammar produced by her culturally impoverished upbringing. Moved by the young woman's talent and determination, the narrator offers Marcia her guidance:

> There could be but one kind of advice to give her—to put away pen and
> ink, and for three years at least devote herself to hard study. She would,
> of course, have none of such counsel. The popular belief in the wings
> of genius, which can carry it over hard work and all such obstacles as
> ignorance of grammar or even the spelling book, found in her a marked
> example. Work was for commonplace talent, not for those whose veins
> were full of the divine ichor. (312–13)

Although the narrator here mocks Marcia's mistaken belief that her native talent obviates the need to work at her craft, the real target of Davis's critique is the Romantic construction of "genius" itself, which had become so widespread by the 1870s that even someone living on an isolated plantation in the Deep South has internalized it.

In Marcia's case, the Romantic view of genius is deadly. She nearly starves to death because she cannot find work and refuses to accept help from anyone and is finally forced to return to her father's plantation as the wife of the overseer, Zack Biron, who has "always 'wanted her'" (314). Marcia's marriage means a return to the "frightful" isolation of the "swamp on one side and the forest of live-oak on the other: [with] nothing to do, nothing to think of," that had driven her mother to madness and drug addiction (311). In the story's final scene, Marcia is already a living dead woman. The newlyweds pay a farewell call on the narrator, who observes that: "Marcia was magnificent in silk and plumes, the costliest that her owner's money could buy. Her little face was pale, however, and she looked nobody in the eye" (316). Marcia informs the narrator that "I shall not return to Philadelphia. I have no wish to return" and refuses the narrator's offer to send reading materials. When the couple is about to leave, Mr. Biron addresses the narrator: "Mrs. Biron has some—rubbish she wishes to leave with you." The "rubbish" is "the old black sachel" [sic] that Marcia had always carried. "Marcia took it in her white-gloved hands, half-opened it, shut it quickly, came up closer. 'These are my manuscripts,' she said. 'Will you burn them for me? All: do not leave a line, a word. I could not do it'" (316). The final sentence refers most logically to the act of burning the papers, but the vague referent "it" allows for an alternative reading of the sentence: what Marcia "could not do" is use her talent to write her way out of the trap of ignorance, isolation, and patriarchal possession. The narrator's characterization of Marcia as an object dressed by "her owner's money," and Marcia's insistence that the narrator send "nothing" to maintain her connection with the world of art and literature, underscores the impossibility of using a patriarchal model of artistic production to liberate women from sexual domination and false consciousness. Mr. Biron's dismissive characterization of Marcia's writing as "rubbish" echoes that of the myriad "real publishers and editors" who had rejected her work for years without even reading it.[58] Marcia is doubly handicapped, Davis suggests: she lacks the kind of access to the literary establishment that would get her work noticed, and her acceptance of the popular conception that genius requires neither education nor hard work to prosper means that when she does finally gain the attention of a cultural authority, she is unwilling to take the proffered advice.

In addition to its analysis of the cultural and economic forces responsible for Marcia's failure, the story suggests that women who do manage to occupy positions of cultural power have a special responsibility to nurture other women, and warns about the failure of female community that is likely to accompany women's successful entry into the brotherhood that is the cultural elite. In making the editor a woman rather than a man (a more realistic choice, since there were few female editors and no female publishers of "quality journals" at the time "Marcia" was written), Davis suggests that the narrator had a responsibility to help a talented young woman, which she ignored, presumably from fear of compromising her own hard-won position as a member of the cultural elite. The narrator's stance as a professional editor, detached, jaded, and immune to the stereotypically feminine appeals familiar from the antebellum period, is made clear in the story's first paragraph, where she describes the letter she expected to find with Marcia's manuscript:

> The letter—truth in every word: formal, hard, practical, and the meaning of it a woman's cry for bread for her hungry children. Every woman who writes such a letter fancies she is the first, that its pathos will move hard-hearted editors, and that the extent of her need will supply the lack of wit, wisdom, or even grammar in her verses or story. Such appeals pour in literally by the thousand every year to every publishing office. (310)

This description distances the narrator, who here identifies herself as a literary professional, from the antebellum model of writing, which encouraged women to substitute financial "need" for literary ability. Marcia's letter confounds the narrator's expectations, however: it "proved not to be of the tragical sort. The writer was 'not dependent on her pen for support'; she had 'avowed herself to literature'" (310). Despite Marcia's appeal to the narrator on purely professional, rather than sentimental or gendered, grounds, and her obvious talent, the narrator is content to give the young woman advice she will "of course" ignore and leaves her to fail on her own. Although she is acutely aware that the "popular belief in genius" is a myth that effectively makes professional writing akin to a secret club to which mostly men, and a few select women, may belong, the narrator is unwilling, or unable, to break with the privileged fraternity she has joined.

The narrator never acknowledges her own complicity in Marcia's failure, but the story's closing sentence, which describes the couple's departure, hints at it: "Mr. Biron was vehement in his protestations of friendship and invitations to visit the plantation. But Marcia did not say a word, even of farewell" (316). Marcia's silence is accusatory. Her refusal to speak to the narrator, her rejection of the narrator's offer to mail books and newspapers, and her final despairing statement that "I couldn't do it," combine to suggest that the narrator is partially responsible for Marcia's return to the prison of silence and ignorance that claimed her mother's life. Marcia's appearance on her doorstep presented the narrator with the opportunity to act unilaterally to challenge the economic and cultural systems that produced Marcia. By mentoring Marcia and helping her learn "the secret of [her] craft," the narrator might have advanced the cause of professionalization, which she clearly espouses, and helped to produce an American genius (311). Her inability to help Marcia suggests that the price the narrator has paid for entrance into the secret society of writers is, in Davis's eyes, dangerously high: not only does the editor turn away from any gender-based allegiance she might owe Marcia, but in allowing Marcia's original American voice go unheard the editor has abnegated her responsibility as a member of the cultural elite dedicated to producing a uniquely American culture in the postbellum period.

A similar failure is at the heart of Constance Fenimore Woolson's 1880 short story "Miss Grief." Both stories end with the death, whether figurative or literal, of the artist, and the destruction of her unpublished work. But whereas Davis foregrounds the structural barriers that lack of education and cultural capital pose to cultivating native genius, Woolson focuses on the anxiety that female genius elicits. Although much ink was spilled on the need for originality in American cultural production by cultural observers of the postbellum period, Woolson suggests that originality in women's art was more feared than celebrated by the cultural authorities who were the gatekeepers of "genius."

"'Miss Grief'" is the story of a series of encounters between a poor but hugely talented woman writer and a successful male writer whom she approaches seeking assistance in getting her work published. Both writers are expatriate Americans, and the story is set in Rome. The story is narrated by the unnamed writer who is, by his own admission, "conceited," and bears at least a passing resemblance to Henry James.[59] Although in many ways "'Miss Grief'" tells the same story as "Marcia"—the work of the female genius is unrecognized and unread, and the central cultural authority figure fails to develop an original American talent—Woolson's story reverses the power relations between the mentor and the aspiring artist. "Miss Grief" is not a supplicant at the narrator's doorstep—she approaches him only after she becomes convinced that he is worthy to read her work.[60] And although in social interactions the narrator is the more powerful of the two by virtue of his higher social and economic status, the balance of power shifts as soon as the discussion turns to art, where Miss Crief's status as a gifted writer and a perceptive reader of the narrator's writing continually remind the narrator of the irreducible fact at the center of their relationship: that Miss Crief possesses genius, and the narrator does not. But merely possessing genius is not sufficient: for without the public validation of the genius as such its existence is meaningless. And it is precisely this validation that the narrator fears conferring, and which Miss Crief dies trying to elicit from him.

The disruptive potential inherent in the encounter with genius is foregrounded even before the two meet. Preceded by her name, which she leaves at the narrator's rooms instead of a calling card, "Miss Grief" produces a sense of foreboding in the narrator, who pushes away thoughts of "whatever she might represent" (249) and envies his valet's ability to "'keep her confined to a particular hour!'" (249). When the two finally meet, the narrator is immediately put on the defensive by Miss Crief's long silence, which stretches to a full five minutes and is finally broken by the visitor, who reminds her host of his privileges: "'You are very happy, are you not, with youth, health, friends, riches, fame?'" (251). But those privileges are not what brought Miss Crief to the writer's doorstep. Rather, it is her decision that the writer is worthy of reading her own work. "'I have read every word you have written'" Miss Crief announces, and proceeds to recite a piece of the narrator's writing, perfectly (252). Not only does she choose a work that "was secretly [the narrator's] favorite," but Miss Crief's delivery of the scene reveals to the narrator that "she had understood me—understood me almost better than I had understood myself. It seemed to me that while I had labored to interpret, partially, a psychological riddle, she, coming after, had comprehended its bearings better than I had, though confining herself strictly to my own words and emphasis" (252–53). Despite his surprised gratification at Miss Crief's insight into his work, he withholds that knowledge from her, preserving his mien of "carelessness" (253). Miss Crief surprises the writer even more by explaining that she considers the scene she has just recited to be the best thing he has done to date and the only work that qualifies him to assess her own: "if you had not written that scene I should not have sought you. Your other sketches are interiors—exquisitely painted and delicately finished, but of small scope. *This* is a sketch in a few bold, masterly lines—work of entirely different spirit and purpose" (253). Despite his secret belief that she is correct, and his frustration that the reading public "had never noticed the higher purpose of this little shaft, aimed not at the balconies and lighted windows of society, but straight up toward the distant stars," the narrator cannot jeopardize his position of power vis-à-vis this shabby ideal reader and withholds his surprised gratification (252). The power struggle continues when the narrator tries to refuse Miss Crief's request that he read her work; she advances toward him, touches his arm, and turns the full power of her "large dark eyes" upon him, causing him to move away uncomfortably, feeling that he had been "magnetized" (254).

The narrator's unease deepens after he reads Miss Crief's work. He finds her work "inspired," full of "passion and power" (256), "unrestrained, large, vast, like the skies or the wind" (265), and strikingly original. Although he had sat up "half the night" to read "Armor," Miss Crief's drama, the narrator carefully preserves his position of power and authority in their meeting the next day, stopping short of paying the author the tribute he knows she deserves. While Miss Crief waits breathlessly to hear the narrator's opinion of her work he thinks to himself:

> It seemed so pitiful that she should be trembling there before me—a woman so much older than I was, a woman who possessed the divine spark of genius, which I was by no means sure (in spite of my success) had been granted to me—that I felt as if I ought to go down on my knees before her, and entreat her to take her proper place of supremacy at once. But there! one does not go down on one's knee, combustively, as it were, before a woman over fifty, plain in feature, thin, dejected, and ill dressed. (257)[61]

The narrator's sense that to tell Miss Crief that he believes she has great talent would be to humiliate himself in front of the shabbily dressed older woman captures the hypocrisy, pretension, and fear that, Woolson suggests, motivates those in positions of cultural power. Although the narrator admits to Miss Crief that he finds her drama to be "full of original power," he withholds his knowledge that her talent is greater than his, a lie of omission that undermines the partial truth he has told (257). The narrator continues to prevaricate throughout the meeting, telling Miss Crief just enough of the truth to encourage her, but balancing his praise with a detailed discussion of the drama's faults and weaknesses. To his surprise, Miss Crief, who had dissolved into tears after the narrator delivered his positive verdict, shows remarkable toughness during this portion of the interview. Despite the narrator's painstaking analysis of each line of the play, he

found that she did not see the blemishes—that she appreciated nothing
I had said, comprehended nothing. Such unaccountable obtuseness
puzzled me. I began again, going over the whole with even greater
minuteness and care. I worked hard: the perspiration stood in beads
upon my forehead as I struggled with her—what shall I call it—obstinacy? But it was not exactly obstinacy. She simply could not see the
faults of her own work. (259)

Miss Crief's blindness is a form of self-preservation. The only power
she holds vis-à-vis the institutional structure to which she must turn for
validation is the power that comes from her deeply held convictions.
Miss Crief's faith in the rightness of her work is such that, when the narrator offers to revise her drama to make it more palatable to "'the world
at large,'" which does not share his appreciation for "'originality and
force'" and "'will not overlook as I do your absolutely barbarous shortcomings on account of them,'" Miss Crief answers simply: "'There shall
not be so much as a comma altered'" (259, 260). Discussing a character
in one of her stories to whom the narrator objects, Miss Crief explains
that she cannot write him out because he "'belongs to the story so close-
ly that he cannot be separated from it'" (263). Confronted with Miss
Crief's refusal to modify her work, the narrator must choose between
his faith in Miss Crief's rare critical discernment, which he has already
conceded by accepting her praise for his own work, and his authority as
a critic. Like the cultural commentators who simultaneously sought to
privilege genius as the source of an original national culture and were
compelled to contain its undemocratic implications, thus making it
something other than "genius," the narrator must choose between
accepting genius on its own terms or making it conform to his own literary standards and risking its destruction.

Resentful of Miss Crief's confidence in her aesthetic judgment, the
narrator submits the drama, a story, and some poems to two friends,
who reject them for reasons similar to those raised by the narrator himself. Having received confirmation of his assessment of Miss Crief's
work, the narrator feels emboldened to alter it, convinced that his and
his friends' aesthetic judgment must, of course, be correct. Under guise
of championing her work, the narrator sets out to prove Miss Crief
wrong: "I was determined that Miss Grief's work should be received. I
would alter and improve it myself, without letting her know: the end
justified the means. Surely the sieve of my own good taste, whose mesh
had been pronounced so fine and delicate, would serve for two. I began;

and utterly failed" (264). Although he assures himself that his own "good taste" will triumph over Miss Crief's "originality and force," the narrator eventually discovers that quite the opposite is true. Turning first to the drama, the narrator finds that Miss Crief's unwillingness to change "so much as a comma" was neither obstinacy nor obtuseness, but an artist's deep understanding of her work:

> I set to work first upon "Armor" [the drama]. I amended, altered, left out, put in, pieced, condensed, lengthened; I did my best, and to no avail. I could not succeed in completing anything that satisfied me, or that approached, in truth, Miss Grief's own work just as it stood. I suppose I went over that manuscript twenty times: I covered sheets of paper with my copies. But the obstinate drama refused to be corrected; as it was it must stand or fall.
>
> Wearied and annoyed, I threw it aside and took up the prose story: that would be easier. But, to my surprise, I found that that apparently gentle "doctor" [the character Miss Crief had said was impossible to remove from the story] would not out: he was so closely interwoven with every part of the tale that to take him out was like taking out one especial figure in a carpet: that is, impossible, unless you unravel the whole. At last I did unravel the whole, and then the story was no longer good, or Aaronna's: it was weak, and mine. All this took time. . . . But, though slowly and at my leisure, I really did try my best as regarded Miss Grief, and without success. I was forced at least to make up my mind that either my own powers were not equal to the task, or else that her perversities were as essential a part of her work as her inspirations, and not to be separated from it. (264–65)[62]

Miss Crief's ability to resist all attempts to change her work to conform to either the narrator's "fine sieve of good taste" or the preferences of "the world at large" is a necessary quality for a woman of genius forced to find validation for her work in the late-nineteenth-century literary world. Miss Crief's work is not destined to be read except by a very small audience, in this case of one, but Woolson here suggests that letting one's work go unread is preferable to allowing it to be altered to conform to the standards of those of lesser talents, though greater cultural power.[63] Although we are never told which of the narrator's choices is true—either he isn't up to editing the work or it is simply uneditable because its flaws are part of its greatness—both choices force him to acknowledge that the shabby woman before whom he would not kneel has brought him to his knees through the sheer power of her work.

The narrator never tells Miss Crief about his failed attempts to edit her work. Instead, at their next meeting, which takes place a few weeks later at her deathbed, he lies and tells her that the drama has been accepted for publication. Sitting by her bedside, the narrator tells Miss Crief "a romance invented for the occasion" about the forthcoming publication of her drama (267). Ever conscious of his status as an artist, the narrator notes that "I venture to say that none of my published sketches could compare with it [the romance]. As for the lie involved, it will stand among my few good deeds, I know, at the judgment bar" (267). Miss Crief dies and her work goes unread—most of it goes to the grave with her—but she manages to extract one final truthful confession from the narrator. In one of their last exchanges, hours before her death, Miss Crief reveals that she has long known what the narrator has tried so hard to conceal: "'Did you wonder why I came to you? It was the contrast. You were young—strong—rich—praised—loved—successful; all that I was not. I wanted to look at you—and imagine how it would feel. You had success—but I had the greater power. Tell me, did I not have it?' 'Yes, Aaronna.' 'It is all in the past now. But I am satisfied'" (268). Miss Crief's triumph is a small one, but her satisfaction is well deserved, for she has managed to elicit from a male authority figure the truth he had struggled to hide.

The story's last word goes to the narrator, of course, but it is an admission that highlights the essential arbitrariness of canons and standards. Thinking about the manuscript of Miss Crief's drama, which he keeps in a locked case, the narrator admits that he reads the play occasionally, "not as a *memento mori* exactly, but rather as a memento of my own good fortune, for which I should continually give thanks. The want of one grain made all her work void, and that one grain was given to me. She, with the greater power, failed—I, with the less, succeeded. But no praise is due to me for that" (269). What, exactly, that "grain" is—a kind of talent or simply being born male and privileged—remains open to interpretation, but the story suggests that whatever the "grain" consists of, its presence or absence is less a literal matter and more a function of perception, positioning, and social and economic circumstances.

Whereas Woolson and Davis highlight the structural barriers to women who seek institutional validation for their identity as "genius," Louisa May Alcott dramatizes the impossibility of any woman occupying that identity. Alcott's close personal relationships with the men who embodied genius in the antebellum United States made her particularly attuned to the worship of genius that permeated the culture, a phenomenon that, Alcott suggests, was deeply destructive to female artists like herself, who hailed from the ranks of the cultural elite. Alcott's anonymous and pseudonymous fiction and her own biography suggest that even for women who enjoy the privileges of access and education that Woolson's and Davis's protagonists lack, genius is an intellectual identity that is both unavailable to and undesirable for women to occupy. For, as Alcott understood, the identity of genius represents a masculine intellectual identity that women—of any class—do not have access to. Moreover, the identity of genius is dependent on a female muse or subject for its existence and that, Alcott demonstrates, both precludes women artists from occupying the identity of "genius" and means that any mentoring relationship between a woman artist and a male genius is doomed to destroy the female artist.

In October 1867 Louisa May Alcott took a room in Boston for the winter to give herself a break from the cold and constant labor of life in her father's home in Concord. Alcott repeated her winter moves to Boston as often as possible for the next decade or so, and she frequently commented in her journal about the pleasure, freedom, and literary productivity that marked these sojourns in the city. Moving to Boston freed Alcott not only of the drudgery of domestic labor but also of the intellectually oppressive influence of the town that was home to some of the most influential thinkers and writers of her time: Emerson, Hawthorne, and Thoreau were all friends and neighbors of the Alcotts. Despite, or perhaps because of, her close personal relationships with leading figures of the American Renaissance, Alcott felt stifled by the intellectual weight of Concord. LaSalle Corbell Pickett records the following conversation with Alcott, in which the author of *Little Women* resists Pickett's assertion that the popular work reflects her "true style of writing":

> "Not exactly that," [Alcott] replied. "I think my natural ambition is for the lurid style. I indulge in gorgeous fancies and wish that I dared inscribe them upon my pages and set them before the public."
>
> "Why not?" I asked. "There seems to be no reason why you should not be gorgeous if you like."
>
> "How should I dare to interfere with the proper grayness of old Concord? The dear old town has never known a startling hue since the redcoats were there. . . . To have had Mr. Emerson for an intellectual god all one's life is to be invested with a chain iron of propriety. . . . I

shall always be a wretched victim to the respectable traditions of Concord."[64]

We now know that when Alcott made this statement she already had a successful career as the creator of lurid thrillers and sensational stories, published anonymously and pseudonymously in popular periodicals and story papers, which paid her well and enabled her to contribute substantially to the support of the Alcott family.[65] Her stated desire to "inscribe [her gorgeous fancies] upon [her] pages and set them before the public" points to Alcott's resentment of the enforced split in her literary identity. That Alcott was forced to channel her "natural ambition" into a well-paying but subliterary mode of production is, of course, due to a complex of personal and cultural factors, of which American transcendentalism's "chain iron of propriety" is only one, but her repeated statements that "Concord has no inspiration for me,"[66] and her observation that she is doomed to "always be a wretched victim to the respectable traditions of Concord" suggest that Alcott's frustration stemmed not only from the financial pressures that forced her to churn out "rubbishy tales" as fast as she could, but also from her ambivalence toward the intellectual tradition available to her.[67] Alcott inscribed her resistance to and frustration with the literary path she had chosen in her journals and fiction, through her repeated moves from Concord to Boston, and in her obsessive exploration of the idea of "genius." Through the last, in particular, Alcott explores her vexed relationship to the male intellectual tradition to which she could never really belong.

Alcott's 1865 novella *A Marble Woman, or The Mysterious Model* reveals that genius is not merely reserved for men; it is deadly for women. The novella, which was serialized in *The Flag of Our Union* in May–June 1865 under the pseudonym A. M. Barnard, features two of Alcott's favorite sensational elements: a manipulative protagonist and drug addiction.[68] But *A Marble Woman* is a rather unusual text in the Alcott oeuvre of sensation writing because its gender roles are conventional: although she usually used the freedom of writing pseudonymously in popular story papers to create strong, smart female characters who use cunning and skill to overcome adversity and triumph, typically at the expense of more powerful male characters, in this work, which explores the power structure of a mentoring relationship between a male genius and a talented female pupil, the female character remains completely powerless throughout. In *The Marble Woman* the genius-mentor destroys the female artist whose talent he claims to wish to develop, leaving her addicted to opium and either unable to or uninterested in working.[69] By portraying male genius as demonic and destructive Alcott points to the shortcomings of the dominant model of "high" intellectual production available to mid-nineteenth-century American artists. Although the power of her critique is muted by the fact of its pseudonymous publication in a work that appeared in sensational story papers, it is precisely this self-censoring that reveals the depth of Alcott's ambivalence about genius. Unlike her acknowledged writings, in which Alcott, like Davis and Woolson, foregrounds the economic pressures facing aspiring artists, in her unacknowledged novella Alcott depicts artists who are free from economic constraints and belong to the cultural elite. The safety, and distance from Concord, afforded by a pseudonym and a "low" genre enable Alcott to depict the American cultural elite as blindly worshiping male genius whose artistic success depends on the existence of the female student, art object, or muse.

The marble woman of the novella's title is twelve-year-old Cecilia, an orphan who has been left in the care of Bazil Yorke, a reclusive sculptor, by her mother, whose lover Yorke was before she married another man. Before Cecilia meets her new guardian, she encounters the boy next door, a friendly child named Alf who gives her a rose and informs her that Yorke doesn't care for flowers because he is "'odd and busy, and a genius, you know.'" Cecilia doesn't know, and she replies: "'I hope that's nothing bad, because I'm going to live with him.'"[70] The child's fear that "genius" is "bad" is eventually confirmed: Yorke uses his genius both to develop her artistic talent and to transform her into the subject of his art.

Yorke's first action upon meeting his new charge is to rename her Cecil, a gesture that both calls attention to her gender and underscores the sculptor's determination to shape and control his ward. Although he initially tells Cecil he can't keep her, Yorke changes his mind after discovering that she has considerable sculpting talent, and he offers the child a home on the condition that she adopt his reclusive ways. The next chapter opens five years later in the studio Yorke shares with Cecil, who has become an accomplished sculptor under Yorke's careful tutelage. Cecil is in the process of receiving a marriage proposal from her childhood friend, Alfred, which she rejects, begging him to "[l]et me be in peace—I'm happy with my work, and my nun's life was pleasant until you came to trouble it with foolish things" (146). Yorke, who has been eavesdropping on the conversation, soon makes his presence known and reminds Cecil of the promise she made when he took her in: "'decide between us two, now and forever, because I will not have your life or mine disturbed by such scenes as this. . . . If you prefer to stop with me, happy in the work you are wonderfully fitted to perform, content with the quiet life I deem best for you, and willing to be the friend and fellow laborer of the old master, then come to him and let us hear no more of lovers'" (147). Yorke's support of Cecil's desire to pursue her work is, ironically, precisely what so many artist figures in fiction from this period lack. But because Yorke's intervention is motivated by his desire to dominate Cecil and "mold" (151) her to suit his own personal and artistic purposes and not by any sincere desire to advance her career, the man who initially appears to be the ideal mentor is soon exposed as a monster whose absolute power over his pupil is at least as destructive as marriage can be: "'Can you be content year after year with study, solitude, steady progress, and in time fame for yourself, but never any knowledge of love as Alfred paints it? . . . Carving Cupid has filled your head with fancies that will do you no good; banish them and be what I would have you'" (150–51). Cecil's response reveals that she understands Yorke's stake in her artistic success more clearly than he thought: "'A marble woman like your Psyche, with no heart to love you, only grace and beauty to please your eye and bring you honor; is that what you would have me?". . . . "Yes, I would have you beautiful and passionless as Psyche, a creature to admire with no fear of disturbing its quiet heart, no fear of endangering one's own'" (151). This exchange suggests that Yorke's desire to promote his talented pupil's artistic career is inseparable from his need to transform her into his muse. She is to become a powerless object to be admired rather than a subject with desires and ambition of her own. Yorke's primary motivation for his insistence that Cecil give up all thought of love is revenge—he wishes to punish Cecil for the pain her mother inflicted upon him years before, when she married another man. As Alcott knew, however, the choice Yorke requires of Cecil is entirely realistic. Marrying Alfred, or anyone, with the possible exception of Yorke himself, would effectively end the young woman's artistic career, and Yorke's insistence that she dedicate herself to her art under his watchful eye is probably the only practical way to ensure that her talent be developed. The choice Alcott depicts here is, then, not only the familiar one between marriage and career, but a more sinister choice between the mentorship of a powerful male genius that enables an artist's career and that same mentor's potential to destroy her very identity as an artist.[71]

Despite her understanding that her mentor wishes to transform her into a object rather than encourage her growth as a subject, Cecil is powerless to resist Yorke, on whom she is dependent for both financial and artistic support. What remains of Cecil's autonomy is soon removed when she agrees to a virgin marriage with her "master" that is intended to put to rest the gossip about their unusual living arrangements (151). Although Cecil is theoretically free to choose another guardian when she reaches eighteen, Yorke's reclusive lifestyle guarantees that she has no other friends and cannot imagine life without him. The possibility that Cecil might live elsewhere and continue her studies under Yorke is not even discussed, presumably because such an arrangement would alter the power structure of the mentor/mentee relationship, which requires the teacher's complete control over his pupil. The offer of a loveless marriage seems to be the only way Cecil can preserve her ties to her teacher and only friend. Yorke promises that "'nothing need be changed between us; to the world we can be husband and wife, here guardian and ward. . . . I shall have the right to protect my little pupil, she to cling to her teacher and her friend. We are both solitary in the world. Why can we not go on together in the old way, with the work we love and live for?'" (172). Yorke's emphasis on the professional motivation for the marriage appears to confirm his commitment to developing Cecil's career, but it soon becomes apparent that Yorke's status as Cecil's mentor is complicated by his own long-dormant ambition. At the wedding reception, which is described only from Yorke's perspective, a male guest offers to buy one of Yorke's works—a statue of Psyche, which is on public display for the first time—"now that he possessed the beautiful model" (174). The offer, and Cecil's beauty, which is also on public display for the first time, "flattered his pride as a man and an artist, enhanced his pleasure in the events of the day, roused his ambition that had slept so long, and banished his last doubt regarding the step he had so hastily taken" (174). Although the marriage has ostensibly been arranged to allow Cecil to develop her artistic talent, its effect is to rekindle Yorke's ambition and motivate him to reclaim the public mantle of his "almost unknown" "genius" (165). Indeed, as the rest of the novella shows, not only is the mentor's reawakened ambition dependent on "possess[ing]" his student/model, but her official status as property/wife precludes the further development of her own talent.

In the wake of the marriage Yorke abandons his reclusive habits and reclaims his place in the city's social world, where he is celebrated as the long-lost genius. The newlyweds are drawn into a social whirl, and the public acclaim both receive—he for his art, she for her beauty—intoxicates Yorke and alters his attitude toward his wife's career:

Wherever she went she won such admiration that his pride was fostered by the praise it fed on, and regarding her as his best work, he could not deny himself the satisfaction of beholding the homage paid his beautiful young wife. She submitted with her usual docility, yet expressed so little interest in anything but her art that he soon grew jealous of it, and often urged her to go pleasuring lest she should grow old and gray before her time, as he had done. (177)

Having urged Cecil to marry him so that she would be free to make "steady progress" and "in time [achieve] fame," Yorke is transformed, seemingly overnight, into a possessive husband, jealous of his wife's preference for her art both because it takes her away from the social whirl that brings him so much pride and because, Alcott implies, he fears that his talented student will soon eclipse him. Her husband's suggestion that Cecil leave her work and "go pleasuring" neatly accomplishes both his objectives: ensuring that the beauty of his "best work" will be preserved, and preventing his only likely rival from developing her talent. This is the last time Cecil's work is mentioned; the rest of the novella revolves around the relationship between Cecil and Yorke, who eventually discover that they love each other, and revealing the identity of the "mysterious model," who turns out to be Cecil's father, whom she had long thought was dead. The novella ends with the happy reconciliation of Cecil and Yorke, but without any indication that Cecil either has done any work since her marriage or intends to do any in the future. The chapter that contains the last reference to Cecil's work also contains the revelation that she has become an opium addict in the year since Alfred proposed and Yorke exacted the promise of isolation as the condition of his continued mentorship. Although the two facts are not explicitly related, their juxtaposition underscores the unequal power structure at the heart of the mentoring relationship between Yorke and Cecil and suggests that the mentee's work may become a pawn in the relationship, which the mentor uses to advance his own needs and desires.

In this case, the mentor's desire is to assert his status as genius publicly. As part of his effort to wean Cecil from her opium addiction, Yorke takes her to the seashore for a month and then to a "summer palace" he buys for her (198). The first thing Cecil sees in her new home is a long hall: "A carpet, green and thick as moss, lay underfoot; warm-hued pictures leaned from the walls, and all about in graceful alcoves stood Yorke's fairest statues, like fit inhabitants of this artist's home" (197).

Although logically the referent of "this artist's home" is Cecil, whose house it is, the grammatical referent is Yorke. The designation of the house as the home of "this artist" rather than "these artists," and the fact that only one of Cecil's works is on display, and that one, "the piping Faun," is placed "among the finer works of [Yorke's] own hands" (201), further suggests that Cecil's identity as an artist has been subsumed into Yorke's, making the home indeed that of one artist, not two. Cecil finds the house a tribute to her "tastes," her "comfort," and her "least whim," but the narrative does not reveal whether it includes a studio for her. We do learn that Yorke's decision to create the "hall of statues" (198) signals his decision to publicly reclaim his status as a "genius."

In giving Yorke a "hall of statues" in which to display his art publicly Alcott invokes the newly designated National Statuary Hall, which was created by a law passed in 1864. The Hall was to occupy a space in the Capitol that had previously been occupied by the House of Representatives, which was relocated to the south wing of the Capitol in 1857. The now-vacant space was dedicated to "display statues of distinguished Americans," produced by American sculptors.[72] In giving Yorke his own "hall of statues" Alcott aligns Yorke's display with that being mounted in the nation's capital, suggesting that both cultural projects institutionalize the conception of genius Yorke embodies, at significant cost to the nation's women artists.[73] Indeed, the implications of Yorke's "hall of statues" are not lost on Cecil; when Germain, a frequent visitor to the house, admires the statues and wonders when Yorke will produce another, noting that he has "been idle of late," Yorke responds confidently "'Never busier in my life. I have a new design in my mind, but it takes time to work it out. Wait a few weeks longer, and I will show you something that shall surpass all these.' 'Unless you have lost your skill.'" This last is whispered by Cecil, as she brushed by her husband, "with a glance that seemed to prophesy a failure for the new design, whatever it might be" (202). Cecil's transformation from admiring student into hostile wife attempting to undermine the artist's confidence has been effected by Yorke himself, whose need to control his potential rival and desire for public acclaim as genius has imposed idleness on his once-promising student, transforming her first into an opium addict and then into a bored woman lounging on a couch in her well-appointed summer "palace," "singing to herself, and playing with a useless fan" while her genius-husband "stroll[s] from alcove to alcove, as if studying the effects [of the sun] among his statues" (200).

The statues receive their first public showing at a masquerade ball that the Yorkes give as a housewarming party, and on that occasion Cecil seems to have abandoned her resentment of Yorke's statues. Disguised by her costume, Cecil strolls among her guests, listening to their reactions to her husband's work with "smiles and tears":

> It was amusing and something more, for as they passed through the glittering throng, or mingled with the groups gathered about each statue-haunted alcove, Cecil saw and heard the wonder, admiration, and reverence her husband's genius inspired. This was the first time his works had been exhibited, and there was something so romantic in the fact that these fine statues had stood unknown, unseen, till they were brought to decorate his wife's home, as if love alone could make him care for fame, that their beauty seemed increased fourfold in the spectators' eyes; and so warm were the commendations bestowed upon the marbles, so varied and beautiful the tributes paid the man, that Cecil glowed behind the mask, and was glad of that screen to hide her smiles and tears. (204–5)

Although the spectators put the most "romantic" interpretation on the artist's new willingness to show his long-hidden work, the reader's access to information about Yorke's motivation places her, along with the narrator, in the position of knowing the truth. The narrator's careful statement that it is "as if love alone could make him care for fame" reminds the reader that it is not, in fact, "love alone" that has made Yorke care for fame again, but a combination of jealousy of his pupil's talent and pride of ownership of the beautiful woman whom he controls.

Alcott's decision to end the text's artistic plot with a scene in which Cecil "glow[s]" with pride for her husband's "genius" while no one, including Cecil herself, seems to remember his pupil's talent, points to her pessimism about the value of male-female mentoring relationships for the woman involved.[74] Finding a powerful male mentor is not a viable solution to the perennial dilemma facing women artists, this novella suggests. Regardless of how "wonderfully fitted to perform" (147) the work of an artist Cecil, or any woman, might be, any offer made by a male genius to mentor a promising female artist so that she will eventually achieve "fame for [her]self" must be viewed with intense skepticism (150). For a male artist to mentor a female is to be willing to accept the possibility that her work may one day surpass his own. The structure of "genius" precludes this possibility, Alcott suggests, since it is always dependent upon the presence of a female object to serve as muse and inspiration, but never colleague or partner.

Although the geographic and social contexts of this novella are left vague, Yorke and Cecil clearly belong to America's social elite. References to Cecil's "good breeding" (138), her familiarity with being waited on by servants, and the fact that she spent much of her childhood traveling through Europe, combined with Yorke's obvious wealth (he has no job, lives in a well-staffed mansion, and is able to purchase summer "palaces" and diamond necklaces apparently on a whim), and the descriptions of the social scene that Yorke steps back into easily—a world of social calls, evening parties, carriages, lavish summer homes, and masquerade balls—all suggest that Yorke and Cecil belong to the social elite of a northeastern American city.[75] The "wonder, admiration, and reverence [Yorke's] genius inspired" in the members of this class, and his willingness to confirm his status as genius at the expense of his pupil/model serve as an indictment both of the Romantic category of genius and of the social elite that supports and produces it.

These portraits of the encounter between female artists and genius are uniformly tragic. Each individual story is a tale of one woman's victimization, but taken together they provide a devastating analysis of the flaws inherent in one of the most important identities available to American artists. Neither Davis, Woolson, nor Alcott offers an alternative to genius, but their portraits of genius suggest that the category itself must be rejected if a truly American art is to thrive. For, as Davis, Woolson, and Alcott demonstrate, outsiders—whether by virtue of their class, education, or gender—cannot occupy the category of "genius," and as long as only insiders can lay claim to the category that was, in the antebellum years, widely seen as representing the highest level of creative accomplishment, American culture will continue to be produced by a relatively small portion of Americans.

At the same time, the Americans writing about genius share a need to find a philosophical and theoretical framework within which to locate both their own intellectual and artistic endeavors and those of the nation. Their search for such a framework led them, often simultaneously, to the figure of the genius and to the legacy of the Civil War, which was regularly invoked by postbellum observers as both a rationale and a metaphor for the urgent cultural nationalism project of the day. In some ways the legacy of the Civil War was a perfect replacement for the category of genius, substituting ideals of communal sacrifice, heroism, and nation building for the undemocratic, self-involved figure of the genius. But as Phelps, Alcott, and Woolson demonstrate, the rhetorical mobilization of the legacy of the Civil War in support of post-bellum cultural nationalism was predicated on many of the same assumptions about gender and class that made the figure of the genius so destructive to American women artists.

CHAPTER FIVE

The Civil War and the Making of the "America of Art"

W RITING in the *Atlantic Monthly* in January of 1867, Thomas Wentworth Higginson articulated a view that would become a truism in the following decades: that to complete the nationalizing process instigated by the Civil War requires an original national culture. America's current quite impressive attainments are meaningless, Higginson argues, because they are not the stuff of history: "as the value of a nation to the human race does not depend upon its wealth or numbers, so it does not depend even upon the distribution of elementary knowledge, but upon the high-water mark of its highest mind. Before the permanent tribunal, copyists and popularizers count for nothing, and even the statistics of the common schools are of secondary value. So long as the sources of art and science are still Transatlantic, we are still a province, not a nation."[1] The anxiety about America's cultural provincialism was as old as the United States itself, but in the wake of the Civil War the need to overcome this historical barrier to national "self-confidence" took on a new urgency.[2] Having won the war, Northern intellectuals turned their attention to its legacy, and most agreed that the most pressing concern facing the United States was bringing the nation's cultural productions up to the level of its industrial and manufacturing achievements.[3] The wave of cultural nationalism that swept through Northern intellectual circles in the decade following the Civil War produced a flood of essays on the topics of art, culture, and "Americanism," most of which sounded a few central themes: that producing American high culture, composed of literature and the visual arts, is a prerequisite to being taken seriously by the rest of the Western world; that such a culture must be original and not imitative, though most commentators agreed that artists and writers must travel abroad to learn from foreign models and methods; that expatriation was a failure of courage, even a form of treason; that the cultural project was a completion, even an extension, of the Civil War's political and moral aims; and that cultural and educational institutions were required if the program of producing a national culture was to extend beyond a relatively small elite, but that an educated elite was essential to creating the conditions in which American culture could thrive.[4] There was a remarkable degree of consensus among the Northern intellectuals engaged in this conversation, both male and female, about the need to produce a national culture and the methods for doing so; but while the women of the transitional generation generally agreed with the goals of the project and sought to participate in it, their analyses consistently challenge the assumptions underlying each of these areas of agreement. For Elizabeth Stuart Phelps, Louisa May Alcott, and Constance Fenimore Woolson, the cultural nationalism of the 1865–85 period presented both an opportunity and a challenge. As members of the educated cultural elite who believed in the necessity of producing a uniquely American culture, and well-respected writers whose work had broad popular appeal, Phelps, Alcott, and Woolson were insiders, uniquely suited to both produce the nation's high culture and advocate for its importance; as women, who had not fought in the Civil War, who did not enjoy the same educational opportunities as their male peers, and whose access to the highest circles of cultural authority was limited, they were outsiders, whose commitment to the cultural nationalism project was tempered by their understanding of the masculine bias and elitism at its core. This doubled vision is evident in the ambivalence toward the Civil War as a source of national cultural production in Phelps's *The Story of Avis* (1877); in the portrayal of expatriation as necessary for women artists' success in Alcott's "Diana and Persis" (ca. 1879); and in Woolson's "The Street of the Hyacinth" (1882), in which she dissents from the view that making great art and art education accessible to Americans would democratize American art.

The Civil War was widely seen by Northern observers as having turned the American states into a nation. As Eric Foner has shown, the industrial and economic requirements of the war had a nationalizing effect: the war produced a tremendous growth in the federal government, which expanded existing agencies and developed new ones to meet the needs of the Union troops for transportation, food, housing, clothing, and medical care. To support the Union army, the federal government created a national paper money, a national debt, a national banking system, new taxes and tariffs, and numerous new federal institutions to encourage everything from immigration (to compensate for the loss of men who had enlisted in the Union army), to settling on western lands, to establishing agricultural and industrial colleges. The Federal government also supported the creation of the transcontinental railroad; all of this was done in the interest of "consolidat[ing] the Union" and strengthening the national state.[5] The creation of national economic structures, in particular, was controversial and required the type of patriotic justification provided by Senator John Sherman, who urged: "'The [economic] policy of this country ought to be to make everything national as far as possible; to nationalize our country so that we shall love our country.'"[6]

The nationalizing effect of the Civil War extended to the realm of cultural identity as well. The importance of achieving a national identity that the United States had hitherto lacked was expressed by Orestes Brownson, who declared in 1865 that: "Among nations, no one has more need of full knowledge of itself, than the United States, and no one has hitherto had less. It has hardly had a distinct consciousness of its own national existence."[7] And that consciousness was to be molded in the image of the North's cultural and political values, whose national dominance was strengthened by the redefinition of the war's moral purpose in the wake of the Emancipation Proclamation and the North's subsequent victory. As early as 1862 a correspondent of James T. Fields suggested that California "'must be northernized thoroughly, by schools, Atlantic Monthlies, lectures, New England preachers, Library Associations, in short, Ticknor & Fieldsism of all kinds,'" expressing the widely held belief—at least among Northern intellectuals—that the model of high culture developed in Boston should and could be exported to the nation.[8] And indeed, Boston's cultural dominance, already significant in the antebellum era, increased in the decades following the Civil War: "The North's victory in the Civil War meant that the national influence of New England culture was dramatically confirmed: the retrospective scripting of the war as a struggle to free the slaves made the New England–based abolitionist movement into the war's victor. Boston was the metropolitan center of New England and its national voice."[9] Its educated elite, grown wealthier thanks to wartime profits, was ready to turn its attention from matters of war to matters of culture;[10] and it was home to Ticknor and Fields, and its house magazine the *Atlantic Monthly*, both of which remained the nation's preeminent belletristic publishing institutions in the decades following the Civil War.[11]

The link between the North's victory in the War and the project of cultural nationalism was regularly made by prominent Northern intellectuals. In an 1870 article titled "Americanism in Literature," Thomas Wentworth Higginson urges Americans to be proud of their nation's recent accomplishment and suggests that this pride will, in turn, produce a national culture:

> We are accustomed to say that the war and its results have made us a nation, subordinated local distinctions, cleared us of our chief shame, and given us the pride of a common career. This being the case, we may afford to treat ourselves to a little modest self-confidence. Those whose faith in the American people carried them hopefully through the long contest with slavery will not be daunted before any minor perplexities of Chinese immigrants or railway brigands or enfranchised women. We are equal to these things; and we shall also be equal to the creation of a literature. We need intellectual culture inexpressibly, but we need a hearty faith still more. "Never was there a great migration that did not result in a new form of national genius." But we must guard against both croakers and boasters; and above all, we must look beyond our little Boston or New York or Chicago or San Francisco, and be willing citizens of the great Republic.[12]

The war has, according to Higginson, made possible the kind of "hearty faith" in America itself that had been impossible while slavery existed, a faith that will, in turn, produce the American nation that the war was fought to create. For Higginson, "intellectual culture," "a hearty faith," and a willingness to identify oneself as a citizen of the "great Republic" rather than of a city or a region are all essential to the task at hand: the "creation of a literature," which is as important, and as difficult a challenge, as mass immigration and corrupt railroad companies. The equation of the cultural enterprise with the social and economic tasks of the period was not unique to Higginson. Writing immediately after the end of the Civil War, Massachusetts clergyman Samuel Osgood declared that the most pressing issue before the country in the aftermath of the war is cultural. All the nation's other problems—Reconstruction, "the Negro," the debt, and so forth—will be settled "in due time and without war," Osgood writes, but the question of educating the children "distances all others in magnitude and interest."[13] And the education Osgood has in mind is not primarily in mathematics and reading, but in "true taste": "Our children are vastly wiser and happier by being taught to distinguish beauty from tinsel pretence, and to see the difference between the fine and the superfine," Osgood argues. "We may begin the reform at the beginning, and apply the ideas of the truly beautiful in the books and magazines that we put before our children."[14] Once a generation of children is raised to appreciate "true taste," America will be ready to take her rightful place in the Western world: "Give us thirty years' fair training of our children in schools and reading, galleries and music-halls, gardens and fields, and our America, the youngest among the great nations, will yield to none the palm of strength or of beauty; and as she sits the queen, not the captive, in her noble domain, her children, who have learned grace under her teaching, shall rise up and call her blessed."[15] In Osgood's formulation, the most pressing task facing the nation still recovering from the wounds of battle is the production of educated citizens who will, in turn, enable the United States to overcome its long-standing sense of cultural inferiority.

The emphasis on the opportunity for cultural growth presented by the Civil War stemmed, in part, from a need to give meaning to the war's losses and, at the same time, from the desire to preserve the wartime sense of purpose and determination and channel it productively. Higginson attempts to do both when he reminds his readers of the war's positive effects:

It is but a few years since we heard it said that the age was dull and mean, and inspiration gone. A single gunshot turned meanness to self-sacrifice, mercenary toil to the vigils of the camp and the transport of battle. It linked boyish and girlish life to new opportunities, sweeter self-devotions, and more heroic endings; tied and loosed the threads of existence in profounder complications. That is all past now; but its results can never pass. The nation has found its true grandeur by war, but must retain it in peace.

Peace too has its infinite resources, after a nation has once become conscious of itself. It is impossible that human life should ever be utterly impoverished, and all the currents of American civilization now tend to its enrichment. . . . Everything is here, between these Atlantic and Pacific shores, save only the perfected utterance that comes with years. Between Shakespeare in his cradle and Shakespeare in Hamlet there was needed but an interval of time, and the same sublime condition is all that lies between the America of toil and the America of art.[16]

Cultural development is cast here as a kind of peace dividend to be reaped both by individuals who have sacrificed for the war effort and by the nation, whose suffering can be redeemed, Higginson implies, by becoming the "America of art." The soaring rhetoric of this statement, and the optimistic belief in the "infinite resources" of peace and in the promise for the improvement of "human life," reflects the intensity of the need to transform the recently ended war, with its tremendous loss of life, into a source of endless opportunity for human growth.[17] While the claim that a prolonged war is an ideal catalyst for the production of national genius might strike twenty-first-century readers as dubious, it was made frequently by social observers in the years immediately after the war, for whom the logic or historical basis of such a claim was clearly less important than its rhetorical effect.

In addition to serving as a rallying cry for those committed to producing the "America of Art," the Civil War also provided a standard for heroism and patriotism that was often invoked by those who viewed the cultural nationalism project as an extension of the war. Writing in 1870, Higginson, who was a colonel in the Union army, invokes the "grandeur" of war as essential to his definition of "Americanism." The "American spirit," which is both the subject and the exemplar of "the higher Americanism" in literature, is the spirit of a soldier:

> It is not important to know whether a man reads Homer or Dante: the essential point is whether he believes the world to be young or old; whether he sees as much scope for his own inspiration as if never a book had appeared in the world. So long as he does, he has the American spirit; no books, no travel, can overwhelm him, but these can only enlarge his thoughts and raise his standard of execution. When he loses this faith, he takes rank among the copyists and the secondary, and no accident can raise him to a place among the benefactors of mankind. He is like a man who is frightened in battle: you cannot exactly blame him, for it may be an affair of the temperament or of the digestion; but you are glad to let him drop to the rear; and to close up the ranks. Fields are won by those who believe in the winning.[18]

Producing culture is transformed here from a reward for fighting the war into a new kind of war. As those who "believe in the winning" stride forward on the "field" of battle, the cowards are left behind to take their place among "copyists and the secondary." In equating the task of producing the "America of art" with fighting the Civil War Higginson genders the "field" of American culture as a masculine territory reserved for courageous soldiers. Those who are unable to withstand the influence of "books and travel" and lose their "pride" are, in Higginson's view, effeminate cowards, best left behind while the real men do the nation's work. Importantly, it is not "books and travel," but "temperament" that is the culprit here. Higginson's definition of the "American spirit" attempts to balance the need for exposure to foreign influences with the danger of becoming "copyists"—that bugbear of American cultural independence. To circumvent this dilemma, which had become more pronounced since midcentury, when growing numbers of American artists had begun traveling to Europe to study and work, Higginson grafts onto the cultural enterprise qualities associated with Americans' westward expansion: he praises exposure to foreign influences, which can "enlarge" the artist's thoughts and "raise his standard of execution," but defines the "American spirit" as the ability to view the cultural world in much the same way as Americans had long viewed the continent itself: as a wide open, uninhabited space, available for colonization, and a canvas for American "inspiration."

A less celebratory view of the Civil War's effects on cultural production is evident in Elizabeth Stuart Phelps's 1877 novel *The Story of Avis,* which opens in the spring of 1861. Although the novel's eponymous heroine is clearly a participant in the project of producing Higginson's "America of art," her promising career as an original American artist never materializes, largely due to the "personal effect of this war" which, the narrator observes, had been "impossible to forecast."[19] In her portrayal of the effects of the war on Avis's career, Elizabeth Stuart Phelps challenges the ubiquitous rhetoric of war and suggests that it is as likely to undermine the postbellum cultural project as to support it.[20]

Avis's status as a member of a new generation of American women artists who take their own and their nation's aspirations seriously is emphasized throughout the early parts of the novel. Before she could pursue her studies, Avis had to convince her father, a widowed professor of philosophy living in Harmouth—a New England college town modeled on Phelps's hometown of Andover—that hers was a serious ambition. Avis recognizes her vocation at the age of sixteen, after reading *Aurora Leigh* (1857), Elizabeth Barrett Browning's prose poem about an artist's struggle to reconcile the demands of heterosexual love and a career.[21] Reading the poem, Avis finally understands "why she was alive; what God meant by making her; what he meant by her being Avis Dobell. . . . Avis Dobell, who had rather take her painting-lesson than go to the senior party" (32). Returning home, Avis informs her father that "I should like to be an artist, if you please" (33). When her father chastises her for missing dinner and causing "more trouble about your domestic duties" Avis repeats herself:

> "I have decided this morning that I want to be an artist. I want to be educated as an artist and paint pictures all my life."
>
> "Poh, poh!" Said the professor. "Nonsense!" . . .
>
> "Nonsense, nonsense!" repeated Professor Dobell. "I can't have you filling your head with any of these womanish apings of a man's affairs, like a monkey playing tunes on a hand-organ." (33)

Seeing his daughter's distress, Professor Dobell relents slightly, telling Avis that she is welcome to continue her drawing lessons: "'Make yourself happy with your paint-box, if you like. That was a very pretty little copy which you made me of Sir William'" (33). Her father's praise for the copy and his dismissive description of her ambition as "apings of a man's affairs" reflect the conventional assumption that women lack the capacity to create original work, an assumption Avis resists vigorously:

> "It was a very pretty little copy," repeated the professor.
>
> "I do not want to make pretty little copies," cried Avis with quivering lip. "*I who love my art would never wish it lower to suit my stature.*" The professor of intellectual philosophy, not being well read in "Aurora Leigh," stared at this alarming quotation. But Avis went headlong on,—
>
> "I want to be educated. I want to be thoroughly educated in art. Mr. Maynard told me, when I drew the Venus, that I should go to Florence." (34)

In rejecting Professor Dobell's condescending assumption that she will produce "pretty little cop[ies]," Avis simultaneously challenges the conventional view of women's artistic limitations expressed by Hawthorne in *The Marble Faun* and inserts herself into the national debate about the nature of American art. Since assertions that American art was merely a copy of British and European originals had long dogged American artists, Avis's rejection of her father's suggestion that she content herself with copies is not only a feminist gesture, but a nationalistic one.

Avis's status as an American is underscored in the chapter describing her years abroad. Having gained her father's permission to stay in Europe after completing the requisite chaperoned Grand Tour, Avis "plunged into a life which extremely few women in America, twenty years ago, found it either possible or desirable to lead"; this observation, coupled with the fact that *Aurora Leigh* is a British work, reminds the readers of the relative paucity of native models of artistic production available to American women and of the novel's role in remedying this very problem. Avis's status as an American ambassador is also emphasized:

> Those who know any thing of art-circles in Italy at that time will recall the impression made upon them by her superb perseverance in mastering the difficulties of her position. . . . The shy American girl of the unquestionable breeding and the yet half-blossomed beauty, trod the mazes of Florentine life with an innocent rapture which protected her like a shining veil.
>
> The prospect of commanding proper surroundings to her venture had seemed, at first, a hopeless one; but one day her friends look about to find that the little Yankee girl had brought her circumstances, like spaniels, to her feet. (36)

This description emphasizes Avis's status as a representative of her nation: in one brief passage she is characterized as both "the shy American" and "the little Yankee girl" who behaves with perfect propriety in unconventional circumstances. Avis's identity as a "Yankee" is clearly important to Phelps: Describing the end of Avis's sojourn in Europe, Phelps describes her as "the New-England girl" (38), and the novel revolves around the question of just what is required to "lead a Yankee girl to glory" (80).

Having spent six years studying in Europe, Avis returns home to United States with the words of her Parisian teacher, Thomas Couture, ringing in her ears: "'I will give you two years to make a reputation'" (37). Arriving shortly before the Civil War begins, Avis settles down to pursue her career as a promising young artist: we learn that she has "got into the newspapers" because one of her pictures has been sold in London and a that "'brilliant future'" is predicted for her (8). The effect of returning home is, initially, invigorating, and Avis seems poised to find in all things American precisely the kind of inspiration that Higginson and his contemporaries theorized was possible. But as the summer of 1861 wears on, Avis still has not found a subject for the "good picture" with which she is to make her reputation (78). The description of Avis's difficulties emphasizes the impact of the United States in general, and the Civil War in particular, on the artist's state of mind:

> Her return to America had been in itself one of those stimulating experiences whose immediate effect is a sedative one.
>
> The elemental loves of kin and country had been stirred in her to the finest fibre of their wide-reaching roots. She had come home to find that the afternoon sun in her father's study, on the picture of Sir William, thrilled her as no glory or story of Vatican, Pitti, or Louvre, had ever done. It meant more to her, at first, just to go out into the garden and bury her face in the young grass, and listen to the squirrels scolding in the pear-trees, and the trustful call of the cows waiting for Jacobs down in the field, than it seemed as if the fair young picture before her could ever mean. Especially she was moved by the spring scents; the breath of the earth, where the overturned loam lay moistly melting shades of brown together . . . ; the aromatic odor of the early bonfires with whose smoke the languid air was blurred and blue; then by the exhalation of small buds, the elm and the grape that borrowed the mantle of the leaf, as wild things do that of the forest, to escape detection. Every sense in her quivered to homely and unobtrusive influences. . . . She would not have exchanged the choirs of St. Peter's for the sound of the old chapel bell calling the students to evening prayers. And then . . . it would have been impossible to forecast the precise personal effect of this war. Life, she thought, had pressed too near her, since she came home, for her to tell the world what it meant. (77–78)

Despite her great pleasure in the sights, sounds, and smells of her native landscape, Avis cannot paint. And although the narrator insists that Avis finds more pleasure in the sights and sounds of her New England home than in the great institutions of European art and culture, its paradoxically "sedative" effect drives the artist to burn her sketches in despair as the time allotted her by Couture's "golden probation" passes inexorably (77). Phelps provides no single explanation for Avis's inability to find inspiration at home, but this description implies that it is her elemental "love of kin and country" itself that allows "life" to infringe on the distance the artist requires for self-expression. And in 1861, life was inextricably bound up with the Civil War.

Avis's inability to find inspiration persists as the hot summer of 1861 wears on, and the descriptions of the artist's despair alternate with references to the war raging far from Harmouth. The sounds of the "college-boys" singing "army songs" permeates Avis's studio, driving her outside into the sultry air, and the next day, instead of "get[ting] to work" as she had planned, Avis joins the town's women, who are rolling bandages and picking lint in the chapel, talking in "hushed voices": "The butchery of Bull Run had fallen upon the mangled land," explains the narrator (78). Later that night, Avis longs for an escape from "the great unholy world, in which seers struggled and sinned for their visions," whose presence she cannot escape even in her locked bedroom:

> Dreamily across the current of her thought, floated the pathetic sound of the boys' voices in the street, still and forever busy with those army songs:—
> "In the beauty of the lilies
> Christ was born across the sea."
> She turned from the window with an abrupt, dejected motion. Who could make a picture till the war was over?
> "Since he died to make men holy,"
> sang on the boys,
> "Let us die to make men free." (79)[22]

Although the novel is set in 1861, it was published in 1877, and to contemporary readers the ubiquity of the boys' misplaced enthusiasm for war would have had the poignancy of knowing just how many young lives were eventually lost. Avis's desire to escape from the "great unholy world" that oppresses her with its nearness is not unpatriotic, Phelps suggests, but essential to the artist, whose task is to interpret the world. Avis cannot live up to the promise of doing "great things" when she is mired in the "elemental love of kin and country" revived by her return from Europe and exacerbated by the war. Unable to escape either the stultifying August heat or the omnipresence of the war, Avis seeks a mental escape: she pulls a bottle of French orange brandy from a locked dressing case and drinks a small amount. The narrator intrudes to clarify the national symbolism of the act, asking: "The wine of a flower has carried many a pretty Parisian to an intrigue or a convent. Could it carry a Yankee girl to glory?" (80). As the liquor affects Avis, she drifts into a slightly drunken stupor and her surroundings recede, freeing her, at least temporarily, from the reality of the war: "The most distinct thought that she had was now a sense of relief that she could not hear the army songs" (80). Silencing the rhetoric of war's "glory" evoked by the college boys' singing is, Phelps suggests, essential to the postbellum project of producing artistic "glory."

In a dreamlike state, Avis sees a succession of images, each of which represents both a possible subject for her painting and a mode of artistic production typically associated with women. In rejecting each of the possible subjects, Avis also rejects its associated model of artistic production, which Phelps deems too limiting to carry a "Yankee girl to glory." The first images Avis sees are drawn from the decorative arts movement:

> Pottery, porcelain, furniture, drapery, sculpture, then flowers, fruits,— a medley of still life,—swept through strange, half-revealed, but wholly resplendent interiors, which glided on indifferently, like languages that said, "what hast thou to do with us?" Now and then, out of the splendid maze, a distinct effect seemed to pause, and poise itself, and woo her through the dark. An open hand, raised, and turned at the wrist like a flower on its stem, held water-lilies drooping and dripping. A sunbeam, upon an empty chair in a student's alcove, focussed [*sic*] upon a child's shoe and a woman's ribbon. . . .
>
> These passed. Avis nodded at them like the children at the visions in Hans Andersen's tales. It was all a kind of bric-à-brac. She had not the ceramic nature. Let them go. (81)

The items Avis sees and rejects are all associated with domesticity. They are the stuff of interior decoration and the kind of "low" art typically assigned to women by the decorative arts movement, which encouraged women to "claim an artistic sphere of their own, rooted in domestic imperatives and the 'minor' arts."[23] The images that seem to "woo her" in particular are feminine and distinctly sentimental, and Avis nods in recognition but moves on. Her dismissive assessment of the images as "a kind of bric-à-brac" further emphasizes their association with femininity and domesticity and aligns Avis with the artistic elite's view of such items as beneath the attention of a serious artist.

Next, a series of nature scenes unfold before Avis, ranging from a wave of color that "held both the passion and the intellect of the sea" to images of desolate forests, mountains, and deserts "'wherein no man had been since the making of the world,'" and culminating in a "mountain-peak, swathed below in gloom, swiftly broken at the summit into glory, on which 'God made himself an awful rose of dawn'" (82). This vision evokes a Romantic model of art based on finding the sublime in nature, which Avis rejects, saying "'[o]nly the high priest enters in.'"

The images of nature's grandeur are followed by visions of human suffering and of Christ:

> When she raised her eyes, they fell upon forms and faces grown gaunt with toil,—an old man sowing sparse seed in a chill place; the lantern-flash on a miner's stooping face; the brow and smile of a starving child; sailors abandoned in a frozen sea; a group of factory women huddling in the wind; the poisoned face of a lead-worker suddenly uplifted like a curse; two huge hands knotted with labor, and haggard with famine, thrust groping out upon the dark.
>
> But her heart cried out, "I am yet too happy, too young, too sheltered, to understand. How dare I be the apostle of want and woe?"
>
> Even with the word the vision changed, and slowly as she leaned to look, swiftly as her heart beat in gazing, there grew the outline of a Face. It was a Face dark, dim, brightening, blinding, beneath a crown of thorns; but she dashed her hand across her eyes and said, "I am unworthy." (82)

Avis's rejection of the mantle of "apostle of woe" is one of the most surprising aspects of Phelps's aesthetic vision. By refusing to speak for the downtrodden, Avis rejects the most familiar and accepted path into self-expression available to female artists. Her assertion that she is "too happy, too young, too sheltered, to understand" others' suffering is a claim virtually no other American woman artist had publicly made before. Avis's statement essentially undoes the traditional association of femininity with suffering that had allowed other sheltered middle-class white women to assert their unique capacity to chronicle the suffering of others not of their class or race.[24] Phelps's endorsement of Avis's refusal to be a Christ figure distances Avis from antebellum conceptions of women's artistic production and further aligns her with the postbellum model of high art, which privileges aesthetic values over ethical ones. These identifications are reaffirmed in the next image, which finally provides the inspiration Avis has been seeking.

On the brink of exhaustion, Avis is disappointed at the failure of her French stimulant when she suddenly sees a peasant girl stooping to pluck some harebells. The single girl metamorphoses into many, and suddenly the room "seemed full of women" (82). Avis first sees famous women from history, mythology, and the Bible, but they soon "moved on solemnly, and gave way to a silent army of the unknown" going through the motions of daily life (82). The women's activities range from the mundane to the horrific, and the narrator explains that "[e]ach, in turn, these figures passed on, and vanished in an expanse of imperfectly-defined color like a cloud, which for some moments she found without form and void to her" (83). The allusion to the creation story in Genesis suggests that these women hold the key to Avis's creative crisis, and indeed, the subject of her next painting soon reveals itself to her:

> Slowly, but surely at last, and with piercing vividness, this unfolded, and she saw in curt outlines, like a story told in a few immortal words, this only:—
>
> She saw . . . in the foreground the sphinx, the great sphinx, restored. The mutilated face patiently took on the forms and the hues of life; the wide eyes met her own; the dumb lips parted; the solemn brow unbent. The riddle of ages whispered to her. The mystery of womanhood stood before her, and said, "Speak for me."
>
> Avis lay back upon her pillow with a sudden, long, sobbing sigh. She was very tired; but she had seen her picture. To-morrow she could work. (83)

But before she can drift into the deep sleep that typically follows her visions, Avis is assaulted by a "panorama of agonies" she cannot shut out. First she see animals suffering under vivisection (Phelps was active in the antivivisection movement), then a bloody battlefield filled with dead and dying soldiers:

> Avis started, with a cry that rang through and through the sleeping house, beating her hands against her eyes, as if she would beat out the very retina on which the shadow of such sight could fall. For now she was pursued by a vision of battles. Martial music filled the room; bright blood-streaked standards waved and sank and rose again; human faces, like a wind-struck tide, surged to and fro; men reeled, threw up their arms, and fell; the floor crawled with the dead and dying; wounded faces huddled in corners, came and vanished on the ceiling, entered and re-entered through the door, gasped their life away upon the bed. The glazing eye, the whitening jaw, the clinching fingers, the ineffectual hoarse effort to breathe a broken name,—all were there; nothing was hidden, hinted, or veiled; nothing was spared her. (83–84)

This sequence of visions, the novel's only detailed account of Avis's creative process, is bracketed by the Civil War: Avis's day was spent rolling bandages for the wounded of Bull Run, as the sound of college boys singing army songs floated in the windows, and her creative repose is shattered by horrific visions of war. The juxtaposition of the war's pervasive presence with Phelps's analysis of the aesthetic choices facing American women artists highlights Avis's identification with the cultural elite and offers a critique of the rhetorical uses of the Civil War by that same elite in the decade after the war. The excruciating detail of Avis's vision of the battlefield—detail penned by a woman writer and seen by a female character—challenges the masculine gendering of the cultural field underlying Higginson's conception of the "American spirit" by suggesting that despite their physical absence from the battlefield, American women of Avis's generation experienced the war with harrowing emotional intensity. Phelps's decision to bring the bloody suffering of the Civil War battlefield itself into the novel, rather than focusing on the epistemological crisis experienced by those left behind by the war (as she had done very successfully in *The Gates Ajar* [1869]), points to her engagement with the rhetorical uses of the war that had become commonplace by 1877. The impulse to cast the war as both a catalyst for cultural production and a standard of execution is misguided, Phelps suggests, because it both masks the true horror and intense suffering revealed in Avis's vision and represents a misuse of what David Blight calls "Civil War memory."[25]

Moreover, in giving Avis the sphinx for the subject of her next painting, Phelps weighs in on the long-standing debate about the "American-ness" of American art, implicitly rejecting the familiar belief that "[t]o analyze combinations of character that only our national life produces, to portray dramatic situations that belong to a clearer social atmosphere,—this is the higher Americanism."[26] Instead, Avis's subject is the sphinx—female, silent, and the eternal object of men's artistic vision; Avis's mission is to make her the speaking subject of her own art, which will take its place as a symbol of "Yankee . . . glory" in a war-torn country desperately in need of heroic images, though not necessarily, Phelps suggests, images drawn from the "glory" of the battlefield.[27] In giving her "Yankee" protagonist an ancient Egyptian subject and a European catalyst for inspiration, Phelps aligns herself with the less common view that art produced by an American artist is, by definition, American: "We may be absolutely confident that just so far as America is American, the literature of America will be American, and whosoever wants more than this is not wise, and, for another thing, will certainly be disappointed; and people who are anxious that our literature should be American may rest assured that it cannot be anything else."[28] The "sedative" effect that Avis's encounter with the American landscape had on her inspiration and the foreign origins of the forces that eventually unlocked her creative energy combine to suggest the limits of the nationalistic chauvinism that permeated the high culture discourse of the period. Avis is unable to live up to her potential to provide the kind of original art "we lack in this country" (205) because she cannot preserve the distance required to interpret the nation to itself, succumbing instead to "the love of . . . country" embodied in a wounded soldier.

For Avis, the unanticipated "personal effect of the war" is her reluctant agreement to marry a former suitor, Philip Ostrander, a promising young member of the Harmouth faculty who was seriously injured at the battle of Bull Run. When Philip recovers sufficiently from his injuries he immediately renews his suit, and this time Avis agrees to marry him, after extracting a promise that she will be free to continue her artistic career. Avis's inability to resist Philip's resumed assault is attributed directly to his wounded state. When the two first meet after he is wounded, Avis cannot conceal her distress at the sight of Philip's feebleness, and the wounded man understands that his weakened state will serve him well: "He felt, that, had he come to her again in the power of his manhood, he might again have gone as he came. It was his physical ruin and helplessness which appealed to the strength in her" (100). Philip's belief that it is the reversal of power roles that appeals to Avis reflects the plot trajectory of such well known British works as Charlotte Brontë's *Jane Eyre* and Browning's *Aurora Leigh,* in which the female protagonist agrees to marry a suitor only after he has been blinded or crippled, thus preserving her own power in a relationship that conventionally requires women's subordination. But Philip's cynical assumption that it is his powerlessness that appeals to Avis may be misplaced; Phelps implies that it is the source of his debility as much as the injury itself that weakens Avis's resolve.

When Avis first sees Philip the narrator explains that although she had followed his progress from "the battle-field, beneath the shot, within the blazing hospital, upon the scorching journey, and at the door of death" from a distance, her imagination had stopped short of visualizing his "shattered" body and "haggard . . . gray" face (99). The first words Avis speaks to Philip express her shock at his altered state: "'Oh!' she said indistinctly. 'I did not think—I did not know?'" (100). The sight of Philip's broken body forces Avis to confront the suffering she had seen in her nightmarish vision of the battlefield, to "know" what she had previously been able to repress by plunging into her work on the sphinx.

The description of Philip's subsequent marriage proposal, which takes advantage of Avis's shock at his changed state to wring an

admission of love from her, is replete with images of death and vivisection that resonate with Avis's battlefield vision and suggest that her
marriage is a form of patriotic sacrifice. After admitting that she had
purposely stayed away from Philip's sickroom because she feared her
emotional response, Avis "seemed like a creature whose throbbing heart
was torn out of her live body" (101). The narrator goes on to describe
Avis's confession of love as a form of death:

> In yielding her confession, she seemed already to have yielded some
> impalpable portion of her personality. In the words of the old story of
> chivalry, "her soul had gone out of her." Her blinding consciousness of
> having taken the first step in a road which led to some indefined [sic]
> but imperative surrender of her nature had an effect upon her incalcu-
> lable to one familiar only with a simpler type of woman. She did not
> look subdued, only startled. And when he reverently extended his thin
> hand again towards her, she shrank, with widening, fear-stricken eyes.
>
> Just then, Ostrander thought her beautiful terror of him more pre-
> cious than her love. (101)

The imagery of vivisection and the language of battle and defeat that fill
this scene link it to Avis's nighttime vision and to Philip's injury. Avis's
tortured psyche and "fear-stricken eyes" resonate with those of the
imaginary "dead and dying" soldiers who "crawled" over the floor of
her room, and her "beautiful terror" masochistically appeals to Philip,
for whom conquering Avis becomes a surrogate for the war that has
feminized him, reducing him to "crawl[ing] weakly towards" Avis, who
stands high above him on a stone wall, straight and strong as "a statue"
(99).[29] It is not Avis who is motivated by the power reversals of Philip's
injury, but Philip himself, whose "shot lung and lifelong feebleness"
paradoxically allow him to "demand" an admission of love from Avis
with "a kind of solemn authority" that restores some of his lost masculinity, enabling him to elicit "terror" from his beloved that is "more
precious than . . . love" because it confirms his power over her. A few
days later, when Philip pressures Avis to agree to a public engagement,
Avis herself articulates the parallel between the Civil War that produced
Philip's injuries and the internal struggle that is sparked by his renewed
suit. Loving a man, Avis informs Philip, "'is like—death,'" and when he
quips "'Then . . . I am ready to die,'" Avis says only "'It is civil war.'"
(106). Avis's civil war is, of course, between her desire to pursue her
career and her knowledge that her marriage is incompatible with her
ambition—a familiar dilemma for women artists in this period. But

Avis's dilemma is complicated by the war; whereas Avis had turned Philip down without qualms the first time he proposed, citing her intention to remain single and pursue a career, once he is "shattered" by the war, she is unable to resist the demands he makes upon her. The spiritual death that she well knows awaits her in marriage is her contribution to the war effort and, perhaps, a form of penance for her desire to shield her eyes from the horrific visions of battle that invaded her psyche on the night after the battle of Bull Run. Unable, by both convention and inclination, to depict the battle on canvas, Avis's road to "glory" is blocked by the same forces that authorize artistic production for Phelps's male colleagues.

In his 1867 Harvard Phi Beta Kappa address on the topic of "Aspects of Culture," Ralph Waldo Emerson confidently declared: "No good citizen but shares the wonderful prosperity of the Federal Union. The heart still beats with the public pulse of joy, that the country has withstood the rude trial which threatened its existence, and thrills with vast augmentation of strength which it draws from this proof. The storm which has been resisted is a crown of honor and pledge of strength to the ship."[30] Within two years, Elizabeth Stuart Phelps produced *The Gates Ajar,* a record of the suffering of the nation's women left to mourn husbands, fathers, and brothers, who found little comfort in the "wonderful prosperity of the Federal Union" in the aftermath of the war. In *The Story of Avis* Phelps expands her critique of the kind of triumphalist rhetoric that had become ever more pervasive in the first decade after the War's end, suggesting that it is not only the suffering of individual women that such uses of the War obscure but the very nationalistic projects that it is designed to support.

The invocation of the "public pulse of joy" that Emerson imagined beating at the prospect of the "vast augmentation of strength" accruing to the "ship" of state was particularly intense when the question of European travel came up, as it did with increasing frequency in the early postbellum years. For H. T. Tuckerman, writing in *Putnam's* in May 1868, Americans' rush abroad in the years immediately after the Civil War is a matter of some concern, since it turned the attention of wealthy, educated Americans away from the work of postwar reconstruction and nation building. Tuckerman depicts the "mania for travel and absenteeism" by "restless pleasure seekers" as the work of middle- and upper-class

American women who lead their reluctant husbands to Europe so that they can social climb and enjoy the domestic ease afforded by running a household with European servants, and warns against the depletion of energy that would be better used in helping to bring the promise of the war to fruition:

> there is a great scope, here and now, not only for enterprise, progress, and political regeneration, but for enlightened citizenship, for private benignity. A national life preserved through such enormous sacrifice of blood and treasure, is surely worth elevating into 'victorious clearness,' concentration into efficient harmony, refining, by all that wealth can bring of art and culture of knowledge, taste, and intellectual sympathy.[31]

In his diatribe against excessive European travel, Tuckerman makes an exception for artists and scholars, whose sojourns abroad support the postbellum cultural project; he applauds "our noble country-men" who "toil . . . bravely in vocations dear to their hearts" in European cities, because they "have or will reflect honor on their native land," and concludes the essay by noting that "[i]t is not of such, but of the butterflies and drones, that we speak, as "'going abroad' to no good purpose."[32] Most cultural observers shared Tuckerman's faith in the importance of artists studying abroad, but the potential for permanent expatriation was widely seen as a serious and growing problem.

Expatriation was an option for a growing number of American artists in the late 1860s and 1870s, and the trend caused considerable consternation among cultural observers. By the end of the Civil War, European travel had become a familiar part of middle-class Americans' lives, and spending time abroad was widely viewed as essential for aspiring artists, both visual and literary.[33] American writers found their way abroad in increasing numbers from the mid-1850s, whether temporarily, as Harriet Beecher Stowe, Nathaniel Hawthorne, and Louisa May Alcott did, or permanently, as Constance Fenimore Woolson and Henry James did. European travel, and especially the encounter with Europe's great art treasures, was for many Americans a breathtaking experience. In *Sunny Memories of Foreign Lands,* an account of her European tour in the early 1850s, Harriet Beecher Stowe frequently describes the pleasure she takes in visiting museums and private art collections, a pleasure that is heightened because of the contrast it provides to her Calvinist upbringing in antebellum America. In one case, just staying near a famous museum is exhilarating: "[The Louvre] is close by. Think of it. To one who has starved all a life, in vain imaginings of what art might be, to know that you are within a stone's throw of a museum full

of its miracles, Greek, Assyrian, Egyptian, Roman sculptors and modern painting, all there!"[34] The contours of the European trip were so
familiar to educated Americans that even those, like Augusta Jane
Evans, whose planned trips never materialized, could imagine their visits in great detail. Writing her friend Rachel Lyons in 1860, Evans paints
a glowing portrait of the trip the two women hoped to take together:
"Just fancy us both safely landed in Rome; once there we could place
ourselves under the protection of Elizabeth Barrett Browning, and her
scarcely less illustrious Lord, Robert. or [sic] if *you* did not particularly
affect the 'pets of Parnassus,' we could doubtless prevail on Charlotte
Cushman or Harriet Hosmer to *Chaperone us*. Apropos! of the two last, I
see they have rented a house and are living together."[35] Evans's reference to Hosmer and Cushman's living arrangements reflects her close
reading of the "quality" periodicals in which such news was reported,
and her expectation of being taken under the wing of prominent
women artists points to her familiarity with the social customs of the
community of expatriate women artists.

Traveling to and studying in Europe were widely viewed as necessary prerequisites for belonging to the American cultural elite, but as
the century progressed growing numbers of artists chose to remain in
Europe and that, most observers agreed, was a problem. The anonymous author of an 1868 essay titled "Sculpture in the United States" is
proud of American sculptors' successes in Italy, but, he wonders,

> can we properly call them American sculptors, or their works Ameri-
> can works? Ward's fine statue of the Indian Hunter belongs to us, and
> a few other meritorious statues; the quaint little people of John Rogers,
> and the production of Clark Mills and Vinnie Ream; but may we claim
> the Lybian Sybil, the Greek Slave, the Zenobia? The subjects of these are
> strange to the people, and the workmanship is foreign. American
> artists dwelling in Europe are in some degree denationalized. While in
> Rome they must do much as the Romans do, and they cannot respond
> fully to our needs and sympathies at home.[36]

The writer's complaint that the subjects of these well-regarded sculptures by America's best known sculptors are "strange to the people"
and their "workmanship is foreign" reflects the oft-expressed belief that
American art must be native in conception and execution in order to
qualify as such. But more pressing than the writer's concern with for-
eignness of subject matter or style is his fear that expatriation "dena-
tionalize[s]" artists and makes them unable, or unwilling, to "respond
fully" to the "needs and sympathies" of the nation they are widely

assumed to represent. For a talented artist to become "denationalized" in 1868—just as the effort to extend the nationalizing effects of the war to the realm of high culture was getting under way—was a severe blow to the project of cultural nationalism. An artist who is more concerned with European standards and customs than with "our needs and sympathies at home" clearly cannot serve as a role model, teacher, or hero for a war-torn nation seeking to unify itself and find its place in the world of Western culture. And the effect of expatriation is not limited to the individuals themselves, the author warns his readers: "Those who emigrate, attaining wider fame, seriously influence those who remain. Few of these are interested in our national art."[37] Not only do expatriate artists lose their motivation to produce art that addresses "our" concerns, but their leaving and their success abroad have a ripple effect on those who stay behind, causing them, too, to lose interest in producing "our national art." Shifting tone slightly, the writer reminds expatriate artists of the special privilege they enjoy as artists in and for a democracy: "Happily, our artists are not often forced to decide between the support of their wise and wealthy patrons and that of the masses; but there can be little hesitation in the minds of those who respect their calling. To model or paint for a person of wealth is comfortable, and to be conscious of a few choice souls is very pleasant; but to model or paint for a nation raises the artist to his true place of a great teacher."[38] The writer of this essay is clearly aware that the American cultural scene in 1868 was, in fact, the province of "a few choice souls" whose wealth or education gave them positions of considerable cultural power, while "the masses" were, for the most part, uninterested in the high art being produced by America's fine artists; but these details are temporarily irrelevant to this polemic, which seems aimed at bullying and cajoling expatriate artists into doing their duty toward their "national art."[39]

For Thomas Wentworth Higginson, expatriation is evidence of a failure of faith in the American political system, a faith that is particularly important to writers and other intellectuals: "It seems unspeakably important that all persons among us, and especially the student and the writer, would be pervaded with Americanism," Higginson begins.[40] He then defines "Americanism" in terms of quasi-religious belief in the political ideal that provides the foundation for the nation's cultural enterprise: "Americanism includes the faith that national self-government is not a chimera, but that, with whatever inconsistencies and drawbacks, we are steadily establishing it here. . . . When a man is heartily imbued with such a national sentiment as this, it is as marrow in his bones and blood in his veins. He may still need culture, but he has the basis of all culture."[41] Lacking this faith causes expatriation: "But if one happens to be born or bred in America without this wholesome confidence, there is no happiness for him; he has his alternative between being unhappy at home and unhappy abroad."[42] Higginson's position is less conciliatory than that of the author of "Sculpture in the United States," whose pride in the accomplishments of American artists abroad is palpable. For Higginson, expatriation is a sign of an ethical failure that has little, if anything, to do with one's personal inclinations, professional ambitions, or the level of the American audience. Not only does expatriation stem directly from a failure of faith in America, but it is, in Higginson's view, almost always an irreversible condition: "Happily, there are few among our cultivated men in whom this oxygen of American life is wholly wanting. Where such exist, for them the path across the ocean is easy, and the return how hard!"[43]

Whereas these two writers see in expatriation a serious threat to the production of a "national art" by "our cultivated men," Louisa May Alcott suggests that it is only by leaving the United States that women artists can find the necessary conditions for contributing to the "America of art." A firm believer in the benefits of European travel, Alcott used her income to support her artist sister May during years of study abroad. Although Alcott frequently resented the fact that May was able to pursue her artistic career at the expense of Alcott's own—it was the income from Louisa's hugely popular children's books, which supplanted her more aesthetically ambitious work for adults, that kept May in Europe—she felt strongly that May's talents could not be developed unless she stayed in Europe for long stretches of time. In "Diana and Persis" (ca. 1879), Alcott portrays a community of American women artists abroad and suggests that expatriation (presumably permanent, since one of the characters marries and settles on the outskirts of Paris) is essential to the development of the current generation of promising young American women artists.

"Diana and Persis" is an unpublished four-chapter fragment of a novel based on the experiences of May Alcott Nieriker, a painter who lived and studied in Europe during the 1870s, and Harriet Hosmer, the American sculptor who was the model for the character of Hilda in Hawthorne's *The Marble Faun*.[44] "Diana and Persis" provides a detailed portrait of a community of women artists in Paris, in the process offering both a critique of strictures against women becoming professional artists and Alcott's own vision of the conditions that must be in place if American women are to develop their talent without succumbing to conventional expectations about women's social roles and artistic abilities. The

central condition, for Alcott, is female community, which need not be
large to be effective. Other conditions include artistic freedom, distance
from the United States, a measure of financial independence or steady
financial support, and, possibly, spinsterhood. One of the story's central
concerns is the possibility of integrating marriage and career, but
because the work is unfinished it is impossible to know how Alcott
intended to resolve this question. Her portrayal of the marriage of Persis (known as Percy) and August Müller, which is modeled on that of
her sister's brief marriage to Ernest Nieriker, a Swiss man, suggests that
Alcott was willing to reconsider her long-held belief that marriage, and
the motherhood that inevitably followed, was fundamentally incompatible with a woman's career. The relationship between Diana (the Hosmer character) and Anthony Stafford, apparently modeled after William
Wetmore Story, is a rewriting of the unequal and destructive relationship between male genius and female artist in *The Marble Woman*. In
"Diana and Persis" the relationship is neither unequal nor destructive,
both because Diana is a mature adult whose sense of artistic self is well
developed when she encounters Stafford, and because the famous
sculptor has been disempowered by the loss of his wife, equalizing the
power relations between the two sculptors and making him profession-
ally vulnerable. For Alcott's characters, moving to Europe is essential,
both because it provides access to teachers who take their work seriously in a society in which artistic ambitions are valued highly, and because
it brings them into contact with men, both foreign and American, who
are capable of taking them seriously as artists and may be capable of
supporting them as wives. In this late story, whose unfinished state is
tantalizing, Alcott began what may have been intended as a summary
of her vision for the future of American women artists, bits and pieces
of which are sprinkled throughout her work from the previous two
decades. That Alcott understood this work as a contribution to an ongoing public debate about the boundaries of women's artistic production
is evident both from its content per se and from the characters' frequent
references to the public scrutiny their actions elicit and to their status as
pioneers.

An important difference between "Diana and Persis" and other of
Alcott's representations of artists is her rejection of the domestic-
tutelary mode and its values. The story opens with Percy's announcement that she has rejected yet another offer of marriage and is returning
to Europe to devote herself to her art. Explaining why she feels compelled to return to Europe to study, Percy provides a snapshot of the
barriers to women's serious artistic accomplishment in late-nineteenth-

century America. Although her work has won "genuine praise," Percy feels that it is more flash than substance:

"I have not *earned* my success, it came by accident. My work is not thoroughly good, only striking; for I aimed high and audacity always tells at first; but when the novelty of style wears off the poverty of the material will show. I know I *can* do better if I can only get more criticism and less praise; find the right atmosphere, the right inspiration, and really do my best."[45]

Percy's analysis of her success implies that the American art establishment is not interested in nurturing promising young female artists by providing the kind of serious criticism necessary to produce high-quality work. Percy's feeling that she gets too much praise and not enough criticism echoes Rebecca Harding Davis's frequent requests that her editor, James T. Fields, forward "intelligent criticism" of her work rather than "sugary reviews."[46] And the "right atmosphere" in which women artists can be challenged rather than be pandered to, Alcott suggests, can only be found in Europe, where they can be free of the persistent expectation that women's art support the domestic ethos.

Although Alcott's own career had conformed to that expectation despite her desire to be a seriously literary artist, Alcott emphatically rejects this assumption on behalf of her characters. Showing Diana her latest painting, of a lark in flight, Percy asks her friend whether the foreground needs to be more clearly defined, explaining that

"Grandmamma said it tired her to think the poor lark had no place to rest in, because no bird that flies is without a nest of some sort, and sings the sweeter for it."

"Pretty sentiment, but the picture is better without it. Anyone can paint a nest but few a sky like that. . . ."

"Thanks. Grandma admired it very much but said, 'If you mean a spirit paint one, my dear, but if you want that bird to be happy give her a comfortable nest full of little responsibilities, for the highest flyers need a home and that lark for all its twittering has got to drop sometimes since it cannot live in the clouds.'" (388)

Representing the persistence of antebellum standards for judging women's art, the grandmother views the painting as a social text rather than an artistic effort. Her literal-minded fear that the bird will be tired, and her thinly veiled advice that her high-flying granddaughter give up living in the clouds and settle down to marriage, a home, and children to fill her "nest" are all familiar responses to women's artistic production, responses for which Alcott clearly has little use. Instead, the prevailing opinion is Diana's—a member of a new class of a women artists who consider their own and their colleagues' work purely in terms of its aesthetic values—who urges her friend: "'Follow the instinct that takes you away from all sickly sentiment before you disgrace yourself'"(388). To fear the contagion of "sickly sentiment" is to distance oneself from the feminine tradition and domestic ethos of an earlier era, though not, as Diana and Persis's relationship reveals, from the friendship and support of women. The two artists' conversation marks the birth of a new generation of women artists whose personal concerns remain similar to those of their foremothers, but whose approach to their art has undergone a profound shift. And for these artists, the only way to get "away" from outdated conceptions of women's artistic production requires physically removing oneself from the "contagion" and seeking the "right atmosphere [and] right inspiration" that can be found only in Europe.

In a chapter devoted to Percy's letters to Diana, who remains behind until she is "ready" for Europe, the painter describes her life in Paris, where she joins a community of young, single English and American women, all dedicated to their work (384). They attend classes daily, paint and draw from live models, live together in small apartments under cooperative domestic arrangements that require minimal housekeeping, and interact freely with their male peers and teachers. Leaving the U.S., Alcott suggests, is essential if women artists are to free themselves from the dominant model of female artistic production and its dual pillars of domesticity and self-sacrifice. The only kinds of sacrifices these women make are for their art. Although as the site of traditional values and the home to the Old Masters Europe threatens to stifle female artistic ambition, as it did to Hawthorne's Hilda, Alcott clearly believes that, under the right circumstances, women's artistic endeavors can prosper in Europe. Percy's letters indicate that Paris is liberating not only because of the practical benefits it provides, but because the very atmosphere is saturated with dedication to and appreciation of artistic work. Percy tells Diana that "the earnestness I find here is most contagious and one cannot take hold of painting superficially when everybody is intent on doing his or her very best. Art pervades the air, everyone paints, all the talk is of pictures" (398). Having fled the "contagion" of domesticity and sentimentality, Percy is happily surrounded by the "contagious" enthusiasm of a continent in which the artistic aspirations of both men and women are valued highly. Whereas at home Percy complained of having "too many pleasures to distract me, too many temptations to let my art go and do as other women do" (386), in Paris she is surrounded by thousands of artists, all fighting for their chance at "glory" (398). Percy's emphasis on the European respect for and tolerance of dedication to one's art alludes to the common view that the United States lacks the kind of broad-based support required for the production of high art, both because of its dedication to industry and material success, and because of its long-standing suspicion of art as potentially immoral. Versions of both arguments were frequently cited as evidence for both the need to produce a national art and the difficulty of doing so. And for women artists, these barriers are compounded by the assumptions about women's inherent inability to produce serious original art, which continued to dominate the American cultural scene until the end of the nineteenth century.

But it is the less-obvious manifestations of gendered barriers to women's artistic activity, such as the expectation of proper feminine behavior, that, Alcott suggests, may be most limiting to aspiring artists. In an indignant letter to Diana, Percy describes her own and her roommates' outraged response to a column by an American correspondent in Paris attacking the relatively new practice of women living alone while they studied abroad, and painting from live models, often in mixed-gender classes. Percy's response reveals that she understands herself and her colleagues as occupying the front lines of a battleground over the future of all American women artists. After rejecting the notion that the appropriate subjects of women's art are limited to "flowers or still life," Percy rebuts the argument that American women artists reflect poorly on their homeland (399). She writes indignantly that she "had rather the French judged us by these brave, rightminded women [who attend the men's classes] than by the frivolous creatures who bring discredit on the name of American girls by their wild pranks and empty heads" (399). This comment suggests that what is at stake in the women's European sojourn is not only individual freedom, but the power to shape the role American women artists are expected to play both at home and abroad. This public role is clearly expressed in Percy's instructions to Diana to "read my protest to all our mates and tell them not to be daunted but to come on, and do their best for every success helps us up" (399). The last comment confirms Percy's acute awareness of both the scrutiny leveled at the pioneering women and of the psychological and public importance of their success. A sojourn in Europe, in Alcott's view, provides not a permanent escape from confining gender roles and a limited public commitment to fine art, but an opportunity to challenge and improve those conditions.

Alcott also holds up for scrutiny another common assumption about women's artistic efforts, that even when they are free to study, their work is inherently inferior to that of their male colleagues, as evidenced by the fact that women received "no medals at the Salon" during Percy's first year abroad (398). In a letter to Diana Percy wonders: "How can we when hitherto we were not allowed to study at the life schools yet expected to do as well in a third of the time and with half the help men have. How few of them get prizes with all their chances. Wait a little, Messieurs, give us a few years of equal teaching, equal opportunities and see what we will do" (399). Alcott immediately clarifies that she does not expect women to wait passively for men to provide the needed opportunities, but rather to create such opportunities through female community. To this end, Alcott introduces Mary Cassatt (thinly disguised as "Miss Cassal"), who occasionally comes to the women's studio to draw. Miss Cassal has both "real genius" and money, which she uses "nobly, not only in helping herself but others" (400). Percy reports that she and Cassal have discussed a plan "[t]o get up a school for women, a studio where we can club together and have the best models and masters and a chance to show what we can do with a clear track and fair judges" (400).[47] Percy concludes this letter by responding to Diana's query about clothes, explaining that she hasn't had any new ones made since she spends all her time and money on her lessons. She then says that "I mean to prove that some women do love art better than dress," underscoring her sense of herself as the object of public scrutiny and a standard bearer for the entire community of American women artists (402).

The chapter ends with an account of Percy's first success: her teacher selects one of her pictures for submission to the Salon, and it is accepted, much to Percy's surprise. Although Percy initially insists that she does not understand why her "insignificant study" (406) receives critical acclaim and recognition, she eventually realizes that her success is the direct result of her professionalism, hard work, and commitment to an aesthetic that rejects both sentimentality and pretension: "I looked at it with new respect and saw that it *was* good, vigorous work; simple in subject and unaffectedly treated. I fancy this very simplicity is the secret of its success, for we too often attempt more than we are equal to, and so fail. It is a good lesson to me and teaches me both humility and a proper regard for patient thoroughness rather than ineffective haste"

(408–9). The painting accepted to the Salon has none of the flash and audacity of the work that earned accolades in America, but it has the quality that Percy knew she could produce with the necessary encouragement. Not only is Percy's success earned, it reflects the seriousness with which both she and her teachers treat her work—a seriousness she could not command at home.

Whereas Percy goes to Europe as a kind of test of her talent, for Diana it is a foregone conclusion that she must leave "the solaces of home" in order to live up to her artistic potential. After Percy leaves for Paris, Diana devotes herself to "laboring always with calm persistence at the purpose of her life, to reach Rome and there do the great work which should unlock the golden future to her longing soul" (391). Diana's conviction that she cannot do her "great work" until she reaches Rome is presented straightforwardly, as a truism, reflecting the widespread view that visual artists of both genders simply could not produce significant work in the United States. Expatriation is especially necessary for an artist like Diana, whose dedication to her art is complete, and whose talent is "masculine" in its power, neither qualities that can be nurtured in a country that expects its women artists to limit their subjects to "flowers or still life" and subordinate their careers to the requirement of building nests.

The "masculine" quality of Diana's talent is the focus of the fourth and final chapter of "Diana and Persis." When Diana finally deems herself "ready" for Europe, she heads for Rome, where her "ever growing ambitions, and . . . sense of power" produce an acclaimed statue (428). The central event of the chapter is a meeting between Diana and Antony Stafford, a famous sculptor and fellow expatriate whose child befriends Diana one afternoon in the Pincio. When the two artists meet it becomes apparent that Diana has acquired a significant reputation of her own by virtue of her sculpture of "Saul," and Stafford asks Diana's permission to visit her and the statue. While she waits for Stafford to pay the promised visit, Diana ruminates on the difference between her work and that of other women:

> She pined to learn his opinion of her statue, for if *he* praised it she would be satisfied. She knew its faults, but she also knew its power, and felt that few women had dared, or if daring had succeeded in doing such bold work as this. Strength had been her aim, not sentiment nor beauty. These women can and have expressed in many shapes with varying success. But power in visible form and undeniable truth is rare

from men's hands, almost unknown from women's, and she thirsted to
hear from his lips whose praise was success the three words, "It is
good."

The masculine fibre in her nature demanded recognition as it does
in all strong natures, and having won it she could permit the softer side
of her character to assert itself without fearing the accusation of weakness, which she hated like a man. (436)

Having finally reached Rome, Diana is finally free to "dare" to leave the
realm of "sentiment" and "beauty" that is the province of American
women artists and produce a "bold" work of great strength and power.
Diana's unabashed desire for praise and recognition further distances
her from the stereotypically feminine qualities of humility and modesty
that female artists had long been expected to exhibit. But despite the
great daring Diana has manifested in producing the work, she requires
the approval of a male authority, and Diana's emphasis on the significance of Stafford's approval suggests that only an artist who has
achieved success in his own right, as Stafford has, can judge her work
without being threatened by its power or limited by conventional
expectations about women's art.

And indeed, Stafford responds to the statue precisely in terms of its
"masculine" power, telling Diana that he is "'glad a woman did" it
"[b]ecause it is so strong! There is virile force in this, accuracy as well as
passion—in short, genius'" (438). Stafford's respect and admiration for
the sculpture pay Diana the highest compliment one artist can give
another, and his praise for the work's masculine power of "genius" is
the highest Stafford can bestow. By focusing on the work's power and
virility Alcott is not suggesting that to succeed women must become
"masculine"; rather, she is arguing that it is not only acceptable but
desirable for women to create work that has the kind of power typically
associated with men. Like Percy's success in the Paris Salon, Diana's
achievement is not only personal, but representative of the potential
accomplishments of all women artists:

> "Few men would say that to a woman." And Diana's voice shook with
> the irrepressible emotion which showed how intense her own anxiety
> had been, how exquisite her joy at such commendation. "Few women
> give us the chance to say it. We have had sentiment enough. Power con-
> quers the proudest, and wrings the truth from the meanest. This is
> noble work, let me study it." (438)

When Stafford is finally done studying her statue he turns to Diana and "offer[s] his hand, giving hers the cordial grasp one man gives another when he says heartily, 'Comrade, well done!'" (438). For Diana, as for Alcott, being treated like a man is synonymous with being taken seriously as an artist. While a modern reader may find the praise of the masculinity of Diana's work a limited, and limiting, capitulation to essentialist conceptions of gender, I would suggest that it represents the triumph of Alcott's feminist aesthetic. For although Alcott challenged existing gender roles in her work and in her own life—she remained single, had a career, was an active supporter of women's rights, and was the first woman in Concord to register to vote in 1879—she, like most of her contemporaries, accepted nineteenth-century essentialist conceptions of "feminine" and "masculine" qualities. Allowing women to develop and be proud of their "masculine" qualities without punishing them or implying that they are desexed is, in nineteenth-century terms, a fairly radical feminist gesture. In Alcott's vision, encouraging women to produce "masculine" work is a necessary step on the path toward taking the work of American women artists seriously. And it is only by leaving the United States, where gendered conceptions of artistic production intensified after the Civil War, that Diana can accomplish her "great work."

Although the debate over expatriation was loud, the choice of expatriation was largely limited to those who belonged to the middle and upper-middle classes and had the education and economic resources to allow them to live abroad. A more pressing concern for many observers was the need for widespread art education, which, it was argued, would accomplish two, related purposes: first, exposing Americans of all classes to great art, in the form of inexpensive lithographs and public art institutions, would transform the great mass of immigrants and newly freed slaves into useful, educated citizens; second, teaching all Americans, and especially children, to recognize and produce the highest quality art (both visual and literary) would produce large numbers of talented American artists and remove American art from the province of the elite, thus producing art that reflected the recent battle to extend the American promise of liberty and equality to all. But American democratic ideals had historically been in tension with the desire to overcome the country's cultural inferiority, and that tension was heightened in the early postbellum years. On the one hand, American art was to be native—produced by and for "the people"—and original in both subject matter and execution. On the other hand, it was widely agreed that education, leisure, and wealth were required in order to produce art that would be taken seriously in European cultural centers, conditions that were available only to a small middle- and upper-middle-class elite that was predominately white, Protestant, male, college educated, and based in the urban centers of the Northeast. And these conditions were required not only to produce artists, but, just as importantly, to create an audience for their work.

In the years immediately after the Civil War the tension between the American ideal of a democratic culture and the belief that producing a "national art" required a cultured elite was heightened by the emergence of an upper class self-consciously organized around high culture, and an increasingly urgent sense of the need to produce "American" culture that was, at least in theory, reflective of America's democratic political ideals and egalitarian social ideals. As Richard Brodhead has demonstrated, the demarcation of a realm of high culture at midcentury was accompanied by the emergence of a new social elite, consisting of various "subgroups" of existing elites whose need to identify themselves as superior drew them together. That elite was defined largely in terms of its relationship to culture: "in the postbellum United States, a now-segregated high culture became a chief sign of elite status and chief weapon of elite social sway. In this period it was the [new elite class] that devoted themselves to high art and founded its social institutions. This group turned out the audience for such art and trained itself to appreciate such art. . . ."[48] At the same time, the widespread dissemination of ideas about high art and culture in the pages of the "quality journals," whose circulation increased and broadened during and after the war thanks to the spread of railroads, and the increased availability of art education and European travel, meant that more Americans from more diverse backgrounds could and did aspire to participate in the task of creating an "America of art."

The combined effect of these social, economic, and demographic changes produced a deep ambivalence among cultural observers, who simultaneously called for a democratization of culture and asserted their belief that the task of transforming the United States from "a province" into "a nation" required a certain degree of elitism.[49] Writing in the *Nation* in 1868, John DeForest outlines the contours of the dilemma facing those who would produce and support American high culture. Taking up the perennial call for the production of "The Great American Novel," DeForest surveys the literary territory and rejects numerous contemporary candidates for the title, including works by Cooper, Irving, Hawthorne, Stowe, Oliver Wendell Holmes, and Rebecca Harding Davis. He then offers four structural reasons for the failure to produce the Great American Novel: the absence of an international copyright law, which would allow works by American writers to compete fairly in the marketplace with European imports; the lack of a generally literate culture of the kind available in England, which DeForest believes contributes to the production of good, but not great, books by large numbers of well-educated but not great writers, and a small number of exceptional ones; the rapid pace of change that characterizes American life, which, DeForest argues, is incompatible with producing serious literary art (a view shared by Higginson and others); and, finally, the social and geographic fragmentation of American culture, which means that there is neither an obvious subject of the Great American Novel nor a single audience for it. Although the existence of a fixed, stable elite is diametrically opposed to American ideals, it is precisely such an elite in England, DeForest argues, that produces both a body of high-quality literature and the audience for it:

> Hundreds of years ago English aristocracy assumed the spiritual nature which it holds with little change to the present day. It had made its code of honor; it had established its relations with the mass of the nation; it had become the model for all proper Englishmen. At this time it is a unit of social expression throughout the kingdom. A large class of people go up to London at the same season, go into the country at the same season, lead very nearly the same lives, have the same ideas and tastes. There you have something fixed to paint; there you have the novelist's sitter; there you have his purchaser. . . . Wealthy, it pays high prices for books; anxious to be amused, it buys them freely. For such a sitter who would not, if possible, learn to paint well. [50]

DeForest's concern that economic pressures, lack of education, and provincialism are inherently incompatible with the postbellum project of producing the "America of art" was widely shared, but he is unusual in his open praise of the British class system. The social stability provided by the English aristocracy—a single, national elite—is required in order to transform the United States from a collection of provinces into a nation, DeForest believes, citing as additional evidence the paucity of great literature in "divided Germany" and "distracted Italy," which he attributes to the fact that they, like the United States, are "nation[s] of provinces."[51] DeForest is remarkable for his unabashed praise of the British social system, but he is not alone in his belief that an educated elite of some kind is necessary for the production of the "America of art."

Higginson's public rhetoric on the question of the proper role of a cultured elite in a democracy is more muted than DeForest's, and he attempts to reconcile his sincere belief in the American democratic ideal with his conviction that artists and writers are in a class of their own by insisting that artists cannot remove themselves from "the people." Although he bemoans the fact that America still lacks "the rudiments of a literary class," Higginson disagrees with DeForest's diagnosis of the reasons for this:[52]

> The chief discouragement of American literature does not seem to me to lie in the want of an international copyright law, as some think, nor in the fact that other pursuits bid higher prices. . . . Nor is it from the want of libraries and collections; for those are beginning to exist, and nature exists always. The true, great want is of an atmosphere of sympathy in intellectual aims. An artist can afford to be poor, but not to be companionless. It is not well that he should feel pressing on him, in addition to his own doubt whether he can achieve a certain work, the weight of the public doubt whether it be worth achieving.[53]

For Higginson, all that American artists require is a supportive atmosphere and some like-minded companionship. And those conditions can be achieved, Higginson argues elsewhere in the essay, through the development of institutions for the promotion of culture, chief among them universities, which are, of course, training grounds for the elite segments of society.[54] Having diagnosed the central barrier to American cultural production as social indifference to the artist's vocation, Higginson turns to artists themselves and reminds them of their responsibility as members of a democratic society. He observes that unlike European and British literature, which is clearly aimed at the educated elites, American literature must appeal to the masses:

> every American writer must address himself to a vast audience, possessing the greatest quickness and common-sense, but with little culture; and he must command their attention as he may. This has some admirable results: one must put some life into what he writes, or his thirty million auditors will go to sleep; he must write clearly, or they will cease to follow him; he must keep clear of pedantry and unknown

tongues, or they will turn to some one who can address them in Eng-lish. On the other hand, the same conditions tempt one to accept a low standard of execution, to substitute artifice for art, and to disregard the more permanent verdict of more select tribunals.[55]

In laying the blame for America's failure to produce a significant high culture at the feet of both artists and their audiences Higginson attempts to imagine a way out of the familiar claims about culture in America: that Americans were too poorly educated, and too consumed with materialism, to support high quality art, and that its self-proclaimed high artists were too insular in their subject matter and style and too disdainful of the popular to appeal to the "vast audience" of Americans. But although Higginson here attempts to convince his read-ers that appealing to 30 million uneducated readers keeps American writers honest, his anxiety about the pressure to write for the lowest common denominator and ignore the "permanent verdict of more select tribunals" is palpable. Stopping short of the blanket rejection of popu-larity that is at the heart of his call for treating "Literature as an Art," which appeared a few months after "A Plea for Culture," Higginson attempts to walk the tightrope of retaining his democratic credentials while expressing an essentially antidemocratic view of culture.[56] To that end, Higginson concludes his article "Americanism in Literature," writ-ten two years later, with this rousing endorsement: "I affirm that demo-cratic society, the society of the future, enriches and does not impover-ish human life, and gives more, not less, material for literary art. Distributing culture through all classes, it diminishes class-distinction and develops distinctions of personal character."[57] In this ideal, culture has a democratizing effect and democracy produces culture.

But, as the author of "Sculpture in the United States" understood, a truly American art, produced by and for the democratic masses, required widespread art education. The central obstacles to such educa-tion, in the author's view, are the Romantic conception of genius and the related mystification about how artists actually produce their art:

> Reform in art . . . depends upon education. False and vague ideas
> regarding the imitative arts are so common and so little resisted that
> progress must be necessarily slow. The vulgar idea of genius is that it
> achieves without effort and without consciousness of its means; that in
> art it evokes statues from marble and pictures from pigments by some
> unknown process and without labor. This is a mischievous and hinder-
> ing notion. Though art is sometimes called a sport, the definition is

inadequate; and the science of art is certainly a matter of labor and patience.[58]

Declaring that art is a "science" and emphasizing the systematic effort required to acquire its basic tenets transforms art from the mysterious provenance of a select few to a field of study accessible to all Americans, especially those who possess the cardinal virtues of "labor and patience." Understanding that the most significant barrier to the democratization of art is its mysterious aura, the author is particularly concerned with demystifying art: "Confused and misty ideas in the popular mind regarding art seem unnecessary, if the subject be approached in a common-sense way, and treated like any other science."[59] For as long as the "the popular mind" considers art something alien and distant, there can be neither an indigenous American art nor an audience for it. Aware of the popular misconception that great artists are born, not made, the author insists: "Imagination is not injured by a proper training of the eye and hand; on the contrary, it can only be revealed and cultivated in imitative art by these means."[60] Such training, which should not be limited to the small, self-selecting group of aspiring artists, but made available to all Americans through the public school system, will "add greatly to future culture and enjoyment of life." The benefit of such widespread training is twofold: it will produce a much larger group of native artists, and it will help develop an educated audience to appreciate their work, thus helping to reverse the tide of expatriation that the author bemoaned at the beginning of the essay:

> Endowing the public with power to appreciate what is now obscure in the best art, and also to detect blunders in means and execution, it would soon do away with meaningless puffery, and obstinate fault finding, substituting for these kind and careful criticism. Then the great power of artists like Greenough, Crawford, Story, and Powers would be utilized, and sculpture could no longer be called an anachronism in America.[61]

In this, the essay's concluding, paragraph, the author issues a call for the democratization of all aspects of the visual arts in America. By making "drawing and modelling . . . one of the elementary branches of knowledge" in the public schools, art education becomes a standard part of the American child's training into citizenship. And teaching American citizens to create, appreciate, and critique art will remove art from the rarefied realm of "genius" and obscurity and speed the development of both a national art and an audience to appreciate it.

The idea that art could be democratized through education is challenged in Constance Fenimore Woolson's "The Street of the Hyacinth" (1882), which reveals the tension inherent in expecting elite experts to participate in the project of democratizing American art. For, as Woolson demonstrates, it is not only the "public" that must change its conception of art, but perhaps more importantly, the cultural authorities who remain both the standard setters for and the educators of that public. But transforming art education, creation, and appreciation from the province of experts into a democratic endeavor open to all is a project postbellum cultural authorities participated in reluctantly, at best.

The short story centers on the encounter between a poorly educated but ambitious young painter from "the West," and a prominent American art critic living in Rome.[62] The protagonist of "The Street of the Hyacinth," Ettie Macks, has sold her farm and arrived in Rome, overdressed mother in tow, expecting that the art critic, Raymond Noel, will superintend her education. The source of Ettie's expectation seems to be simply Noel's status as a respected art critic whose writings are widely distributed in the United States. Ettie's understanding that Noel's writing serves a public educational function is made explicit early in the story's first scene, when Ettie informs Noel that since his work, which is "scattered about in the magazines and papers" (174), is not easy for someone living in Tuscolee Falls to obtain, she "'feel[s] a friendly interest in your taking measures to introduce your writings into the community where I lived. It is a very intelligent community. Naturally, a writer wants his articles read. What else does he write them for?' 'Perhaps a little for his own entertainment,' suggested her listener" (172). While Noel's rejection of Ettie's supposition that he is looking for an audience, and his subsequent assertion that "'[s]uccessfully to entertain one's self—that is one of the great successes of life'" (172), are slightly tongue-in-cheek, they do reflect a fundamental gap between Ettie's and Noel's understandings of the cultural function of the art critic. Tuscolee Falls is exactly the kind of place that would benefit from the systematic art education called for by the author of "Sculpture in the United States": it is a small farming town in the "West" where vulgar mid-Victorian standards of taste prevail, if Ettie's mother's brightly colored clothes are anything to judge by; where even the landed gentry, such as it is, has little leisure for cultural pursuits; and where the highest level of artistic education available is that provided by the occasional visiting art teacher and the local Young Ladies Seminary. But Noel resists the notion

that he might be interested in helping Ettie bring his art criticism to Tuscolee Falls. Regardless of the reasons for his resistance—we never find
out if Noel thinks Ettie's townspeople are too stupid to understand his
work or simply too uneducated—the arrogance of his refusal is obvious. His half-joking suggestion that he might be writing only for his
own entertainment implies that keeping himself amused is a better use
of his time than educating his readers. In dismissing Ettie's suggestion
that he might wish to participate in educating the people of Tuscolee
Falls, Noel insists on his status as an authority speaking for and to a
small educated audience and resists the democratizing implications of
the fact that his writing is widely distributed in the United States. This
exchange reveals the tensions at the heart of the postbellum attempts to
make art education the purview of public education rather than the preserve of an elite minority.

Indeed, Ettie understands the responsibility of the cultural authority quite differently: by writing art criticism and allowing it to be widely
distributed, Noel is stepping into the role of teacher, and it is that role
she expects him to play in her career. When Ettie first presents herself to
Noel, she explains that it was his belief that "no one could do well in
painting who had not seen and studied the old pictures" in Europe that
prompted her to sell the farm and leave the United States (174).
Although they have neither met nor corresponded before her arrival in
Rome, Ettie expects Noel to evaluate her paintings, help her choose a
teacher, and act as her guide through Rome's art galleries. "I haven't
any hesitation in asking" she explains, "because I am sure you will feel
interested in a case like mine, and because it was your writings really
that brought me here, you know" (174). Ettie's certainty that Noel will
"feel interested" in her presumably stems from the fact that she is an
aspiring American artist, and, as such, automatically of interest to a cultural authority like Noel. Ettie assumes that Noel will be interested in
her because she expects him to understand that, in the absence of any
kind of organized system for art education and mentoring, he has a
responsibility to those of his readers who are deeply influenced by his
writing and see him as a mentor and guide. She is taken aback by Noel's
refusal of this role, and puzzled by the fact that the lively intelligence
and "interest" evident in his writing seems to missing from the man
himself:

> "I desire but one thing, and that is to have you guide me. . . . Why, think
> of it: here I have come all this long distance, bringing mother, too, just
> to study, and to see you. I shall study hard; I have a good deal of

perseverance. It took a good deal to get here in the first place, for we are poor. But I don't mind that at all; the only thing I should mind, the only thing that would take my courage away, would be to have you desert me. In all the trouble that I thought might happen, I assure you, I never once thought of *that*, Mr. Noel. I thought, of course, you would be interested. Why, in your books you are all interest. Are you different from your books?" (179)

Ettie's assumption that the "interest" Noel expresses in his books—presumably in the need for developing American artists—would translate into a willingness to put himself out for an actual aspiring artist who appears on his doorstep is naïve, of course, but it stems from the realities of the cultural context of the 1870s, in which the story is set. Given the ubiquity of writing on the subject of cultural nationalism in postbellum periodicals and newspapers, and the absence of any system for widespread art education, Ettie's expectation that Noel will "of course" help her seems not unreasonable. Indeed, Ettie's belief that she can make these demands on Noel makes sense only when they are placed in that context. At their first meeting in Ettie's apartment she chastises Noel for taking "so long—three days" to answer her summons; when Noel pleads previous engagements, Ettie responds, "Yes, but this was a little different, wasn't it? This was something important—not like an invitation to lunch or dinner, or the usual idle society talk" (171). Ettie's response is "quite in earnest," and her belief that beginning her artistic training is "something important" that bears no delay is not merely egocentrism (though it is that too), but a reflection of the tone of much of the published writing on the subject, which depicted the need to develop American culture as crucial to the task of postwar reconstruction. The belief that Noel must share the national burden that Ettie has shouldered in coming to Rome is made explicit later in this same meeting, when Ettie explains to Noel that she is acting upon the idea that "in the lives of all—almost all—artists, there comes a time when they have to live on hope and their own pluck more than upon anything tangible that the present has to offer" (174), an idea she has clearly picked up from her reading; she concludes simply: "They have to take that risk. Well, I have taken it; I took it when we left America. And now I will tell you what it is I want from *you*" (174). As far as Ettie can tell, she has done her part by rising to the challenge posed by the myriad calls for the development of American art and artists. She has risked the security of both herself and her mother in the interest of pursuing an artistic career; it seems quite self-evident to her that, as an art authority whose writings prompted her to "take that risk," Noel has a part to play in her future.

The other assumption underlying Ettie's behavior is that the American work ethic applies to the realm of art just as it does to any other. In this she seems to have absorbed the critique of the "mischievous and hindering" idea that genius does not require work; indeed, Ettie's capacity for hard work is commented on throughout the story, both by Ettie herself and by the narrator: she has memorized Noel's art criticism before arriving in Rome; once there she intends to "devote [herself] entirely to [her] work" (175); "study hard" and apply "perseverance" (179) to the project at hand; she is willing to "study up to" Noel (186); and, when he finally does start teaching her, she applies "systematic industry" to her lessons and "work[s] hard" at learning everything Noel has to teach her (188). The autobiography Ettie narrates to Noel underscores her confidence in the dual pillars of the American success story: hard work and "determination": "'I have always had a great deal of ambition; by that I mean that I did not see why things that had once been done could not be done again. It seemed to me that the point was—just determination. And then, of course, I always had the talent'" (173). Ettie's belief that she has "the talent" has been shored up by her mother, who has not only kept all the pictures Ettie drew as a child, but seems to have brought them to Rome. "'I can show them to you'" Ettie explains to Noel, pointing out, in case he had missed the implications, "'It is just like all the biographies, you know. They always begin in childhood, and astonish the family'" (173). Ettie here frames her narrative in terms of the generic expectations of the biographical sketches of successful Americans that appeared regularly in the nineteenth-century American periodical press, complete with the requisite account of childhood precociousness. Ettie works very hard to accomplish her cherished goal, and she has clearly internalized the belief that hard work and "dedication" will ensure her success. What she has not bargained for is that talent, taste, and aesthetic standards are susceptible neither to hard work and determination nor to democratic debate.

Although Ettie seeks out Noel precisely because he is an art authority, she has no qualms about the fact that her aesthetic judgments differ from his. Indeed, Ettie expects that Noel will engage her in a dialogue on those issues on which they disagree. Very early in their acquaintance Ettie tells Noel that she has a history of disagreeing with art authorities, and she seems to expect the art world to be much like the political realm: an arena where ideas that one disagrees with can be either ignored or debated. Ettie first encounters an art authority whose opinions differ from hers before she leaves the United States; after completing her studies at the Young Ladies Seminary near Tuscolee Falls, where "everyone," including Ettie herself, "was astonished at [her] progress" and "[a]ll sorts of things are prophesied out there about [her] future," Ettie had taken lessons with a visiting art teacher from New York (173). A consumptive young man visiting Tuscolee Falls for his health, the teacher "wasn't of much use to [Ettie] in actual work" because "[h]is ideas were completely different from those of my other teachers, and, indeed, from my own" (174). Ettie ignored most of this teacher's advice, though she did take his recommendation to read Noel's "art-articles," and went to great lengths to track down and read everything Noel had written. But, as Ettie informs Noel early in their acquaintance, although his ideas "made a great impression upon" her, "I doubt . . . whether we should ever entirely agree" (174). To her surprise, Noel makes no effort to change her mind, simply conceding, "That is very probable, Miss Macks" (174). Ettie finds Noel's reply "odd," observing to her mother later, "Now, any one would suppose that he would have answered that he would try to make me agree, or something like that. Instead, he just gave it right up without trying! But I expect he sees how independent I am, and that I don't intend to *reflect any* one" (174). But Ettie is wrong: Noel "gave it right up without trying" to change Ettie's mind not because he understands that she has that quintessentially American quality of independence, but because he doesn't care to make the effort that would be required in order to change her mind, nor does he care to find out why Ettie disagrees with him. What Ettie doesn't realize is that, as an arbiter of cultural standards, Noel is hugely confident in his judgments, which he knows are shared by his peers and colleagues, and sees no need to convince Ettie that he is right. He expects her to simply accept his views as true.

That expectation is explicitly challenged later in the story, when Ettie finally gets Noel to serve as her guide and teacher in the Roman art galleries. During their first walk Ettie "gave Noel a close attention, almost always a comprehension, but seldom agreement. Her disagreement she did not express in words, but he could read it in her eyes" (184). When Noel asks for her frank opinion of a number of the pictures they have just seen, Ettie does not hesitate: A Raphael double portrait is "'very ugly'"; a Sebastian del Piombo portrait of Andrea Doria, is "'uglier still'"; a Velasquez is "'Ugliest of all'"; and two large works by Claude Lorraine are "'Rather pretty; but insipid'" and lack "'any reality or meaning'" (185). In rejecting these famous paintings, which Noel has designated as "the best" (184) in the gallery, Ettie challenges both Noel's opinions and the very canon of art itself, largely on the basis of her own standards of beauty. Ettie's approach to evaluating the art she sees in Rome would have undoubtedly pleased the author of "Sculpture in the United States": she is not intimidated by the mystique of art, but rather systematic and open minded—her list of twenty galleries to visit is much broader than Noel's, who "had supposed there were but nine in Rome" (186); she is uncowed by conventional standards; and she forms her opinions systematically, collecting and evaluating the evidence available to her, which includes both her own opinions and those of Raymond Noel. She does not shrink from expressing opinions that are different from those of the expert whom she admires deeply, because she views their relationship as essentially democratic. In this and subsequent visits to Rome's art galleries Ettie never loses her confidence in her own aesthetic opinions, though she records every word Noel says and studies his pronouncements until she can recite them verbatim. Puzzled by the apparent contradiction, Noel wonders "'Why do you care for my opinions . . . when you do not agree with them?'"

> "Why do I care? Because they are yours, of course."
> "Then you think I know?"
> "I am sure you do."
> "But it follows, then, that you do not."
> "Yes; and there is where my work comes in; I have got to study up to you. I am afraid it will take a long time, won't it?"
> "That depends upon you. It would take very little if you would simply accept noncombatively."
> "Without being convinced? That I could never do."
> "You want to be convinced against your will?"
> "No; my will itself must be convinced to its lowest depth." (186)

Ettie's strong desire to be "convinced" rather than simply accept the authoritative opinions Noel offers is at odds with her equally strong belief that Noel is an authority who "know[s]" while she "do[es] not," and that it is up to her to "study up to" Noel. But for all her respect for Noel's knowledge and standing as an authority, Ettie is unwilling to suspend her quintessentially American independence and "*reflect any one*," even Noel. That tension is irreducible, because it encapsulates the struggle between democratizing culture and preserving cultural authority that is at the heart of the postbellum invocation of the Civil War— with its retrospective scripting as a struggle to extend principles of equality and democracy to all Americans—as the rationale for the urgent project of national cultural development.

Noel and Ettie's relationship is a microcosm of these tensions, as Ettie's determination to apply the American qualities of hard work and independent judgment to her career runs up against Noel's unbending aesthetic standards and his sense of himself as a cultural authority whose judgment is never in doubt. Ettie's artistic aspirations fall victim to this clash. Although she works hard for over a year, Ettie does not become an artist because she comes to accept the assessment of no fewer than five cultural authorities that she has no talent. The process of accepting this judgment is prolonged unnecessarily because she ignores the views of the first authority she encounters—the consumptive young art teacher from New York—and the next two authorities whose opinions she seeks, Raymond Noel and Horace Jackson, the English art teacher to whom Noel refers Ettie, both lie to her. Both men's lies are lies of omission and evasion motivated by Ettie's gender and, in Noel's case, by his unwillingness to fully accept the role of public educator that is engendering by his career as a widely published art critic. Initially, Noel wonders "whether it would be better to decline clearly and in so many words the office she had thrust upon him, or trust to time to effect the same without an open refusal. He decided upon the latter course; it seemed the easier, and also the kinder to her" (176). When Ettie finally forces Noel to look at her paintings, he again avoids telling Ettie the unpleasant truth—that in his opinion her paintings "were all extremely and essentially bad"— because he believes that

> where women were concerned, a certain amount of falsity was some-
> times indispensable. There were occasions where a man could no more
> tell the bare truth to a woman than he could strike her; the effect would
> be the same as a blow. He was an excellent evader when he chose to
> exert himself, and he finally got away from the little high-up apartment
> without disheartening or offending its young mistress, and without
> any very black record of direct untruth. . . . (181)

Noel's belief that that he had managed to avoid "direct untruth" notwithstanding, he has clearly lied to Ettie insofar as he fails to tell her that her work is, in his view, utterly without promise. The gap between Ettie's expectations that she can trust Noel because he is an authority and the art critic's actual behavior is attributable both to Noel's unwillingness to ignore the gender conventions that lead him to believe that dealing with women requires "a certain amount of falsity," and to his inability to live up to the responsibility that accompanies his status as an American cultural authority. The third authority Ettie consults is Horace Jackson, who fails to tell Ettie the truth about her talent because he falls in love with her. Noel referred Ettie to Jackson because he has "a reputation of being the most incorruptibly honest teacher in Rome," and Noel hopes that he will deliver the unpleasant news that Noel himself wishes to avoid (183). When he pays Jackson a visit to see what he thinks of his new pupil, Noel is somewhat surprised to discover that Jackson "seemed to think that Miss Macks had talent" and that he had "turned her back to the alphabet" and was willing to "see what she could do" "in time" (183). Despite his surprise, and his awareness that Ettie has a tendency to put her entire faith in the hands of the authorities she respects, Noel does not confront Jackson. When Ettie next shows him her work, months later, Noel "saw at once that the Englishman had not kept his word. He had not put her back upon the alphabet, or, if he had done so, he had soon released her, and allowed her to pursue her own way again. The original faults were as marked as ever. In his opinion all was essentially bad" (190). But Noel neither confronts Jackson nor tells Ettie his true opinion. Conscious that he has again abdicated his responsibility, Noel, who is leaving Rome for the summer, assuages "a little stir at the edges of his conscience" by promising to send Ettie books "that are rather good," which he hopes will do the job for him (192). They don't.

When Ettie and Noel next meet, two years have passed, during which Ettie received a proposal from the art teacher, Jackson, who subsequently died, and has finally learned what both Noel and Jackson have believed all along—that she has no future as an artist. This realization does not come easily: it takes the brutal honesty of the teacher she turns to after Jackson's death, who tells her that she "had not a particle of talent; that all [her] work was insufferably bad," and of the second teacher she seeks out, who confirms his colleague's assessment. To Noel's observation that "'Bellot [the first teacher] is always a brute!'" (196) Ettie responds simply: "'If he told the truth brutally, it was still the truth; and it was the truth I needed'" (197). Bellot is the first cultural authority Ettie has encountered who treats her as an adult capable of hearing the truth rather than as a child in need of "kindness" and protection. Although Ettie no longer "feels bitterly towards [Noel]" she makes no bones about the fact that she holds him responsible for his lies: "'My hopes were false ones, and had been so from the beginning; you knew that they were, yet you did not set me right'" (196).

Although it is possible to read this story as an indictment of the male-dominated art scene's inability to appreciate and nurture female art, as other critics have, Woolson gives us no grounds to judge whether Ettie has talent that is overlooked or whether she has mistaken desire for ability. The assessment of Ettie's mother, Mrs. Spurr, her teachers at the Young Ladies' Seminary, the people of Tuscolee Falls, and Ettie herself is pitted against the unanimous view of five cultural authorities, and the reader is left to determine whose opinions to accept.[63] There is no doubt that the aesthetic standards of Tuscolee Falls lack refinement: Ettie's mother's speech is "voluble" and uncultured; she calls Noel "Mr. No-ul" and thanks him for being "real kind" to her daughter (191). Her color is extremely "high"—due to her girth and asthmatic condition—and her clothes, which are commented on repeatedly, do nothing to minimize either: "her high color . . . was surmounted by an imposing cap, adorned with large bows of scarlet ribbon; a worsted shawl, of the hue known as 'solferino,' decked her shoulders; under her low-necked collar reposed a bright blue necktie, its ends embroidered in red and yellow; and her gown was of a vivid dark green. But although her colors swore at each other, she seemed amiable" (191). Ettie herself dresses much more conservatively, but she lacks what art authorities view as an artist's eye. When he meets Ettie by chance one morning while she is shopping for vegetables, Noel, who "was very fond of the old streets" of Rome, falls into step with her, "curious to see whether she would notice the colors and outlines that made their picturesqueness. She noticed nothing but the vegetable-stalls, and talked of nothing but her pictures" (180). Ettie's greatest, indeed only, strength as an artist seems to be originality. When she shows Noel the work she has been doing under Jackson's direction, he points to the painting he "thought the worst" and asks what the Englishman thinks of it. "'He admires the idea greatly,'" Ettie replies; "'he thinks it very original. He says that my strongest point is originality.' . . . 'He means—ah—originality of subject?' 'Oh yes; my execution is not much yet. But that will come in time. Of course, the subject, the idea, is the important thing; the execution is secondary'" (190). As she talks, it dawns on Ettie that Noel disagrees with her view that "the execution is secondary" to the subject matter, and she quotes at length from one of his articles to that effect, observing, "'It would be dreadful for me if you were right!' . . . 'I thought you believed that I was always right,' . . . 'You are—in everything but that'" (192). Noel's view that originality of subject cannot compensate for poor execution is the dominant one, and it is the one that Ettie eventually comes to accept. But Woolson leaves the reader no way to judge whether Ettie is a highly original American artist whose talent has been lost because the male-dominated institutions and cultural authorities are incapable of nurturing an artist whose vision is different from theirs, or whether Jackson's praise for Ettie's "originality" is simply his euphemistic way of avoiding telling the truth to someone with whom he is in love.

But to read "The Street of the Hyacinth" primarily as a tale of Ettie's victimization is to miss the larger cultural implications of Woolson's story. At stake in Woolson's story is the struggle over the competing demands of the postbellum impulse to democratize American culture and the long-standing view that educated elites were essential to the creation of the "America of art." The postbellum conversation about democratizing art that took place in articles such as those written by the fictional Noel produced a generation of young people who, like Ettie Macks and Davis's Marcia, left the tiny backwaters of their birth and headed to big cities and even to Europe, armed only with the conviction that they had talent and the encouragement they gleaned from reading numerous essays about the nature of art and genius in the periodicals of the day. But without institutional validation of some kind, a desire to create art and a conviction that one has talent are simply not enough. The cultural authorities who encounter these young artists fail to live up to the role that they had been asked to play in the postbellum cultural project of developing American art, both because they are intent on protecting their own power and privilege and because creating art is not, finally, a democratic endeavor. The irreducible tension at the heart of the postbellum project of cultural nationalism is that institutions, standards, and experts are essential for American high art to exist. And these institutions, and the people who populate them, are, Woolson and Davis demonstrate, inherently conservative and resistant to work that fails to conform to established standards and expectations.

Melville called upon Americans to "foster all originality, though, at first, it be crabbed and ugly as our own pine knots," and cultural observers frequently celebrated originality as essential to both genius and postbellum American culture, but "Marcia," "'Miss Grief'," and "The Street of the Hyacinth" suggest that the postbellum desire to democratize art was fundamentally incompatible with the critical establishment's inability to support highly original but "crabbed and ugly" work produced by women.

This litter of dead and failed female artists serves as a counterpoint to the soaring rhetoric of cultural nationalism that filled the pages of the nation's elite publications in the two decades after the Civil War. The postbellum project of producing an "America of art" was essentially contradictory: authorized by the Civil War, yet destroyed by the demands of wartime patriotism; designed to nationalize a collection of provinces, but undermined by the persistence of provincialism; defined as essentially native, yet requiring expatriation; conceived as the expression of democracy, but dependent on increasingly rigid classifications of culture and class. Writing by American women underscores these contradictions and, at the same time, articulates, even if through negative examples, a vision that insists on American women artists' full participation in the project of producing American "national" culture. Although each member of the "transitional generation" had a successful career and received considerable critical acclaim, none achieved full participation in the high literary culture of the period. Economic pressures, disagreements with James T. Fields, and her commitment to social realism all conspired to push Rebecca Harding Davis out of the elite literary culture and toward journalistic and popular writing; Louisa May Alcott's success as a children's writer and her embrace of the domestic-tutelary model of authorship barred her from producing "the American Novel";[64] Elizabeth Stuart Phelps's persistent interest in social issues such as temperance, her commitment to an ethically based aesthetic, and her public disagreement with the tenets of American high realism combined to marginalize her from the realm of high culture in the latter years of her career; and Constance Fenimore Woolson's premature death cut short the promising career of the one writer in this group who might have become, along with her friend and colleague Henry James, a central contributor to American high culture. But the failure to achieve a secure place in the ranks of those who are remembered for their role in shaping American literature in the postbellum years is less important, finally, than the fact that they understood themselves as participating in their era's central cultural endeavor. Furthermore, the fiction produced by Stowe, Evans, Davis, Alcott, Phelps, and Woolson, with its engagement with every aspect of the project of cultural nationalism itself and with female artists' place in it, was essential to the emergence of a generation of serious, self-consciously literary female writers in the late-nineteenth and early-twentieth centuries that includes Sarah Orne Jewett, Edith Wharton, and Willa Cather, among others.

It is difficult to identify any single aesthetic vision binding these writers together: Stowe and Evans both view religious faith as essential to aesthetics, and their feminist aesthetics define their own modes of work as examples of the kind of art essential to producing a national culture; Alcott seeks to preserve the category of "genius" and imagine ways that women could gain access to it, through expatriation, membership in feminist communities, and extra-market economic systems; Phelps and Davis both struggled to articulate aesthetic visions that combine social and ethical concerns with high literary art; and Woolson stresses originality and the independence of one's aesthetic judgments. But it is precisely the disparities in these visions, combined with the striking similarities in their assessments of the social, institutional, and economic barriers to women artists' success, that makes this body of writing so important, both for students of American women's literature and for historians of the literary and cultural transformations in the second half of the nineteenth century.

NOTES

Notes to Introduction

1. Fanny Fern, *Ruth Hall* (New Brunswick: Rutgers University Press, 1986), 136.

2. Louisa May Alcott, *The Journals of Louisa May Alcott*, eds. Madeleine Stern, Joel Myerson, and Daniel Shealy. (Boston: Little Brown, 1989), 92, 95.

3. Elizabeth Stuart Phelps, *Chapters from a Life* (Cambridge: Riverside, 1896), 78–79.

4. Thomas Wentworth Higginson, "A Plea for Culture," *Atlantic Monthly* (Jan. 1867), 37.

5. The term "quality journals" was widely used in the nineteenth century to denote a group of periodicals that published a mix of nonfiction and fiction, with a special emphasis on relatively rigorous pieces on literature and science. The group of "quality journals" includes the *Atlantic Monthly*, the *Nation*, the *Century*, *Harper's New Monthly*, and others that came and went over the second half of the decade. For detailed discussions of the role these magazines played in shaping American high culture during the postbellum years, see Ellery Sedgwick, *The Atlantic Monthly 1857–1909, Yankee Humanism at High Tide and Ebb* (Amherst: University of Massachusetts Press, 1994); Richard Brodhead, *The School of Hawthorne* (New York: Oxford University Press, 1986); and Brodhead, *Cultures of Letters: Scenes of Reading and Writing in Nineteenth-Century America* (Chicago: University of Chicago Press, 1993). In *Reading for Realism: The History of a U.S. Institution 1850–1910* (Durham and London: Duke University Press, 1997), Nancy Glazener identifies what she calls the "Atlantic Group" magazines, a somewhat expanded group of the "quality journals" listed here, which shared a common set of aesthetic values and cultural purposes.

6. Examples include Nathaniel Hawthorne, *The Marble Faun* (1860); Rebecca Harding Davis, "Life in the Iron Mills" (1861), *Earthen Pitchers* (1874), and "Marcia" (1876); Louisa May Alcott, *A Marble Woman, or, The Mysterious Model* (published anonymously in 1865), *Little Women* (1868), and "Diana and Persis" (an unfinished fragment, ca. 1879); Henry James, *Roderick Hudson* (1875); Elizabeth Stuart Phelps, *The Story of Avis* (1876); Helen Hunt Jackson, *Mercy Philbrick's Choice* (1876); and Constance Fenimore Woolson, "'Miss Grief'" (1880), "The Street of the Hyacinth" (1882), and "At the Château of Corinne" (1886).

7. I view these four writers as the key figures in this generation, which also includes Elizabeth Drew Stoddard (1823–1902), Helen Hunt Jackson (1830–85), Emily Dickinson (1830–86), Gail Hamilton (Mary Abigail Dodge; 1833–96), Harriet Prescott Spofford (1835–1921), Celia Thaxter (1835–94), and numerous other,

lesser-known authors, for a number of reasons: Each had a successful career that combined popular success and considerable respect from the high literary establishment; each was as prominent a public figure as a respectable woman could be during this period; and each produced numerous works that thematized the aesthetic questions central to her own career and to the cultural nationalist project of the day. I have chosen to exclude Emily Dickinson's work for the obvious reason that it was mostly unpublished during the period of this study and therefore did not participate in the public conversation about women's authorship that I trace here. I have chosen not to include Sarah Orne Jewett's (1849–1909) work because, as I will discuss below, although her lifetime coincides with that of the writers I focus on, she is widely viewed as the first American woman writer to consider herself a serious literary Artist—and to be considered so by the literary establishment. She is, in that sense, a member of the next generation of women writers, which includes Edith Wharton, Willa Cather, and others.

8. The phrase "domestic-tutelary" refers to Richard Brodhead's classification of the models of authorship available to American writers at midcentury into three categories: the high literary mode, "writing as a tutelary activity in support of the domestic ethos"; and the "industrial" or hack writer, identified with popular dime novels and story papers (*Cultures of Letters* 82). Women writing from within the domestic-tutelary model of authorship typically depicted themselves as driven to write for financial reasons; portrayed writing as an extension of domestic work; denied artistic ambition—a quality that was considered unseemly in a woman and that was inconsistent with these writers' stated intention of remaining within their own "sphere"; downplayed their achievements as accidental; and depicted themselves as mediums for a divine message rather than as originators of an aesthetic message of their own. See Ann D. Wood, "'The 'Scribbling Women' and Fanny Fern: Why Women Wrote," *American Quarterly*, Vol. 23, No. 1 (Spring 1971): 3–24; Nina Baym, "Introduction," *Woman's Fiction: A Guide to Novels by and about Women in America 1820–1870* (1978. 2nd ed. Urbana: University of Illinois Press, 1993); and Mary Kelley, *Private Woman Public Stage: Literary Domesticity in Nineteenth-Century America* (New York: Oxford University Press, 1984), chapters 5–8. The business relationships of popular women writers are the subject of Susan Coultrap-McQuin, *Doing Literary Business: American Women Writers in the Nineteenth Century* (Chapel Hill: University of North Carolina Press, 1990). In *The Artistry of Anger: Black and White Women's Literature in America, 1820–1860* (Chapel Hill and London: University of North Carolina Press, 2002), Linda Grasso complicates Kelley's model in important ways, by focusing on the ways in which antebellum women used their anger as both a motivating factor and an aesthetic strategy. As I will discuss below, the model of authorship described by Kelley, Baym, Wood, and Coultrap-McQuin and adopted, with some variations, by most white, middle-class American women writers in the antebellum era was the dominant one available to the women who are my subjects.

9. For a description of the institutional structures supporting American visual artists at midcentury, see Neil Harris, *The Artist in American Society: The Formative Years 1790–1860* (New York: George Braziller, 1966); and Roger B. Stein, *John Ruskin and Aesthetic Thought in America, 1840–1900* (Cambridge: Harvard University Press, 1967). For an overview of the literary field during the 1850s, see Brodhead, *The School of Hawthorne.*

10. Ruskin's *Modern Painters I* appeared in England in 1843 and was published in the United States in 1847; *The Seven Lamps of Architecture* appeared in 1849, and the first volume of *The Stones of Venice* in 1851. Popular anthologies of Ruskin's work began appearing within a decade. *Modern Painters* had an immediate effect on American intellectuals: both Emerson and Whitman read it shortly after it appeared, and it was widely and enthusiastically reviewed in American journals (Stein, *John Ruskin and Aesthetic Thought*, 40–44). For an analysis of the appeal of Ruskin's writing for American intellectuals seeking an alternative to the Scottish Common Sense approach, see Stein, chapters 1–5.

For general discussions of the Common Sense view of art and its effect on both literature and the visual arts, see Neil Harris, *The Artist in American Society* (New York: George Braziller, 1966) and Terence Martin, *The Instructed Vision: Scottish Common Sense Philosophy and the Origins of American Fiction* (Bloomington: Indiana University Press, 1961). For the transcendentalists' role in modifying the assumptions governing antebellum artistic production, see Lawrence Buell, *New England Literary Culture, From Revolution through Renaissance* (Cambridge: Cambridge University Press, 1986).

11. The most comprehensive recent discussion of the emergence of an American literary tradition in conjunction with the marketplace is Cathy Davidson, *Revolution and the Word: The Rise of the Novel in America* (New York: Oxford University Press, 1986). Numerous other scholars have analyzed the impact of the marketplace on antebellum authors and authorship. Key studies include Michael T. Gilmore, *American Romanticism and the Marketplace* (Chicago: University of Chicago Press, 1985); William G. Rowland Jr., *Literature and the Marketplace: Romantic Writers and Their Audiences in Great Britain and the United States* (Lincoln: University of Nebraska Press, 1996); and Michael Newbury (*Figuring Authorship in Antebellum America.* Stanford: Stanford University Press, 1997). The relationship between the figure of the popular women writers and the demarcation of a realm of literary high culture in the 1850s and beyond is the subject of chapter 3.

12. *Putnam's Magazine,* which was founded in 1853, prefigured the *Atlantic's* commitment to promoting high-quality American literature and to promulgating standards of literary quality that were explicitly defined in opposition to the tradition of sentimental writing. This commitment was abandoned in 1856, however, when the editorial leadership at *Putnam's* changed, leaving the *Atlantic,* which was founded a year later, as the foremost arbiter of national literary standards and shaper of an emerging literary high culture in the late 1850s and beyond. For discussions of *Putnam's* editorial practices, see Sarah Robbins, "Gendering the History of the Antislavery Narrative: Juxtaposing *Uncle Tom's Cabin* and *Benito Cereno, Beloved* and *Middle Passage,*" *American Quarterly* 49.3 (1997), and Sheila Post-Lauria, "Magazine Practices and Melville's *Israel Potter,*" in Kenneth M. Price and Susan Belasco Smith, eds., *Periodical Literature in Nineteenth-Century America* (Charlottesville and London: University Press of Virginia, 1995).

13. James Russell Lowell, "The Origins of Didactic Poetry," *Atlantic Monthly* (Nov. 1857), 112.

14. Both of Phelps's grandfathers were ministers. Her maternal grandfather, the Reverend Moses Stuart (1780–1852), brought German Biblical Criticism to Andover Theological Seminary in the early decades of the nineteenth century, an introduction that revolutionized the field of biblical study in the United States. Her father, Austin

Phelps, was appointed Professor of Rhetoric and Homiletics at Andover in 1848, where he remained for the rest of his life.

15. For the friendship between Stowe and Phelps, see Elizabeth Stuart Phelps, *Chapters from a Life* (Cambridge: Riverside, 1896), chapter 7, and Joan Hedrick, *Harriet Beecher Stowe: A Life* (New York: Oxford University Press, 1994), especially chapter 21.

16. Alcott, *Journals* 99.

17. Sharon L. Dean, *Constance Fenimore Woolson: Homeward Bound* (Knoxville: The University of Tennessee Press, 1995), 1–6.

18. Woolson maintained most of her literary relationships by correspondence, both because she lived in Europe for much of her adult life and because of her increasing deafness, which made conversation difficult (Dean, *Constance Fenimore Woolson,* 6, 83, 178).

19. Augusta Evans to William Seaver, March 20, 1875; reprinted in Rebecca Grant Sexton, ed., *A Southern Woman of Letters, The Correspondence of Augusta Jane Evans Wilson* (Columbia: University of South Carolina Press, 2002), 154.

20. Evans published widely in Southern magazines and newspapers, but her work never appeared in Northern periodicals, despite evidence in her letters that she was invited to contribute to at least one Northern art magazine. Evans's well-publicized sectional loyalty meant that her work was always viewed through the prism of her identity as a Southern writer, and that Evans never got to be an active part of the New York (or any other) literary scene. As I discuss in chapter 2, however-er, Evans very much wanted to play a central role in the intellectual and cultural life of the nation, and she gives her fictional surrogates precisely such a role.

21. Brodhead, *Cultures of Letters,* 87–88.

22. See, for example, Rebecca Harding Davis, *Bits of Gossip* (Boston: Houghton Mifflin, 1904) 36–41, and Alcott, *Journals,* 109, 119, for accounts of Davis and Alcott's mutual admiration and respect for each other's work. Elizabeth Stuart Phelps's memoir, *Chapters from a Life,* is littered with references to the work of her female peers and predecessors, most of them admiring; the same is true of Annie Fields, ed., *Life and Letters of Harriet Beecher Stowe* (1897; Detroit: Gale Research, 1970). Augusta Jane Evans makes frequent references to the popular literature of the day; see Sexton, *A Southern Woman of Letters.* Since Constance Fenimore Woolson's surviving letters and journals are unpublished, it is difficult to know what her opinion of her female peers was.

23. Phelps, *Chapters from a Life,* 146–47. Both Alcott and Davis had somewhat more difficult relationships with Fields than Phelps did. Early in Alcott's career, Fields had recommended that she give up writing and confine herself to teaching, a recommendation that Alcott ignored, noting in her journal "Being wilful [*sic*], I said, 'I won't teach; and I can write, and I'll prove it'" (Alcott, *Journals,* 109). Fields's comment clearly rankled Alcott, since she returns to it repeatedly. Recording her pleasure at the success of *Hospital Sketches,* Alcott writes: "A year ago I had no publisher & went begging with my wares; now *three* have asked me for something. . . . There is a sudden hoist for a meek & lowly scribbler who was told to 'stick to her teaching,' & never had a literary friend to lend a helping hand!" (*Journals,* 121). She mentions the comment again in a letter to Louise Chandler Moulton in 1883 (*The Selected Letters of Louisa May Alcott* [eds. Madeleine Stern, Joel Myerson, and Daniel Shealy. Boston: Little Brown, 1987], 160, n. 2). Although Alcott knew the Fields family well—

she stayed with them while teaching school in Boston in 1862—Brodhead suggests that she felt like a "poor relation" rather than a literary "find" and legitimate participant in the Fields' sparkling literary salon (Brodhead, *Cultures of Letters*, 87–88).

Sharon M. Harris suggests that Fields had been looking for an excuse to drop Davis from the *Atlantic* when he ended their relationship on grounds of breach of contract after Davis published *Waiting for the Verdict* in *The Galaxy* in 1868—this despite the fact that Davis had long been in breach of her exclusive contract with the *Atlantic* by publishing in *Peterson's* (*Rebecca Harding Davis* [Philadelphia: University of Pennsylvania Press, 1991], 138–39). It was during Fields's tenure as editor (1861–71) that the *Atlantic* stopped accepting the work of both Davis and Alcott.

24. Quoted in Sharon M. Harris, *Rebecca Harding Davis and American Realism* (Philadelphia: University of Pennsylvania Press, 1991), 137. Many of James's reviews of his American peers of both genders are reprinted in Henry James, *Literary Criticism* (New York: The Library of America, 1984). Joan Hedrick argues that the *Nation*'s hostility toward women writers was part of an effort to reclaim the cultural and political power that women writers of domestic fiction had amassed during the antebellum period by addressing matters of social and political reform in their fiction: "At a time when women lacked the vote, the *Nation* insisted that the important issues of Reconstruction should be decided in the political arena and literary women should give up their pulpits, pens, and podiums. The *Nation*'s method was to attack the literary excellence of women writers in the name of 'art'" (*Harriet Beecher Stowe*, 349).

25. No one has conducted a systematic study of the gendering of high culture in the nation's "quality journals" during the postbellum era, but many critics have noted the phenomenon in passing. Only publication patterns in the *Atlantic* have been studied in detail. Ellery Sedgwick observes that although approximately 50 percent of the contributions to the inaugural issue of the *Atlantic* were by women, they were represented exclusively in the fiction department (Sedgwick also asserts that this ratio held throughout the nineteenth century, a fact that Sharon Harris disputes). In *Rebecca Harding Davis and American Realism*, Sharon Harris notes that although both Fields and Howells retained a ratio of 25 percent of contributions by women, under Fields's editorship of the *Atlantic*, "23 percent of fiction and essays published were by women authors and 77 percent by men. When Howells began his editorship, the percentage for women dropped to 17 percent, leaving 83 percent of the fiction and essays to be produced by the journal's male contributors" and relegating women's contributions to poetry (167). Richard Brodhead notes that "the *Atlantic* underwent a palpable stiffening of its selection criteria in the mid-1860s" when it stopped accepting work by Alcott and Davis (*Cultures of Letters*, 87–88). A systematic gender analysis of the content of the *Atlantic* and of its reviewing patterns is in Anne E. Boyd, "'What! Has she got into the '*Atlantic*'?': Women Writers, the *Atlantic Monthly*, and the Formation of the American Canon," *American Studies* 39:3 (Fall 1998): 5–36. The most cursory survey of the tables of contents of other prominent magazines reveals similar trends: although a significant proportion of contributions are by women, they are almost exclusively fiction and poetry, along with the occasional nonfiction essay on a "feminine" subject.

26. Discussing the common critical misconception that Rebecca Harding Davis didn't have a well-thought-out theoretical program, Sharon Harris observes that "because she, like the majority of early nineteenth-century women realists, explicated the premises of her theory in fiction rather than by writing a separate theoretical

tract, her contributions to the development of these concepts have been virtually ignored by scholars" (*Rebecca Harding Davis and American Realism*, 10–11).

27. I believe that Phelps's *Chapters from a Life* (1896) and Davis's *Bits of Gossip* (1904) are the first published memoirs by American women writers. Although both discuss their vocations and careers, Phelps confines her aesthetic manifesto to a single chapter, at the very end of the book, and Davis provides no organized statement about her literary program. As discussed in chapter 3, Alcott fully expected that her journals and letters would be published after her death, but she wrote no formal memoir.

28. Alcott, *Letters* 144, n. 17.

29. Baym, *Woman's Fiction*, 32.

30. Susan Coultrap-McQuin points out that "the model of the Gentleman Publisher presupposed that the publisher was male. Although women had often been involved in printing and publishing during colonial days, by the nineteenth century few of them were publishers in their own right of books or magazines until the last two decades of the century" (*Doing Literary Business*, 33). Women did influence publishing decisions made by husbands and fathers—John P. Jewett's wife recommended that he publish *Uncle Tom's Cabin*; Susan Warner's *The Wide Wide World* was accepted by G. P. Putnam only after his mother read the manuscript and urged its publication; and James T. Fields's wife, Annie, influenced her husband's decision to publish Elizabeth Stuart Phelps's *The Gates Ajar* (*Doing Literary Business*, 35). A recent collection that demonstrates the myriad ways in which women writers did participate in the periodical press of the nineteenth century is Cane and Alves, eds., *The Only Efficient Instrument: American Women Writers & The Periodical, 1837–1916* (Iowa City: University of Iowa Press, 2001).

31. Buell, *New England Literary Culture*, 47.

32. Lawrence W. Levine, *Highbrow/Lowbrow: The Emergence of Cultural Hierarchy in America* (Cambridge: Harvard University Press, 1988).

33. Brodhead, *Cultures of Letters*, 85.

34. "Evans and the Waning of Woman's Fiction" is the title of the final chapter of *Woman's Fiction: A Guide to Novels by and about Women, 1820–1870*. Although Baym observes at the end of *Woman's Fiction* that "the flowering of this fiction created the ground from which, after the Civil War, a group of women who were literary artists developed along with an audience to appreciate them" (298), the process by which this group developed is outside the purview of Baym's study. Subsequent literary historians of the period have accepted and repeated both Baym's timeline and her implication that this change took place either imperceptibly or organically or both. Elizabeth Ammons notes that for those who wanted to continue to produce popular fiction identified with domesticity and aimed primarily at female readers, "identification as a woman writer posed little problem." But "for many women late in the nineteenth and then early in the twentieth century, the mid-nineteenth-century mainstream American image of the domestic novelist no longer applied. . . . Increasingly, women writers as a group were determined to assert their right to write not simply to make a living but for the same reasons that ambitious men (and a few women) had always turned to novel writing: to create original works of art" ("Gender and Fiction," *The Columbia History of the American Novel*, ed. Emory Elliott [New York: Columbia University Press, 1991], 272). Richard Brodhead echoes Baym's and Ammons's sense that American women's writing was qualitatively dif-

ferent by the end of the nineteenth century, observing that "[w]hen women writers began to hang quotations from Flaubert over their writing desks—as Sarah Orne Jewett did in fact and as Kate Chopin must have done *in pectore*—we know that something has changed" (*The School of Hawthorne*, 13). Brodhead also argues that Sarah Orne Jewett was the first American woman to write from within the vision of the literary that had been articulated by the *Atlantic:* Jewett's "career plan . . . set a figure of authorship—aligning women's writing with high-cultural aspirations, with antifamilial careerism and profound artistic seriousness," which numerous women writers followed (*Cultures of Letters*, 175).

35. In her influential study *Conflicting Stories: American Women Writers at the Turn into the Twentieth Century* (New York: Oxford University Press, 1991), Elizabeth Ammons argues: "What is significant about the group [of seventeen turn-of-the-century writers] I am discussing is not that they are unprecedented, but that before them no historically coherent *group* of women of comparable artistic ambition and accomplishment aspired to succeed as artists working primarily in fiction in the United States. They were the pioneer generation. Before them were scattered individuals struggling with the problems of reconciling gender and art or gender, race, and art. At the turn of the century, however—as books in the period about women artists attest—there erupted a whole group of women struggling with the issues" (12).

36. Harriet Beecher Stowe, *Sunny Memories of Foreign Lands* (Boston: Phillips, Sampson, and Company, New York: J. C. Derby, 1854), Vol. II, 351.

37. Stowe, *Sunny Memories*, Vol. I, 325.

Notes to Chapter 1

1. Charles Edward Stowe, *Life of Harriet Beecher Stowe, Compiled from her Letters and Journals* (Boston: Houghton, Mifflin, and Co., 1889), 32. Hereinafter abbreviated as *Life of HBS*.

2. Joan Hedrick, *Harriet Beecher Stowe, A Life* (New York: Oxford University Press, 1994), 87, 119. Hereinafter abbreviated as *HBS*.

3. Hedrick, *HBS*, 138–39.

4. Ibid., 239–40.

5. Despite their chronological proximity, these three texts are not typically read as being in dialogue with each other. Although Nina Baym discusses them together, she calls these works Stowe's "religious novels" and views all three novels as virtually identical in their depiction of female characters who are not human but "[p]erfected beings [who] have no functions to perform vis-à-vis themselves; their purpose is to validate religious belief and the spiritual world for others, including the audience" (*Woman's Fiction: A Guide to Novels by and about Women in America 1820–1870*. 1978. 2nd ed. Urbana: University of Illinois Press, 1993), 233.

6. Harriet Beecher Stowe, *Sunny Memories of Foreign Lands* (Boston: Phillips, Sampson, and Company, New York: J. C. Derby, 1854). Vol. II, 351.

7. Stowe, *Sunny Memories*, Vol. I, 325.

8. John Gatta has established definitively that Stowe joined the Trinity Episcopal Church in Hartford sometime between 1864 and 1866 ("The Anglican Aspect of Harriet Beecher Stowe," *The New England Quarterly* Sept. 2000; 425).

Charles Foster argues quite convincingly that Stowe never completely rejected
Calvinism as the fundamental intellectual and theological framework that shaped
her life and work. See *The Rungless Ladder: Harriet Beecher Stowe and New England
Puritanism* (Durham: Duke University Press, 1954), especially chapter 7. Gatta does
not disagree with this view entirely, although he ascribes more importance to the
religious aspects of Stowe's "involvement" with Anglicanism than does Foster,
arguing that it helped shape "the aesthetic spirituality, the enlarged vision of human
salvation, and the feminized theology of divine love that characterize most of her
fiction" (432–33).

9. Harriet Beecher Stowe, "New England Ministers," *Atlantic Monthly* (Feb.
1858), 487.

10. "Heart" religion refers to Horace Bushnell's view that the heart rather than
the head was the source of religious knowledge; God's "'purity, goodness, beauty,
and gentleness . . . can never be sufficiently apprehended by mere intellect. It
requires a heart, a good, right-feeling heart, to receive so much of heart as God opens
to us in the Gospel of Christ'" (quoted in James Turner, *Without God, Without Creed:
The Origins of Unbelief in America* [Baltimore: Johns Hopkins University Press, 1985],
111). For an account of the transformation of Protestant theology from a focus on
knowledge of God to an emphasis on feeling God, see Turner, chapter 3. For a discussion of the way in which "heart religion" coexisted with the ideology of domesticity see Ann Douglas, *The Feminization of American Culture* (1977; New York:
Anchor, 1988), especially chapters 4–7. In her *Common Sense Applied to Religion, or The
Bible and the People* (1857) Catharine Beecher articulated her belief, which drew on
the work of Bushnell and other liberal theologians as well as on her own years of
religious turmoil, that salvation was available to all who sought it, thus removing
the central barrier Calvinism posed to those who sought eternal life. See Kathryn
Kish Sklar, *Catharine Beecher: A Study in American Domesticity* (New Haven and
London: Yale University Press, 1973), chapter 16.

11. Stowe, *Agnes of Sorrento* (1862. Rpt. *The Writings of Harriet Beecher Stowe*, New
York: AMS, 1967), 127.

12. Ellery Sedgwick, *The Atlantic Monthly 1857–1909, Yankee Humanism at High
Tide and Ebb* (Amherst: University of Massachusetts Press, 1994), 24.

13. On the gender dynamics of the institutionalization of high culture at midcen-
tury and beyond, see Brodhead, *The School of Hawthorne* (New York: Oxford
University Press, 1986); Lawrence W. Levine, *Highbrow/Lowbrow: The Emergence of
Cultural Hierarchy in America* (Cambridge: Harvard University Press, 1988); and
Hedrick, *HBS*, especially chapter 23.

14. James Russell Lowell, "The Origins of Didactic Poetry," *Atlantic Monthly*
(Nov. 1857), 110–12.

15. The attitude toward "morals" expressed in this poem is a distinct departure
from antebellum views of the proper relationship between morality and art.
Although transcendentalism was based in part on rejecting Johnsonian views of
art's purpose, it did not give rise to an aesthetic that divorced morality from art.
Lawrence Buell explains that in the early part of the nineteenth century the standard
of judgment of art changed from "Does this book make vice attractive?" to "Does it
make virtue beautiful?" Buell notes: "Transcendentalist aesthetics went one step further, referring the moral power of great literature to the act of creation (which
Emerson, like Coleridge, saw as a quasi-religious experience), rather than to the

work's reinforcement or promotion of accepted moral standards. At this point, in theory, an aesthetics completely divorced from morality became possible—Poe's Coleridge-based aesthetic, for example; but in New England this did not happen. Emerson continued to make art subordinate to the moral and religious experience that underlay it and that it, in turn, was designed to provoke in the reader" (Lawrence Buell, *New England Literary Culture, From Revolution through Renaissance* [Cambridge: Cambridge University Press, 1986], 65). The effect, Buell points out, is a philosophy of art that wasn't very far removed from the didactic moralistic aesthetics from which Transcendentalism initially distinguished itself.

16. Sedgwick, *The Atlantic Monthly,* 30.

17. Hedrick, *HBS,* 289. Women were invited to one of the *Atlantic's* dinner meetings in 1859, but only two women (Stowe and Harriet Prescott [later Spofford]) attended, and the atmosphere was tense and uncomfortable. Women were not invited to the *Atlantic's* meetings again until late in the century, and even then it was only on rare, celebratory occasions (the Holmes breakfast in 1880 and the celebration of Stowe's eightieth birthday in 1882). For detailed discussions of the cultural and practical barriers to women's participation in the editorial and business sides of literary culture in the nineteenth century, see Hedrick, *HBS,* chapter 23, and Susan Coultrap-McQuin, *Doing Literary Business: American Women Writers in the Nineteenth Century* (Chapel Hill: University of North Carolina Press, 1990).

18. Ibid., 291. For a detailed discussion of the institutional ambivalence toward women writers that permeated the *Atlantic Monthly* during the first four decades of its existence, see Ann E. Boyd, "'What! Has she got into the '*Atlantic*'?': Women Writers, the *Atlantic Monthly,* and the Formation of the American Canon," *American Studies* 39:3 (Fall 1998): 5–36.

19. As numerous scholars of nineteenth-century women's writing have demonstrated, antebellum women commonly used their fictional pulpits to critique the excessive materialism, individualism, and other social ills of the period and to endorse social reform based on extending the "feminine" values of the domestic sphere into the broader world. Stowe's critique in *The Minister's Wooing* text differs from this pattern in that the solution she imagines is based on aesthetic rather than primarily moral activity.

20. Roger B. Stein, *John Ruskin and Aesthetic Thought in America, 1840–1900* (Cambridge: Harvard University Press, 1967), 41.

21. As Stein notes, "It was not so much the guidebook information with which Ruskin supplied [Americans] that contributed to his growing popularity . . . as it was the way he helped them to resolve the normative questions of the value of nature, religion, and art with what they felt to be a satisfying epistemology" (*Ruskin and Aesthetic Thought,* 86–87).

22. There is no record of the books in the Stowe family library, so we can't know with certainty what Harriet Beecher Stowe read, but she was clearly very familiar with the ideas about the Italian middle ages and Renaissance advanced by Ruskin and others. In *Sunny Memories of Foreign Lands* she records her great pleasure at meeting Mrs. Anna Jameson, a British writer "whose works on art and artists were for years almost my only food for a certain class of longings" (Vol. I, 107). Stein notes that Mrs. Jameson's works, along with those of Ruskin and Lord Lindsay, were among the primary vehicles for introducing Americans to ideas about Medieval art (*Ruskin and Aesthetic Thought,* 76).

23. Stowe, *Sunny Memories of Foreign Lands*, Vol. II, 249.

24. Harriet Beecher Stowe, *The Minister's Wooing* (1859. Rpt. *Harriet Beecher Stowe, Three Novels*. New York: Library of America, 1982), 600, 599, 598, 600, 598. Hereinafter cited parenthetically.

25. Stowe's critique of utilitarianism and her rejection of Calvinist strictures on beauty are not new ideas for her. They are central themes of *Sunny Memories of Foreign Lands*, where statements on the topic are sprinkled throughout the two volumes of travel writing, sandwiched between accounts of social events and minor tourist mishaps and descriptions of people, meals, and hotels. One of her more pointed critiques of utilitarianism is inspired by a trip through beautiful Alpine meadows, where Stowe marvels at the beauty of wildflowers and argues that the "great Artist" who created them "is no utilitarian, no despiser of the fine arts, and no condemner of ornament; and those religionists, who seek to restrain every thing within the limits of cold, bare utility, do not imitate our Father in heaven" (Vol. II, 249). Noting that the natural world is filled with beauty that seems to lack a purpose, Stowe argues that beauty itself is divine: "The instinct to adorn and beautify is from him; it likens us to him, and if rightly understood, instead of being a siren to beguile our hearts away, it will be the closest affiliating band" (Vol. II, 250).

26. "The Position of the Artist," *The Crayon* (March 28, 1855), 193. Although most of the articles in the *Crayon* were anonymous, more than half of the pieces in the magazine's first three volumes were written by founder and coeditor, William James Stillman. His coeditor and financial backer was John Durand, son of American painter Asher B. Durand (Stein, *Ruskin and Aesthetic Thought*, 102, 106).

27. "The Art of the Present," *The Crayon* (May 9, 1855), 289.

28. Ibid., 289–90.

29. James Jackson Jarves, *Art-Hints. Architecture, Sculpture, and Painting* (New York: Harper & Brothers, 1855), 10.

30. Stowe's comments on the destructive effect of Puritan culture on aesthetic sensibilities are strongly autobiographical; in *Sunny Memories of Foreign Lands* Stowe recounts with some bitterness her feeling of having had her soul "starved" by the lack of access to art and beauty, not only by virtue of living in a country relatively poor in works of art, but, more fundamentally, by the Calvinist tradition's strictures against aesthetic pleasure. Describing her stay in a Paris house close to the Louvre, Stowe writes: "[The Louvre] is close by. Think of it. To one who has starved all a life, in vain imaginings of what art might be, to know that you are within a stone's throw of a museum full of its miracles. . . . (Vol. II, 159). Commenting on the French love of beauty, Stowe mourns the paucity of beauty in her own life: "With all New England's earnestness and practical efficiency, there is a long withering of the soul's more ethereal part,—a crushing out of the beautiful,—which is horrible. Children are born there with a sense of beauty equally delicate with any in the world, in whom it dies a lingering death of smothered desire and pining, weary starvation. I know, because I have felt it.

One in whom this sense has long been repressed, in coming into Paris, feels a rustling and waking within him, as if the soul were trying to unfold her wings, long unused and mildewed" (Vol. II, 392).

31. Describing her first encounter with some of the great Italian Renaissance art about which she had read, Stowe records her ambivalence toward paintings of sacred subjects by Murillo and Raphael and concludes, "Protestant as I am, no

Catholic picture contents me" (*Sunny Memories*, Vol. 1, 323). For an excellent discussion of antebellum Americans' ambivalent relationship with Catholicism and Stowe's engagement with Catholic Italy in *Agnes of Sorrento*, see Jenny Franchot, *Roads to Rome: The Antebellum Protestant Encounter with Catholicism* (Berkeley: University of California Press, 1994).

32. Jarves, *Art-Hints*, 13.

33. "The Position of the Artist," 193.

34. Stowe had evidently been thinking about the gendered nature of the "soul artist" long before she created the character of Mary Scudder; her description of Mrs. Anna Jameson, a well-regarded British art historian whom she met during her 1854 visit to England, depicts the writer as a kind of "soul artist": "Mrs. Jameson is the most charming of critics, with the gift, often too little prized, of discovering and pointing out beauties rather than defects; beauties which we may often have passed unnoticed, but which, when so pointed out, never again conceal themselves. This shows itself particularly in her *Characteristics of Shakespeare's Women*, a critique which only a true woman could have written" (*Sunny Memories*, Vol. II, 107). As in the description of the "soul artist" in *The Minister's Wooing*, the ability to praise rather than criticize—a characteristic stereotypically associated with male critics—and to call the reader's attention to little-noticed qualities in the object being examined, whether a person or a work of art, are understood by Stowe as specifically feminine qualities.

35. Barton Levi St. Armand, *Emily Dickinson and Her Culture: The Soul's Society* (Cambridge and New York: Cambridge University Press, 1984), 115.

36. Stowe, "New England Ministers," 487.

37. Stowe, *Life of HBS*, 25.

38. Ibid., 29.

39. Charles Stowe was apparently aware of the tension revealed by his mother's letters to her brother Edward in which she challenged the solution he offered to her religious difficulties, but he persistently reads those tensions teleologically. He notes, "A letter written to her brother Edward in Boston, dated March 27, 1828, shows how slowly she adopted the view of God that finally became one of the most characteristic elements in her writings" (*Life of HBS*, 42). In the revised edition of the biography, published in 1911, Charles is only slightly more forthcoming about Stowe's ambivalence towards her siblings' theological views. He suggests that the crisis of faith his mother experienced in her late teens was prompted by her inability to reconcile "the powerful and somewhat contradictory influences brought to bear upon her mind by her father, her brother Edward, and her sister Catherine." But, he insists, "She is naturally drawn to the winning and restful conception of God as like Jesus Christ which both her brother Edward and her sister Catherine unite in presenting to her, but at the same time she shows how the iron of her father's Calvinism has passed into her soul. It may make her very unhappy and depressed, but still she cannot let it go immediately. For dull, lethargic souls Calvinism may be a most excellent tonic under given conditions, but on her artistic and sensitive nature it acted like a subtle poison. It appealed to her reason and left her heart unsatisfied,—nay, even wounded and bleeding (Charles Edward Stowe and Lyman Beecher Stowe, *Harriet Beecher Stowe: The Story of Her Life*, Boston: Houghton Mifflin, 1911), 57–58. In keeping with this narrative, Charles Stowe makes only passing reference to the repeated religious crises Stowe experienced throughout her adult life. For accounts of these,

see Foster, *The Rungless Ladder,* esp. chapters 3–5, and Hedrick, *HBS,* chapters 14–15, 22.

40. Among modern critics, Dorothy Berkson originated the emphasis on Candace as the bearer of Stowe's theological vision, arguing that the novel is one of a number of Stowe's works dedicated to imagining a matriarchal millennial society "that will result from th[e] wedding of Christian and feminine virtues" and will be opposed to "patriarchal Calvinism." For her, "Candace's maternal, New Testament philosophy is egalitarian, inclusive and participatory. The disciple, not the ruler, determines his own salvation. This, for one of Stowe's background was radical theology with equally radical political implications" ("Millennial Fiction and the Feminine Fiction of Harriet Beecher Stowe," in Elizabeth Ammons, ed., *Critical Essays on Harriet Beecher Stowe,* Boston: G. K. Hall, 1980), 245–46, 248. For Armand Barton St. Levi, Stowe is a "sentimentalist" redefiner of Calvinism (17). He argued that "[w]hile Stowe's Sentimental Love Religion parodies the patriarchal nature of Calvinism by caricaturing its God as a desiccated New England deacon, it affirms the matriarchal amplitude of the New testament by extending the dogma of the immaculate conception to all women" (94). Summarizing the development of sentimental love religion as an alternative to Calvinist theology, Marianne Noble points out that comparisons of God to mothers "are particularly prominent in nineteenth-century sentimental fiction; indeed, sentimental fiction plays an important role in developing and disseminating them," noting that "[i]n *The Minister's Wooing,* Mrs. Marvyn nearly goes insane trying to love the wrathful, masculine God who appears to have damned her son for all time, but she is able to love God when her black servant, Candace, compares him to her own maternal self . . ." (Marianne Noble, *The Masochistic Pleasures of Sentimental Literature,* Princeton: Princeton University Press, 2000, 67). John Gatta argues that in *The Minister's Wooing* "Stowe renounces austere Calvinism. . . . She proposes instead a 'feminized' Christianity that stresses the motherly compassion of Jesus. . . ." The vehicle for Stowe's "repudiation of Calvinist demands for a discrete moment of conversion" are the "unordained women like Candace and Mary" whose "charisma of spiritual maternity . . . emerges from a kind of priesthood whose power derives from a personal knowledge of affliction and identification with the bleeding heart of the Mother of God'" (417, 418).

Although Joan Hedrick's reading of the novel, and of Stowe's relationship with Calvinism, is considerably more nuanced than that of many critics, she, too, focuses on Candace at the expense of Mary Scudder as the bearer of Stowe's vision in the novel. Hedrick argues that "in the figures of Mrs. Marvyn and Candace, Stowe splits herself into two mothers, a white mother who sorrowed and a black mother who comforted. Making Candace the high priest of suffering was consistent with Stowe's view of the outrages slave mothers had experienced and with her view, articulated in *The Minister's Wooing,* that only those who had experienced 'a great affliction' were fit to guide those who are struggling in it" (*HBS,* 282). For other insightful discussions of Stowe's relationship to Calvinism in *The Minister's Wooing,* see Lawrence Buell, "Calvinism Romanticized: Harriet Beecher Stowe, Samuel Hopkins, and *The Minister's Wooing,*" in Elizabeth Ammons, ed., *Critical Essays on Harriet Beecher Stowe;* and Buell, *New England Literary Culture,* chapter 2.

41. Foster, *The Rungless Ladder,* 114.

42. Sklar, *Catharine Beecher,* 43.

43. Stowe, *Life of HBS,* 33–34.

44. Although Henry Ward Beecher became the best-known public spokesman for liberal "heart" religion in the second half of the nineteenth century, it is unlikely that he was much of an influence on Harriet, since he was two years her junior. During her formative years, Edward, Catharine, and, of course, Lyman Beecher were by far the strongest influences on Stowe. See Stowe, *Life of HBS*, and Hedrick, *HBS*.

45. Stowe, *Life of HBS*, 40.

46. There is no written record of Stowe's conversations about religion with Catharine from this time since the two lived and worked together. As correspondence from later in life reveals, however, Stowe was extremely close to her sister and strongly influenced by her theological views, which Catharine published in numerous treatises including *The Elements of Mental and Moral Philosophy, Founded upon Experience, Reason, and the Bible* (1831); *Letters on the Difficulties of Religion* (1836); and *Common Sense Applied to Religion, or The Bible and the People* (1857). For a detailed discussion of Beecher's struggles with Calvinism and the theological solutions she developed, see Sklar, *Catharine Beecher*.

47. See chapter 14 of Hedrick, *HBS*, for a detailed discussion of this difficult time in Stowe's life.

48. Harriet Beecher Stowe to Calvin E. Stowe, September 4, 1842. Quoted in Hedrick, *HBS*, 149. ˙

49. Hedrick, *HBS*, 155.

50. Ibid., 153. Quotations from Stowe are from a letter to Thomas Beecher, March 16, 1844. The belief in the necessity of submitting completely to the divine will was a cornerstone of Lyman Beecher's strain of Calvinism. Any failure to submit cast doubt on one's regeneration and capacity to achieve grace and could bring about further trials. See Sklar, *Catharine Beecher*, 28–32. See also Hedrick, *HBS*, 150–53.

51. Letter from HBS to Thomas Beecher, March 16, 1844. Quoted in Hedrick, *HBS*, 155.

52. Foster, *Rungless Ladder*, 95.

53. Sklar, *Catharine Beecher*, 239.

54. Stowe, *Life of HBS*, 322.

55. Ibid., 322; Foster, *Rungless Ladder*, 98.

56. See Foster, *Rungless Ladder*, 96–106.

57. Turner, *Without God, Without Creed*, 153.

58. Ibid., 156.

59. Ibid., 186.

60. Ibid., 187.

61. Ibid., 146.

62. Ibid., 147.

63. In his classic article "American Intellectuals and the Victorian Crisis of Faith" (*American Quarterly* [December 1975]), D. H. Meyer offers a detailed overview of what he calls the "internal crisis of faith" (586) produced by these challenges to religion; but his analysis of the postbellum period focuses exclusively on male intellectuals such as Theodore Munger, Thomas Henry Huxley, Robert G. Ingersoll, William James, Herbert Spencer, and others. See also Jerry Wayne Brown, *The Rise of Biblical Criticism in America, 1800–1870, The New England Scholars*, whose "New England Scholars" are, of course, all men; D. H. Meyer, *The Instructed Conscience: The Shaping of the American National Ethic* (Philadelphia: University of Pennsylvania Press, 1972); and Turner, *Without God, Without Creed*. Literary critics and cultural historians have

similarly viewed the Victorian crisis of faith as a strictly masculine affair. See, for example, David S. Reynolds, *Faith in Fiction: The Emergence of Religious Literature in America* (Cambridge: Harvard University Press, 1981), and T. J. Jackson Lears, *No Place of Grace: Antimodernism and the Transformation of American Culture, 1880–1920* (New York: Pantheon, 1981). Recent work by religious historians has begun to focus on women's participation in American religious life in the 19th century, but the mid-century crisis of faith has not yet been the subject of the newer scholarship.

64. Charles Foster discovered that the letter Mary sends to Dr. Hopkins in the "Evidences" chapter, in which she resists the doctor's attempts to plant doubts and elaborates on the source of her faith, is drawn almost word for word from a letter Roxanna Foote wrote her then-fiancé Lyman Beecher in 1798; see *The Rungless Ladder,* 115–17. For a discussion of Roxanna Foote's symbolic function in the Beecher family in general, and in Stowe's life in particular, see Hedrick, *HBS,* chapters 1–2.

65. Stowe, "New England Ministers," 487.

66. Harriet Beecher Stowe, *Uncle Tom's Cabin* (1852. Rpt. *Harriet Beecher Stowe, Three Novels.* New York: Library of America, 1982), 460.

67. See Hedrick, *HBS,* especially chapters 14 and 15, for examples of Calvin Stowe's religious doubts.

68. Stowe, *Uncle Tom's Cabin,* 344.

69. I am purposely focusing quite narrowly here on one aspect of the sentimental plot—conversion and Christ-like sacrifice—because it is fundamental to antebellum women writers' authorial self-conception. As Mary Kelley and Ann Douglas have shown, antebellum women harnessed their need, or desire, to write for publication to the culturally sanctioned conception of women as modest, self-effacing repositories of the family's and the nation's religious values. Antebellum women writers' emphasis on their religious motivation for writing fiction enabled them to justify, for themselves and their public, their violation of proper womanly behavior by defining their literary activities as entirely consistent with that behavior. For if they wrote to "do good," "to share the gospel of St. John that 'God is Love'; and to "'bring forth much fruit to [God's] glory,'" then their literary activities were, by definition, both consistent with acceptable feminine behavior and a form of doing God's work (Mary Kelley, *Private Woman, Public Stage: Literary Domesticity in Nineteenth Century America* [New York: Oxford University Press, 1984]), 286, 288, 292, 293). For the women who adopted this rationale for writing fiction, the central mechanism for doing God's work was effecting conversions in their readers by depicting conversions in their texts. And conversion, in domestic fiction, is almost always to a belief in the loving maternal God of Bushnell's "heart religion." Not all heroines of sentimental novels die, of course. But as readers have long noted, the death of a child or a young woman who has achieved conversion and becomes Christ-like is a staple of sentimental fiction. And for those heroines who don't die, successful growth to adulthood is dependent on learning to practice Christ-like self-denial; as Jane Tompkins points out, the death or self-sacrifice at the center of the sentimental novel "enact[s] the drama of the idea, central to Christian soteriology, that the highest human calling is to give one's life for another" (*Sensational Designs: The Cultural Work of American Fiction, 1790–1860* [New York: Oxford University Press, 1985], 128). To privilege Christ-like self-sacrifice and/or the untimely death of children and young women as a vehicle of conversion is, in the mid-nineteenth century, to identify oneself with a particular constellation of beliefs about religion, women, and women authors.

There is a large and rich body of scholarship on the cultural work of the sentimental which has extended the terms of the discussion beyond the narrow ones first outlined by Ann Douglas and Jane Tompkins of being, as June Howard has noted recently, either "'for' or 'against'" sentimentality ("What Is Sentimentality?" *ALH* [Spring 1999], 65). Some of the key contributions to the expanded critical dialogue include Shirley Samuels, ed., *The Culture of Sentiment: Race Gender, and Sentimentality in Nineteenth Century America* (1992); Karen Sánchez-Epplar, *Touching Liberty: Abolition, Feminism, and the Politics of the Body* (1993); Lora Romero, *Home Fronts: Domesticity and Its Critics in the Antebellum United States* (1997); Lori Merish, *Sentimental Materialism: Gender, Commodity Culture, and Nineteenth-Century American Literature* (1999); Marianne Noble, *The Masochistic Pleasures of Sentimental Literature* (2000). These studies take account of the various ways in which the sentimental functions as a cultural discourse that both participates in and challenges the social, political, and economic structures of antebellum America. There is also a growing body of work that revisits the notions of sympathy and sentiment and interrogates the critical response to them in the last three decades of the twentieth century. See, for example, Joanne Dobson, "Reclaiming Sentimental Literature," *American Literature* 69 (1997); June Howard "What Is Sentimentality?," and an expanded version in chapter 5 of *Publishing the Family* (2001). For a useful overview of the trends in the critical discussion of sentimentality, see the Preface to the new edition of Mary Kelley, *Private Woman, Public Stage* (2002) and Sharon Harris's review essay, "'A New Era in Female History': Nineteenth-Century U.S. Women Writers," *American Literature* 74 (September 2002).

Although all of this work has greatly expanded the frameworks within which critics read and understand sentimental novels, it has not displaced the original insights of Ann Douglas, Jane Tompkins, and Mary Kelley about the central ways in which sentimental religion authorized literary production by white, middle-class women.

70. In "Harriet Beecher Stowe's Conversation with *The Atlantic Monthly*: The Construction of *The Minister's Wooing*" (*Studies in American Fiction*, Vol. 28, No. 1), Dorothy Z. Baker argues that the marriage between Mary Scudder and James Marvyn represents Stowe's rejection of the marriage plots common to fiction published alongside *The Minister's Wooing* in the pages of the *Atlantic Monthly*, in which the protagonist rejects the dashing but unsuitable young man of her choice and marries an older, stable man of her mother's choosing. Baker asserts, however, that Mary's "decision to accept James Marvyn as her husband is informed by her consultation with a French woman" who "teache[es] Mary about the emotional and sexual components of marriage" and urges her not to accept a loveless marriage out of duty (33). Baker's reading overlooks the fact that Mary actually rejects Virginie de Frontigniac's argument in favor of breaking off the engagement with Doctor Hopkins and that the final resolution of the plot has very little to do with Mary's agency and is made possible by Miss Prissy's intervention, which leads the minister to voluntarily release Mary from her betrothal.

71. Hedrick, *HBS*, 297. For a discussion of the autobiographical elements in *The Pearl of Orr's Island*, see *HBS*, 297–98.

72. For details of the lengthy composition of *The Pearl of Orr's Island*, see Foster, *The Rungless Ladder*, 64–65, 69, 86–87. *The Pearl of Orr's Island* was published in two parts; the first few chapters appeared in the *Independent* newspaper from January to

April 1861. Stowe halted the story after chapter 17, when Mara and Moses are still children, explaining to her readers that she had a previous commitment to fulfill and promising to continue the story in the fall. *Agnes of Sorrento* was serialized in the *Atlantic* between May 1861 and April 1862. Stowe resumed publication of *The Pearl of Orr's Island* in December 1861, and the two stories were published concurrently for part of 1862 (Hedrick, *HBS*, 297–302).

73. The novel has received very little critical attention from contemporary critics, but the first part was widely praised by nineteenth-century readers. See Foster, *The Rungless Ladder*, chapter 6, for a summary of these responses and one of the few published extended analyses of the novel. See also Hedrick, *HBS*, 296–302.

74. Harriet Beecher Stowe, *The Pearl of Orr's Island* (1862. Rpt. *The Writings of Harriet Beecher Stowe* [New York: AMS, 1967]), 158–59.

75. Stowe, *The Pearl of Orr's Island*, 163.

76. Hedrick, *HBS*, 301.

77. Hedrick observes that Stowe's choice of a male pseudonym is rather puzzling, since she was by this time a world-famous author whose contributions were sought by magazine and newspaper editors because her name on the masthead helped boost sales. Hedrick attributes Stowe's choice of a male pseudonym to the changes in the American literary scene in the 1860s, suggesting that "speaking in a male voice was the price of admission to the *Atlantic* club" (*HBS*, 314).

78. The Civil War began on April 12, 1861. *Agnes of Sorrento* was serialized in the *Atlantic* from May 1861 to April 1862. Stowe wrote most of *Agnes* before the war began, however. The novel was influenced by the three trips the Stowes took to Europe during the 1850s. Stowe began writing the story in Italy in 1859 and finished it after returning to the States, in 1860 and 1861 (Hedrick, *HBS*, 292–301).

79. HBS to James and Annie Fields; n.d. [ca. February, 1861], Fields Papers, HL; quoted in Hedrick, *HBS*, 295.

80. HBS to James T. Fields, January 16, 1861, quoted in Hedrick, *HBS*, 298.

81. In *The Myth of the Renaissance in Nineteenth-Century Writing* (New York: Oxford University Press, 1994), J. B. Bullen explains that in the nineteenth century the word "Renaissance" had controversial, "morally unorthodox associations" that have disappeared in the twentieth century. For earlier writers the word "represented a change in values or an ontological shift; it suggested a substitution of pagan values, or the assertion of individualism for religious or moral attitudes established in the Middle Ages. This change could be interpreted in very different ways. For some—Ruskin and Montalembert, for example—the Renaissance brought about a change for the worse. For them it was the source of contemporary social ills, and in their view it continued to be a model for contemporary dissipation and decadence. For others—Pater and Michelet, for example—Renaissance art and Renaissance life offered models of freedom of expression, freedom of emotion, and intellectual liberty denied to them by Victorian culture" (10).

82. Although Pugin's work was known to American architects, it never achieved the kind of widespread popular appeal that Ruskin's did. Stein suggests that Ruskin's "Protestant restatement and development of [Pugin's] ideas . . . gained the popular hearing Pugin had forfeited" because of his conversion to Catholicism (*Ruskin and Aesthetic Thought*, 65).

83. Bullen, *Myth of the Renaissance*, 90. Bullen writes that Rio's central evaluative standard was the degree of "Christian poetry" in a work of art and that in his

approach to art history Rio privileged intuition over reason and made "few demands on historical knowledge in his reader, and even less on technical expertise. 'Your heart will tell you the difference between good art and bad art,' he claims, trust that and you cannot go wrong.' The mystical in art is, he says, inaccessible to reason, hence the limitation of the historian when dealing with outstanding 'Christian' artists. 'It is here that the competence of those popularly called *connoisseurs* ends,' he says, 'the particular appreciative faculty which one applies to the creations of which we are about to speak is no longer that by which one judges ordinary works of art.' 'Mysticism is to painting,' he adds, 'what ecstasy is to psychology'" (quoted in Bullen, 83).

84. *Contrasts* [1841], 9 n. Pugin's emphasis; quoted in Bullen, *Myth of the Renaissance*, 102.

85. Thomas Wentworth Higginson, "Literature as an Art," *Atlantic Monthly* (Dec. 1867), 746.

86. Stowe, *Agnes of Sorrento* (1862. Rpt. *The Writings of Harriet Beecher Stowe*, New York: AMS, 1967), 62. Hereinafter cited parenthetically.

87. Ronald M. Steinberg, *Fra Girolamo Savonarola, Florentine Art, and Renaissance Historiography* (Athens: Ohio University Press, 1977), 30.

88. Ibid., 4.

89. Ibid., 28.

90. The lack of time to write, and the necessity of squeezing her literary work in-between her myriad domestic responsibilities, is a constant theme of the letters reprinted in Annie Fields, ed., *Life and Letters of Harriet Beecher Stowe* (1897. Detroit: Gale Research, 1970). The subject is also discussed in detail in Hedrick, *HBS.*

91. According to Steinberg, the San Marco "School of Art" was largely a nineteenth-century invention: "As nineteenth-century writers became increasingly more interested in *quattrocento* art and more confirmed in their belief that the glory of the art resided in its dependence upon an intensely spiritual Catholicism, the more attention the 'San Marco school' began to receive. This attention was vastly augmented by the foundation in the nineteenth century of spiritual brotherhoods of painters and other artists who, in imitation of what they thought existed before the 'pagan' sixteenth century, actually formed cloistered religious groups with conventual labors" (*Fra Girolamo Savonarola*, 8). Steinberg explains that although Savonarola did indeed urge his fellow Dominicans to earn their livings by practicing the arts, he "did not advise the practice of the 'fine arts' of painting or sculpture as the nineteenth-century writers assumed; for Savonarola the fine arts were in no way distinguished from the other manufacturing arts" (9).

92. This quote is from a letter written by Stowe's close friend, Annie Howard, in which she recounts a conversation with Stowe in the mid-1850s; the letter is reprinted in Annie Fields, ed., *Life and Letters of Harriet Beecher Stowe*, 163. A similar description of Stowe's motivation for writing is also given in Stowe, *Life of HBS*, chapter 7. Although Stowe's oft-quoted statement that "God wrote" *Uncle Tom's Cabin* appears to have been made only toward the end of her life, she disclaimed authorial agency in writing the novel as soon as she began to be asked about her motives for writing. For the anecdote in which Stowe declared that "God wrote it [*Uncle Tom's Cabin*]" see Fields, *Life and Letters*, 377. For other, undated examples of similar declarations see Stowe, *Life of HBS*, 156.

93. During the 1860s, the question of originality was a subject of much consider-

ation, often as part of discussions of genius and American cultural identity, and sometimes as a topic in its own right. The topic is discussed in chapters 3, 4, and 5.

94. When Stowe does speak publicly about women writers, in "How Shall We Learn to Write?" (*Hearth and Home*, January 16, 1869), it is to observe that "the best writing is done by men," because of their superior educations, and to suggest not that women seek better education, but that they stick to writing about what they know best—the domestic; Stowe assures her readers, "There is a great deal of writing, very charming, very acceptable, and much in demand, which consists simply in painting by means of words the simple and homely scenes of every-day life"—in effect warning them away from attempting to challenge the boundaries of the literary sphere that had long been allotted to American women writers.

Notes to Chapter 2

1. Augusta Evans to Rachel Lyons, August 28, 1860; reprinted in Rebecca Grant Sexton, *A Southern Woman of Letters: The Correspondence of Augusta Jane Evans Wilson* (Columbia: University of South Carolina Press, 2002), 19–20. Hereinafter abbreviated as *SWL*. Evans met Lyons in the fall of 1859, during her visit to New York City, where Evans was attending to the publication of *Beulah*.

2. Augusta Evans to Rachel Lyons, July 30, 1860 (Sexton, *SWL*, 18).

3. Evans's first novel, *Inez, A Tale of the Alamo* (1855), is an anti-Catholic love story that also functions, as Elizabeth Moss has argued, as a piece of "proslavery propaganda" (*Domestic Novelists in the Old South* [Baton Rouge and London: Louisiana State University Press, 1992], 154). The protagonists of her three subsequent novels, *Beulah* (1859), *Macaria* (1864), and *St. Elmo* (1866), are all artists who serve as vehicles for Evans's exploration of questions of aesthetics and cultural nationalism. Although each of these novels is written in Evans's erudite, often-difficult style, all three were successful, establishing Evans as one of the most popular authors of her day: *Beulah* brought the Evans family financial security; royalties from *Macaria*, which was smuggled through the blockade and printed in the North in 1864, provided Evans with much-needed cash after the end of the Civil War; and *St. Elmo* was a tremendous commercial success, although it is difficult to establish precisely how many copies were sold. The publisher, G. W. Carleton, couldn't keep up with demand when the book was first published and claimed to have sold one million copies in the first four months after the book's publication (Mary Kelley, *Private Woman, Public Stage: Literary Domesticity in Nineteenth Century America* [New York: Oxford University Press, 1984], 25). See also William P. Fidler, *Augusta Evans Wilson 1835–1909, A Biography* (Tuscaloosa: University of Alabama Press, 1951), chapter 11. During the years of her marriage to Lorenzo Wilson, from 1868 until 1891, Evans wrote very little; and when she took up her pen again after Wilson's death, she produced two works of fiction, *The Speckled Bird* (1902) and *Devota* (1907), in which a love story serves as a vehicle for Evans's conservative views about women's social roles.

4. Augusta Evans to J. L. M. Curry, July 15, 1863 (Sexton, *SWL*, 65).

5. Ibid. (Sexton, *SWL*, 66).

6. Ibid.

7. Evans was born into a prominent Southern family in Columbus, Georgia. Her father, Matthew Evans, lost most of his fortune to bad investments and an economic

downturn during the 1840s; the family moved to Mobile, Alabama, where they lived in straitened circumstances until Evans's work as a writer brought the family financial security. The only book length biography of Evans is Fidler, *Augusta Jane Evans*. Summaries of Evans's life and career and of the plots of Evans's novels can be found in Anne Sophie Riepma, *Fire & Fiction: Augusta Jane Evans in Context* (Amsterdam and Atlanta, GA: Rodopi, 2002).

8. Evans is classified by Mary Kelley as the youngest of the literary domestics, and by Baym as the last in the line of writers producing "woman's fiction," because of her immense popularity, which rivaled Susan Warner's and Harriet Beecher Stowe's, and because her plots rarely deviate from the standard formula that Baym outlines in *Woman's Fiction: A Guide to Novels by and about Women in America 1820–1870* (1978. 2nd ed. Urbana: University of Illinois Press, 1993). Subsequent scholars have elucidated the differences between the Northern and Southern domestic novel and focused on Evans as a specifically Southern practitioner of the form (Anne Goodwyn Jones, *Tomorrow Is Another Day: The Woman Writer in the South, 1859–1936* [Baton Rouge: Louisiana State University Press, 1981], and Elizabeth Moss, *Domestic Novelists in the Old South*). Drew Gilpin Faust has explored the role that Evans's writing played in supporting the Confederacy during the Civil War (*Mothers of Invention: Women of the Slaveholding South in the American Civil War* [Chapel Hill: University of North Carolina Press, 1996]), but Evans's status as a "domestic novelist" is unquestioned by these scholars.

9. Augusta Evans, *St. Elmo* (1866; reprint, Tuscaloosa: University of Alabama Press, 1992), 107.

10. [Augusta Jane Evans], "Southern Literature," *Mobile Daily Advertiser*, Nov. 6, 1859 [2].

11. See Drew Gilpin Faust, *A Sacred Circle: The Dilemma of the Intellectual in the Old South, 1840–1860* (Baltimore and London: The Johns Hopkins University Press, 1977), chapter 1, for an overview of the conditions of intellectual activity in the South.

12. The members of the "Sacred Circle" Faust studies include William Gilmore Simms, a novelist; James Henry Hammond, a politician; Edmund Ruffin, an agricultural reformer; and two professors: Nathaniel Beverley Tucker and George Frederick Holmes. For a detailed discussion of the proslavery writings of these five men, see chapter 6 of *Sacred Circle*.

13. See the Introduction to Elizabeth Moss, *Domestic Novelists in the Old South*, for an account of the significant ways in which the popular domestic novels produced by Southern writers differed from those produced by Northern writers.

14. *The International Magazine of Literature, Art and Science* (March 1852), 420.

15. "Southern Literature," *Putnam's Monthly* (Feb. 1857), 207, 208.

16. Ibid., 209.

17. Ibid., 210.

18. The *Atlantic Monthly* was conceived, initially, by Francis Underwood, in order to "'give the active support of letters to the anti-slavery cause,'" a purpose that was obvious to readers in both the North and the South. George William Bagby, editor of the *Southern Literary Messenger*, declared, after the magazine's second issue appeared, "This magazine has appeared before the world challenging the patronage of all lovers of polite learning by articles of the highest excellence in point of style and sentiment . . . all enlisted in making attractive a work the object of which is to

wage war on Southern society'" (quoted in Ellery Sedgwick, *The Atlantic Monthly 1857–1909: Yankee Humanism at High Tide and Ebb* [Amherst: University of Massachusetts Press, 1994], 62). In the first three years of the *Atlantic's* existence, strongly abolitionist articles appeared in almost every issue of the magazine, all written by Robert Lowell, the magazine's first editor, or his "radical abolitionist" friends (Sedgwick, 62). After James T. Fields assumed the editorship in 1862, Lowell continued to contribute much of the political writing that appeared in the magazine, and he and R. W. Emerson, became "the magazine's principal spokesmen on emancipation" (101). Thomas Wentworth Higginson, who was an outspoken abolitionist and the commander of the first regiment of freed slaves and who was also a regular contributor to the magazine, wrote "sympathetic accounts of the slave revolts of Toussaint L'Overture, Denmark Vesey, and Nat Turner" (101). *Putnam's* was equally strongly aligned with abolitionism; according to Frank Luther Mott, it was widely viewed by the editors of Southern periodicals such as *De Bow's* and *Southern Literary Messenger* as the unofficial organ of the Republican Party; that view is supported both by the tone and the content of the political writing that appeared in the magazine during the early 1850s and by the fact that Associate Editor Parke Godwin "wrote the first platform of the Republican party, basing it on an article he had contributed to the magazine in January 1856" (*A History of American Magazines, 1850–1865* [Cambridge: Harvard University Press, 1957], 423). For a discussion of the ways in which literary nationalism and abolition were inextricably linked in the pages of *Putnam's* magazine, which was founded in 1853 with the explicit goal of "promoting high-quality, 'resolutely American' literature," see Sarah Robbins, "Gendering the History of the Antislavery Narrative: Juxtaposing *Uncle Tom's Cabin* and *Benito Cereno, Beloved* and *Middle Passage, American Quarterly* 49.3 [1997], 547).

19. "Northern Literature," *Mobile Daily Advertiser,* Oct. 16, 1859, [p. 2]. Although the articles appeared anonymously, Evans biographer William Fidler definitively identified Evans as the author of the articles (*Augusta Evans Wilson,* 70), and it seems likely that her identity was not a secret, at least in Mobile in 1859, since she frequently published anonymous newspaper articles, which she equally frequently alludes to in her letters. She refers to the articles offhandedly in a letter to Rachel Lyons from Jan. 4, 1860, as part of her apology for not responding to her friend's letter more promptly (Sexton, *SWL,* 7). The four articles are "Northern Literature," which appeared in two parts on October 10 and 16, 1859, and "Southern Literature" which appeared on October 30 and November 6, 1859. The articles all appeared on p. 2 of the newspaper. All further references to these articles will be made parenthetically, by date. I am extremely grateful to Melissa J. Homestead for locating the only extant copies of these articles (in the Library of Congress) and sharing her transcription of them with me.

20. As my analysis in the rest of this chapter will demonstrate, I disagree with Rebecca Grant Sexton's assessment that Evans was unable or unwilling to admit that she wrote "as a means of self-fulfillment" (xxii).

21. Augusta Evans to Rachel Lyons, July 30, 1860 (Sexton, *SWL,* 18).

22. Augusta Evans to Rachel Lyons, August 28, 1860 (Sexton, *SWL,* 19–20).

23. Augusta Evans to Rachel Lyons, July 30, 1860 (Sexton, *SWL,* 18). I am using a nineteenth-century notion of "literary" here, rather than a postmodern one. In a subsequent letter Evans expresses her pleasure that her friend has "*really* contemplated writing" and gives the novice writer some professional advice: "Elaborate your plot,

trace clearly to the end, your grand leading aim, before you write *a line* and then you will find no trouble I think in weaving the details, arranging your—chiaroscuro—in fine—polishing the whole. Let me beg of you not to waver in this project; set to work, and your labor will gather wonderful charms for you. I know you *can write*, and I believe you will, if you only once set about it" (Augusta Jane Evans to Rachel Lyons, Nov. 15, 1860 [Sexton, *SWL*], 21–22).

24. Quoted in Ann D. Wood, "'The 'Scribbling Women' and Fanny Fern: Why Women Wrote," *American Quarterly*, Vol. 23, No. 1 (Spring 1971), 8.

25. Susan Warner to Dorothea Dix, August 27, 1852; quoted in Kelley, *Private Woman, Public Stage*, 293. Anna Warner, *Susan Warner*, 264; quoted in Kelley, 293. Warner's novel, like many of the most popular antebellum novels by women, traces the development of a young, orphaned girl through numerous trials and challenges. The heroine of such novels triumphs over adversity through hard work, self-control, and Christian faith, which is typically sorely tried by both circumstances and the heroine's own pride and anger, which she must overcome before being rewarded with marriage to a desirable man and a comfortable middle-class life. For a description of this familiar plot and detailed analysis of the ways in which different antebellum writers used it, see Nina Baym, *Woman's Fiction: A Guide to Novels by and about Women in America 1820–1870* (1978; Second edition, Urbana: University of Illinois Press, 1993). For competing views of the "cultural work" these novels perform, see Ann Douglas, *The Feminization of American Culture* (1977. New York: Anchor, 1988) and Jane Tompkins, *Sensational Designs: The Cultural Work of American Fiction, 1790–1860* (New York: Oxford University Press, 1985).

26. Annie Fields, ed., *Life and Letters of Harriet Beecher Stowe* (1897. Detroit: Gale Research, 1970), 377.

27. Maria Cummins to Annie Fields, September 16, 1862, quoted in Kelley, *Private Woman, Public Stage*, 293.

28. Mary Kelley has demonstrated that the "literary domestics" rarely admitted, even in their private correspondence and diaries, that their careers provided the kind of intellectual satisfaction and purpose that Evans describes here. Kelley attributes this reluctance to claim either ambition or satisfaction from one's literary endeavors as indicative of a kind of internal psychic split produced by the disjuncture between the "literary domestics'" career choices and their socialization as proper nineteenth-century women. I see it as a rhetorical strategy adopted, indeed even internalized, by Evans's predecessors because it was a convention that permitted them to pursue a literary career and preserve their status as "true women."

29. The recommendation to read Ruskin is in a letter from Evans to Lyons from December 8, 1859. A few weeks later Evans tells Lyons that she is reading Dante whose "great work I consider far superior to 'Paradise Lost.' I believe I wrote you of Ruskin." Evans continues, "Fully to appreciate 'Modern Painters,' one must possess an intimate knowledge of Dante" (Augusta Evans to Rachel Lyons, Jan. 4, 1860; Sexton, *SWL*, 8).

30. Susan K. Harris has theorized that popular fiction by nineteenth-century women writers frequently contains an "overplot" that functions as a "cover—or— cover up for a far more radical vision of female possibilities embedded in the text" (*19th-Century American Women's Novels: Interpretive Strategies* ([Cambridge: Cambridge University Press, 1990], 12–13).

31. The centrality of domestic life to preserving Southern culture and values was

the subject of domestic fiction produced by antebellum Southerners. As Elizabeth Moss explains, "Planter women, southern domestic fiction contended, had the privilege and the obligation to serve as the center of their immediate and extended community; they could not shirk their responsibilities if that community were to endure" (*Domestic Novelists in the Old South*, 10). In addition to serving as apologists for slavery, the authors of Southern domestic novels had a message for their Southern readers: "southern women of privilege must take an active role in protecting their region from northern encroachment; only through the efforts of the planter class, specifically planter-class women, could the northern threat [to the Southern way of life] be averted" (23).

32. Faust, *A Sacred Circle*, 7.

33. Augusta Evans to J. L. M. Curry, July 15, 1863 (Sexton, *SWL*, 65).

34. Ibid., 66.

35. Ibid., 67.

36. Ibid., 65.

37. Ibid., 66.

38. Ibid., 66.

39. Ibid.

40. Perhaps because she is writing privately, Evans is remarkably frank about the limits of citing history in defense of slavery; she reminds Curry that except for "Penelope and Lucretia, I can recall no examples worth adducing in favor of slavery," and she dismisses the common claim that Christianity distinguishes the slaveholding South from other slave societies, asking, "Sir, do you find the status of the mass of women in Christian Russia, any more encouraging" than that of the "semi-barbarism" and "degradation" of women in the "East where the institution has been maintained from time immemorial" (Sexton, *SWL*, 66–67).

41. Augusta Jane Evans, *Macaria, or, Altars of Sacrifice* (1864; reprint, Baton Rouge: Louisiana State University Press, 1992), xiii. Hereinafter cited parenthetically.

42. Augusta Evans to Rachel Lyons, June 14, 1864 (Sexton, *SWL*, 104).

43. For a detailed discussion of these views of art's social and religious function, see chapter 1.

44. References to Ruskin are sprinkled throughout *Macaria* (e.g., 190, 356, 409) and Evans's personal correspondence. For a detailed discussion of Ruskin's influence on American aesthetic thought in the 1850s, see chapter 1.

45. Augusta Evans to J. L. M. Curry, July 15, 1863 (Sexton, *SWL*, 66).

46. Evans seems to have been quite willing to use her sources selectively; she invokes John Stuart Mill's authority here, but in *St. Elmo* she strongly attacks Mill's liberal social views.

47. Augusta Evans, *Beulah* (1859; reprint, Baton Rouge: Louisiana State University Press, 1992), 331. As Drew Gilpin Faust points out, the Civil War drastically changed the expectation of most elite Southern women that all but a small minority of them would marry. Although, as Faust notes, the war made possible heroines like Electra and Irene, and Evans's embrace of singleness at the end of *Macaria* offers Southern women an alternative world view for facing the postbellum world, many Southern readers of *Macaria* were uncomfortable with the novel's willingness to envision a world without men. See *Mothers of Invention*, chapters 6 and 7.

48. Drew Gilpin Faust argues in the Introduction to *Macaria* that the religious emphasis at the end of the novel undermines the subversiveness of Evans's portrait

of female independence and self-sufficiency: "Evans redefines the work that is at the center of both Irene's and Electra's self-fulfillment as but a special form of divine worship. . . . The self-assertion implicit in the pursuit of artistic or intellectual goals is thus subsumed within the larger context of religious submission" (xxiii). Faust quite rightly notes Evans's redefinition of women's intellectual work as a form of divine worship, but her suggestion that this act of redefinition is a last-minute effort to contain overly subversive material misses the point of Evans's project both in *Macaria* and in her other work from this period. As all three of Evans's novels from this period, and as her 1860 letters to Rachel Lyons, demonstrate, religious faith is the source of Evans's feminist aesthetic, not antithetical to it. Such a redefinition neatly inverts the formula that had authorized female literary production during the first half of the century and allows Evans, and Harriet Beecher Stowe, to preserve both their religious faith and their socially conservative views about women's proper role, even as they argued for the centrality of women's aesthetic work to the cultural projects of their regions.

49. Evans's work was reviewed widely in the newspapers of the day, but it received virtually no attention from the more prestigious literary periodicals such as the *Atlantic Monthly*.

50. One of Evans's earliest biographers, Louise Manly, praises the decision to avoid explicitly sectarian themes in *St. Elmo* as "an act of rare self-control . . . and . . . high wisdom" which, she suggests, Evans made in an attempt to "lift . . . herself and her readers out of the overwhelming seas around them and place . . . them in a region of peace and prosperity, to which only the most sanguine hope then beckoned the stricken inhabitants of the South" ("Augusta Evans Wilson, 1835–1909," *Library of Southern Literature*, 1909. Eds. Edwin Anderson Alderman et al. [New Orleans: Martin & Hoyt, 1907–1913], Vol. 13, 5843). Fidler speculates that Evans chose to ignore the war both because "[u]nlike many of her sentimental compatriots, Augusta quickly realized that the Southern cause, as interpreted and defended by Confederates, was lost forever" and because she "believed that she could lay greater emphasis upon the lasting values of former times, upon the noble impulses associated with good living in the ante-bellum South, if she developed the love story of Edna Earl and St. Elmo among stable, seemingly permanent conditions" (*Augusta Evans Wilson*, 124–25).

51. As Melissa Homestead has shown in her analysis of Evans's business relationships during and after the war, Evans was quite capable of presenting herself in different lights to different correspondents, in order to advance her interests. See Melissa J. Homestead, *American Women Authors and Literary Property, 1822–1869* (Cambridge and New York: Cambridge University Press), forthcoming, 2005. It is quite possible, indeed likely, that when writing to fellow Confederate loyalists, Evans played to her audience and accentuated her hostility toward the North. There is no evidence, however, that her decision to set the novel in the antebellum era and avoid all but the most muted sectional references was motivated by a conciliatory impulse of any kind.

52. Augusta Evans to Mrs. J. H. Chrisman, Feb. 3, 1866 (Sexton, *SWL*, 116).

53. Augusta Evans to General Beauregard, March 30, 1867 (Sexton, *SWL*, 138).

54. "A Chat with Mrs. Wilson," *N.Y. World*, undated; in the Augusta Evans Wilson Collection, Alabama Department of Archives and History. The interview is probably from sometime in 1878 or slightly later, since in it Evans refers to her 1868 marriage as taking place "ten years ago."

55. Augusta Evans to Orville James Victor, Dec. 1, 1860 (Sexton, *SWL*, 25).

56. Augusta Evans to William Seaver, Dec. 31, 1859 (Sexton, *SWL*, 5). I have been unable to find a specific reference to the dinners Evans alludes to, but Delmonico's was a fashionable New York restaurant patronized by members of New York's cultural and business elite and was the site of many famous dinners for literary celebrities as well as regular gatherings by groups of men associated through business. See Lately Thomas, *Delmonico's: A Century of Splendor* (Boston: Houghton Mifflin, 1967).

57. Augusta Evans to J. L. M. Curry, Oct. 7, 1865 (Sexton, *SWL*, 109). Evans assures Curry that she met "only such people as Ben Woods of the 'Times,' who had proved their detestation of the war party and policy"; she omits mention of calling on J. C. Derby in order to collect the considerable royalties from sales of *Macaria* that Derby had accumulated on her behalf. In *American Women Authors and Literary Property, 1822–1869*, Melissa J. Homestead speculates that Evans's visit to New York immediately after the end of the war was motivated as much by a desire to collect this money as by her wish to seek medical attention for her brother.

58. Augusta Evans to William Seaver, Sept. 26, 1866 (Sexton, *SWL*, 130).

59. Augusta Evans to William Seaver, March 20, 1875 (Sexton, *SWL*, 154).

60. Augusta Jane Evans, *St. Elmo* (1866; reprint, Tuscaloosa: University of Alabama Press, 1992), 114. Hereinafter cited parenthetically.

61. In calling Manning's magazine "Maga," Evans was invoking the general tradition of elite literary magazines established in Edinburgh by *Blackwood's Magazine* (1817–1980), which was dubbed "Maga" by its founder and was emulated by numerous Americans in the 1850s and 1860s. See http://www.pmpc.napier.ac.uk/scob/blackhist.html

She might also have intended to allude to *Putnam's Monthly*, which was often referred to as 'Maga' by magazine insiders and whose virulently anti-Southern views Evans would have undoubtedly been familiar with (for an example of these views see the article titled "Southern Literature," discussed earlier in this chapter). *Putnam's* existed from 1853 through 1857 and was revived briefly in 1868, after *St. Elmo* was published; but it was a very influential magazine during the 1850s, and it seems likely that readers who were at least Evans's contemporaries or older would have been aware of the allusion. I am indebted to Melissa J. Homestead for information about the history of the name "Maga" in the United States.

62. Even as she was giving the fictional Manning the belief that "women never write histories" Evans was intending to do just that; she shelved her plans to write a definitive history of the Confederacy when she learned that Confederate Vice President Stephens intended to do the same. Despite her self-censorship and her frequent assertions that she was no "Xenophon," Evans clearly viewed this proposed project as materially different from her fiction writing. She told J. L. M. Curry, "My history, I intend to make the *great end of all my labors* in the realm of letters . . ." (Augusta Evans to J. L. M. Curry, October 7, 1865 [Sexton, *SWL*, 107]).

63. "Female Authors," *The North American Review* (Jan. 1851), 151, 152.

64. Harriet Beecher Stowe, "How Shall I Learn to Write," *Hearth and Home* (Jan. 16, 1869).

65. For a detailed discussion of the role of literary periodicals like the *Atlantic Monthly* in the stratification of American culture during the second half of the nineteenth century, see Brodhead, *The School of Hawthorne*, and Glazener, *Reading for Realism*.

66. Sarah Hale declared, in 1831, "It is only on emergencies, in cases where duty demands the sacrifice of female sensitiveness, that a lady of sense and delicacy will come before the public, in a manner to make herself conspicuous," explaining that she had taken up literary work only after being widowed, and out of a need to "obtain the means of supporting and educating her children in some measure as their father would have done." Following Hale's lead, American women regularly declared, usually quite truthfully, that they had been driven to the unladylike measure of publication only because of economic necessity brought on by the death or financial failure of the male relatives whose responsibility it was to support them and their children. Hale's quotation is from *Lady's Magazine* 4 (1831), 2–4; quoted in Ann D. Wood, "Scribbling Women," 10. For a detailed discussion of the economic bases for women's authorship in the antebellum period, see Kelley, *Private Woman, Public Stage*, especially chapter 6.

67. This attack is somewhat ironic, in light of her own significant economic motivation for writing, but it seems obvious from Evans's letters and her autobiographical portraits of women writers that she never considered herself motivated to write for purely economic reasons.

68. "Female Authors," *North American Review*, 153.

69. Evans seems to have had both the ancient and the contemporary meanings of "hierophant" in mind. According to the *OED*, the ancient meaning is "An official expounder of sacred mysteries or ceremonies, esp. in ancient Greece"; by the late seventeenth century the meaning of "an initiating or presiding priest" had come into use, and by the early-nineteenth century the word was commonly used to mean "an expounder of sacred mysteries; an interpreter of an esoteric principle."

70. As Susan K. Harris points out, Edna's thorough classical education and her knowledge of ancient languages put her in distinctly masculine territory: she had "fulfilled the requirements for the Christian ministry. It would be difficult to imagine a more radical appropriation of elite male intellectual culture than Edna achieves" (*19th Century American Women's Novels*, 67). See chapter 2 of Harris's study for a detailed discussion of the ways in which Edna's erudition might have served as an example and motivational model for the novel's readers.

71. James Russell Lowell, "The Origins of Didactic Poetry," *Atlantic Monthly* (Nov. 1857), 112.

72. I discuss the gender/genre split in detail in the Introduction.

73. William Fidler claims that Evans was ambivalent about the popular success of *Beulah:* "The erudition in her writing indicates that she hoped to attract intellectual readers, but when it became evident that the masses and not the intelligentsia were her constituents, she professed to be pleased that her audience was composed of unsophisticated commoners who follow the dictates of their heart and conscience, even in matters of art" (*Augusta Evans Wilson*, 48). Whatever Evans's initial reaction to her popular success may have been—Fidler provides no evidence that her pleasure was "professed"— it seems to me that by the time she published *St. Elmo*, she had developed an aesthetic vision based on her own experience of gaining a broad audience and popular success for fiction that challenges its readers in ways that most popular nineteenth-century fiction does not.

74. One of the rare references to the dates of the action is given toward the end of the novel, in a description of Edna's satisfaction with her professional and social successes: "Only one cause of disquiet now remained. The political storm of 1861

alarmed her, and she determined that if the threatened secession of the South took place, she would immediately remove to Charleston or New Orleans, link her destiny with the cause which she felt was so just, so holy, and render faithful allegiance to the section she loved so well" (Evans, *St. Elmo*, 360).

75. Faust, *A Sacred Circle*, 47.

76. I know of only a few other examples, including Fanny Fern, *Ruth Hall* (1855). Although Jo March returns to writing in sequels to *Little Women,* at the end of that novel she has, at least temporarily, given up her career in favor of marriage and motherhood. Alcott's "Diana and Persis" (1879) was left unfinished, so it is impossible to know if Alcott intended to allow either of the protagonists to continue their artistic careers.

77. Augusta Evans to Rachel Lyons, July 30, 1860 (Sexton, *SWL*, 18).

78. See, for example, Elizabeth Fox Genovese's Introduction to the reprint edition of *Beulah;* Anne Goodwyn Jones's discussion of *Beulah* in *Tomorrow Is Another Day,* chapter 2; Drew Gilpin Faust's Introduction to the reprint edition of *Macaria* and her discussion of *Macaria* in *Mothers of Invention,* 168–78; Mary Kelley's discussion of *St. Elmo* in *Private Woman, Public Stage,* 190–92. For a reading that argues that the focus on the marriages at the end of Evans's novels is misplaced, see Susan K. Harris, *19th-Century American Women's Novels,* chapter 2.

79. Similarly, I read the fact that Evans's second novel is a conservative analysis of "the only true and allowable and womanly sphere of feminine work" (*St. Elmo,* 337), which appears at the height of Edna's prominence in New York's intellectual scene, not as a sign of Edna's decline into domesticity, but as an indicator of Evans's commitment to imagining a woman writer who can function successfully in both intellectual realms.

80. Baym, *Woman's Fiction,* 296.

81. Harris, *19th-Century American Women's Novels,* 1–38.

Notes to Chapter 3

1. "Woman in the Domain of Letters," *Knickerbocker Monthly: A National Magazine* (July 1864), 83. I'm assuming that this writer is a man not only because most such essays were written by men, but also because it opens with a comic description of "our" distress at discovering women ice-skating publicly on the Boston Common "in broad daylight" (83).

2. "Woman in the Domain of Letters," 84.

3. David Reynolds has found that the image of a marketplace flooded with popular fiction by women in the late-antebellum period, culminating in the so-called "feminine fifties," is a myth. According to Reynolds, "The only time that female-authored American volumes had anything close to a numerical parity with male-authored ones was during the earliest stage of American fiction, between 1784 and 1810, when 41 percent of all volumes were written by women and 44 by men (the remaining volumes were published anonymously). By the 1830–1860 period the proportion of female-authored volumes had fallen to 23 percent, while the proportion of male volumes had risen to 57 percent" (David S. Reynolds, *Beneath the American Renaissance: The Subversive Imagination in the Age of Emerson and Melville* [Cambridge: Harvard University Press, 1988], 338).

But these numbers can be misleading, because although women published far fewer volumes than men, the percentage of best-selling titles by women was disproportionate to the numbers of woman-authored volumes. According to Susan Coultrap-McQuin, who compiled statistics from a variety of sources, "in the 1850s, nearly 50 percent of the best-selling titles were by women, any one work selling more than writings of Nathaniel Hawthorne, Herman Melville, Henry David Thoreau, and Walt Whitman combined. This success was apparently matched by equally high percentages of women submitting and having works accepted. By 1872, nearly three-quarters of American novels were written by women" (*Doing Literary Business: American Women Writers in the Nineteenth Century* [Chapel Hill and London: The University of North Carolina Press, 1990], 47).

As both Mary Kelley and Susan Coultrap-McQuin have shown, a significant percentage of the women who entered the literary marketplace earned at least some income from their literary work, and many earned quite a bit. Each of the twelve "literary domestics" Mary Kelley profiles earned a living from her writing, and some, such as Harriet Beecher Stowe and Augusta Evans, became quite wealthy. Although the concept of "bestseller" did not come into being until midcentury, books by the "literary domestics" all sold extremely well in the context of their times. For example, Catherine Maria Sedgwick's *Hope Leslie* (1827) had a first edition of 2,000 copies, at a time when selling more than that was rare (Kelley, *Private Woman, Public Stage: Literary Domesticity in Nineteenth Century America* [New York: Oxford University Press, 1984], 13). By the late 1840s and 1850s, the numbers involved were much higher: Mary Virginia Terhune's *Alone* (1854), which Terhune was initially required to publish herself, eventually sold over 100,000 copies (Kelley, 17); Susan Warner's *The Wide Wide World* (1850) sold over 40,000 copies in the first year, was reprinted 67 times, and, its publishers claimed, eventually sold over a million copies (Kelley, 18). For detailed discussions of American women writers' popularity and relationship to the market, see Kelley, especially chapters 1 and 7; see also Susan Coultrap-McQuin, *Doing Literary Business: American Women Writers in the Nineteenth Century*.

4. My thinking on this topic is informed by the work of Sonia Hofkosh, who argues that existing categories through which we understand British romanticism ignore and devalue women's literary work, not because it didn't exist, but "precisely because it was so formative, so responsible to and resonant with the literate culture's emerging concerns, desires, aspirations, with the empowerment of and also contestation within bourgeois, literate culture itself." Hofkosh's goal is not to add any particular text or group of texts to the canon, but rather to uncover how romanticism was constructed: "In remarking the exclusionary practices operative in romantic aesthetics," she writes, "I am specifically interested in how that aesthetics is haunted at its very foundation by the vision of women it can never quite occlude" (Sonia Hofkosh, *Sexual Politics and the Romantic Author* [Cambridge: Cambridge University Press, 1998], 11).

5. Although there had been a publishing industry in the United States since Colonial times, it was small, localized, and published mostly pirated British reprints until the early-nineteenth century. Charles Brockden Brown and Susannah Rowson both published fiction in the late-eighteenth and early-nineteenth centuries, but Washington Irving and James Fenimore Cooper were the first American writers to enjoy significant popularity and sales, in the early 1820s. For accounts of the emergence of a literary marketplace and a market for literature in antebellum America

see, for example, William Charvat, *The Profession of Authorship in America, 1800–1870* (Ed. Matthew J. Bruccoli, Columbus: The Ohio State University Press, 1968); Cathy Davidson, *Revolution and the Word: The Rise of the Novel in America* (New York: Oxford University Press, 1986); John Tebbel, *Between Covers: The Rise and Transformation of Book Publishing in America* (New York: Oxford University Press, 1987); and Michael Newbury, *Figuring Authorship in Antebellum America* (Stanford: Stanford University Press, 1997).

6. Nina Baym, *Novels, Readers, and Reviewers: Responses to Fiction in Antebellum America* (Ithaca: Cornell University Press, 1984), 45.

7. Lawrence Buell, *New England Literary Culture: From Revolution through Renaissance* (Cambridge: Cambridge University Press, 1986), 58.

8. The prominent "Gentleman Publishers" were William Ticknor, James T. Fields, Daniel Appleton, Charles Scribner, George P. Putnam, Joshua B. Lippincott, and James Osgood (Coultrap-McQuin, *Doing Literary Business*, 32–33).

9. Coultrap-McQuin, *Doing Literary Business*, 44.

10. Buell, *New England Literary Culture*, 59.

11. Ibid., 63.

12. Richard Brodhead, *The School of Hawthorne* (New York: Oxford University Press, 1986), 55.

13. Ibid., 56. Brodhead points out that "Fields the canon-former and institution-builder is the agent, in the literary domain, of a general social process . . . through which American culture was reorganized on a more steeply hierarchical plan, featuring sharp gradations of levels of cultural values" (56). Fields's work was a direct continuation of that of Evert Duycknick, the famous New York editor and champion of American literature who, Brodhead argues, should be understood more accurately not merely as a "cultural nationalist but specifically as the proponent of an indigenous American *high* culture" (53); but Fields's canons were much more discriminating than Duycknick's because Fields "represents this process [of differentiation] in its fullness," whereas Duycknick embodied a "transition phase, which already values a culture it thinks of as high but does not yet insist on the hierarchical differentiations such a culture would require. Fields's American library is emphatically discriminating, Duycknick's still a very mixed affair; unlike Fields's it includes both men and women [Margaret Fuller], both established writers and newcomers [the Melville of *Typee*], both literature and nonfiction. . . ." (56). For detailed discussions of these processes of differentiation in the literary world, see *The School of Hawthorne*, especially chapter 3, and Jane Tompkins, *Sensational Designs: The Cultural Work of American Fiction, 1790–1860* (New York: Oxford University Press, 1985), chapter 7. For descriptions of the processes of differentiation taking place simultaneously in other realms of American life, see Lawrence W. Levine, *Highbrow/Lowbrow: The Emergence of Cultural Hierarchy in America* (Cambridge: Harvard University Press, 1988), and Burton J. Bledstein, *The Culture of Professionalism: The Middle Class and the Development of Higher Education in America* (New York: W. W. Norton, 1976).

14. Yunok Park chronicles the correlation between the shift in the style and substance of Melville's writing, his waning popularity, and his changing conception of authorship in chapter 1 of "Masculine Genius and the Literary Marketplace: A Study of Melville's Fiction in the 1850s" (unpublished dissertation, Washington State University, 1996). Richard Brodhead situates this phase of Melville's career in rela-

tion to the emerging realm of "high" literary production in chapter 2 of *The School of Hawthorne*.

15. From an 1849 letter to Melville's English publisher (quoted in Brodhead, *The School of Hawthorne*, 22).

16. Quoted in Brodhead, *The School of Hawthorne*, 21.

17. Melville to Lemuel Shaw, Oct. 6, 1849 (quoted in Park, "Masculine Genius," 19).

18. Brodhead, *The School of Hawthorne*, 23.

19. Nathaniel Hawthorne to William D. Ticknor, January 1855 (*The Centenary Edition of the Works of Nathaniel Hawthorne*, Vol. XVII, The Ohio State University Press, 1987), 304.

20. Herman Melville, "Hawthorne and His Mosses" (1850; reprinted in Baym et al., *The Norton Anthology of American Literature*, 4th ed. [New York: W. W. Norton, 1994]), 2205, 2207. Nominally a review of Hawthorne's short story collection *Mosses from an Old Manse* (1846), the essay is actually Melville's literary manifesto.

21. Ibid., 2202, 2203.

22. Ibid., 2205.

23. Ibid., 2207.

24. Ibid., 2208.

25. Ibid., 2207. As numerous Melville scholars have pointed out, Melville never earned enough from his writing to support his large family and was frequently in debt. See Park, "Masculine Genius and the Marketplace," 11–16.

26. Such ambivalence toward popularity and the marketplace is not necessarily a defensive response to failure; William G. Rowland, Jr., suggests that Longfellow is paradigmatic of this tendency among American Renaissance authors: "Despite his great commercial success, Longfellow could still disparage any attempt to associate literature and trade" (*Literature and the Marketplace: Romantic Writers and Their Audiences in Great Britain and the United States* [Lincoln and London: University of Nebraska Press, 1996], 35). Rowland's survey of Longfellow's statements on the subject of the poet's relationship to the reading public and the marketplace suggests that Longfellow shared Melville's and Higginson's belief that artistic greatness and popular acceptance and success are fundamentally incompatible (36–37).

Interestingly, contemporary critics of Longfellow's work either bracket the question of his popularity, or, if they discuss it at all, see it as an indication both of the quality of his poetry and of the improvement in the tenor of the American reading public's taste. When Longfellow's popularity was discussed, it was almost always aligned with that of Washington Irving, while other writers and poets who had achieved popular and critical success in the antebellum period were simply ignored. See, for example, George W. Curtis, "Longfellow," *Atlantic Monthly* (Dec. 1863), 769. British critics were far more likely than American ones to comment on Longfellow's popularity, typically pointing out that Longfellow's American popularity was initiated by the warm critical reception he received in Britain. See, for example, "American Literature. Longfellow," *Dublin University Magazine*, reprinted in *Eclectic Magazine* in 1850 and in Kenneth Walter Cameron, ed., *Longfellow among His Contemporaries* (Hartford: Transcendental Books, 1978), 34–40; and "Longfellow," *The National Review*, reprinted in *Littell's Living Age* in 1859 and in *Longfellow among His Contemporaries*, 63–66. Among American observers, Longfellow's ability to appeal to a popular audience despite his status as a learned Harvard professor was widely seen as a great strength. But it is precisely this status as a member of the literary and cultural elite, and his independent income, which was often alluded to in periodical pieces, that combined to give Longfellow's popularity a different cultural meaning from that associated with the popular female novelists of the period. The differences in gender and genre are significant too: as a male poet, Longfellow occupied an identity that commanded literary respect in a way the female novelist—a relatively recent arrival on the literary scene—did not.

27. For a detailed discussion of this shift see *Cultures of Letters: Scenes of Reading and Writing in Nineteenth-Century America* (Chicago: University of Chicago Press, 1993), especially chapter 3.

28. Of course, many others participated in the conversation that defined high culture and explained its importance to middle-class readers, but Higginson stands out in both the number and the length of his contributions to the *Atlantic*, which was one of the institutional centers of this process.

29. Higginson also commanded the first unit of black soldiers to be mustered into the Union army, and he wrote about his war-time experiences in the *Atlantic* and in *Army Life in a Black Regiment* (1869). His "Letter to a Young Contributor" (1862) prompted Emily Dickinson to send him some poems, and their epistolary friendship lasted, intermittently, until her death. For a detailed overview of Higginson's career as an activist and writer, see the Introduction to *The Magnificent Activist: The Writings of Thomas Wentworth Higginson, 1823–1911*, edited by Howard N. Meyer (Da Capo Press, 2000).

30. Thomas Wentworth Higginson, "Literature as an Art," *Atlantic Monthly* (Dec. 1867), 746.

31. Ibid., 746.

32. Ibid., 747.

33. Melville, too, relied on the labor of the women in his household to support his career; his wife, sisters, and, eventually, his daughters all proofread, copied, and produced fair-copies of his manuscripts—no small task, since Melville's handwriting was illegible and his spelling atrocious. Of course, Melville's female relatives performed these tasks in addition to their own domestic work, which would have been considerable, since the family included many children and relatively few servants (Park, "Masculine Genius and the Literary Marketplace," 4).

34. Higginson was an ardent support of women's rights and a firm believer in women's intellectual equality to men. He would have undoubtedly argued that a woman was just as capable of producing literary art as a man, under the right circumstances, which were, of course, not usually available to women. While it unlikely that he understood his views as excluding women writers in any practical sense, the rhetorical weight of the attack on the popular has precisely that effect.

35. Higginson, "Literature as an Art," 751.

36. Ibid.

37. Ibid., 753.

38. Although the *Atlantic Monthly* and its sister high-culture magazines paid authors much more generously than antebellum periodicals had, a writer could not earn a living, much less support a family, by producing only the kind of writing that Higginson privileges as literary art.

39. Alcott's letters and journals are full of remarks about her frustration at being forced to produce lucrative work she considered inferior; although neither was

published in her lifetime, she knew that both would be published after her death, and she frequently edited her journals accordingly (see the Introduction to Alcott's *Journals* for a complete discussion of her editorial practices). Davis and Phelps both published memoirs late in life which, while not particularly revealing by modern standards, nevertheless bespeak an awareness of themselves as literary artists whose lives and opinions are of interest to their readers. Woolson, who died young, probably by her own hand, left no memoir, but she did leave specific instructions about the disposition of her papers and letters, not all of which were followed. Readings of her surviving letters in Sharon Dean's *Constance Fenimore Woolson*, Lyndall Gordon's *A Private Life*, and Joan Weimer's Introduction to *Women Artists, Women Exiles* all reveal that she considered herself an artist first and foremost, although the financial aspects of her career were always of great concern to her.

40. Fanny Fern, *Ruth Hall* (1855; reprint, New Brunswick: Rutgers University Press, 1986), 136.

41. Entry for June, July, August 1862; Louisa May Alcott, *The Journals of Louisa May Alcott*, eds. Madeleine Stern, Joel Myerson, and Daniel Shealy (Boston: Little Brown, 1989), 109. The "L" of the entry is Frank Leslie, the editor of *Frank Leslie's Illustrated Newspaper*.

42. Entry for February and March, 1873; Alcott, *Journals*, 187.

43. Entry for February, 1865; Alcott, *Journals*, 139.

44. Sharon M. Harris, *Rebecca Harding Davis and American Realism* (Philadelphia: University of Pennsylvania Press, 1991), 72.

45. Carol Farley Kessler, *Elizabeth Stuart Phelps* (Boston: Twayne, 1982), 117.

46. Brodhead, *Cultures of Letters*, 87–88.

47. Alcott, *Journals*, 131. The story did appear in the November/December 1864 issue of the *Boston Commonwealth*. No Alcott stories appeared in the *Atlantic* after 1864 (*Journals*, 136 n. 34, 36).

48. Rebecca Harding Davis, *Earthen Pitchers* (1874; reprinted in *A Rebecca Harding Davis Reader*, ed. Jean Pfaelzer, Pittsburgh: University of Pittsburgh Press, 1995), 226. Hereinafter cited parenthetically.

49. Stowe, *Agnes of Sorrento* (1862; reprinted in *The Writings of Harriet Beecher Stowe*, New York: AMS, 1967), 127. Augusta Evans, *St. Elmo* (1866; reprint, Tuscaloosa: University of Alabama Press, 1992), 107.

50. The lack of a community of like-minded women and men was a significant problem for Davis early in her career. Sharon Harris notes that Davis regularly asked James T. Fields to forward to her "intelligent criticism" of her work so that she could learn from it. Fields didn't, or perhaps couldn't, oblige, sending only what Davis called "'sugary' reviews" (*Rebecca Harding Davis*, 74).

51. Although she had been a successful journalist, Jane's career path was forced upon her by circumstances. Early in the novella Jane rejects the notion that she is "a woman of genius," explaining that writing is not her real calling: "I have covered up my real character in a reputation for wit and fancy just as I hid the bare walls with those pictures, which don't belong to me. It is shop-work with me. I read this book and that to find a style. I scour the country for ideas and facts as capital. . . . If I were older and had enough money saved I think I'd go into trade. I could make a fortune at that" (Davis, *Earthen Pitchers*, 226).

Jane's hostility toward Audrey may stem, at least in part, from her resentment at having been forced into one of the few professions open to women despite her inclination for "trade."

52. *Edinburgh Review* 33 (Jan. 1820), 79. Quoted in Richard Ruland, ed., *The Native Muse* (New York: Dutton, 1972), 156.

53. Roger B. Stein, *John Ruskin and Aesthetic Thought in America, 1840–1900* (Cambridge: Harvard University Press, 1967), 14–15.

54. Although most observers shied away from defining originality in any specific terms, there was widespread consensus that being original did not simply mean being new. The central argument of an essay titled "Originality" is that since nothing can truly be new in the world, originality lies rather in one's way of interpreting universal, familiar truth. For D. A. Wasson there are two principles on which any "sufficient doctrine of literature and literary production" rest: "First, that the perfect truth of the universe issues, by vital representation, into the personality of man. Secondly, that this truth *tends* in every man, though often in the obscurest way, toward intellectual and artistic expression." If you accept these two truths, Wasson argues, then the fact that no one can ever say anything truly original does not matter, because "it is the verity, the vital process, the depth of relationship, which concerns us. Nay, in one sense, the older his truth, the *more* the effects of originality lie central to him" (D. A. Wasson, "Originality," *The Atlantic Monthly,* [July 1862], 66). Wasson's definition essentially leaves the judgment about a work's originality to the critic or audience who, presumably, will recognize it when he or she sees it.

The relationship between originality and nationality was a source of considerable anxiety among observers of Longfellow's career, who viewed his work as a literary translator, his deep knowledge of world literatures, and his willingness to borrow from those literatures as a threat to Longfellow's status as the preeminent American poet. But virtually all came to the conclusion that Longfellow could be defined as an American genius despite his failure to be "original"; for many, his interest in American historical subjects was the saving grace—transforming poetry that might have been derivative into something truly original by virtue of its subject matter. For others, it was the harder-to-pin-down category of style that exempted Longfellow from the category of the merely imitative. See, for example, "Longfellow's Song of Hiawatha," *Putham's* (Dec. 1855): 578–87, in which the author devotes the first half of the review to defending Longfellow from charges of imitation, carefully distinguishing between "servile reproductions" (578) and "free and fruitful reproductions" (579) which, in the hands of a talented artist like Longfellow, can produce work that is highly original in style if not in substance (581). Similar arguments in defense of Longfellow's status as an original American artist inform George W. Curtis, "Longfellow," *Atlantic Monthly* (Dec. 1863), and "Henry Wadsworth Longfellow," *The North American Review* (April 1867).

55. Harriet Beecher Stowe, *Sunny Memories of Foreign Lands* (2 Vols. New York: J. C. Derby, 1854), Vol. I, 189.

56. Stowe, *Sunny Memories of Foreign Lands*, Vol. II, 165–66.

57. Thomas Wentworth Higginson, "Americanism in Literature," *Atlantic Monthly* (Jan. 1870), 63.

58. Ralph Waldo Emerson, "Quotation and Originality," *North American Review* (April 1868), 555.

59. Higginson, "Americanism in Literature," 57.

60. Thomas Wentworth Higginson, "A Plea for Culture," *Atlantic Monthly* (Jan. 1867), 36.

61. James Parton, "Popularizing Art," *Atlantic Monthly* (March 1869), 350, 355. For a discussion of Louis Prang's influential work as a lithographer see Peter C. Marzio, *The Democratic Art: Pictures for a 19th Century America: Chromolithography 1840–1900* (Boston: David R. Godine, 1979), chapter 6.

62. Parton, "Popularizing Art," 354.

63. Ibid.

64. Ibid., 355.

65. Ibid.

66. Although American Renaissance writers were certainly concerned with the effects of industrialization on the author, these anxieties tend to be expressed in terms of the artist's labor rather than the object he produces. See Michael Newbury, *Figuring Authorship in Antebellum America* (Stanford: Stanford University Press, 1997) for a discussion of the ways in which antebellum writers of both genders used various rhetorics of labor to negotiate their positions within the changing field of literary production.

67. Nathaniel Hawthorne to William D. Ticknor, January 1855 (*The Centenary Edition of the Works of Nathaniel Hawthorne*, Vol. XVII, The Ohio State University Press, 1987) 304.

68. Nathaniel Hawthorne, *The Marble Faun* (1860; reprint, New York: Penguin, 1990), 55. Hereinafter cited parenthetically.

69. Hawthorne's companion portrait of female originality, in the character of Miriam, suggests that, if not contained and channeled, female originality is tremendously destructive. Numerous critics have focused on the figure of the copyist in *The Marble Faun*, frequently reading Hilda as emblematic of Hawthorne's own anxieties about his place in the American art canon. See, for example, Robert Brooke, "Artistic Communication and the Heroines' Art in Hawthorne's *The Marble Faun*," *ESQ: A Journal of the American Renaissance* 29 (1983); Robert H. Byer, "Words, Monuments, Beholders: The Visual Arts in Hawthorne's *The Marble Faun*," in David C. Miller, ed., *American Iconology: New Approaches to Nineteenth-Century Art and Literature* (New Haven: Yale University Press, 1993); Carol Hanbery MacKay, "Hawthorne, Sophia, and Hilda as Copyists: Duplication and Transformation in *The Marble Faun*," *Browning Institute Studies: An Annual of Victorian Literary and Cultural History* 12 (1984). Deborah Barker has situated *The Marble Faun* in relation to contemporary views about women's limited artistic abilities and "properly" limited role as transmitters rather than creators of culture. Barker reads *The Marble Faun*, as I do, in conjunction with Phelps's *The Story of Avis*, but our readings differ significantly in their emphases. Barker situates Phelps's rejection of the role of copyist in relation to the figure of the Sphinx, the subject of Avis's painting, which Barker suggests is "a symbol of the alien Other in all its diverse manifestations"—blacks, women, immigrants, Jews, and the working class, which "relates to American fears of the devolutionary threat of the alien Other" (*Aesthetics and Gender in American Literature: Portraits of the Woman Artist* [Lewisburg: Bucknell University Press, 2000], 65).

70. "Culture"—by which most antebellum observers meant European painting, sculpture, music, and literature—was integral to the emergence of an elite class in postbellum America, a class that coalesced, in large part, around its appreciation and consumption of culture. At the same time, the project of "civilizing" immigrants,

former slaves, and working-class people by exposing them to "culture" and incul-
cating in them a respect both for the objects themselves and for the institutions that
were their custodians, was central to attempts by Northeastern Protestant elites to
control the large numbers of workers moving into cities, bringing with them their
own cultural habits and leisure-time activities. There was a widespread belief that
everyone who could not afford access to original art, whether it be housed in
European galleries or in the American museums that began to be built soon after the
Civil War, could benefit from owning inexpensive reproductions of great art. For a
discussion of the development of an American elite class coalescing around high culture see Brodhead, *Cultures of Letters*, 122–24. For a discussion of the uses and abus-
es of culture in controlling and educating poor and working-class populations in
large American cities, see Alan Trachtenberg, *The Incorporation of America: Culture and
Society in the Gilded Age* (New York: Hill and Wang, 1982), especially chapter 5.

71. From the mid-1860s on, a number of manufacturers offered large catalogues
of lithograph reproductions of famous paintings that sold for anywhere from $1.50
to $10. Portraits and busts of famous men (and a few women) were also inexpen-
sive and widely used to decorate middle-class parlors (Louise L. Stevenson, *The
Victorian Homefront: American Thought and Culture, 1860–1880* [New York: Twayne
Publishers, 1991], 5–6). The definitive history of lithography is Marzio, *The
Democratic Art.*

72. Copyists were essential to the process of chromolithography. According to
Catharina Slautterback, Associate Curator of Prints and Photographs, The Boston
Athenaeum, chromolithographs, or chromos, as they were popularly called, were
produced by copying a design onto a lithographic stone which was then used for
printing color copies. Since lithographic stones were extremely heavy and not easily transported, lithographic reproductions of famous paintings housed in European
museums were produced using a secondary source such as an engraving, a hand-
painted copy, or, more rarely, a photograph. In some cases, paintings were transported to the lithographer's studio, where the lithographic artist copied them directly onto the stones. (Information is from the author's personal correspondence with
Ms. Slautterback.)

73. Elizabeth Stuart Phelps, *The Story of Avis* (1877; reprint, New Brunswick:
Rutgers University Press, 1992), 37. Hereinafter cited parenthetically.

74. Phelps's views about producing American culture, and the role of the Civil
War in destroying the career of an artist who seemed poised to produce just what the
war-torn nation required, are discussed in detail in chapter 5.

75. The original of Avis's *Sphinx* eventually returns to Harmouth, the property of
local millionaire Stratford Allen, who is known for the "many fine pictures" that
hang in his house (243). Ironically, it is Allen who inadvertently precipitated the
marriage that ended Avis's career, by retrieving Philip Ostrander from the Army
hospital where he might have died of his battle wounds and bringing him to his own
Harmouth home, where he was nursed back to health by Stratford's sister Barbara.
As if to add insult to injury, Avis learns at the same time that she hears of the *Sphinx*'s
purchase that since his sister Barbara's marriage, Stratford Allen has hired a new
housekeeper, one Susan Jessup, née Wanamaker, whom Philip Ostrander had jilted
years before he met Avis. The fact that the ownership and domestic care of Avis's
Sphinx—the symbol of the wasted promise of her career—are in the hands of the man
who saved Philip from almost-certain death, and the woman whose marriage to

Philip might have saved Avis from the artistic death of marriage, underscores the complex interrelations between marriage and the marketplace that precipitated the sale of the *Sphinx* in the first place.

76. Louisa May Alcott, *Little Women* (1868; reprint, New York: Oxford University Press, 1994), 443. Hereinafter cited parenthetically.

77. Hawthorne, *The Marble Faun*, 55.

78. That Alcott considered her fiction a forum for shaping public opinion is evident throughout her journals and letters. She makes this point explicit in a letter to her family from 8 July 1870 in which she describes Theodore Tilton's attempts to persuade her to write for the *Revolution*, Elizabeth Cady Stanton's feminist newspaper: "I think I'd rather keep to my own work and lecture the public in a story, than hold forth . . . in the papers" (*The Selected Letters of Louisa May Alcott* [eds. Madeleine Stern, Joel Myerson, and Daniel Shealy. Boston: Little Brown, 1987], 144 n. 17).

79. Louisa May Alcott, *An Old Fashioned Girl* (1870; reprint, New York: Puffin, 1991), 237, 238. Hereinafter cited parenthetically.

80. Alcott, *Little Women*, 443.

Notes to Chapter 4

1. Warren G. French, "'Honor to Genius': The Complimentary Festival to Authors, 1855," *The New York Historical Society Quarterly* (Oct. 1955), 361.

2. French, "Honor to Genius," 366.

3. Kerry Charles Larson, "Betrayers and the Betrayed: The Cult of Genius in the Age of Emerson" (unpublished dissertation, Johns Hopkins University, 1982).

4. Although historians of realism typically discuss realism's rejection of genius in some detail, their discussions imply that attitudes toward genius remained unchanged from the 1850s through the 1880s, when leading realists began critiquing genius. For example, Christopher Wilson has only this to say about authorship in the Gilded Age before the emergence of realism: "Eventually, the oppositional culture of Transcendentalism only collapsed back into the sentimental genteel mainstream of the Gilded Age. Upper-class and amateur associations of authorship had persisted. Even the postbellum bohemian communities, for which Whitman himself became something of a patron saint, had only sustained the aristocratic ideology he detested. Bohemian enclaves had hardly been congenial to the values (work, timeliness, responsibility) basic to a professionalized orientation" (*The Labor of Words: Literary Professionalism in the Progressive Era* [Athens: The University of Georgia Press, 1985], 9).

In contrast, Daniel Borus is clearly aware of the debates about cultural nationalism in the early postbellum years, but he simply writes, "The issue of American literary contribution seemed especially compelling in the postwar nationalism that followed Reconstruction. What began as a new series of calls for an American literature that matched the greatness of the nation's institutions became part of the debate over realism" (*Writing Realism: Howells, James, and Norris in the Mass Market* [Chapel Hill: University of North Carolina Press, 1989], 81).

5. Margaret C. Ervin, "Re-Placing Genius: Reconciling the Aesthetic and the Political in Margaret Fuller's Writing" (unpublished dissertation, SUNY Albany, 1997), 19.

6. Raymond Williams, *Culture and Society 1780–1950* (New York: Columbia University Press, 1983), xvi.

7. Christine Battersby, *Gender and Genius: Towards a Feminist Aesthetics* (Bloomington: Indiana University Press, 1989), 3. See pp. 52–90 for a discussion of the historical gendering of genius as masculine. Although, as I will show, the concept of genius was put to specifically American uses during the nineteenth century, the understanding of genius as a specifically masculine quality was adopted in the American context without revision.

8. Marlon B. Ross, *The Contours of Masculine Desire: Romanticism and the Rise of Women's Poetry*, (New York: Oxford University Press, 1989), 16.

9. Description of Sand is from Nina Baym, *Novels, Readers, and Reviewers: Responses to Fiction in Antebellum America* (Ithaca: Cornell University Press, 1984), 262. Of course, the characterization of the female genius as monstrous was common in England as well. See Battersby, *Gender and Genius,* chapters 11 and 12, for a discussion of the ways in which monstrosity, madness, and degeneracy were all allied at various times with femininity as part of changing conceptions of genius.

10. Louisa May Alcott, *The Journals of Louisa May Alcott* (eds. Madeleine Stern, Joel Myerson, and Daniel Shealy. Boston: Little Brown, 1989), 101.

11. Alcott, *Journals,* 95.

12. Louisa May Alcott, *Little Women* (1868; reprint, New York: Oxford University Press, 1994), 257. Hereinafter cited parenthetically.

13. This portrayal of Jo echoes Melville's conception of writing as "'a certain something unmanageable in us, that bids us do this or that, and be done it must— hit or miss'" (from an 1849 letter to his English publisher; quoted in Brodhead, *The School of Hawthorne* [New York: Oxford University Press, 1989], 22). Emerson expresses a similar belief in "The Poet" where he observes, "The poet knows that he speaks adequately, then, only when he speaks somewhat wildly," and "the imagination intoxicates the poet" (*Ralph Waldo Emerson,* Richard Poirier, ed. [New York: Oxford University Press, 1990], 208, 209). Interestingly, Alcott, who described her own bursts of intense creative activity as "fits" and "a vortex," seems to have understood the "vortex" as a state she could choose to bring upon herself. In a journal entry for January 1879 she writes that she has "[g]ot two books well started but had too many interruptions to do much, & dared not get into a vortex for fear of a break down" (*Journals,* 213).

14. It is by now a critical commonplace to read Jo March as an autobiographical figure who illuminates Alcott's desires and anxieties about her literary career; see, for example, Elizabeth Lennox Keyser, "Alcott's Portraits of the Artist as Little Woman," *International Journal of Women's Studies* 5 (November–December 1982); Veronica Bassil, "The Artist at Home: The Domestication of Louisa May Alcott," *Studies in American Fiction* 15 (Autumn 1987); Beverly Lyons Clark, "A Portrait of the Artist as a Little Woman," *Children's Literature* 17 (1989); and the essays on *Little Women* in Madeleine B. Stern, ed., *Critical Essays on Louisa May Alcott* (Boston: Hall, 1984).

15. Edward Young, *Conjectures on Original Composition* (1759); quoted in Williams, *Culture and Society,* 37.

16. For a discussion of the historical conditions that produced the Romantic conception of genius, see Williams, *Culture and Society,* chapter 2.

17. Ervin, "Re-Placing Genius," 20.

18. For a useful overview of the discourse of genius in the early decades of the nineteenth century, see Ervin, "Re-Placing Genius," 22–34. For a brief summary of the history of American cultural anxiety, see Daniel Borus, *Writing Realism: Howells, James, and Norris in the Mass Market*, 81–83.

19. Fisher Ames, "American Literature," *Works of Fisher Ames* (Boston: T. B. Wait, 1809 [458]). Quoted in Ervin, "Re-Placing Genius," 23.

20. Herman Melville, "Hawthorne and His Mosses" (1850; reprinted in Baym et al., *The Norton Anthology of American Literature*, 4th ed. [New York: W. W. Norton, 1994]), 2201, 2208. For discussions of the place of "Hawthorne and His Mosses" in Melville's career, see Richard Brodhead, *The School of Hawthorne*, chapter 2. For a detailed analysis of Melville's gendering of genius as masculine in the essay as part of his effort to "rescue" Hawthorne from the feminizing effects of popularity, see Yunok Park, "Masculine Genius and the Literary Marketplace: A Study of Melville's Fiction in the 1850s" (unpublished dissertation, Washington State University, 1996), chapter 1.

21. Melville, "Hawthorne and His Mosses," 2208.

22. What, exactly, constitutes "American-ness" in literature was a question that was hotly debated during the second half of the nineteenth century in the pages of quality magazines and newspapers. Although commentators differed in the details of their positions, there was a consensus that literature that depicted American people, places, and things and somehow captured the essence of the American spirit was the ideal to which a national literature aspired. A few examples of contributions to this discussion include Higginson, "Americanism in Literature," *Atlantic Monthly* (Jan. 1870); John DeForest, "The Great American Novel," *The Nation* (Jan. 9, 1868); Emerson, "Quotation and Originality," *North American Review* (April 1868); and "Literature Truly American" (*The Nation,* Jan. 2, 1868). There were scores of others.

23. For discussions of the ways in which realism was institutionalized as the preferred mode of American high literary culture and was self-consciously defined in opposition to antebellum genres such as the "romance" and popular sentimental fiction, see Nancy Glazener, *Reading for Realism: The History of a U.S. Institution 1850–1910* (Durham and London: Duke University Press, 1997). Barbara Hochman argues in *Reimagining Books and Reading in the Age of American Realism* (Amherst: University of Massachusetts Press, 2001) that the high-realist aesthetic requirement of authorial self-erasure was produced by a conscious attempt to distance realism from antebellum assumptions about the "friendly" relationship between the reader and the author.

24. Wilson, *The Labor of Words*, 204, n. 3.

25. The paraphrase of Howells is from *Criticism and Fiction* (1891); Norris's comments are from "Novelists to Order—While You Wait," in *Responsibilities of the Novelist* (1903). Both quoted in Borus, *Writing Realism,* 70.

26. Daniel Borus points out, "Unlike the emerging industrial proletariat, writers did not suffer erosion of work skills, sell their labor, punch a time clock, or toil under direct supervision. For all the editorial intervention of the Gilded age, they kept control of their work process and retained the ability to initiate production. Even the most harried paragrapher did not turn out a standardized product in the way that a machine toolmaker did. The notion that the writer was a laborer did, however, have an ideological function. Unlike antebellum writers, who had no use for anything so

common as work, postbellum writers delighted in the implication that they, like farmers or craftsmen, were an integral part of American life. In claiming that their value was in their productivity, they ceased to be 'aristocratic' dabblers and became useful citizens instead" (*Writing Realism*, 66).

27. Brown likely has in mind the transcendentalist version of genius, theorized by Emerson, which Margaret C. Ervin notes, "exaggerates the role of the individual to the almost complete exclusion of place and nation" (Ervin, "Re-Placing Genius," 29).

28. J. Brownlee Brown, "Genius," *Atlantic Monthly* (Feb. 1864), 138.

29. Ibid., 148.

30. Ibid., 148–49.

31. Ibid., 154.

32. The son of a Harvard professor and a graduate of Harvard Divinity School, Frederic Henry Hedge (1805–1890) was instrumental in bringing Transcendentalism to the United States. A member of the intellectual circle that included Emerson and Margaret Fuller, Hedge published "Coleridge's Literary Character" in the *Christian Examiner* in 1833. The article surveyed Coleridge's transcendental ideas and their origins in German philosophy. After founding the transcendental club that published *The Dial*, Hedge gradually distanced himself from transcendentalism, which he criticized for its antichurch positions. Hedge served as a Unitarian minister for various New England congregations and became a leader of the Unitarian church and influential in shaping nineteenth-century liberal theology. Source: Garraty and Carnes, eds., *American National Biography*, 491–92.

33. F[rederic] H[enry] Hedge, "Characteristics of Genius," *Atlantic Monthly* (Feb. 1868), 150.

34. Ibid., 153.

35. Self-control and discipline were the two cardinal virtues of the Victorian middle class. As Louise Stevenson explains, "Victorians believed that civilized people should be punctual, industrious, neat, modest, and temperate—in other words, self-controlled. Self-control regulated the interaction between people, ensuring that they would be free both to compete with one another and to develop their better natures. If all were self-controlled, the world would be orderly. Individuals who worked hard would succeed because of their admirable personal traits, not because of chance" (*The Victorian Homefront: American Thought and Culture, 1860–1880* [New York: Twayne Publishers, 1991]), xxii.

36. Hedge, "Characteristics of Genius," 153.

37. Ibid., 153–54.

38. For example, in "A Plea for Culture," *Atlantic Monthly* (Jan. 1867), Thomas Wentworth Higginson argues that the establishment of universities, as opposed to colleges, is a prerequisite for the development of an American high culture. In "Books for Our Children" (*Atlantic Monthly* [Dec. 1865]) Samuel Osgood anticipates a time when widespread aesthetic education produces a new breed of cultured citizens: "Give us a thirty years' fair training of our children in schools and reading, galleries and music-halls, gardens and fields, and our America, the youngest among the great nations, will yield to none the palm of strength or of beauty; and as she sits the queen, not the captive, in her noble domain, her children, who have learned grace under her teaching, shall rise up and call her blessed" (732). Similar views are expressed in "Sculpture in the United States," *The Atlantic Monthly* (Nov. 1868), and

"American Art," *Scribner's Monthly* (Nov. 1876), among other places. This topic is discussed in detail in chapter 5.

39. Hedge, "Characteristics of Genius," 154–55.

40. Ibid., 155.

41. Ibid., 158.

42. Ibid.

43. Daniel T. Rodgers, *The Work Ethic in Industrial America, 1850–1920* (Chicago: The University of Chicago Press, 1978), 6.

44. Eric Foner, *Reconstruction: America's Unfinished Revolution, 1863–1877* (New York: Harper and Row, 1988), 29.

45. For a detailed account of the Puritan roots of the American work ethic and of its subsequent development in the popular imagination, see Rodgers, *The Work Ethic in Industrial America*, chapter 1.

46. Hedge, "Characteristics of Genius," 158. Hedge's assertion that artistic merit was measured numerically ("So many readers, so many copies sold, so much merit") is not empty rhetoric but is rather a slight exaggeration of common antebellum reviewing practices, which evaluated a work's popularity and sales as a sign of its aesthetic merits. For a more detailed discussion of these practices see Nina Baym, *Novels, Readers, and Reviewers.*

47. John DeForest expresses such a view in "The Great American Novel" (*The Nation*, Jan. 9, 1868); Thomas Wentworth Higginson's analysis of the need for American universities in "A Plea for Culture" is based on similar reasoning (*Atlantic Monthly*, Jan. 1867: 29–37).

48. Hedge, "Characteristics of Genius," 150.

49. Brown, "Genius," 141.

50. Ibid.

51. Single middle-class women often worked as teachers before marriage, but their pay rates were extremely low—barely enough to maintain a middle-class standard of living or reputation (Stevenson, *The Victorian Homefront*, xxiv).

52. See Rodgers, *The Work Ethic in Industrial America*, chapter 7, for a complete discussion of the changing attitudes toward women's work both inside and outside the home. For an account of the many varieties of unpaid work that middle-class women did outside the home, in benevolent organizations and in the abolitionist and other social change movements, see Lori D. Ginzberg, *Women and the Work of Benevolence: Morality, Politics, and Class in the Nineteenth-Century United States* (New Haven: Yale University Press, 1990).

53. Harriet Hosmer, "The Process of Sculpture," *Atlantic Monthly* (Dec. 1864), 736. Hereinafter cited parenthetically.

54. The practice of employing skilled assistants at every stage of producing the large neoclassical statues favored by Hosmer and her peers was routine. In addition to making it possible for artists of all sizes to produce statues that significantly outweighed their creators, employing skilled craftsmen also enabled sculptors to reproduce their works and sell multiple versions of a single "conception." According to William H. Gerdts, "[I]t was a time honored tradition that such work [of shaping the clay and carving the stone] was handed over to [skilled craftsmen]. . . . For the neoclassic sculptor, the workmen were men of talent, the artist were men of genius, and the distinction was carefully maintained" (*American Neo-Classic Sculpture: The Marble Resurrection* [New York: Viking, 1973], 17–18).

55. For a survey of contemporary debates about the scientific basis of gender (in)equality, see Louise Michele Newman, ed., *Men's Ideas/Women's Realities: Popular Science, 1870–1915* (New York: Pergamon, 1985).

56. Thomas Wentworth Higginson, "A Plea for Culture," *Atlantic Monthly* (Jan. 1867), 37.

57. Rebecca Harding Davis, "Marcia" (1876; reprinted in *A Rebecca Harding Davis Reader*, ed. Jean Pfaelzer. [Pittsburgh: University of Pittsburgh Press, 1995], 311. Hereinafter cited parenthetically.

58. Marcia tests the editors to whom she submits her work by placing a black thread between the third and fourth pages of her manuscript. The manuscript is always returned with the thread undisturbed ("Marcia," 312).

59. Constance Fenimore Woolson, "'Miss Grief'," (1880); reprinted in Constance Fenimore Woolson, *Women Artists, Women Exiles, "Miss Grief" and Other Stories*, ed. Joan Myers Weimer (New Brunswick and London: Rutgers University Press, 1988), 248. Hereinafter cited parenthetically.

For discussions of what Weimer calls Woolson's "difficult relationship with Henry James" (xxxv) and its effect on her work, see Cheryl Torsney, *Constance Fenimore Woolson: The Grief of Artistry* (Athens: University of Georgia Press, 1989), and Sharon Dean, *Constance Fenimore Woolson: Homeward Bound* (Knoxville: The University of Tennessee Press, 1995). Both studies set out to challenge the long-standing claims, initially introduced as media rumors and later validated by Henry James's biographers and editors, that Woolson killed herself because of her unre-quited love for James. Most recently, Lyndall Gordon's biography, *A Private Life of Henry James: Two Women and His Art* (New York: W. W. Norton, 1999), has highlight-ed the importance of the James-Woolson relationship to both writers and has revealed the extent to which Woolson's work influenced James's. For a nuanced reading of "'Miss Grief'" in the context of Woolson's relationship with Henry James and James's attitudes toward women writers, see Anne E. Boyd, "Anticipating James, Anticipating Grief: Constance Fenimore Woolson's "'Miss Grief,'" in Victoria Brehm, ed., *Constance Fenimore Woolson's Nineteenth Century: Essays* (Detroit: Wayne State University Press, 2001).

60. Miss Grief's name is actually Aarona Moncrief, which she shortens to "Crief"; the narrator initially misunderstands his valet, but he continues to call her "Miss Grief" in his own mind even after he sees the name spelled out because it reflects his dread of her power of the aura of sadness that clings to her.

61. Miss Crief is not actually "so much older" than the narrator: although he thinks that she is over 50, she is, in fact, just 43; he is "over thirty," though he looks younger (260). Wondering how to address her, the narrator suggests that he might call her "Aunt," though Miss Crief tells him her first name, Aaronna, which he pro-ceeds to use. The idea of calling Miss Crief "Aunt" and the emphasis on the dispar-ity in the two characters' ages echo Woolson's own attitude vis-à-vis Henry James; Lyndall Gordon quotes from a letter from Woolson to James in which she says, "I do not come in as a literary woman at all, but as a sort of—of admiring aunt" (Letter from Woolson to James, 18 Feb. 1882; Gordon, *A Private Life*, 170). Gordon points out that although Woolson was only three years older than James, she "pretended to be aged, fat, and unapproachable" (170).

62. Henry James's short story "The Figure in the Carpet" was published in 1896. Lyndall Gordon speculates that the James story "may be a private tribute to

Woolson," whom, Gordon suggests, James "singled out as his true reader" during a visit to Woolson's rooms in Rome in the spring of 1881, during which he discussed his work in progress—*The Portrait of a Lady*—with her (*A Private Life*, 177, 175–76).

63. Lisa Radinovsky argues that Elizabeth Stoddard came to a similar conclusion in her own struggle with the label of "genius." See "Negotiating Models of Authorship: Elizabeth Stoddard's Conflicts and Her Story of Complaint," in Brehm, *Constance Fenimore Woolson's Nineteenth Century.*

64. LaSalle Corbell Pickett, *Across My Path: Memories of People I Have Known* (New York: Brantano's, 1916), 107–8. Pickett does not date her recollections, saying only that the conversation took place "in Boston" after publication of *Little Women* (1868) but before that of *A Modern Mephistopheles* (1877).

65. Alcott's career as a writer of sensational tales and thrillers remained a secret until Madeleine B. Stern began recovering and identifying the anonymous and pseudonymous works in the 1970s. Stern's work has been invaluable in establishing the full range of Alcott's literary career. Over the past two decades, Alcott's sensational writing has been reprinted in numerous collections with various titles and overlapping tables of contents, making it difficult to refer the interested reader to the most comprehensive editions. The best place to start is with the two original collections of Alcott's sensational stories, *Behind a Mask: The Unknown Thrillers of Louisa May Alcott* (1975), and *Plots and Counterplots: More Unknown Thrillers of Louisa May Alcott* (1976), both edited by Stern.

A wealth of biographical information is available about Alcott: the Introductions to the *Selected Letters of Louisa May Alcott* and *The Journals of Louisa May Alcott* provide detailed overviews of her life and career. The most recent biography is Martha Saxton's, *Louisa May, A Modern Biography of Louisa May Alcott* (1977). Although not generically a biography, Sarah Elbert, *A Hunger For Home: Louisa May Alcott's Place in American Culture* (1987) reads much of Alcott's work through the lens of her life. Earlier biographies such as Madeleine B. Stern's *Louisa May Alcott* (1950) and Ednah D. Cheney's *Louisa May Alcott, Her Life, Letters, and Journals* (1889) are useful gauges of attitudes toward Alcott's work at different points in the past century.

66. Alcott, *Journals*, 204.

67. Ibid., 139. As Richard Brodhead has shown, as the cultural scene became increasingly differentiated and categories of "high" and "low" hardened in the 1860s and beyond, writers were required to choose one model with which to identify. Alcott chose, quite consciously, Brodhead argues, to reject the sensational story paper writing that was so lucrative early in her career and align herself with the "domestic tutelary" model, which met both her economic and her emotional needs. For Brodhead, Alcott's lifelong struggle to control her temper and what was defined by her parents as selfish willfulness, a struggle attested to in her *Journals* and fictionalized in *Little Women's* Jo March, made the juvenile form, which she never liked writing, attractive for precisely that reason. It allowed her to "demonstrate that she had overcome her selfish will" because it "signified self-sacrifice, signaled that she had set aside personal pleasure for socially useful work" (*Cultures of Letters*, 88). My own view is that cultural and economic forces shaped Alcott's professional decisions far more profoundly than the psychological motivation of intentional self-sacrifice that Brodhead suggests but does not demonstrate convincingly. Indeed, Alcott's lifelong resentment of the derailment of her serious literary career is reflected throughout her *Journals* and *Letters*, and her pride in her ability to support her entire family

with her pen is marked by a deep ambivalence about the personal sacrifices that were the price of her popular success.

68. See Madeleine B. Stern's Introduction to *Plots and Counterplots: More Unknown Thrillers of Louisa May Alcott* (New York: William Morrow, 1976) for an overview of the plots and thematic elements Alcott used regularly in her sensational fiction.

69. Alcott takes up the question of the genius-mentor relationship again in *A Modern Mephistopheles* (1877), which was published anonymously as part of Howells's "No Name Series," to considerable acclaim. In that novel the genius-mentor, a Faustian figure, destroys an aspiring male artist, who sells his soul for fame (there is also a female artist figure, but she is not the central focus of the novel). For an interesting discussion of Alcott's depiction of gender and genius in two stories not discussed here, see Gustavus Stadler, "Louisa May Alcott's Queer Geniuses," *American Literature* Vol. 71, No. 4 (Dec. 1999): 657–77.

70. Louisa May Alcott, *A Marble Woman, or, The Mysterious Model* (1865; reprinted in *Plots and Counterplots: More Unknown Thrillers of Louisa May Alcott*), 134. Hereinafter cited parenthetically.

71. The Faustian echoes are no accident; Alcott loved Goethe and reread him often. A January 1869 diary entry is typical: "Refreshed my soul with Goethe, ever strong and fine and alive" (*Journals*, 171).

72. Gerdts, *American Neo-Classical Sculpture*, 104.

73. The law establishing the creation of the National Statuary Hall was signed on July 12, 1864; Alcott's *novella* was published almost a year later, in May 1865, so it is likely that Alcott was aware of the law's passage and purpose, although none of the statues had been commissioned or displayed at the time of the novella's publication. The first statue was placed in the Hall in 1870, the most recent in 2003. Fewer than ten of the 98 sculptures eventually commissioned and displayed are of female subjects, and perhaps ten of the sculptors are women. See, Gerdts, *American Neo-Classical Sculpture*, 104–5, and the Web site of the Architect of the Capitol, http://www.aoc.gov/cc/art/nsh/nsh_states.htm

74. The novella doesn't end here, but the rest of it is devoted to reuniting Cecil with her long-lost father and revealing Cecil and Yorke's love for each other.

75. One of the few details Alcott does provide identifies the setting as American; when Cecil first meets Yorke, she explains that she and her mother had spent the final year of her mother's life "here in America" after living in England, Germany, and elsewhere in Europe for much of her childhood (137).

Notes to Chapter 5

1. Thomas Wentworth Higginson, "A Plea for Culture," *The Atlantic Monthly* (Jan. 1867), 36.

2. Thomas Wentworth Higginson, "Americanism in Literature," *The Atlantic Monthly* (Jan. 1870), 57.

3. Politicians and businessmen, of course, had other priorities, but among the intellectuals writing in the nation's "quality journals," the need to produce a national culture was widely viewed as the pressing issue of the day.

4. Nancy Glazener observes that the intensity of cultural nationalism had ebbed and flowed throughout the nineteenth century, often in concert with wars: "if the

nationalist polemics in *Putnam's* were galvanized by the Mexican War, as seems likely, the early nationalist polemics in the *Atlantic* and its kindred magazines took their force from the North's victory in the Civil War and the urgent task of providing cultural instruction and reconstruction for the South and West" (*Reading for Realism: The History of a U.S. Institution 1850–1910* [Durham and London: Duke University Press, 1997], 44). Glazener is one of the few literary historians to comment on the cultural nationalism of the early postbellum period, but her focus is not on the terms of the discussion itself, but on the way in which realism emerged as the preferred genre of the "high" cultural realm solidified in and through the cultural nationalism of the period.

5. Eric Foner, *Reconstruction: America's Unfinished Revolution, 1863–1877* (New York: Harper and Row, 1988), 21.

6. Quoted in Foner, *Reconstruction,* 24.

7. Orestes Brownson, *The American Republic* (Boston, 1865), 2. Quoted in Foner, *Reconstruction,* 24.

8. Warren S. Tryon, *Parnassus Corner: A Life of James T. Fields, Publisher to the Victorians* (Boston: Houghton Mifflin, 1963), 260. Quoted in Glazener, *Reading for Realism,* 28.

9. Glazener, *Reading for Realism,* 27.

10. For the North, the Civil War years were the most prosperous years in history, a prosperity fueled by wartime inflation and speculation in stocks and gold ventures. In addition, northern and mid-western industries such as railroads, meat packing (Chicago), textiles (New England and mid-Atlantic states), and related industries such as banking all profited from hugely increased demand during the war years (Foner, *Reconstruction,* 18–19).

11. For discussions of the expanding influence of the New England cultural establishment in the postbellum years, see Louise Stevenson, *The Victorian Homefront: American Thought and Culture, 1860–1880* (New York: Twayne Publishers, 1991), chapter 3; and Glazener, *Reading for Realism,* chapter 1. For an analysis of the centrality of Boston elites to the trend toward the professionalization of cultural and philanthropical work and institutions, see Peter Dobkin Hall, *The Organization of American Culture, 1700–1900: Private Institutions, Elites, and the Origins of American Nationality* (New York: New York University Press, 1982).

12. Higginson, "Americanism in Literature," 57.

13. Samuel Osgood, "Books for Our Children," *Atlantic Monthly* (Dec. 1865), 724.

14. Ibid., 731.

15. Ibid., 732

16. Higginson, "A Plea for Culture," 37.

17. As David Blight has shown, similar rhetoric was frequently used in ceremonies to memorialize the Civil War dead in the decades immediately following the war (*Race and Reunion: The Civil War in American Memory* [Cambridge and London: Harvard University Press, 2001] chapter 3).

18. Higginson, "Americanism in Literature," 63.

19. Elizabeth Stuart Phelps, *The Story of Avis* (1877; reprint, New Brunswick: Rutgers University Press, 1992), 78. Hereinafter cited parenthetically.

20. The familiar view of the Civil War as "unwritten" has recently begun to be challenged by scholars. For a discussion of the myriad ways in which women writers engaged with the Civil War in a variety of genres, see Elizabeth Young, *Disarming the Nation: Women's Writing and the American Civil War* (Chicago and London: The

University of Chicago Press, 1999). Other recent studies of the literary culture sur-
rounding the Civil War include Kathleen Diffley, ed., *Where My Heart Is Turning Ever:
Civil War Stories and Constitutional Reform, 1861–1874* (Athens: University of Georgia
Press, 1992), and Alice Fahs, *The Imagined Civil War: Popular Literature of the North &
South, 1861–1865* (Chapel Hill and London: University of North Carolina Press,
2001).

21. In her autobiography Phelps credits *Aurora Leigh* with inspiring her to pursue
a literary career: "what Shakespeare or the Latin Fathers might have done for some
other impressionable girl, Mrs. Browning—forever bless her strong and gentle
name!—did for me. I owe to her, distinctly, the first visible aspiration (ambition is
too low a word) to do some honest, hard work of my own in the World Beautiful,
and for it" (*Chapters from a Life* [Cambridge: Riverside, 1896], 65–66).

Other details of *The Story of Avis* are also biographical: Like Avis, Phelps lost
her mother, a successful writer, at the age of eight, when she died soon after giving
birth to her third child. Phelps was raised by her father, Austin Phelps, a respected
theologian and a professor at Andover Theological Seminary whose conservatism
about women's roles was a serious source of disagreement between the father and
the daughter, causing Phelps considerable distress throughout her lifetime. Unlike
her fictional creation, however, Phelps did not marry until 1888, when her career
was well established, and she continued to write until her death in 1911.

22. The boys are singing Julia Ward Howe's "The Battle Hymn of the Republic."

23. Kathleen D. McCarthy, *Women's Culture: American Philanthropy and Art,
1830–1930* (Chicago: University of Chicago Press, 1991), 37. Although it encouraged
women to limit their artistic productions to conventionally feminine art forms,
Candace Wheeler's decorative arts movement also "constituted the first major artistic crusade created, managed, and promoted under female control" (37). The decorative arts movement did not provide a stepping stone for women into other institutional involvement in the arts, however. According to McCarthy, "Throughout the
nineteenth century . . . women shaped their most successful institutional mandates
around the arts of design. Moreover, they were best able to maintain the institutions
they created if they were clearly oriented toward female constituencies, domestic
ends, and (rhetorically) limited gains." A related phenomenon was women's "lingering reticence to speak on behalf of the community as a whole when the subject
was the visual rather than the decorative arts" (77). Avis's rejection of the decorative
arts in this scene is thus not only a form of distancing herself from conventionally
feminine art forms but also an indication of Phelps's willingness to offer a public
statement about visual arts.

24. Avis's refusal to speak for mill workers and other poor and exploited people,
and her insistence on her need for distance from the world, can be and has been seen
as a failure of compassion for which she is later punished by her own suffering and
the failure of her career. Although Avis does eventually develop compassion for others' suffering and a deeper appreciation for the kind of ethically driven work that
she rejects here, I would argue that such readings overlook Phelps's emphasis on the
personal and national loss represented by Avis's stunted career. Although Phelps
developed an aesthetic based on the centrality of the artist's ethical vision over the
course of her lifetime, Avis's rejection of the role of "apostle of want and woe" and
her subsequent rejection of the opportunity to become a Christ figure point to
Phelps's commitment to imagining an alternative model of female artistic produc-

tion, one that depends neither on the suffering of others nor on self-sacrifice. For examples of readings that view Avis's failed career as stemming from her lack of compassion and her rejection of the traditional moral foundation for feminine artistic endeavor, see Jack H. Wilson, "Competing Narratives in Elizabeth Stuart Phelps's *The Story of Avis*," *American Literary Realism* 26 (Fall 1993); Susan S. Williams, "Writing with an Ethical Purpose: The Case of Elizabeth Stuart Phelps," in Steven Fink and Susan S. Williams, eds., *Reciprocal Influences: Literary Production, Distribution, and Consumption in America* (Columbus: The Ohio State University Press, 1999); and Deborah Barker, *Aesthetics and Gender in American Literature: Portraits of the Woman Artist* (Lewisburg: Bucknell University Press, 2000), chapter 3.

25. Blight, *Race and Reunion*, 6.

26. Higginson, "Americanism in Literature," 63. This view was not, of course, new in the postbellum period. Writing in 1854, Harriet Beecher Stowe expresses a similar sentiment when she asserts, "The literature of a people must spring from the sense of its nationality; and nationality is impossible without self-respect, and self-respect is impossible without liberty" (*Sunny Memories of Foreign Lands* [New York: J. C. Derby, 1854], Vol. I., 189). As I have demonstrated in the preceding chapters, the changing cultural and religious climate in the 1850s contributed to a profound shift in the way elite Americans thought of the role that art should play in the nation's identity; that shift was compounded by the Civil War, and in the early postbellum years the conversation about the need for American cultural nationalism took on a new intensity. For discussions of cultural nationalism in the antebellum era and before, see Richard Ruland, ed., *The Native Muse* (New York: Dutton, 1972); Robert E. Spiller, ed., *The American Literary Revolution: 1783–1837* (New York: New York University Press, 1967); Benjamin T. Spencer, *The Quest for Nationality, An American Literary Campaign* (Syracuse: Syracuse University Press, 1957); and Neil Harris, *The Artist in American Society: The Formative Years 1790–1860* (New York: George Braziller, 1966).

27. Deborah Barker sees *The Story of Avis* as Phelps's critique of European Romantic aesthetics and German idealist philosophy. For a fascinating reading of Phelps's sphinx in the context of the profusion of sphinxes in nineteenth-century art, see chapter 3 of *Aesthetics and Gender in American Literature: Portraits of the Woman Artist* (Lewisburg: Bucknell University Press, 2000).

28. "Literature Truly American," *The Nation* (Jan. 2, 1868), 8.

29. Phelps repeatedly uses the image of a grown person "crawling" to denote extreme powerlessness; whereas in the early parts of the novel the verb is used exclusively to describe the stricken soldiers on the battlefield and the injured Philip Ostrander, after her marriage the verb is increasingly used to describe Avis.

30. Ralph Waldo Emerson, "Aspects of Culture," *The Atlantic Monthly* (Jan. 1868), 86.

31. H. T. Tuckerman, "Going Abroad," *Putnam's* (May 1868), 531, 535, 535.

32. Ibid., 538.

33. According to Richard Brodhead, "Europe"—traveling to it, understanding and appreciating its art, and so on—became in the 1860s and beyond "the chief requisite for American artists seeking high-artistic careers, and in the late 1860s the ability to display this knowledge became the chief literary ticket in" (*Cultures of Letters: Scenes of Reading and Writing in Nineteenth- Century America* [Chicago and London: University of Chicago Press, 1993], 97).

34. Stowe, *Sunny Memories of Foreign Lands*, 159.

35. Augusta Jane Evans to Rachel Lyons, January 21, 1860 (reprinted in Rebecca Grant Sexton, ed., *A Southern Woman of Letters* [Columbia: University of South Carolina Press, 2002], 9).

36. "Sculpture in the United States," *Atlantic Monthly* (Nov. 1868), 558–59. The sculptures this writer refers to were the work of William Wetmore Story (*The Libyan Sybil*, 1860–61); Hiram Powers (*The Greek Slave*, 1843); and Harriet Hosmer (*Zenobia*, 1859).

37. Ibid., 559.

38. Ibid., 561.

39. Indeed, most of the rest of the essay is a call for the development of art-education programs in elementary schools so that "the masses" can acquire the basic knowledge required to transform them into an intelligent audience for fine art.

40. Higginson, "Americanism in Literature," 56.

41. Ibid.

42. Ibid., 57.

43. Ibid.

44. "Diana and Persis" is the name given by Sarah Elbert to the four-chapter manuscript she discovered in the Alcott family papers at Harvard's Houghton Library and subsequently arranged to have reprinted in 1978. The fragment has been reprinted in its entirety in *Alternative Alcott*, where the editor, Elaine Showalter, has reversed the order of the third and fourth chapters of Elbert's edition. I find Showalter's arguments for re-ordering the chapters convincing and have referred to her version throughout this discussion. See the Introduction to *Alternative Alcott* for a complete discussion of Showalter's reasoning.

45. Louisa May Alcott, "Diana and Persis" (ca. 1879; reprinted in *Alternative Alcott*, Elaine Showalter, ed. (New Brunswick: Rutgers University Press, 1988), 385. Hereinafter cited parenthetically.

46. Sharon M. Harris, *Rebecca Harding Davis and American Realism* (Philadelphia: University of Pennsylvania Press, 1991), 74.

47. Although Mary Cassatt befriended other women artists both in Paris and in the United States, her career as an art collector and broker is marked by her dedication to the male Impressionists whose circle she joined in 1877, at the invitation of Edward Degas, who became her mentor. Kathleen D. McCarthy observes that "[r]ather than promoting her own works, or those of other women painters such as her friend Berthe Morisot, Mary Cassatt used her influence to steer wealthy American patrons toward the works of her male colleagues within the Impressionist circle" (*Women's Culture: American Philanthropy and Art, 1830–1930* [Chicago: University of Chicago Press, 1991], 108). Somewhat ironically, Cassatt's own art was actively promoted by a female contemporary, Louisine Havemeyer, who collected Cassatt's paintings along with those of her male contemporaries.

48. Brodhead, *Cultures of Letters*, 124. The new elite Brodhead describes was composed of "inheritors of older wealth and of older local-gentry status, mercantile and managerial groups grown rich in the new corporations, the new-order professionals of this professionalizing period; and elements of the earlier self-articulated middle class eager to distinguish themselves from a now more clearly defined working class strongly identified with this new elite formation as well, especially after the 1860s" (124).

49. Higginson, "A Plea for Culture," 36.

50. John DeForest, "The Great American Novel," *The Nation* (Jan. 9, 1868), 29.

51. Ibid.

52. Higginson, "Literature as an Art," *Atlantic Monthly* (Dec. 1867), 746.

53. Higginson, "A Plea for Culture," *Atlantic Monthly* (Jan. 1867), 33.

54. Higginson argues specifically for the establishment of universities, as opposed to colleges, which he lambastes for their limited and parochial curriculum and provincial attitudes. Universities, in Higginson's conception, are explicitly imagined as training grounds for the acquisition of "high culture": "The demand for high culture outruns the supply," Higginson notes, as evidenced by the large number of young people being sent to Europe for instruction. "What we need," he continues, "is the opportunity of high culture somewhere,—that there should be some place in American where a young man may go and study anything that kindles his enthusiasm, and find there instrumentalities to help the flame" ("A Plea for Culture," 30, 31).

55. Higginson, "A Plea for Culture," 36.

56. In "Literature as an Art" Higginson defines high culture and popularity as incompatible when he declares, "Indeed, a man may earn twenty thousand dollars a year by writing 'sensation stories,' and have nothing to do with literature as an art. But to devote one's life to perfecting the manner, as well as the matter, of one's work; to expatriate one's self long years for it, like Motley; to overcome vast physical obstacles for it, like Prescott or Parkman; to live and die only to transfuse external nature into human words, like Thoreau; to chase dreams for a lifetime, like Hawthorne; to labor tranquilly and see a nation imbued with one's thoughts, like Emerson,—this is to pursue literature as an art" (747). The qualities Higginson valorizes as hallmarks of the "literary" are all associated with the American social elite: leisure, education, and masculinity. For a detailed discussion of the gender implications of this stance, see chapter 3.

57. Higginson, "Americanism in Literature," *Atlantic Monthly* (Jan. 1870), 62

58. "Sculpture in the United States," 563.

59. Ibid., 563–64.

60. Ibid., 564.

61. Ibid., 563, 564.

62. Constance Fenimore Woolson, "The Street of the Hyacinth" (1882), reprinted in *Women Artists, Women Exiles: "Miss Grief" and Other Stories* (New Brunswick and London: Rutgers University Press, 1988), 173. Hereinafter cited parenthetically.

63. Sharon Dean also reads "The Street of the Hyacinth" in terms of its assessment of truth and authority, but she asserts that Noel "lies about his assessment of the quality of her [Ettie's] paintings" when in fact he fails to do even that (*Constance Fenimore Woolson: Homeward Bound* [Knoxville: The University of Tennessee Press, 1995], 182). For readings of the story in terms of Ettie's victimization at the hands of the male cultural establishment, see Dean, *Constance Fenimore Woolson*, 180–85, and Cheryl Torsney, *Constance Fenimore Woolson: The Grief of Artistry* (Athens: University of Georgia Press, 1989), chapter 7.

64. A reviewer of Alcott's *Little Men* (1871) took the opportunity to assess Alcott's career as a serious writer of fiction for adults: "That Miss Alcott has sufficient artistic power to succeed in a longer story, with more variety, incident, and machinery, it would not be safe to infer; she certainly had not when she wrote *Moods*. But between

that and her later works is an almost immeasurable advance: we say immeasurable, because it seems a positive change in *kind* as well as quality of work. However, while she will give us simple stories which all boys and girls read with delight and profit, and all fathers and mothers laugh and cry over after their boys and girls have gone to bed, we may well be content, without desiring that she should attempt that impossible thing, the American Novel" (*Scribner's Monthly* [Aug. 1871], 446–47).

BIBLIOGRAPHY

Alcott, Louisa May. *A Marble Woman, or, The Mysterious Model.* 1865. In *Plots and Counterplots: More Unknown Thrillers of Louisa May Alcott.* Ed. Madeleine B. Stern. New York: William Morrow, 1976.

———. *Little Women.* 1868. Introduction by Valerie Alderson. New York: Oxford University Press, 1994.

———. *An Old Fashioned Girl.* 1870. New York: Puffin, 1991.

———. *A Modern Mephistopheles.* 1877. Ed. Madeleine B. Stern. New York: Praeger, 1987.

———. "Diana and Persis." 1879. Reprint in *Alternative Alcott.* Ed. Elaine Showalter. New Brunswick: Rutgers University Press, 1988.

———. *The Selected Letters of Louisa May Alcott.* Eds. Madeleine Stern, Joel Myerson, and Daniel Shealy. Boston: Little Brown, 1987.

———. *The Journals of Louisa May Alcott.* Eds. Madeleine Stern, Joel Myerson, and Daniel Shealy. Boston: Little Brown, 1989

"American Art." *Scribner's Monthly.* Nov. 1876.

Ammons, Elizabeth (Ed.). *Critical Essays on Harriet Beecher Stowe.* Boston: G. K. Hall, 1980.

———. *Conflicting Stories: American Women Writers at the Turn into the Twentieth Century.* New York: Oxford University Press, 1991.

———. "Gender and Fiction." In *The Columbia History of the American Novel.* Ed. Emory Elliott. New York: Columbia University Press, 1991.

"The Art of the Present." *The Crayon.* May 9, 1855.

Baker, Dorothy Z. "Harriet Beecher Stowe's Conversation with *The Atlantic Monthly: The Construction of The Minister's Wooing."* *Studies in American Fiction.* Vol. 28, No. 1 (2000): 27–38.

Barker, Deborah. *Aesthetics and Gender in American Literature: Portraits of the Woman Artist.* Lewisburg: Bucknell University Press, 2000.

Bassil, Veronica. "The Artist at Home: The Domestication of Louisa May Alcott." *Studies in American Fiction* 15 (Autumn 1987).

Baym, Nina. *Woman's Fiction: A Guide to Novels by and about Women in America 1820–1870.* 1978. 2nd ed. Urbana: University of Illinois Press, 1993.

———. *Novels, Readers, and Reviewers: Responses to Fiction in Antebellum America.* Ithaca: Cornell University Press, 1984.

Beecher, Catharine. *Treatise on Domestic Economy.* 1841. New York: Source Book, 1970.

Berkson, Dorothy. "Millennial Politics and the Feminine Fiction of Harriet Beecher Stowe."

Bledstein, Burton J. *The Culture of Professionalism: The Middle Class and the Development of Higher Education in America.* New York: W. W. Norton, 1976.

Blight, David W. *Race and Reunion: The Civil War in American Memory.* Cambridge and London: Harvard University Press, 2001.

Borus, Daniel H. *Writing Realism: Howells, James, and Norris in the Mass Market.* Chapel Hill: University of North Carolina Press, 1989.

Boyd, Anne E. "'What! Has she got into the '*Atlantic*'?": Women Writers, the *Atlantic Monthly,* and the Formation of the American Canon." *American Studies* 39:3 (Fall 1998): 5–36.

Brehm, Victoria (Ed.). *Constance Fenimore Woolson's Nineteenth Century: Essays.* Detroit: Wayne State University Press, 2001.

Brodhead, Richard H. *The School of Hawthorne.* New York: Oxford University Press, 1986.

———. *Cultures of Letters: Scenes of Reading and Writing in Nineteenth-Century America.* Chicago: University of Chicago Press, 1993.

Brooke, Robert. "Artistic Communication and the Heroines' Art in Hawthorne's *The Marble Faun.*" *ESQ: A Journal of the American Renaissance* 29 (1983).

Brown, Gillian. *Domestic Individualism: Imagining Self in Nineteenth Century America.* Berkeley and Los Angeles: University of California Press, 1990.

Brown, J. Brownlee. "Genius." *Atlantic Monthly.* Feb. 1864: 137–55.

Brown, Jerry Wayne. *The Rise of Biblical Criticism in America, 1800–1870, The New England Scholars.* Middletown: Wesleyan University Press, 1969.

Buell, Lawrence. "Calvinism Romanticized: Harriet Beecher Stowe, Samuel Hopkins, and *The Minister's Wooing.*" In *Critical Essays on Harriet Beecher Stowe.* Ed. Elizabeth Ammons. Boston, MA: G. K. Hall & Co. 1980.

———. *New England Literary Culture, From Revolution Through Renaissance.* Cambridge: Cambridge University Press, 1986.

Bushnell, Horace. "Unconscious Influence." *The American National Preacher* 20 (1846).

Byer, Robert H. "Words, Monuments, Beholders: The Visual Arts in Hawthorne's *The Marble Faun.*" In *American Iconology: New Approaches to Nineteenth-Century Art and Literature.* Ed. David C. Miller. New Haven: Yale University Press, 1993.

Cameron, Kenneth Walter (Ed.). *Longfellow among His Contemporaries: A Harvest of Estimates, Insights, and Anecdotes from the Victorian Literary World and an Index.* Hartford: Transcendental Books, 1978.

Cane, Aleta Feinsod, and Susan Alves (Eds.). *"The Only Efficient Instrument": American Women Writers & The Periodical, 1837–1916.* Iowa City: University of Iowa Press, 2001.

Chai, Leon. *The Romantic Foundations of the American Renaissance.* Ithaca: Cornell University Press, 1987.

———. *Aestheticism: The Religion of Art in Post Romantic Literature.* New York: Columbia University Press, 1990.

Charvat, William. *The Profession of Authorship in America, 1800–1870.* Ed. Matthew J. Bruccoli. Columbus: The Ohio State University Press, 1968.

"A Chat with Mrs. Wilson." *N.Y. World.* N.d. Copy in the Evans Surname File at the Alabama Department of Archives and History.

Cheney, Ednah D. (Ed.). *Louisa May Alcott, Her Life, Letters, and Journals.* Boston: Roberts Brothers, 1889.

Clark, Beverly Lyons. "A Portrait of the Artist as a Little Woman." *Children's Literature* 17 (1989).

Conrads, Margaret C. *Winslow Homer and the Critics: Forging a National Art in the 1870s.* Princeton: Princeton University Press, 2001.

Cott, Nancy. *The Bonds of Womanhood: 'Woman's Sphere' in New England, 1780–1835.* New Haven: Yale University Press, 1977.

Coultrap-McQuinn, Susan. *Doing Literary Business: American Women Writers in the Nineteenth Century.* Chapel Hill: University of North Carolina Press, 1990.

Cummins, Maria. *The Lamplighter.* London: Charles H. Kelly. 1854.

George W. Curtis, "Longfellow." *Atlantic Monthly* (Dec. 1863): 769–75.

Davidson, Cathy. *Revolution and the Word: The Rise of the Novel in America.* New York: Oxford University Press, 1986.

Davidson, Cathy (Ed.). *Reading in America: Literature and Social History.* Baltimore: Johns Hopkins University Press, 1989.

Davis, Rebecca Harding. *Margaret Howth, A Story of Today.* 1862. Afterword by Jean Fagan Yellin. New York: Feminist Press, 1990.

———. *Bits of Gossip.* Boston: Houghton Mifflin, 1904.

———. *A Rebecca Harding Davis Reader.* Ed. Jean Pfaelzer. Pittsburgh: University of Pittsburgh Press, 1995.

Dean, Sharon L. *Constance Fenimore Woolson: Homeward Bound.* Knoxville: University of Tennessee Press, 1995.

DeForest, John. "The Great American Novel." *The Nation.* Jan. 9, 1868.

Diffley, Kathleen (Ed.). *Where My Heart Is Turning Ever: Civil War Stories and Constitutional Reform, 1861–1874.* Athens: University of Georgia Press, 1992.

Dobson, Joanne. "Reclaiming Sentimental Literature." *American Literature* 69 (1997): 263–88.

Douglas, Ann. *The Feminization of American Culture.* New York: Anchor, 1988.

Elbert, Sarah. *A Hunger for Home: Louisa May Alcott's Place in American Culture.* New Brunswick and London: Rutgers University Press, 1987.

Emerson, Ralph Waldo. "Aspects of Culture." *Atlantic Monthly.* Jan. 1868.

———. "Quotation and Originality." *North American Review.* April 1868.

Ervin, Margaret C. "Re-Placing Genius: Reconciling the Aesthetic and the Political in Margaret Fuller's Writing." Unpublished Dissertation, SUNY Albany, 1997.

Evans, Augusta Wilson. *Beulah.* 1859. Introduction by Elizabeth Fox-Genovese. Baton Rouge: Louisiana State University Press, 1992.

———. *Macaria, or, Altars of Sacrifice.* 1864. Introduction by Drew Gilpin Faust. Baton Rouge: Louisiana State University Press, 1992.

———. *St. Elmo.* 1866. Introduction by Diane Roberts. Tuscaloosa: University of Alabama Press, 1992.

———. Unpublished letter to Mrs. J. H. Chrisman, Feb. 3, 1866. In Augusta Evans Wilson Collection, Alabama Department of Archives and History.

Fahs, Alice. *The Imagined Civil War: Popular Literature of the North & South, 1861–1865.* Chapel Hill and London: University of North Carolina Press, 2001.

Faust, Drew Gilpin. *A Sacred Circle: The Dilemma of the Intellectual in the Old South, 1840–1860.* Baltimore and London: Johns Hopkins University Press, 1977.

———. *Mothers of Invention: Women of the Slaveholding South in the American Civil War.* Chapel Hill: University of North Carolina Press, 1996.

"Female Authors." *The North American Review.* Jan. 1851: 151–77.

Fern, Fanny. *Ruth Hall.* 1855. Introduction by Joyce W. Warren. New Brunswick: Rutgers University Press, 1986.

Fidler, William Perry. *Augusta Evans Wilson 1835–1909. A Biography.* Tuscaloosa: University of Alabama Press, 1951.

Fields, Annie (Ed.). *Life and Letters of Harriet Beecher Stowe*. 1897. Detroit: Gale Research, 1970.

Filene, Peter G. *Him/Her/Self: Gender Identities in Modern America*. 3rd ed. Baltimore: Johns Hopkins University Press, 1998.

Foner, Eric. *Reconstruction: America's Unfinished Revolution, 1863–1877*. New York: Harper & Row, 1988.

Foster, Charles H. *The Rungless Ladder: Harriet Beecher Stowe and New England Puritanism*. Durham: Duke University Press. 1954.

Fox, Richard W., and T. J. Jackson Lears (Eds.). *The Power of Culture: Critical Essays in American History*. Chicago: University of Chicago Press, 1993.

Franchot, Jenny. *Roads to Rome: The Antebellum Protestant Encounter with Catholicism*. Berkeley: University of California Press, 1994.

French, Warren G. "'Honor to Genius': The Complimentary Festival to Authors, 1855." *The New York Historical Society Quarterly* (Oct. 1955).

Fuller, Margaret. *Woman in the Nineteenth Century*. 1845. Ed. Donna Dickenson. Oxford: Oxford University Press, 1994.

Gallagher, Catherine. *Nobody's Story: The Vanishing Acts of Women Writers in the Marketplace, 1670–1820*. Berkeley: University of California Press, 1994.

Garraty, John A. and Mark C. Carnes (Eds.). *American National Biography*. New York: Oxford University Press, 1999.

Gatta, John. "The Anglican Aspect of Harriet Beecher Stowe." *The New England Quarterly* (Sept. 2000): 412–33.

Gerdts, William H. *American Neo-Classic Sculpture: The Marble Resurrection*. New York: Viking, 1973.

Ginzberg, Lori D. *Women and the Work of Benevolence: Morality, Politics, and Class in the Nineteenth-Century United States*. New Haven: Yale University Press, 1990.

Glazener, Nancy. *Reading for Realism: The History of a U.S. Institution 1850–1910*. Durham and London: Duke University Press, 1997.

Gordon, Lyndall. *A Private Life of Henry James: Two Women and His Art*. New York: W. W. Norton, 1999.

Hall, Peter Dobkin. *The Organization of American Culture, 1700–1900: Private Institutions, Elites, and the Origins of American Nationality*. New York: New York University Press, 1982.

Halttunen, Karen. *Confidence Men and Painted Women: A Study of Middle-Class Culture in America, 1830–1870*. New Haven: Yale University Press, 1982.

Harris, Neil. *The Artist in American Society: The Formative Years 1790–1860*. New York: George Braziller, 1966.

Harris, Sharon M. *Rebecca Harding Davis and American Realism*. Philadelphia: University of Pennsylvania Press, 1991.

———. "'A New Era in Female History': Nineteenth-Century U.S. Women Writers." *American Literature* 74 (Sept. 2002): 603–18.

Harris, Susan K. *Nineteenth-Century American Women's Novels: Interpretive Strategies*. Cambridge: Cambridge University Press, 1990.

———. "The Female Imaginary in Harriet Beecher Stowe's *The Minister's Wooing*." *The New England Quarterly* 66 (June 1993).

Hawthorne, Nathaniel. *The Marble Faun*. 1860. Introduction by Richard Brodhead. New York: Penguin, 1990.

———. *The Centenary Edition of the Works of Nathaniel Hawthorne.* Columbus, OH: The Ohio State University Press, 1987.

Hedge, F[rederic] H[enry]. "Characteristics of Genius." *Atlantic Monthly.* Feb. 1868: 150–59.

Hedrick, Joan D. *Harriet Beecher Stowe: A Life.* New York: Oxford University Press, 1994.

"Henry Wadsworth Longfellow." *The North American Review.* April 1867: 531–40.

Higginson, Thomas Wentworth. "A Plea for Culture." *Atlantic Monthly.* Jan. 1867: 29–37.

———. "Literature as an Art." *Atlantic Monthly.* Dec. 1867: 745–54.

———. "Americanism in Literature." *Atlantic Monthly.* Jan. 1870.

Hochman, Barbara. *Getting at the Author: Reimagining Books and Reading in the Age of American Realism.* Amherst: University of Massachusetts Press, 2001.

Hofkosh, Sonia. *Sexual Politics and the Romantic Author.* Cambridge: Cambridge University Press, 1998.

Homestead, Melissa J. *American Women Authors and Literary Property, 1822–1869.* Cambridge and New York: Cambridge University Press, forthcoming 2005.

Hosmer, Harriet. "The Process of Sculpture." *Atlantic Monthly.* Dec. 1864: 734–37.

Howard, June. "What Is Sentimentality?" *ALH.* (Spring 1999): 63–81.

———. *Publishing the Family.* Durham and London: Duke University Press, 2001.

Howells, William Dean. *Selected Literary Criticism 1859–1897.* Eds. Ulrich Halfmann and Christoph K. Lohmann. Bloomington: Indiana University Press, 1993.

Jackson, Helen Maria (Fiske) Hunt. *Mercy Philbrick's Choice.* Boston: Roberts Brothers, 1876.

James, Henry. *Literary Criticism.* New York: The Library of America, 1984.

Jarves, James Jackson. *Art-Hints. Architecture, Sculpture, and Painting.* New York: Harper & Brothers, 1855.

Jones, Anne Goodwyn. *Tomorrow Is Another Day. The Woman Writer in the South, 1859–1936.* Baton Rouge: Louisiana State University Press, 1981.

Kelley, Mary. *Private Woman, Public Stage: Literary Domesticity in Nineteenth-Century America.* New York: Oxford University Press, 1984.

———. "Preface." *Private Woman, Public Stage.* Chapel Hill and London: University of North Carolina Press, 2002.

Kessler, Carol Farley. *Elizabeth Stuart Phelps.* Boston: Twayne, 1982.

Keyser, Elizabeth Lennox. "Alcott's Portraits of the Artist as Little Woman." *International Journal of Women's Studies* 5 (Nov.–Dec. 1982).

Kilcup, Karen L. and Thomas S. Edwards (Eds). *Jewett and Her Contemporaries: Reshaping the Canon.* Gainesville: University Press of Florida, 1991.

Larson, Kerry Charles. "Betrayers and the Betrayed: The Cult of Genius in the Age of Emerson." Unpublished Dissertation, Johns Hopkins University, 1982.

Lears, T. J. Jackson. *No Place of Grace: Antimodernism and the Transformation of American Culture, 1880–1920.* New York: Pantheon, 1981.

Levine, Lawrence W. *Highbrow/Lowbrow: The Emergence of Cultural Hierarchy in America.* Cambridge: Harvard University Press, 1988.

"Literature Truly American." *The Nation.* Jan. 2, 1868.

"Little Men." Review of *Little Men,* by Louisa May Alcott. *Scribner's Monthly.* Aug. 1871: 446–47.

"Longfellow's Song of Hiawatha." *Putnam's.* Dec. 1855: 578–87.

Lowell, James Russell. "The Origins of Didactic Poetry." *Atlantic Monthly.* Nov. 1857: 110–12.

Lowry, Richard S. *'Litttery Man': Mark Twain and Modern Authorship.* New York: Oxford University Press, 1996.

MacKay, Carol Hanbery. "Hawthorne, Sophia, and Hilda as Copyists: Duplication and Transformation in *The Marble Faun.*" *Browning Institute Studies: An Annual of Victorian Literary and Cultural History* 12 (1984).

Manly, Louise. "Augusta Evans Wilson, 1835–1909." In *Library of Southern Literature.* 1909. Eds. Edwin Anderson Alderman, Joel Chandler Harris, and Charles William Kent. New Orleans: Martin & Hoyt, 1907–13. Vol. 13: 5841–46.

Martin, Terence. *The Instructed Vision: Scottish Common Sense Philosophy and The Origins of American Fiction.* Bloomington: Indiana University Press, 1961.

Marzio, Peter C. *The Democratic Art: Pictures for a 19th Century America: Chromolithography 1840–1900.* Boston: David R. Godine, 1979.

McCarthy, Kathleen D. *Women's Culture: American Philanthropy and Art, 1830–1930.* Chicago: University of Chicago Press, 1991.

Melville, Herman. "Hawthorne and His Mosses." 1850. Reprinted in *The Norton Anthology of American Literature.* 4th ed. Eds. Baym et al. New York: W. W. Norton, 1994.

Merish, Lori. *Sentimental Materialism: Gender, Commodity Culture, and Nineteenth-Century American Literature.* Durham: Duke University Press, 1999.

Meyer, D. H. *The Instructed Conscience: The Shaping of the American National Ethic.* Philadelphia: University of Pennsylvania Press, 1972.

———. "American Intellectuals and the Victorian Crisis of Faith." *American Quarterly.* Vol. XXVII, No. 5 (Dec. 1975): 585–603.

"Miss Augusta J. Evans." *The Democratic Watchtower,* Talladega, Alabama 27th Mar. 1867. Copy in the Evans Surname File of the Alabama Department of Archives and History.

Mott, Frank Luther. *A History of American Magazines, 1850–1865.* Cambridge: Harvard University Press, 1957.

Newbury, Michael. *Figuring Authorship in Antebellum America.* Stanford: Stanford University Press, 1997.

Newman, Louise Michele (Ed.). *Men's Ideas/Women's Realities: Popular Science, 1870–1915.* New York: Pergamon, 1985.

Noble, Marianne. *The Masochistic Pleasures of Sentimental Literature.* Princeton: Princeton University Press. 2000.

Osgood, Samuel. "Books for Our Children." *Atlantic Monthly.* Dec. 1865: 724–35.

Park, Yunok. "Masculine Genius and the Literary Marketplace: A Study of Melville's Fiction in the 1850s." Unpublished dissertation, Washington State University, 1996.

Parton, James. "Popularizing Art." *Atlantic Monthly.* March 1869: 348–57.

Pfaelzer, Jean. *Parlor Radical. Rebecca Harding Davis and the Origins of American Social Realism.* Pittsburgh: University of Pittsburgh Press, 1996.

Phelps, Elizabeth Stuart. *The Gates Ajar.* Boston: Fields, Osgood, & Co. 1868.

———. *The Story of Avis.* 1877. Introduction by Carol Farley Kessler. New Brunswick: Rutgers University Press, 1992.

———. *Chapters from a Life.* Cambridge: Riverside, 1896.

Pickett, LaSalle Corbell. *Across My Path: Memories of People I Have Known.* New York: Brantano's, 1916.

"The Position of the Artist." *The Crayon.* March 28, 1855.

Post-Lauria, Sheila. "Magazine Practices and Melville's *Israel Potter.*" In *Periodical Literature in Nineteenth-Century America.* Eds. Kenneth M. Price and Susan Belasco Smith. Charlottesville and London: University Press of Virginia, 1995.

Railton, Stephen. *Authorship and Audience: Literary Performance in the American Renaissance.* Princeton: Princeton University Press, 1991.

Reynolds, David S. *Faith in Fiction: The Emergence of Religious Literature in America.* Cambridge: Harvard University Press, 1981.

———. *Beneath the American Renaissance: The Subversive Imagination in the Age of Emerson and Melville.* Cambridge: Harvard University Press, 1988.

Riepma, Anne Sophie. *Fire & Fiction: Augusta Jane Evans in Context.* Amsterdam and Atlanta, GA: Rodopi, 2002.

Robbins, Sarah. "Gendering the History of the Antislavery Narrative: Juxtaposing *Uncle Tom's Cabin* and *Benito Cereno, Beloved* and *Middle Passage.*" *American Quarterly* 49.3 (1997): 531–73.

Rodgers, Daniel T. *The Work Ethic in Industrial America, 1850–1920.* Chicago: University of Chicago Press, 1978.

Romero, Lora. *Home Fronts: Domesticity and Its Critics in the Antebellum United States.* Durham: Duke University Press, 1997.

Romines, Ann. *The Home Plot. Women, Writing and Domestic Ritual.* Amherst: University of Massachusetts Press, 1992.

Rosenfeld, Natania. "Artists and Daughters in Louisa May Alcott's *Diana and Persis.*" *The New England Quarterly* 64 (March 1991).

Ross, Marlon B. *The Contours of Masculine Desire: Romanticism and the Rise of Women's Poetry.* New York: Oxford University Press, 1989.

Rowland, William G., Jr. *Literature and the Marketplace: Romantic Writers and Their Audiences in Great Britain and the United States.* Lincoln: University of Nebraska Press, 1996.

Ruland, Richard (Ed.). *The Native Muse.* New York: Dutton, 1972.

Samuels, Shirley (Ed.). *The Culture of Sentiment: Race, Gender, and Sentimentality in Nineteenth-Century America.* New York: Oxford University Press, 1992.

Sánchez-Epplar, Karen. *Touching Liberty: Abolition, Feminism, and the Politics of the Body.* Berkeley: University of California Press, 1993.

Santayana, George. *The Genteel Tradition: Nine Essays.* Ed. Douglas L. Wilson. Cambridge: Harvard University Press, 1967.

Saxton, Martha. *Louisa May: A Modern Biography of Louisa May Alcott.* Boston: Houghton Mifflin, 1977.

Schiller, Emily. "The Choice of Innocence: Hilda in *The Marble Faun.*" *Studies in the Novel* 26 (Winter 1994).

"Sculpture in the United States." *The Atlantic Monthly.* Nov. 1868.

Sedgwick, Ellery. *The Atlantic Monthly 1857–1909, Yankee Humanism at High Tide and Ebb.* Amherst: University of Massachusetts Press, 1994.

Sexton, Rebecca Grant (Ed.). *A Southern Woman of Letters, The Correspondence of Augusta Jane Evans Wilson.* Columbia: University of South Carolina Press, 2002.

Shumaker, Conrad. "'Daughter of the Puritans': History in Hawthorne's *The Marble Faun.*" *The New England Quarterly* 57 (March 1984).

Sklar, Kathryn Kish. *Catharine Beecher: A Study in American Domesticity.* New Haven and London: Yale University Press, 1973.

Smith, Lannom. "Howells and the Battle of Words over 'Genius.'" *American Literary Realism 1870–1910* (Spring 1980): 101–7.

Spencer, Benjamin T. *The Quest for Nationality: An American Literary Campaign.* Syracuse: Syracuse University Press, 1957.

Spiller, Robert E. (Ed). *The American Literary Revolution: 1783–1837.* New York: New York University Press, 1967.

St. Armand, Barton Levi. *Emily Dickinson and Her Culture: The Soul's Society.* Cambridge and New York: Cambridge University Press, 1984.

Stadler, Gustavus. "Louisa May Alcott's Queer Geniuses." *American Literature.* Vol. 71, No. 4 (Dec. 1999): 657–77.

Stein, Roger B. *John Ruskin and Aesthetic Thought in America, 1840–1900.* Cambridge: Harvard University Press, 1967.

Steinberg, Ronald M. *Fra Girolamo Savonarola, Florentine Art, and Renaissance Historiography.* Athens: Ohio University Press, 1977.

Stern, Madeleine B. *Louisa May Alcott.* Norman: University of Oklahoma Press, 1950.

Stern, Madeleine B. (Ed.). *Behind a Mask: The Unknown Thrillers of Louisa May Alcott.* New York: William Morrow, 1975.

———. *Plots and Counterplots: More Unknown Thrillers of Louisa May Alcott.* New York: William Morrow, 1976.

———. *Critical Essays on Louisa May Alcott.* Boston: Hall, 1984.

Stevenson, Louise L. *The Victorian Homefront: American Thought and Culture, 1860–1880.* New York: Twayne, 1991.

Stowe, Charles Edward. *Life of Harriet Beecher Stowe, Compiled from Her Letters and Journals.* Boston: Houghton, Mifflin, and Co., 1889.

Stowe, Charles Edward and Lyman Beecher Stowe. *Harriet Beecher Stowe: The Story of Her Life.* Boston: Houghton Mifflin, 1911.

Stowe, Harriet Beecher. *Uncle Tom's Cabin.* 1852. Reprint *Harriet Beecher Stowe, Three Novels.* New York: Library of America, 1982.

———. *Sunny Memories of Foreign Lands.* 2 Vols. New York: J. C. Derby, 1854.

———. "New England Ministers." *The Atlantic Monthly.* Feb. 1858: 485–92.

———. *The Minister's Wooing.* 1859. Reprint *Harriet Beecher Stowe, Three Novels.* New York: Library of America, 1982.

———. *Agnes of Sorrento.* 1862. Reprint *The Writings of Harriet Beecher Stowe,* New York: AMS, 1967.

———. *The Pearl of Orr's Island.* 1862. Reprint *The Writings of Harriet Beecher Stowe.* New York: AMS, 1967.

———. "How Shall I Learn to Write?" *Hearth and Home.* Jan. 16, 1869.

Thomas, Lately. *Delmonico's: A Century of Splendor.* Boston: Houghton Mifflin, 1967.

Thompson, Lou. "The Contagion of Guilt and the Women in Hawthorne's *The Marble Faun.*" *Lamar Journal of the Humanities* 10 (Spring 1984).

Tompkins, Jane. *Sensational Designs: The Cultural Work of American Fiction, 1790–1860.* New York: Oxford University Press, 1985.

Torsney, Cheryl B. *Constance Fenimore Woolson: The Grief of Artistry.* Athens: University of Georgia Press, 1989.

Trachtenberg, Alan. *The Incorporation of America: Culture and Society in the Gilded Age.* New York: Hill and Wang, 1982.

Tuckerman, H. T. "Going Abroad." *Putnam's.* May 1868: 530–38.

Turner, James. *Without God, Without Creed: The Origins of Unbelief in America.* Baltimore: Johns Hopkins University Press, 1985.

Warner, Susan. *The Wide Wide World.* 1850. Introduction by Jane Tompkins. New York: Feminist Press, 1987.

Williams, Raymond. *Culture and Society 1780–1950.* New York: Columbia University Press, 1983.

Williams, Susan S. "Writing with an Ethical Purpose: The Case of Elizabeth Stuart Phelps." In *Reciprocal Influences: Literary Production, Distribution, and Consumption in America.* Eds. Steven Fink and Susan S. Williams. Columbus: The Ohio State University Press, 1999.

Wilson, Christopher P. *The Labor of Words: Literary Professionalism in the Progressive Era.* Athens: University of Georgia Press, 1985.

———. "Tempests and Teapots: Harriet Beecher Stowe's *The Minister's Wooing.*" *The New England Quarterly* 58 (December 1985).

Wilson, Jack H. "Competing Narratives in Elizabeth Stuart Phelps's *The Story of Avis.*" *American Literary Realism* 26 (Fall 1993).

"Woman in the Domain of Letters." *Knickerbocker Monthly: A National Magazine.* July 1864: 83–86.

Wood, Ann D[ouglas]. "The 'Scribbling Women' and Fanny Fern: Why Women Wrote." *American Quarterly.* Vol. 23, No. 1 (Spring 1971): 3–24.

Woolson, Constance Fenimore. *Women Artists, Women Exiles: "Miss Grief" and Other Stories.* Ed. Joan Myers Weimer and Introduction by Weimer. New Brunswick and London: Rutgers University Press, 1988.

Young, Elizabeth. *Disarming the Nation: Women's Writing and the American Civil War.* Chicago and London: The University of Chicago Press, 1999.

INDEX